# INDIAN EDUCATION
# PROGRESS AND CHALLENGES

# INDIAN EDUCATION
# PROGRESS AND CHALLENGES

M.A. Rahman
Sukanta Sarkar

ISBN : 978-93-5128-090-3

Price : 990

First Published, 2015

*Published by*

Kalpaz Publications
C-30, Satyawati Nagar,
Delhi-110052, Ph. : 9212142040
E-mail: kalpaz@hotmail.com

*Laser Typesetting* : Future Computer, Delhi
*Printed at* : G. Print Process, Delhi

Cataloging in Publication Data—DK
Courtesy: D.K. Agencies (P) Ltd. <docinfo@dkagencies.com>

**Indian education :** progress and challenges / Prof M.A. Rahman, Dr Sukanta Sarkar.

pages ; cm
Contributed articles.
Includes bibliographical references and index.
ISBN 9789351280903

1. Education—India. 2. Education and state—India. I. Rahman, M. A. (Professor), editor. II. Sarkar, Sukanta, editor.

DDC 370.954 23

*This book is dedicated to my**

**Guru Prof B.K. Panda**

**with reverence and due affection**

# Contents

# Preface

Education in its general sense is a form of learning in which the knowledge, skills, and habits of a group of people are transferred from one generation to the next through teaching, training, or research. Systems of schooling involve institutionalised teaching and learning in relation to a curriculum, which itself is established according to a predetermined purpose of the schools in the system. Schools systems are sometimes also based on religions, giving them different curriculum. Universalisation of upper primary education in India is normally discussed in terms of enrolling and retaining all children belonging to the group 11 to 14. This seems more to be a desirable goal to be achieved in the long run than a realisable target at the present level of development of primary education. Universal Primary Education (UPE) is a goal stated in many national development plans and pursued with vigour by governments of most developing countries. The United Nations Millennium Development Goal is to achieve universal primary education by the year 2015, by which time they aim to ensure that all children everywhere regardless of race or gender, will be able to complete primary schooling. In the Indian context, balanced development of education is critical for nation building. Education is one of the most important components of the inclusive development model of the emerging Indian democracy, which was well articulated even in the 1960s in the report of the Education Commission (1963-64). Historical forces have largely influenced the policy-planning processes and growth trends in education, both in developed and low-income countries.

In this connection, we want to place on record our deep appreciation to Prof Ajay Pathak, Vice-Chancellor, ICFAI University, Tripura, Agartala for providing valuable inputs.

We desire to express our heartiest thank to Prof B.K. Panda, Department of Economics, Berhampur University, Odisha who despite his busy schedule and hectic academic engagements, all the time encouraged and supported us. I have also beholden to Dr N.G. Pandse, Department of Economics, Rani Durgabati University, Jabalpur who's erudite and scholarly tidbits for preparing such a vast work are still fresh in our minds. I also thanks to Dr Pradeep Kumar Pandey, Centre of Judicial Studies, Dibrugarh University, Assam; Dr Suman Kalan Chaudhury, Department of Business Administration, Berhampur University,

Odisha; Dr Rakesh Joshi, Department of Economics, Saurashtra University, Gujarat; Dr D. Pulla Rao, Department of Economics, Andhra University; Dr Vibhuti Patel, Professor-cum-Director, Centre for Study of Social Exclusion and Inclusive Policy, SNDT Women's University, Mumbai; Dr. Wakar Amin, Department of Social Work, University of Kashmir, J and K.; Dr. Shazia Manzoor, Assistant professor Department of Social Work, University of Kashmir, J & K; Dr Pallab Kanti Ghoshal, Department of Commerce, Netaji Subhas College, Udaipur, for their valuable suggestions and moral support.

We are heartily grateful to Prof R. Prasad, Prof Ashish Kumar Shrivastava and Prof L.S. Nigam, Pandit Ravishankar Shukla University, Raipur, Chhattisgarh who always encouraged us to carry on this constructive work. Further, we express our heartily thankfulness to each and every person who directly/indirectly helped us in preparing this work.

It is hoped that this book will be very useful in society in general and students of education in particular. Comments and suggestions are welcomed

**Prof M.A. Rahman**
**Dr Sukanta Sarkar**

# List of Contributors

**Amitra Sudan Chakraborty:** Assistant Professor, School of Legal Studies, GLOCAL University, Uttar Pradesh.

**Dipankar Biswas:** Assistant Professor and Head, Dept. of Education, Iswar Chandra Vidyasagar College, Tripura.

**Anil Chandra Basak:** Professor, College of Agricultural Sciences of International University of Business Agriculture and Technology, Dhaka, Bangladesh.

**Manaswini Patra:** Librarian I/C, R.P. Padhi Library, Berhampur University, Odisha

**P.K. Ghoshal:** Associate Professor, Department of Commerce, Netaji Subhas College, Udaipur, Tripura.

**Rakesh Joshi:** Associate Professor, Department of Economics, Saurashtra University, Rajkot, Gujarat.

**S.K. Chaudhury:** Faculty Member, Department of Business Administration, Berhampur University, Odisha.

**P.K. Pandey:** Assistant Professor, Centre of Judicial Studies, Dibrugarh University, Assam.

**N.G. Pandse:** Professor, Department of Economics, Rani Durgabati University, Jabalpur, Madhya Pradesh.

**Sukanta Sarkar:** Assistant Professor, School of Management Studies, ICFAI University, Agartala, Tripura.

**D. Pulla Rao:** Professor, Department of Economics, Andhra University, Andhra Pradesh.

**Satish Chand Bhadwal:** Professor, Department of Education, H.P. University, Shimla, Himachal Pradesh.

**Anil Kumar Agnihotri:** Principal, Mehar Chand College of Education, Bhanupali, District Ropar (Panjab).

**Sarika Manhas:** Assistant Professor, P.G. Department of Home Science, University of Jammu, Jammu and Kashmir.

**B.K. Panda:** Professor and Head, Department of Economics, Department of Economics, Berhampur University, Odisha.

**Mohammad Afsar Alam:** Assistant Professor and Head, Department of Geography, Adi-Keih College of Arts and Social Sciences, Eritrea, N.E. Africa.

**N.C. Patnaik:** Principal, Lingaraj Law College, Berhampur University, Odisha.

**R. Prasad:** Professor and Head, Department of Economics, Pandit Ravi Shankar Shukla University, Raipur, Chhattisgarh.

**Md. Ataur Rahman:** Director of Centre for Global Environmental Culture (CGEC) and Professor of College of Agricultural Sciences of International University of Business Agriculture and Technology, Dhaka, Bangladesh.

**Farzana Alim:** Professor and Head, Department of Home Science, Aligarh Muslim University, Aligarh, Uttar Pradesh.

**Ravi Saini:** Assistant Professor, Sachdeva Institute of Education, Mathura, Uttar Pradesh.

**Manzoor Hussain:** Assistant Professor, Department of Sociology, University of Kashmir, Srinagar, Jammu and Kashmir.

**Rajib Mallik:** Assistant Professor and Academic Co-ordinator, School of Management, National Institute of Technology, Agartala, Tripura.

**Fouziya Qadiri:** Research Scholar, P.G. Department of Home Science, University of Jammu, Jammu and Kashmir.

**Meenu:** Research Scholar (JRF), Department of Education, Panjab University, Chandigarh.

**Niranjan Thengal:** Lecturer, Department of Education, D. R. College, Golaghat, Assam.

**Prahelika Roy:** Student, Women's College, Agartala, Tripura.

**Renu Pachauri**: Assistant Professor, Sachdeva Institute of Education, Mathura, Uttar Pradesh.

**Sachin Sachdeva:** Research Scholar, NIMS University, Jaipur, Rajasthan.

# Abbreviations

| | | |
|---|---|---|
| AAMR | : | American Association on Mental Retardation |
| AB | : | Accreditation Board |
| ACM | : | Association for Computing Machinery |
| ADEA | : | Association for the Development of Education in Africa |
| AEP | : | Adult Education Programme |
| AHPL | : | Art of Healthy and Productive Living |
| AICTE | : | All India Council of Technical Education |
| AIDS | : | Acquired Immune Deficiency Syndrome |
| AIE | : | Alternate Innovative Education |
| AIPMT | : | All India Pre-Medical Test |
| AISHE | : | All India Survey on Higher Education |
| AISSCE | : | All India Senior School Certificate Examination |
| AIU | : | Association of Indian Universities |
| AIWEFA | : | All India Women's Education Fund's Associations |
| ANP | : | Applied Nutrition Programme |
| APPEP | : | Andhra Pradesh Primary Education Project |
| AS | : | Akshara Sankranti |
| ASER | : | Annual Status of Education Report |
| ASME | : | American Society of Mechanical Engineers |
| ASTM | : | American Society for Testing and Materials |
| AYUSH | : | Ayurveda, Yoga and Naturopathy, Unani, Siddha and Homoeopathy |
| | | |
| B.ED | : | Bachelor of Education |
| BAIF | : | Bhartiya Agro Industrials Foundation |
| BAOU | : | Dr Babasaheb Ambedkar Open University |
| BCI | : | Bar Council of India |
| BRAOU | : | Dr B.R. Ambedkar Open University |
| | | |
| CABE | : | Central Advisory Board of Education |
| CABE | : | Commission for Architecture and the Built Environment |
| CBSE | : | Central Board of Secondary Education |

| | | |
|---|---|---|
| CCE | : | Continuous and Comprehensive Evaluation |
| CCH | : | Central Council of Homoeopathy |
| CCIM | : | Central Council of Indian Medicine |
| CD-ROM | : | Compact Disc, Read-Only-Memory |
| CEC | : | Consortium for Educational Commutation |
| CEE | : | Centre for Environment Education |
| CII | : | Confederation of Indian Industry |
| CIS | : | Commonwealth of Independent States |
| CISCE | : | Council for the Indian School Certificate Examinations |
| CMU | : | Carnegie Mellon University |
| COA | : | Council of Architecture |
| COL | : | Commonwealth of Learning |
| CP | : | Chaduvula Panduga |
| CSIR | : | Council of Scientific and Industrial Research |
| CSS | : | Common School System |
| CTE | : | Colleges of Teacher Education |
| DCI | : | Dental Council of India |
| DEC | : | Distance Education Council |
| DGS | : | Directorate General of Shipping |
| DIET | : | District Institutes of Teacher Education |
| DL | : | Digital Libraries |
| DLI | : | Digital Library of India |
| DPEP | : | District Primary Education Programme |
| EASS | : | East African Submarine Cable System |
| EBB | : | Educationally Backwards Block |
| EC | : | European Commission |
| ECCE | : | Early Childhood Care and Education |
| EE | : | Environmental Education |
| EFA | : | Education for All |
| EGS | : | Education Guarantee Scheme |
| EMIS | : | Educational Management Information System |
| EMRS | : | Eklavya Model Residential Schools |
| FCI | : | Food Corporation of India |
| FEP | : | Foreign Education Provider Foreign education institutions, |
| FOSS | : | Free and Open Source Software |
| FRLHT | : | Foundation for Revitalisation of Local Health Traditions |
| GEI | : | Global Education Initiative |
| GEP | : | Girls Education Programme |

GLOBE : Global Learning and Observations to Benefit the Environent

GOI : Government of India

GSDL : Greenstone Digital Library Software

HEI : Higher Educational Institutions

IASE : Institutes of Advanced Study in Education

IB : International Baccalaureate

ICAR : Indian Council for Agriculture Research

ICC : International Co-operation Cell

ICDS : Integrated Child Development Services

ICMR : Indian Council of Medical Research

ICSE : Indian Certificate of Secondary Education

ICSSR : Indian Council of Social Science Research

ICT : Information and Communications Technology

IDMI : Infrastructure Development of Minority Institute

IGNOU : Indira Gandhi National Open University

IIITH : International Institute of Information Technology, Hyderabad

IIPS : International Institute for Population Sciences

IISC : Indian Institute of Science

ILO : International Labour Organisation

IMC : Indian Medlars Centre

IMLS : Institute of Museum and Library Services

INC : Indian Nursing Council

INDCAT : Indian Catalog of University Libraries in India

INDEST : Indian National Digital Library in Engineering Sciences and Technology

INSAT : Indian National Satellite System

ISC : Indian School Certificate

ISI : Institute for Scientific Information

IT : Information Technology

KSOU : Karnataka State Open University

KVS : Kendriya Vidyalayas

LCD : Liquid-Crystal Display

LIS : Library and Information Science

LWE : Left Wing Extremism

MCI : Medical Council of India

MDG : Millennium Development Goal

MDMS : Mid Day Meal Scheme

| | | |
|---|---|---|
| MHRD | : | Ministry of Human Resource Development |
| MLL | : | Minimum Levels of Learning |
| MoEF | : | Ministry of Environment and Forests |
| MPBOU | : | Madhya Pradesh Bhoj Open University |
| NAAC | : | National Assessment and Accreditation Council |
| NACO | : | National Aids Control Organisation |
| NARA | : | National Accreditation Regulatory Authority |
| NBA | : | National Board of Accreditation |
| NCERT | : | National Council of Educational Research and Training |
| NCHER | : | National Commission for Higher Education and Research |
| NCTE | : | National Council for Teacher Education |
| NEAC | : | National Environment Awareness Campaign |
| NFEC | : | National Fundamental Education Centre |
| NGO | : | Non Governmental organisations |
| NIC | : | National Informatics Centre |
| NIEPA | : | National Institute of Educational Planning and Administration |
| NIN | : | National Institute of Nutrition |
| NIOS | : | National Institute of Open Schooling |
| NLA | : | National Library of Australia |
| NLM | : | National Literacy Mission |
| NNMB | : | National Nutrition Monitoring Bureau |
| NOS | : | National Open School |
| NOU | : | Nalanda Open University |
| NPE | : | National Policy of Education |
| NPEGEL | : | National Programme for Education of Girls at Elementary Level |
| NP-NSEP | : | National Programme of Nutritional Support to Primary Education |
| NSDC | : | National Skill Development Corporation |
| NSOU | : | Netaji Subhas Open University |
| NVS | : | Navodaya Vidyalayas |
| OBB | : | Operation Black Board |
| OBC | : | Other Backward Classes |
| OCW | : | Open Course Ware |
| ODL | : | Online Distance Learning |
| OECD | : | Organisation for Economic Co-operation and Development |
| OHP | : | Over Head Projector |
| PCI | : | Pharmacy Council of India |
| PCT | : | Patent Co-operation Treaty |

| | | |
|---|---|---|
| PPP | : | Public–Private Partnership |
| PRA | : | Participatory Rural Appraisal |
| PSLE | : | Primary School Leaving Examination |
| PSSOU | : | Pt. Sunderlal Sharma Open University |
| PTA | : | Parent Teacher Association |
| QA | : | Quality Assurance |
| RCI | : | Rehabilitation Council of India |
| RMSA | : | Rashtriya Madhyamik Shiksha Abhiyan |
| RRA | : | Rapid Rural Appraisal |
| RRA | : | Regional Resource Agency |
| RTE | : | Right of Children to Free and Compulsory Education |
| RTE | : | Right to Education |
| SACON | : | Salim Ali Centre for Ornithology and Natural History |
| SC | : | Scheduled Castes |
| SCERT | : | State Council Educational Research and Training |
| SCI | : | Science Citation Index |
| SIS | : | State Implementation Societies |
| SITE | : | Society for Information Technology and Teacher Education |
| SPQEM | : | Scheme for Providing Quality Education in Madrasas |
| SSA | : | Sarva Siksha Abhiyan |
| SSCI | : | Social Science Citation Index |
| ST | : | Scheduled Tribes |
| STD | : | Sexually Transmitted Diseases |
| TNOU | : | Tamil Nadu Open University |
| UDCT | : | University Department of Chemical Technology |
| UDHR | : | Universal Declaration of Human Rights |
| UEE | : | Universal Elementary Education |
| UGC | : | University Grants Commission |
| UK | : | United Kingdom |
| UNDP | : | United Nations Development Programme |
| UNESCO | : | United Nations Educational, Scientific and Cultural Organisation |
| UNFPA | : | United Nations Population Fund |
| UNICEF | : | United Nations Children's Fund |
| UPE | : | Universal Primary Education |
| UPRTOU | : | U.P. Rajarshi Tandon Open University |

| | | |
|---|---|---|
| VEC | : | Village Education Committee |
| VMOU | : | Vardhman Mahaveer Open University |
| VVS | : | Vidya-Volunteer Scheme |
| WEF | : | World Economic Forums |
| WIPO | : | World Intellectual Protection Organisation |
| WWW | : | World Wide Web |
| YCMOU | : | Yashwantrao Chavan Maharashtra Open University |

# PART I – PRIMARY EDUCATION

# 1

# Primary Education in India: Progress and Challenges

***Prof. N.G.Pandse and Dr.Sukanta Sarkar***

*"Intelligence plus character-that is the goal of true education."*

**-Martin Luther King Jr.**

## Introduction

Education in general sense is a form of learning in which the knowledge, skills and habits of a group of people are transferred from one generation to the next through teaching, training, or research. Systems of schooling involve institutionalized teaching and learning in relation to a curriculum, which itself is established according to a predetermined purpose of the schools in the system. Schools systems are sometimes based on religions, giving them different curricula. According to some learned people, the word "*Education*" has been derived from the Latin term *"Educatum"* which means the act of teaching or training. A group of educationists say that it has come from another Latin word *"Educare"* which means *"to bring up" or "to raise"*. All these meanings indicate that education seeks to nourish the good qualities in man and draw out the best in every individual. The real meaning of education is the process of becoming an educated person. It entails the delivery of skills, knowledge and information from the teachers to the students. An educated person has the access to many optimal states of mind.

The Indian State is well aware of the importance of ensuring universal basic education. In 1950, the Constitution had resolved in Article 45 under the Directive Principles of state Policy that the '*...State shall endeavour to provide, within a period of ten years from the commencement of this Constitution, for free and compulsory education for all children until they complete the age of fourteen*'. Since then, many documents including every Five Year Plan, the 1968 National Policy on

Education, and the revised 1992 National Policy on Education have attempted to refine India's efforts at Universal Elementary Education (UEE). The 42nd Amendment to the Constitution in 1976 brought education, which was largely a state responsibility, into the Concurrent List and made universalising elementary education the responsibility of both the central and state governments. In 2002, Government of India took another significant step by making elementary education a fundamental right through the 86th Constitutional Amendment. In 2009, India went further and passed the Right of Children to Free and Compulsory Education Act (2009).

## Concept

Primary education is the first stage of compulsory education. In most countries, it is compulsory for children to receive primary education although it is permissible for parents to provide it. In countries such as the United States and Canada, primary education generally covers the first six or seven years of school life. In many countries, although primary education is compulsory, it can be permissible for parents to provide this level at home. However this education is provided, its importance is undeniable. The United Nations has explicitly identified universal primary education by 2015 as one of its Millennium Development Goals. The relative priority of various areas, and the methods used to teach them are an area of considerable political debate. Typically, primary education is provided in schools, where the child will stay in steadily advancing classes until they complete it and move on to high school/secondary school. Children are usually placed in classes with one teacher who will be primarily responsible for their education and welfare for that year. This teacher may be assisted to varying degrees by specialist teachers in certain subject areas, often music or physical education.

## Importance of Primary Education

Primary education fulfills the special needs of students during the first few years of their schooling life. It has specific goals that make it an exceedingly important component of an educational system as a whole. Parents can elect to send children to either public or private institutions when it comes time for them to receive primary education. In these institutions, primary education can last from five to seven years. It usually begins at kindergarten and continues until grades five to seven, depending on the particular system. Primary education lays the groundwork for future learning and future success. The skills and values that primary education instills are no less than foundational, and serve as bases for all future learning, whether formal or informal. Students build on their primary education in their succeeding years in the educational system.

Universal Primary Education (UPE) is a goal stated in many national development plans and pursued with vigour by governments of most developing countries. Primary Education is seen as the first step in laying the foundation for future educational opportunities and life long skills. Through the skills and knowledge imbued, primary education enables people to participate in the social, economic and political activities of their communities to their fullest potential. It is also seen as a basic human right that frees human beings from a state of ignorance and helps to reduce the negative effects of poverty, relating in particular to health and nutrition. Educated girls are more productive at home and better paid in the workplace, and more able to participate in social, economic and political decision-making.

**Primary Education in India**

In ancient times, India had the *Gurukula* system of education in which anyone who wished to study went to a teacher's (Guru) house and requested to be taught. If accepted as a student by the guru, he would then stay at the guru's place and help in all activities at home. This not only created a strong tie between the teacher and the student, but also taught the student everything about running a house. The modern school system was brought to India, including the English language, originally by Lord Thomas Babington Macaulay in the 1830s. The curriculum was confined to *"modern"* subjects such as science and mathematics. Teaching was confined to classrooms and the link with nature was broken, as also the close relationship between the teacher and the student. The Uttar Pradesh Board of High School and Intermediate Education was the first Board set up in India in the year 1921 with jurisdiction over Rajputana, Central India and Gwalior. In 1929, the Board of High School and Intermediate Education, Rajputana, was established. Later, boards were established in some of the states. In 1952, the constitution of the board was amended and it was renamed Central Board of Secondary Education (CBSE). Universal and compulsory education for all children in the age group of 6-14 was a cherished dream of the new government of the Republic of India. This is evident from the fact that it is incorporated as a directive policy in article 45 of the constitution. Each state in the country has its own Department of Education that runs its own school system with its own textbooks and evaluation system. The curriculum, pedagogy and evaluation method are largely decided by the SCERT in the state, following the national guidelines prescribed by the NCERT. Each state has three kinds of schools that follow the state curriculum. The government runs its own schools in land and buildings owned by the government and paying the staff from its own resources. These are generally known as government schools.

Research suggests that pre-primary education is very important for the development of young children before they enter formal school. It helps in cognitive development of children at the early grades of primary education and it has strong bearing on attendance and participation of children once they enter primary school. Pre-primary education is considered to be very important for the child as it is the first step towards entering the world of knowledge as well as a healthy and purposeful life. Pre-primary education helps children become more independent and confident as well as promoting the all round development of the children. The National policy on Education 1986 and its Plan of Action have placed immense importance on pre-school education. At national or state level it is partially supported by the ongoing flagship educational programme Sarva Siksha Abhiyan (SSA) which includes a major component of ECCE. The Government of India launched the Integrated Child Development Services (ICDS) scheme in 1975. The Department of Women and Child Development has been implementing the scheme which seeks to provide health care facilities, supplementary nutritional support and to improve children's communication and cognitive skills as a preparation for entry into primary school. Initially the programme started as a project in some states but presently it covers many rural and tribal areas along with some urban pockets targeting mainly underprivileged children.

A strong education system is the cornerstone of any country's growth and prosperity. Over the last decade, India has made great strides in strengthening its primary education system. In 2012 that 95percent of India's rural populations are within one kilometer of primary schools. The 2011 Annual Status of Education Report (ASER), which tracks trends in rural education, indicated that enrollment rates among primary-school-aged children were about 93percent, with little difference by gender. About 20% of Indian children between the ages of six and 14 are not enrolled in school. Even among enrolled children, attendance rates are low and 26percent of pupils enrolled in primary school drop out before Grade 5. The situation is worse in certain sectors of the population i.e. poor who living in rural areas and those living in some states, such as Bihar and Rajasthan. Realizing the importance and the critical state of primary education in India today, many organizations on many levels are focusing on this issue. International agencies, such as UNESCO and UNICEF are deeply involved. UNESCO has pledged to work with national governments and development partners to achieve universal free primary education by 2015, as was agreed upon at the World Education Forum in Dakar. UNICEF also has primary education as part of its mission. Both are supporting the Government of India in its task with funds and expertise. Many NGOs in India run schools for poor children. Some organizations, such as Katha, Pratham, and Prayas, have made universal primary education their focus and operate education centers for children in slum areas. Others NGOs are niche players that target particular segments of the child population with innovative programs.

Children with disabilities and working children are two other categories that have not enjoyed the benefits of universal schooling. The education departments are not generally dealing with issues concerning these sets of children. Legislations for the disabled and for child labour form the concern of other ministries and departments which have very little coordination with the education department. One hopes that the new legislation on education would tackle this issue at least to some extent. Teachers have a pivotal role to play in schools, especially in rural areas where they are the sole representatives of the education system. Much of school quality in fact depends on the teacher. Many teachers are experiencing a growing disconnect with children. Several systemic and structural deficiencies characterize the functioning of government schools. There are exceptions but by and large, the quality of rural and even urban schooling is abysmal. With few exceptions, the quality of public school infrastructure even in cities and urban areas is abysmal. Several suggestions have been made for improving school effectiveness. Schools need to become pro-actively inclusive and inspirational. Decentralization of management is advanced as the solution for improving the performance of schools. Reports from across the country suggest the many benefits of decentralized management of schools. While the benefits of decentralization are more evident in financial and administrative decision making, it is less so in its impact on enhancing the quality of education.

On the whole, there has been a steady increase in school enrolment starting from 1990. The acceleration in enrolment in recent yeas is plausible, given a number of schemes such as the recruitment of local teachers, increasing proximity of schools, serving of hot-cooked meals in schools, and incentives for girls do encourage children to enroll in schools. On the matter of enrolment, parental indifference has often been identified as a major factor that keeps children out of school. Despite aggregate improvements in education levels, glaring inequalities in basic education continue to persist. Disparities between regions (states) and across gender, caste, class, religious groups; and other marginalized sections of society continue to present the biggest challenge for policy makers and educationists. A large proportion of minority groups and principal among them, Muslims remain deprived of access to basic education. The availability of census data by religion for the first time allows looking at the trends in the education levels of religious groups such as the Muslims. In addition, the recently released Sachar Committee Report (2006) also provides a broad perspective on the education of Muslims in India. It points out that the *'condition of Muslims is of grave concern....Despite overall improvements in educational status the rate of progress has been the slowest for Muslims (compared to other socio-religious groups).'* As many as 25 per cent of Muslim children in the age group 6–14 years are currently not enrolled in any school. In some instances the relative share of Muslims is lower than even the SCs who are victims of a long standing caste system. Such relative deprivation calls for a significant policy shift, in the recognition of the problem and in devising corrective measures, as well as in the allocation of resources.

The landmark passing of the Right of Children to Free and Compulsory Education (RTE) Act 2009 marks a historic moment for the children of India. For the first time in India's history, children will be guaranteed their right to quality elementary education by the state with the help of families and communities. Few countries in the world have such a national provision to ensure child-centered, child-friendly education to help all children develop to their fullest potential. There were an estimated eight million six to 14-year-olds in India out-of-school in 2009. India's education system over the past few decades has made significant progress. According to India's Education For All Mid Decade Assessment, in just five years between 2000 and 2005, India increased primary school enrolment overall by 13.7 per cent and by 19.8 per cent for girls, reaching close to universal enrolment in Grade 1. The number of out-of-school children has declined from 25 million in 2003 to 8.1 millions in mid–2009. The most significant improvements have been in Bihar, Jharkhand, Manipur and Chhattisgarh. The percentage of out-of-school children in highly populated states like Uttar Pradesh, West Bengal, Orissa and Bihar remains a cause of concern. Although there have been significant improvements in the proportion of children from socially disadvantaged groups in school, persistence gaps remain. Girls are still less likely to enroll in school than boys. In 2005, for upper primary school (Grades 6-8) girls' enrolment was still 8.8 points lower than boys for Scheduled Tribes (ST) the gender gap was 12.6 points and 16 points for Scheduled Castes (SC). Children have the right to have at least one qualified and trained teacher for every 30 pupils. Currently, the national average is about 1 teacher to every 34 students, but in states such as Jharkhand, Madhya Pradesh and West Bengal one teacher works with more than 60 students. Approximately 1.2 million additional teachers need to be recruited to fill this gap. Currently, about one in five primary school teachers do not have the requisite minimum academic qualification to ensure children's right to quality learning. UNICEF is committed to ensuring all children to have access to quality education and complete their schooling. UNICEF works with its partners to improve children's developmental readiness to start primary school on time, especially for marginalized children. Technical support on education quality, school retention and achievement rates are also given. UNICEF is also working to reduce gender and other disparities to increase access and completion of quality basic education. In emergencies, UNICEF helps to restore education to affected populations.

Among one of the leading priorities for the UNICEF worldwide is its commitment to ensure that every girl and every boy completes a quality, primary-school education. The number of children attending school has gone up many-fold since the time of India's Independence increasing from around 19.2 million in 1950-51 to 113.8 million in 2000-01. But several problems persist. Among the many contributing factors is the quality of the physical space that children inhabit. Of India's 700,000 rural schools, only one in six have toilets deterring children especially girls from going to school, and if enrolled, in remaining there. The persistence of class and caste differences and the prevalence of child labour further complicate this scenario, obstructing both girls and boys from having equal opportunities to education. The rate of school attendance is better than ever before with more and more children between the ages of six and 14 enrolling at schools, the education system is inadequately developed i.e. wracked by a shortage of resources, schools, classrooms and teachers. Often, due to the resulting, poor quality of teaching, many children drop out before completing five years of primary school and many of those who stay on, learn little. Government efforts have been intensified in recent years following the launch of various programmes including the District Primary Education Programme (DPEP) in 1992, the Minimum Levels of Learning (MLL) initiative and more recently the Sarva Shiksha Abhiyan (or the National Programme for Universal Elementary Education). UNICEF is an active partner in the Sarva Shiksha Abhiyan supporting its objective to ensure all children complete five years of school and have access to good quality education.

Since the late 1980s, government efforts to augment rural primary education have been supplemented by the emergence of an intervention-based non-governmental system that spans multiple institutional types. While private schools have emerged as a parallel system over the last two decades, their impact is limited because they serve less than 13percent of India's rural primary-school children. Some organisations are attempting to innovate with new formats and systems of education. The Indian government at every level recognizes the need for educational reform and has made a conscientious effort to achieve it. The midday-meal plan, for example, is a highly publicized nationwide program through which government school children across India are provided with a midday meal every day of the school week. The program is largely considered a success. In 2012, the Central Government enacted the Right to Education (RTE) Act, under which every child between the ages of six and 14 receives a free and compulsory education. In addition to regulating access to education, the act contains certain provisions that could positively impact the quality of education. Education in India has improved dramatically over the last three decades. Schools are accessible to most children, both student enrollment and attendance are at their highest level, and teachers are adequately remunerated. The RTE Act guarantees a quality education to a wider range of students than ever before. However, challenges in implementing and monitoring high standards in teaching and learning outcomes across regional, cultural and socioeconomic subsets prevent India from fully achieving this goal.

**Millennium Development Goals**

The United Nations Millennium Development Goal is to achieve universal primary education by the year 2015, by which time they aim to ensure that all children everywhere regardless of race or gender, will be able to complete primary schooling. Due to the fact that the United Nations is specifically focusing on Sub-Saharan Africa and Southern Asia, as they are both home to the vast majority of children out of school, they hypothesize that they might not be able to reach their goal by 2015. In order to achieve the goal by 2015, the United Nations estimates that all children at the official entry age for primary school would have had to be attending classes by 2009. This would depend on the duration of the primary level as well as how well the school schools retain students until the end of the cycle.

Meeting the Education Goal will speed progress toward every other Millennium Goal. Educating children helps reduce poverty and promote gender equality. It helps lower child mortality rates and promotes concern for the environment. UNICEF advocates quality basic education for all, with an emphasis on gender equality and eliminating disparities of all kinds. In particular, getting girls into school and ensuring that they stay and learn has what UNICEF calls a *"multiplier effect"*. UNICEF stages global information campaigns on the importance of getting children to school, especially girls, and has committed $233 million to these efforts. Education for Every Child' campaign is about raising awareness, generating public support and mobilizing resources for *'25 by 2005'*, an accelerated effort to get girls in school in 25 countries. Such campaigns involve a wide range of partners from children and teachers to religious leaders and popular sports such as soccer and cricket to help get the word out. UNICEF also works directly with governments to highlight and address issues of gender discrimination or other roadblocks to education, such as school fees or forced child labour. UNICEF serves as the lead agency for the United Nations Girls' Education Initiative (UNGEI), a group of partners dedicated to achieving gender parity and equality targets in education.

### Challenges

India's education system has not achieved strong learning outcomes for reasons that are as diverse and nuanced as the country itself. Key among these reasons is poor teaching quality, which results from a multitude of factors.

1. Teachers working in primary schools across rural India have a difficult job.
2. Primary education in India has lack of methodical approach.
3. A key factor affecting the quality of primary education appears to be low levels of teacher motivation. In 2002-2003, 25per cent of primary-school teachers in rural India were absent on any given day. The impact of absenteeism is exacerbated by the fact that the average primary school in India has a workforce of no more than three teachers.
4. In India, rote learning has been institutionalized as a teaching methodology. Primary school teachers in rural India often try to educate students by making them repeat sections of text over and over again.
5. Finally, India's linguistic diversity creates unique challenges for the nation's education system. The country's 22 official languages and hundreds of spoken dialects often differ considerably from the official language of the state or region.
6. Many of the Indian schools are not yet converted into new pattern books.

### Conclusion

Primary education is more important for socio-economic development of any country. The Importance of Primary education has been neglected in India knowingly or unknowingly since independence and the government of India is now realized and willing to improve wise primary education by making legislation and planning to cover all the sections of age group of 6 – 14 years of age and assuring for the deserved free education. India has demonstrated considerable progress in the past decade on improving primary school access, infrastructure, pupil-teacher ratios, teacher salaries, and student enrollment. Nevertheless, student learning levels and trajectories are disturbingly low. The landmark passing of the Right of Children to Free and Compulsory Education (RTE) Act 2009 marks a historic moment for the children of India. The United Nations Millennium Development Goal is to achieve universal primary education by the year 2015, by which time they aim to ensure that all children everywhere regardless of race or gender, will be able to complete primary schooling.

## References


1. A. K. Shiva Kumar & Preet Rustagi (2010). *Elementary education in India: Progress, Setbacks, and Challenges,* Retried from http://www.oxfamindia.org/sites/default/files/III.%20Elementary%20Education%20in%20India-Progress,%20 Setbacks,%20and%20Challenges.pdf.
2. Anthony Wilson (2005). *Creativity in Primary Education*, First edition, Learning Matters Limited.
3. Archana Gelda, Vinay Narayan, Meghana Mudiyam, Karan Raturi and Nikhil Seshan (2013). *Need improvement: Despite progress, Indian primary education system has a way to go,* Retrieved from http://knowledge.wharton.upenn.edu/article/needs-improvement-despite-progress-indias-primary-education-system-has-a-ways-to-go/
4. Brian Woolland (1993). *The teaching of drama in the primary school,* First edition, Longman.
5. Colin Richards (1984). *The Study of Primary Education:* A Source Book, Volume 1, Falmer Press.
6. Carol Elston (2007). *Using ICT in the Primary School,* First edition, SAGE.
7. David Dunn (2011). *How to be an Outstanding Primary School Teacher*, First edition, Continuum.
8. Dr. V. Sasi Kumar, *The education system in India,* Retrieved from http://www.gnu.org/education/edu-system-india.html.
9. Education sector development programme: primary education development plan (2002-2006), Basic Education Development Committee.
10. Edward Conrad Wragg & George Brown (2001). *Questioning in the Primary School,* First edition, Routledge Falmer.
11. Eve Bearne (2002). *Differentiation and Diversity in the Primary School,* First edition, Taylor & Francie.
12. *Education-India- UNICEF,* Retrieved from http://www.unicef.org/india/education.html.
13. John Lancaster (1990). *Art in the Primary School,* First edition, Routledge.
14. Malcolm Clarkson (1988). *Emerging issues in primary education*, First edition, Falmer Press.
15. Marilyn Leask, & John Meadows (2000). *Teaching and Learning with ICT in the Primary School,* First edition, Psychology Press.
16. Penelope Harnett (2008). *Understanding Primary Education: Developing Professional Attributes,* Knowledge and Skills, First edition, Routledge.

17. *Pre primary education in India (2010).* Retrieved from http://www.create-rpc.org/pdf_documents/India_Policy_Brief_1.pdf.
18. *Primary school years,* Retrieved from http://www.unicef.org/india/children_166.htm.
19. Ranjani Iyer Mohanty, *Primary education in India,* Retrieved from http://birbhum.gov.in/DPSC/reference/19.pdf.
20. R. F. Dearden (1968). *The philosophy of primary education,* First edition, Routledge & Kegan Paul.
21. *The Importance of Primary Education,* Retrieved from http://www.ehow.com/about_6574902_importance-primary-education.html.
22. Webb Rosemary (2006). *Changing Teaching and Learning in the Primary School,* First edition, McGraw-Hill International.
23. http://www.pngbuai.com/300socialsciences/education/policy/globalization/ed-global-1.html.
24. http://www.unicef.org/mdg/education.html.

# 2

# Progress of Upper Primary Education in India: A Comparative Study of Pre and Post Reform Period

***Prof D. Pulla Rao***

*"Live as if you were to die tomorrow. Learn as if you were to live forever."*

**— Mahatma Gandhi**

## Introduction

One of the important characteristic features of democracy is that it presupposes an educated and enlightened society. Democracy, both as a form of the government and as a way of life, cannot function when the society is uneducated and ignorant. Education and modernisation are the two wheels of the same cart. Both, when combined together, lead to a rapid socio-economic development of a nation. Economists have been arguing with sufficient empirical evidence that education contributes positively to development. A number of studies have been undertaken by researchers to establish the relationship between literacy and socio-economic development. It is, however, necessary to remember that primary education is pivotal for achieving literacy. Universalisation of Elementary Education (UEE) is a constitution provision and a national commitment in India. Universalisation implies education all children up to the age of 14 which is equivalent to completion of upper primary level of education. Over the years, efforts by the government towards achieving the goal of UEE were focussed more on the primary stage then on the upper primary level of education. With the expansion of enrollment at the primary level of education, the pressure for expansion of the upper primary level of education has increased. The present study was an effort to analyse implication for provision of upper primary education facilities to ensure that this level of education is provided to all eligible children. This implies creation of easy geographical access conditions to enroll all the eligible children in upper primary schools, provision reasonable level of physical and infrastructural facilities in upper primary schools and teaching learning materials in the classrooms to facilitate meaningful curriculum transaction.

Universalisation of upper primary education in India is normally discussed in terms of enrolling and retaining all children belonging to the group 11 to 14. This seems more to be a desirable goal to be achieved in the long run than a realisable target at the present level of development of primary education. Enrollment is a function of the relevant the group at the primary level of education. However, enrolment in upper primary schools is more a function of primary education completion rates than a function of the relevant the group (11 to 14) cannot be enrolled in upper primary classes unless they complete primary level of education. In other words, all relevant the group children can be provided upper primary education only when all children of the primary school going age group are enrolled, retained and successfully complete the primary stage of education. Since primary education is not yet universalised, this implies that universalisation of upper primary education means providing upper primary education for all children who have successfully completed primary level of upper primary education in India. However, once universalisation of primary education is attained, then there cannot be any difference between providing upper primary level education to all the group children and those who complete primary stage of education. The efforts at present needs to be to improve the inter-stage transition ratios from primary to upper primary level in education.

**Present Structure of School Education in India**

India, being a union of states, has accepted a uniform structure of school and college education popularly known as 10+2+3 pattern of school and college education. This pattern visualised 10 years of general education including eight years of elementary followed by two years of secondary education; two years of senior secondary followed by three years of college education leading to the award of the first degree. Until recently there existed several different patterns such as 8+3+3, 10+1+3, or 10+2+2. But, in pursuance of the recommendations of the Education Commission (1964-66) and the proposals of the National Policy on Education, 1968, most of the States have adopted 10+2+3 pattern. The National Policy on Education (NPE)-1986 also reiterated the need for adopting a common pattern, namely, the 10+2+3 in the whole country. The NPE-1986 also proposed adopt of a common structure of elementary education consisting of eight years of schooling – five years of primary and three years of upper primary education. Therefore, the present structure of school education can be represented as {(5+3) +2+2}. A child is admitted to class I, normally, at the age of six years and is supposed to complete primary education up to Class V at the age of 11 years, and elementary education up to Class VIII, at the age of 14 years. Up to this stage the state is constitutionally obliged to provide for free and compulsory education to all children under Article 45 of the Constitution of India. Elementary education is followed by two years of secondary education popularly known as *'High School'*.

**Objectives**

1. To examine the growth of enrollment of students in upper primary schools by sex and the corresponding growth in the number of schools.
2. To estimate the trends in the student-teacher ratio in upper primary education, and
3. To compare the development of upper primary education in pre-reform period and post-reform period.

**The Data**

The secondary data relating to the number of recognised schools, enrolment by sex and number of teachers appointed by sex in upper primary schools for selected years of more than five decades period from 1965-66 to 2009-10 are obtained from annual reports for various years, Ministry of Human Resource Development, Government of India and from Selected Educational Statistics for various years, Ministry of Human Resource Development, Government of India. In as much as the terminal year of our study is 2009-10, it cannot adequately reflect upon the phenomenal changes that have taken place in the upper primary educational set up in the more recent past especially pre-reform period and post-reform period. This is a limitation of the study. The progress of UEE in India may be analysed in terms of three identifiable periods in history after independence.

1. Before Education Commission (1966)
2. Between Education Commission and the National Policy on Education - 1986, and
3. After National Policy on Education – 1986.

Our study is limited to 1965-66 to 2009-10. We have divided our study period into two phases for estimation of annual compound growth rate of schools, enrolment and teachers by sex. Phase one refers to the period between the years 1965-66 and 1985-86. It may be called pre-reform period. And phase two refers to the period between 1990-91 and 2009-10 and this may be called post-reform period.

**Progress of Upper Primary Education**

From Table 2.1 it may be observed that there were only 75798 upper primary schools in the country in 1965-66 and this number continuously increased to 367745 in 2009-10. The index of upper primary schools recorded a much higher increase than that of index of primary schools. The annual compound growth rate of upper primary schools was 3.57 per cent for the entire period of study. The rate is much higher in phase two (4.54 per cent) than in phase one (2.92 per cent). There were 10.5 million children enrolled in upper primary schools in 1965-66, of which 2.8 million were girls. They constitute only 26.67 per cent of the total enrollment. The total enrollment in these schools had increased to 27.3 million in 1985-1986 in which they were 17.7 million boys and 9.6 million girls. The enrollment in upper primary schools ultimately reached to 51.2 million in 2004-05, of which 22.7 million were girls with 44.33 per cent of the total enrollment and it is just decreased to 51 million but there is hike in girl's enrollment with 45.88 per cent of total enrollment in 2009-10. An interesting trend which can easily be observed is that enrollment of girls has grown at a higher rate than boys during the period of study in upper primary education. It is emphasised that the index of girls' enrollment in upper primary education is much higher than that of index of girls' enrollment in primary education. It is a positive sign and shows the improvement of upper primary education in the country during the study period. The annual compound growth rate of enrollment of total children in phase one was 4.89 per cent and it is much higher than that of the growth rate in phase two (2.05 per cent) and total period (3.57 per cent). It is interesting that the growth rate of enrollment in the case of girls is more than that of boys over the period.

**Student-Teacher Ratio in Upper Primary Schools**

As noted earlier, the student-teacher ratio shows the quality of education. Here, we examine the growth in the number of teachers employed in the upper primary schools in the country during the period under study. The data are presented in Table 2.2. It is observed that there were 5, 28,000 teachers employed in upper primary schools in 1965-1966, of which 1, 39,000 were women, with 26.32 per cent of the total. By 2009-10, the total number of teachers in upper primary schools increased to 19, 12,000 from which 8, 01,000 are women with 41.89 per cent.

The number of women teachers reached on all time high in 2009-10 (801,000) and they constitute 41.89 per cent of the total teachers, indicating that women teaching community has been on the increase all through. One should consider this to be a healthy sign for the reasons, (1) that it contributes to gender equality and (2) that women teacher's exhibit care and patience, their general traits, in teaching children. The number of both in male and female teachers in upper primary schools shows an increasing trend over the period of our study. The index of female teachers recorded a much higher increase than that of the male teachers. This may be due to implementation of reservation policies in some states in the country in favour of women.

The annual compound growth rate of total teachers was 3.08 per cent in first phase. It is higher than the growth rate of total teachers in second phase (2.93 per cent). It is interesting that the growth rate of female teachers was 4.01 per cent and it was higher than that of the male teachers at 2.70 per cent in those one. In the

**Table 2.1: Enrollment and Number of Recognised Upper Primary Schools in India: 1965-1966 to 2009-10**

| *Year* | *Upper Primary Schools* | *Index* | *per cent growth rate over previous period* | *No. of Boys enrolled (11-14 years) (in millions)* | *Index* | *per cent growth rate over previous period* | *No. of Girls enrolled (11-14 years) (in millions)* | *Index* |
|---|---|---|---|---|---|---|---|---|
| 1965-66 | 75798 | 100 | — | 7.7 | 100 | — | 2.8 | 100 |
| 1970-71 | 90621 | 119 | 19.55 | 9.4 | 122 | 22.08 | 3.9 | 139 |
| 1975-76 | 106571 | 141 | 17.60 | 11 | 143 | 17.02 | 5 | 179 |
| 1980-81 | 118571 | 156 | 11.26 | 13.9 | 180 | 26.36 | 6.8 | 243 |
| 1985-86 | 134846 | 177 | 13.72 | 17.7 | 230 | 27.34 | 9.6 | 343 |
| 1990-91 | 151456 | 200 | 12.3 2 | 21.5 | 279 | 21.47 | 12.5 | 446 |
| 1995-96 | 171216 | 226 | 13.05 | 25 | 324 | 16 .28 | 16 | 571 |
| 1999-2000 | 198004 | 261 | 15.64 | 25.1 | 326 | 0.40 | 17 | 607 |
| 2004-05 | 274731 | 362 | 38.75 | 28.5 | 370 | 13.54 | 22.7 | 811 |
| 2009-10 | 367745 | 485 | 33.85 | 27.6 | 358 | -3.16 | 23.4 | 836 |
| 1st phase | 2.92 | | | 4.25 | | | 6.35 | |
| 2nd phase | 4.54 | | | 1.26 | | | 3.19 | |
| Total period | 3.57 | | | 2.88 | | | 4.83 | |

Sources: 1. Annual reports of Ministry of Human Resource Development, Government of India. 2. Selected Educational Statistics, Ministry of Human Resource Development, Government of India.

second phase the growth rate of female teachers was 4.14 per cent and it was higher than that of male teachers at 2.21 per cent. The growth rates gradually decreased in phase two in male teachers, but the growth rates of female teachers have been higher than that of male teachers in both the phases and also total period of our study. During the period under study, the increase in the number of teachers was 13,84,000 that means at the beginning the total number of teachers in 1965-66 was 5,28,000 and it is increased to 19,12,000 in 2009-10. As the enrollment in upper primary schools showed an increasing trend, it resulted in a favourable change in student-teacher ratio. It is observed that the ratio was 20:1 in 1965-66 and it increased to 28:1 in 1985-1986. Later, the ratio gradually increased to 35:1 in 1995-1996. By 2009-10 the ratio decreased and stood at 27:1. Anyhow, this figure is less than the student-teacher ratio of 40 recommended by the government for aided schools.

**Conclusions**

It is a common knowledge that India achieved freedom from the British imperialism on 15th August, 1947. Many decades have elapsed since. Yet in matters of education in general and primary education in particular the country is enviably placed. Economic backwardness of the country may have to do with mass illiteracy and ignorance of the people. But economic backwardness alone cannot explain educational backwardness. Kerala, though not particularly a rich state in the country, has achieved the

**Table 2.2: Number of Teachers Employed by Sex in Upper Primary Schools in India: 1965-1966 to 2009-10 (in 000s)**

| *Year* | *Male* | *Index* | *Percentage of growth rate over previous period* | *Female* | *Index* | *Percentage of growth rate over previous period* |
|---|---|---|---|---|---|---|
| 1965-66 | 389 | 100 | —— | 139 | 100 | —— |
| 1970-71 | 463 | 119 | 19.02 | 175 | 126 | 25.90 |
| 1975-76 | 554 | 142 | 19.65 | 224 | 161 | 28.00 |
| 1980-81 | 598 | 153 | 7.94 | 253 | 182 | 12.95 |
| 1985-86 | 663 | 170 | 10.87 | 305 | 219 | 20.55 |
| 1990-91 | 717 | 184 | 8.14 | 356 | 256 | 16.72 |
| 1995-96 | 756 | 194 | 5.44 | 409 | 294 | 14.89 |
| 1999-2000 | 829 | 213 | 9.66 | 469 | 337 | 14.67 |
| 2004-05 | 992 | 255 | 19.66 | 597 | 429 | 27.29 |
| 2009-10 | 1111 | 286 | 11.99 | 801 | 576 | 34.17 |
| 1st phase | 2.70 | | | 4.01 | | |
| 2nd phase | 2.21 | | | 4.14 | | |
| Total period | 2.36 | | | 3.97 | | |

*Sources:* 1. Annual reports of Ministry of Human Resource Development, Government of India. 2. Selected Educational Statistics, Ministry of Human Resource Development, Government of India.

objective of universalisation of primary-education. The population explosion in the country could not have been unrelated to the illiteracy of its people. We have examined here the effect of the initiatives of the government in the field of primary-education. More specifically, we examined the trends in upper primary-education in particular pre- reform-period and post reform period. The focus is on (1) enrollment of children by sex (2) size of the teaching staff by sex, and (3) student-teacher ratio at the upper primary stage. Our data on the trends in the enrollment of children at the upper primary level showed that it was not commensurate with the growth of population in the relevant age group, notwithstanding the fact that universalisation of elementary education has been the avowed objective of the government. The quantitative growth of enrollment has been faster in the case of girls than in the case of boys throughout the study period in upper primary education. Besides, the enrollment of students has increased at a higher - rate than the number of schools and teachers.

To reflect upon the quality of education we arrived at student-teacher ratios. Let it be told that the significance of women teachers has been increasing over time and this should contribute positively to the growth and development of children. The student-teacher ratio at the upper primary level stood at 27:1 in 2009-10 and this compares highly favourable with the accepted norm of 40:1 ratio. This no doubt augurs well for upper primary-education. There is, however, a further need to effect improvements in upper primary-education. As the child goes into the upper primary set up from primary set up there will be greater demands on the quality of teachers, of school buildings, of other infrastructure including toilets. These need to be strengthened. Mere increase in the number of teachers does not satisfy the demands of the pupils. This aspect has to be borne in mind if we want to ensure that the upper primary set up expands fast. The expansion of upper primary-education had been the highest during the 1st phase than 2nd phase in enrollment, teachers except in schools. One important reason of the downfall in the quality and standard of school education during the recent decades may be the uneven growth of enrollment, number of teachers and number of schools, the enrollment growing faster than the other two. As a conservative estimate, the population of children in the age group 6-14 years, at present, may be about 200 million of which about 160 million might be attending elementary schools. This leads to the conclusion that about 40 million children are still out of school, which constitute about 20 per cent of the relevant age group. It is reported that 22 per cent of the total out of school children of the world are in India.

According to our study, we have not been able to achieve the goal of the UEE as guaranteed in article 45 of our constitution. Though, there has been a massive expansion of schooling facilities during the reform period, the goal has moved farther with the number of out of schools children increasing. Moreover, there are glaring disparities in what has been achieved, which are based on caste, sex, religion, and rural-urban areas. There are good reasons to believe that India will not be able to achieve this goal of UEE even by 2030 unless some effective and efficient alternative strategies are planned and implemented.

## References


1. Chalam, K.S. (1985): Educational Development of the Scheduled Castes in the Districts of Andhra Pradesh, (Mimeo), School of Economics, Andhra University, Visakhapatnam.
2. Chalam, K.S. (1988): *Education and Weaker Sections,* Inter India Publication, New Delhi.
3. Chauhan, B.R. and others (1975): *Scheduled Castes and Education,* Anu Publications, Meerut.
4. Gopinathan Nair, P.R. (1981): *Primary Education, Population Growth and Socio-Economic Change,* Allied Publishers, New Delhi.
5. Government of India (1986): National Policy on Education 1986: Programme of Action, New Delhi.
6. Government of India (1994): 'Development of Education in India (1993-94)', MHRD, New Delhi.
7. Govinda, R. (2002): *"India education report:* A profile of basic education", NIEPA, Oxford, New Delhi.
8. Govinda, R. and Varghese (1992): *"Quality of primary education: an empirical study"*, Journal of Educational Planning and Administration, Vol. 6, No. 1, January, New Delhi.
9. Kabra, G.D. (1984): *Development of Weaker Sections,* Inter-India Publications, New Delhi.
10. Naik, J.P. (1975): *Elementary Education in India* – a Promise to Keep, Allied Publishers, Bombay.
11. Rajaiah, B. (1987): *Economics of Education, Mittal Publication,* New Delhi.
12. Rajput, J.S. (1994): *"Elementary Education – Alternative Strategies",* The Hindustan Times, June 10, New Delhi.
13. Saini, S.K. (1980): *"Development of Education in India",* Cosmo Publications, New Delhi.

# 3

# Employee Stress Management in Private School: An Analysis

*Ms. Sachin Sachdeva*

*"The educated differ from the uneducated as much as the living differs from the dead."*

**—Aristotle**

## Introduction

Stress is a psychological and physical response of the body that occurs whenever we must adapt to changing conditions, whether those conditions be real or perceived, positive or negative, although everyone has stress in their lives, people respond to stress in different ways. Some people seem to be severely affected while others seem calm, cool, and collected all the time. Stress is an unpleasant state of emotional and physiological arousal that people experience in situations that they perceive as dangerous or threatening to their well-being. Stress is a common experience. We may feel stress when we are very busy, have important deadlines to meet, or have too little to finish all our tasks. Often people experience stress because of problems at work or in social relationships. Stress can have both positive and negative effects. It is a threat. It signals danger and prepares us to take defensive action. Fear of things that pose realistic threats motivates us to deal with them or avoid them. It is an inevitable concomitant of organisational life. Its source is an organisation task or role related. Stress affects the employee's performance that indirectly affects the organisation survival because if employee reduces their work efficiency and can't work best for their organisation performance but also affects the mental health of the teachers.

### Stress: Hans Selye's General Adaptation Syndrome

Hans Selye was a Canadian endocrinologist who did many experiments about the effects of stress, in particular prolonged stress. For ethical reasons, Selye could not do his research on human participants and instead elected to do it on rats. Selye exposed these rats to stressors such as exposing them to extreme heat or cold, electric shocks, tying their legs together for around 24 hours, giving them bacterial infections and pulling their tails. He noticed that all the different stressors he had exposed them to had the same basic physiological response: weightloss occurred, the rats developed stomach ulcers, the immune system's vital glands shrunk and the adrenal glands became enlarged. In the alarm stage, the person first becomes aware of the stressor.

### Stage One: Alarm Reaction

In this stage, the person first becomes aware of the stressor. After becoming aware to the stressor, the body goes into a state of shock. In the state of shock, the blood pressure and body temperature drop, and temporary loss of muscle control is experienced. While in shock, the body's ability to deal with the stressor is below its normal level. Shock is just temporary though, and is then replaced with countershock. During countershock, the animal or human becomes highly alert as it prepares to deal with the stressor. The heart and respiratory system speed up, which supplies the muscles with more energy to enable the body to either fight or run away.

### Stage Two: Resistance

If the stressor is not immediately dealt with, the person or animal enters a stage of resistance, in which they try to adapt to the stressor, and cope with it. All unnecessary processes in the body, such as growth, menstruation and sex drive are shut down to save energy, so that all of it is directed towards resisting the stressor. Hormones are released into the bloodstream, which supports resistance but damages your immune system, which messes up your body's ability to fight disease.

### Stage Three: Exhaustion

If the stressor has still not been dealt with, the body enters a state of exhaustion. The person or animal can no longer deal with the effects of the stressor, and their resources are depleted. Resistance to disease is very weak, and the organism is vulnerable to physical and mental disorders. Being in this stage for too long may cause heart disease and high blood pressure, because if the hormones (adrenalin and cortisol) released during stage two are at a high level in the body for a long amount of time, they can damage the heart and the functioning of the immune system. Selye's General Adaptation Syndrome model has much strength, such as the fact that it includes the idea that resources can become depleted, increasing a person's vulnerability to disease. It also has weaknesses, the biggest being that it is a "one size fits all" model. It doesn't allow for individual differences, and ignores the fact that some people may interpret the same stressor differently (A model that does do that is the Lazarus and Folkman's transactional model of stress and coping). Critics have also argued that because most of the research the model is based on was experimenting on animals, the findings may lack relevance to humans.

**Sources of Stress**

One can experience stress from four basic sources:

1. *The Environment:* The environment can bombard with intense and completive demands to adjust,e.g., weather, noise, crowding, pollution, traffic, unsafe and substandard housing, crime etc.

2. *Social Stressors:* Multiple stressors can arise social roles, such as parents, spouse, caregiver, and employee. Some other examples of social stressors include deadline, financial problems, job interviews, loss of loved ones, divorce, etc.

3. *Physiological:* Situations and circumstances affecting our body can be experienced as physiological stressors. e.g., Include sleep disturbance, accidents, lack of exercise, poor nutrition. etc.

4. *Thoughts:* Your brain interprets and perceives situations as stressful, difficult, painful or pleasant. Some situations in life are stress provoking, but it is our thoughts that determine whether they are problem for us.

**Types of Stressors**

Situations that are stress provoking called stressors. Stress is not always a bad thing. Stress is simply the body's response to changes that create taxing demands.

1. *Positive Stress*: Which motivates, focuses energy, it is perceived as within our coping abilities, it improves performance. e.g., promotion at work, new job, new home, holiday and retirement.

2. *Negative Stressors:* Causes anxiety, can be of short term or long term, it is perceived as outside of our coping abilities, feels unpleasant such as death of loved ones, money problems, unemployment, job insecurity, conflicts. etc.

**Effects of Stress**

Stress is difficult to define because it is a highly subjective phenomenon. Things that are distressful for some individual can be pleasurable for others. There are numerous physical as well as emotional responses. Few of them are as follows: Frequent headaches, neck pain, back pain, muscle spasm, sweating, blushing, cold and, frequent urination, low sexual drive, disturbed appetite, irritability, confusion, difficulty in concentration, reduced work productivity, feeling of loneliness or worthlessness, weight gain or loss without dieting, social withdrawal, etc.

**Objectives**

Objectives of this study are (a) To analyse the level of occupational stress among school teachers, and (b) To identify different methods and techniques to reduce job related stress.

**Methodology of the Study**

The sample selected from the private schools in Rewari. Questionnaire were distributed and collected.

**Research Design**

The study is explorative as well as descriptive in nature. Tool: The information was collected from school teachers. Interviews were conducted with the teachers for gathering information on their perception about their organisation and the problems which they face both directly and indirectly. Stress Management Questionnaire was given to the teachers.

**Result and Discussions**

This paper also includes an analysis of data collected by representing it in tabular form along with interpretations. The information collected were analysed for arriving at proper conclusion on the topic.

**Table 3.1**

**Percentage of Teachers Who Felt Stressed in Life**

| *Category* | *Percentage of Teachers* |
|---|---|
| Stressed | 74 |
| Not Stessed | 26 |

Source: Field Survey.

From the table it is indicated that majority of teachers in private schools were stressed in their lives, only few were not stressed.

**Table 3.2**

**Attributes of Stress**

| Causes | Percentage of Teachers |
|---|---|
| Time Management | 20 |
| Work Place Stress | 18 |
| Overload | 22 |
| Demand for high performance | 14 |

Source: Field Survey.

From the Table No. 3.2, it is informed that major causes of stress among the school teachers are excess of workload (22 percent) and lack of time management skills (20 per cent). Hence it was found the teachers felt that they were facing severe work pressure, Time stress is created by a real or imaginery deadlines.

**Table 3.3**

**Steps to Overcome the Stress Levels of Teachers**

| *Steps* | *Percentage of Teachers* |
|---|---|
| Good Environment | 23 |
| Continous Training | 15 |
| Recreational Activities (yoga) | 35 |
| Personal Time | 27 |

*Source:* Field Survey.

## Limitations

The limitations of the study are:

1. The Participants in the study will possess a great deal of knowledge about the teaching profession which may affect the outcomes of the results. Participants may also have much greater intense in the subject matter, which may also lead to results that are non-conforming of other teachers.

2. Since Participants will be asked to respond to items that review past experience of stress, the way in which they respond may be affected by their memory recall. Participants may have a tendency to under report undesirable results because they do not want to portray the teaching profession in a negative way.

## Future Research Directions

Based on the findings from this study, there is an opportunity to increase the existing literature on teacher stress and coping behaviours. While it seems that qualitative data is currently the main method used to study teacher stress and coping behaviours, researchers may consider using quantitative methods to investigate this topic in the future. By doing so, researchers can numerically measure teacher stress and coping behaviours to discover the most frequent causes of stress and coping behaviours used by teachers. Also, the literature is limited on stress within the teaching profession specifically. An opportunity exists to study this profession and to explore the major causes of stress and coping behaviours utilised by its primary employees. Finally, there is very little research at all on school teacher stress. The literature that does exist on teacher stress focuses on either elementary or secondary teachers. Research involving school teachers exclusively is necessary to learn more about this population-group and their perceptions and experiences with stress. The participants in this study felt strongly that non-teaching duties were more stressful than teaching duties. These duties included paperwork, administering assessments and parent conferences. It may be beneficial for researchers to examine the amount of time teachers are actually performing these non-teaching duties throughout the school day in order to see why these duties are considered so stressful. Participants also agreed that documentation procedures were unreasonable. Participants explained that as a teacher, you have to re-write the same information about each student on multiple documents.

## References


1. Bachkirova, T. (2005). Teacher stress and personal values: An exploratory study. *School Psychology International*, 26(3), 340-352.
2. Bindhu, C.M., and Sudheeshkumar, P.K. (2006). Job satisfaction and stress coping skills of primary school teachers. Calicut: Department of Education, Farook Training College.
3. Berryhill, J., Linney, J.A., and Fromewick, J. (2009). The effects of education accountability on teachers: Are policies too stress provoking for their own good? *International Journal of Education Policy and Leadership*, 4(5), 1-14.
4. Chaney, E., Burke, S., and Rager, R. (in review). Development of an instrument to assess stress, depression, and coping among Latino Migrant Seasonal Farmworkers.
5. Creswell, J.W. (2007). *Qualitative inquiry and research design* (2nd ed.). Sage Publications: Thousand Oaks, CA.
6. Cuseo, J. (2007). The empirical case against large class size: Adverse effects on the teaching, learning, and retention of first year students. *Educational Research,* 1-26.
7. Crisis Intervention and Suicide Prevention Centre of British Columbia (2010). Coping with Stress. Retrieved April 16, 2010, from www.crisiscentre.bc.ca/get-help/coping-withstress/.
8. The Definition of Coping (2010). *www.dictionary.com.* Retrieved February 27, 2010, from http://dictionary.reference.com/
9. National Union of Teachers (2010). Retrieved April 8, 2010, from www.teachers.org.uk.

# 4

# Development of Primary Education among Scheduled Tribes in Andhra Pradesh

***Prof D. Pulla Rao***

*"A primary object should be the education of our youth in the science of government. In a republic, what species of knowledge can be equally important? And what duty more pressing than communicating it to those who are to be the future guardians of the liberties of the country?"*

**—George Washington**

## Introduction

In the traditional caste system (*Varna vyavastha*), the Indian society has been divided into four groups, known as castes, on the basis of occupations. But, in the modern Indian social system there are two more marginalised caste groups namely, Scheduled Castes (SCs) and Scheduled Tribes (STs). The term SC has a long historical origin. Prior to the year 1935, when the Government of India Act was enacted, the communities suffering from the stigma of untouchability were being referred to as *'untouchables'* or *'exterior'* or *'depressed'* classes or by various caste names most of which were derogatory. As a part of the social and political changes sought to be introduced in 1935 the various castes, which suffered social disabilities, were listed in a Schedule and from that time onwards they came to be described as SCs. After the Constitution of India was enacted, the list of scheduled castes was notified by the President of India in accordance with the provisions of Article 341 of the Constitution. The SCs thus represent constitutionally declared groups of castes or communities with the characteristic of being suffering from *'untouchability'*. In terms of the provisions in Article 341, they have been specified separately in relation to each of the States and Union Territories.

The caste-based stratification of society adversely affected the equality of educational opportunities to the disadvantage of these groups as they were engaged in traditional family occupations, which did not require any kind of education or special training. This situation persisted through the ages and the depressed classes continue to be deprived of educational opportunities, which were cornered by the upper castes.

**Policies and Programmes**

The Government of India is adopting the following measures to bring the SCs literacy rates on par with others. The central focus in SCs' educational development is their equalisation with the non-SC population at all stages and levels of education, in all areas and in the entire four dimensions-rural male, rural female, urban male and urban female. The measures contemplated for this purpose include: Incentives to indigent families to send their children to school regularly till they reach the age of 14; Pre-matric scholarship scheme for children of those families engaged in occupations such as scavenging, flaying and tanning to be made applicable from class I onwards. All children of such families, regardless of income, will be covered by this Scheme and time bound programmes targeted on them will be undertaken; Constant micro-planning and verification to ensure that the enrollment, retention and successful completion of courses by SC students do not fall at any stage, and provision of remedial courses to improve their prospects for further education and employment; Recruitment of teachers from Scheduled Castes; Provision of facilities for SC students in students' hostels at district headquarters, according to a phased programme.

Since SCs lack of primary education this paper focussed its attention on several variants with special reference to Andhra Pradesh, The Government of Andhra Pradesh has taken up several projects to promote primary education in the State. These include Operation Black Board (OBB), Andhra Pradesh Primary Education Project (APPEP), District Primary Education Programme (DPEP), Chaduvula Panduga (CP), Akshara Sankranti (AS), Sarva Shiksha Abhiyan (SSA), Vidya-Volunteer Scheme (VVS), Mid-day Meal Scheme, etc. These programmes may have had some impact on enrollment of all children including SCs, recruitment of teachers including SC teachers, and student-teacher ratios. The present Study examined their impact on primary education of SC children. In the process, it also analysed the trends in primary education in Andhra Pradesh, for the period 1959-60 to 2007-08.

**Objectives and Methodology**

Against the background the present Study aims at: (a) To compare SC literacy rates with the overall literacy rates. (b) To estimate and compare the rates of growth of enrollment of SCs and all children, and (c) To examine the district-wise enrollment ratios of SC children and all children.

While pursuing these objectives it was also provided a gender-dimension to the study — literacy rates and enrollment rates of boys and those of girls and the relative significance of male and female teachers are highlighted. The secondary data relating to the number of children enrolled and the number of teachers working in primary schools by caste group are obtained from the office of the Bureau of Economics and Statistics, Government of Andhra Pradesh and the Commissioner and Director of School Education, Government of Andhra Pradesh. It was found that there are some discrepancies in the data supplied by these offices. Therefore, it is important to throw in some caveats at the very beginning, that the data are to be analysed cautiously. First, there is a difference between enrollment in primary school and enrollment of primary stage. The former excludes the enrollment in primary sections of the upper primary schools, whereas the latter, includes such enrollment. Only the latter definition was considered in the analysis of the enrollment of primary stage. But, in the case of teachers, the number of teachers working only in primary schools, as per the data provided by the offices of the Bureau of Economics and Statistics; and Commissioner and Director of School Education were considered.

**Disparities in Literacy Rates between Scheduled Castes and All Communities**

Literacy plays a vital role of all the social factors. As per the figures based on 2001 census, SCs constitute 16.19 per cent of the total population of Andhra Pradesh. In the field of literacy, the disparities between males and females are still large. Table 4.1 shows the gap between the literacy rates of all males and SC males, all females and SC females and total literacy (total males + total females) and SC literacy rate. It shows how the gap has been persisting since 1961. In 1961, SC male's literacy rate was 13.4 per cent as against 30.2 per cent among all males. The disparity index (ratio of all male literacy rates to SC male literacy rate) in 1961 was 2.2. The literacy rate of SC males rose to 63.5 per cent in 2001 even as the rate for all males increased to 70.8 per cent. The disparity index in 2001 was 1.1. It shows the disparity in literacy rate between SC males and all males has come down from 2.2 in 1961 to 1.1 in 2001.

In the case of females, the literacy rate of SCs as recorded in 1961 was 3.4 per cent as against 12.0 per cent among all females. The disparity index in 1961 was 3.5. The literacy rate was 43.3 per cent among SC females in 2001 as against 51.2 per cent among all females. The disparity index has decreased from 3.5 in 1961 to 1.2 in 2001. Understandably the female literacy rates at all points of time are lower than those for males. This is true irrespective of whether one considers SCs or all persons. Also, the disparity in literacy rates between all persons and SCs is higher among females than among males. The total literacy rate of SCs was 8.5 per cent as against the overall rate of 21.2 per cent in 1961. The disparity index in 1961 was 2.5. The total literacy rate was 53.5 per cent among SCs in 2001 as against overall rate of 61.1 per cent. The disparity index decreased from 2.5 in 1961 to 1.1 in 2001.

**Table 4.1: Gender-wise Literacy Rates among All Persons and SCs in Andhra Pradesh**

| | *Male literacy rates* | | | *Female literacy rates* | | | | | *Total* |
|---|---|---|---|---|---|---|---|---|---|
| *Year* | *All* | *SC* | *Disparity Index** | *All* | *SC* | *Disparity Index** | *All* | *SC* | *Disparity Index** |
| 1961 | 30.2 | 13.4 | 2.2 | 12.0 | 3.4 | 3.5 | 21.2 | 8.5 | 2.5 |
| 1971 | 33.2 | 15.9 | 2.1 | 15.8 | 5.3 | 3.0 | 24.6 | 10.7 | 2.3 |
| 1981 | 39.3 | 24.8 | 1.6 | 20.4 | 10.3 | 2.0 | 29.9 | 17.7 | 1.7 |
| 1991 | 55.1 | 41.9 | 1.3 | 32.7 | 20.9 | 1.6 | 44.1 | 31.6 | 1.4 |
| 2001 | 70.8 | 63.5 | 1.1 | 51.2 | 43.3 | 1.2 | 61.1 | 53.5 | 1.1 |

*Note:* *Disparity Index: Ratio of literacy rate among all persons to that among SCs.

*Source* : Census of India, different periods.

### Enrollment of SC Children versus All Children in Primary Stage

Literacy rate is but one dimension of the progress of education of a community. Another dimension of the progress is the enrollment ratio of children at the primary stage. Table 4.2 shows that the number of children enrolled in primary stage in 1959-60 was 28.06 lakhs. Of this, 62.12 per cent were boys and 37.88 per cent were girls. Enrollment of students in general increased to 91.12 lakhs by 1999-2000 recording a 52 per cent boys and 48 per cent increase among girls. By 2007-08 enrollment of students in general noticed a declining trend to 71.73 lakhs, consisting of 50.75 per cent of boys and 49.25 per cent of girls. An interesting trend which can be observed is that enrollment of girls has grown at a higher rate than that of boys during the period of study. The annual compound growth rate of enrollment of girls was 2.53 per cent as against 1.54 per cent among boys.

In the case of SCs, the total enrollment in 1959-60 was 3.91 lakhs. Of those enrolled, 64 per cent were boys and 36 per cent were girls and the proportion of the enrollment of SC children to all children was 14 per cent. The enrollment of SC children reached 18.83 lakhs by 1999-2000. Of this, 52 per cent were boys and 48 per cent were girls. In 1999-2000, the proportion of the enrollment of SC children to all children was 21 per cent. After that the enrollment of SC children has been declined to 13.65 lakhs and the SC boys recorded 50.52 per cent and the SC girls recorded 49.48 per cent. The trend growth rate shows that the enrollment of SC girls has been higher at 3.34 per cent than that of SC boys at 2.12 per cent during the period of our study. The fact that the special programmes and initiatives taken to motivate SCs to enroll their children in ever-larger numbers in primary schools are bearing fruit and it is evident from the data presented in Table 4.2. The annual compound growth rate of enrollment during the period 1959-1960 to 2007-08 was 1.54 per cent and 2.12 per cent for all boys and SC boys and 2.53 per cent and 3.34 per cent for all girls and SC girls.

### District-wise Enrollment of SC Children versus All Children in Primary Stage

The enrollment of all children in the primary stage in Andhra Pradesh during the academic year 2007-08 was 71.73 lakhs of which 50.75 per cent were boys and

49.25 per cent were girls. The highest per centage of enrollment of all boys was recorded in Rangareddy District (in Telangana) viz, 51.74 per cent. It was around 50 per cent in the remaining districts of the State. Enrollment of girl children in the Districts of Guntur and Hyderabad are higher compared to the boys among the districts of the State. Rangareddy district recorded only 48.26 per cent enrollment, the lowest rate among the districts of the State. The gross enrollment ratio at the primary stage in the state was 96.40 per cent, 96.19 per cent among boys and 96.62 per cent among girls during the academic year 2007-08. Barring a couple of exceptions, enrollment ratio was uniformly lower, albeit marginally, among girls than among boys. The ratio was the highest among boys in the Rayalaseema region and the lowest in the Coastal Andhra — the most developed of the three regions. In respect of girls, however, the enrollment ratio was the highest in Coastal Andhra and the lowest in Rayalaseema.

In the case of SCs, the enrollment ratio of boys was the highest at 51.68 per cent in Kurnool district and the lowest at 49.34 per cent in Visakhapatnam district. The gross enrollment ratio at the primary stage in the State among the SCs was 112.78 per cent for boys and 113.94 per cent for girls. As in the case of the enrollment ratio of all boys was the highest in Rayalaseema and it was the lowest in Coastal Andhra. The ratio of SC boys was the highest in Rayalaseema and the lowest in Coastal Andhra. This is in contrast to the case of girls, where the enrollment ratio was the highest in Coastal Andhra and the lowest in Rayalaseema. The enrollment among SC boys as a per centage of all boys and SC girls as a per centage of all girls was calculated using the district-wise and region-wise data. The following points emerge from this exercise. (1) Barring three, enrollment ratio was relatively more among SC boys than among SC girls in all districts, (2) Enrollment ratio was the highest in the Coastal Andhra, for boys as also for girls, (3) The highest proportion of the enrollment of SC boys to all boys was 29.33 per cent in Guntur District and it was the lowest (8.26 per cent) in Visakhapatnam District, and (4) In the case of SC girls, the highest proportion of enrollment (28.74 per cent) was recorded in Prakasam District and the lowest proportion ( 8.40 per cent) in Hyderabad District. The gross-enrollment ratio at the primary stage in Andhra Pradesh among SC children was 113.3–112.78 among SC boys and 113.94 among SC girls.

The information relating to the enrollment of boys and girls from I to V standards during the academic year 2007-08. One interesting aspect is that the enrollment ratio of SC boys is equal to all boys except in II and V standards. One expects this to be because of the existence of social welfare hostels and Ashram schools. As food and clothes are provided freely, SCs are prompted to enroll their children here. Another important aspect which is noticed here is that SC girl's enrollment ratio is more than all girls enrollment ratio in II and V standards and in the remaining standards they are equal. In recent years, a number of steps have been taken up by the Government of Andhra Pradesh to strengthen the educational base of SCs. Ideally, the enrollment of SCs in educational process should be as per their proportion in the total population of the

**Table 4.2: Enrollment of All and SC Students by Sex in Primary Stage in Andhra Pradesh: 1959-60 to 2007-08**

| | Overall enrollment | | | SC enrollment | | | | | |
|---|---|---|---|---|---|---|---|---|---|
| *Year* | *Boys* | *Girls* | *Total* | *Boys* | *Proportion of SC boys to all boys* | *Girls* | *Proportion of SC girls to all girls* | *Total* | *Proportion of SCs all children* |
| 1959-60 | 1743486 | 1062965 | 2806451 | 251760 | 14.44 | 139567 | 13.13 | 391327 | 13.94 |
| | (62.12) | (37.88) | (100.00) | (64.33) | | (35.67) | | (100) | |
| 1969-70 | 2331634 | 1572320 | 3903954 | 293483 | 12.59 | 200605 | 12.76 | 494088 | 12.66 |
| | (59.72) | (40.28) | (100.00) | (59.40) | | (40.60) | | (100) | |
| 1979-80 | 3024697 | 2130618 | 5155315 | 580572 | 19.19 | 392992 | 18.44 | 973564 | 18.88 |
| | (58.67) | (41.33) | (100.00) | (59.63) | | (40.37) | | (100) | |
| 1989-90 | 4205423 | 3115165 | 7320588 | 819177 | 19.48 | 609325 | 19.56 | 1428502 | 19.51 |
| | (57.45) | (42.55) | (100.00) | (57.35) | | (42.65) | | (100) | |
| 1999-00 | 4702696 | 4409365 | 9112061 | 977601 | 20.79 | 905790 | 20.54 | 1883391 | 20.67 |
| | (51.61) | (48.39) | (100.00) | (51.91) | | (48.09) | | (100) | |
| 2007-08 | 3640320 | 3533217 | 7173537 | 689936 | 18.95 | 675744 | 19.12 | 1365680 | 19.03 |
| | (50.75) | (49.25) | (100) | (50.52) | | (49.48) | | (100) | |
| Percentage Growth rate in 2007-08 over 1959-60 | 108.79 | 232.39 | 155.61 | 174.04 | | 384.17 | | 248.99 | |
| Annual compound growth rate | 1.54 | 2.53 | | 1.97 | 2.12 | | 3.34 | | 2.64 |

**Note:** Figures in brackets indicate percentage to the total.

*Sources:* 1. Commissioner and Director of School Education, Government of Andhra Pradesh, Hyderabad,

2. Statistical Abstracts of Andhra Pradesh for various years, Government of Andhra Pradesh.

State. Though, overall progress in this direction is satisfactory, yet much work is to be done to bridge the educational disparities in enrollment. The dropout rates of children at the primary stage, and it may be concluded that (1) it is slightly higher for boys (19.1per cent) than girls (18.48 per cent) in general, and also slightly higher for boys (21.45 per cent) than girls (20.16 per cent) among SCs, (2) between all children and SC children, it is much higher for the latter (20.82 per cent) compared to the former (18.79 per cent).

The student-teacher ratio in the primary schools in Andhra Pradesh during the academic year 2007-08 was recorded at 42.94. In Coastal Andhra it was 42.02, in Rayalaseema region 43.79 and in Telangana 43.69. It is interesting that in the case of student-teacher ratio it was the lowest (33.32) in Cuddapah District and it was the highest (60.90) in Kurnool District. The student-teacher ratio of 40 students per teacher for aided schools is the norm. Low student-teacher ratio affects the quality of education at the primary level, because the school teacher does not find any motivation to teach if the ratio is low, let alone paying the much-needed individual attention, which is so essential at the primary stage of education.

## Conclusions

The present study sought to place SCs vis-à-vis total population in respect of literacy rates, and enrollment ratio at the primary-education stage. Besides, it also tried to focus on the relative significance of SC school teachers compared to all teachers. While gender dimension is provided in the study throughout, the inter-temporal data were also in the analysis of literacy rates and enrollment ratios. For the reason that Andhra Pradesh exhibits wide regional variations at district/regional level, variations in the variables were taken into consideration. The major conclusions, as they emerge from the study are while females generally lag behind males in literacy rates, the disparity in the rate between all persons and SCs is higher among females than among males. Government's initiatives aimed at motivating the SCs to enroll their children in increasing numbers are bearing fruit especially in respect of enrollment of boys. Enrollment-ratio does not seem to be related to the development of a region. In fact the backward Telangana is found to have recorded high enrollment in respect of boys. The drop out rate among SC girls is much higher than that of SC boys and, between all children and SC children, it is much higher for the latter. The opportunity cost of sending SC children to primary school, notwithstanding the incentives provided by the government to them, seems to be very higher. Student-teacher ratio, as seen from the district-level averages, seems to be promising. However, wide variations between schools, with some schools reporting an extremely adverse ratio could be noticed. The study concludes that females are yet to gain considerable foothold as teachers in schools and this is much more so in respect of SC females.

## References

1. Chalam, K.S. (1985): *Educational Development of the Scheduled Castes in the Districts of Andhra Pradesh, (Mimeo),* School of Economics, Andhra University, Visakhapatnam.

2. Chalam, K.S. (1988): *Education and Weaker Sections*, Inter India Publication, New Delhi.
3. Chauhan, B.R. and others (1975): *Scheduled Castes and Education,* Anu Publications, Meerut.
4. Gopinathan Nair, P.R. (1981): *Primary Education, Population Growth and Socio-economic Change*, Allied Publishers, New Delhi.
5. Government of India (1986): *National Policy on Education 1986: Programme of Action,* New Delhi.
6. Kabra, G.D. (1984): *Development of Weaker Sections*, Inter-India Publications, New Delhi.
7. Naik, J.P. (1975): *Elementary Education in India – a Promise to Keep*, Allied Publishers, Bombay.
8. Rajaiah, B. (1987): *Economics of Education*, Mittal Publication, New Delhi.

# 5

# A Study of Academic Attainment among Class I Students of Himachal Pradesh

**Dr Satish Chand Bhadwal and Dr Anil Kumar Agnihotri**

"*A liberal education is at the heart of a civil society, and at the heart of a liberal education is the act of teaching.*"

**— A. Bartlett Giamatti**

**Introduction**

Universalisation of Elementary Education (UEE) has been accepted as a national goal in India since Independence. The founding fathers of Indian Constitution recognised UEE as a crucial input for nation building. In this context, about 60 years ago, Article 45 of the Indian Constitution (1950) stated that: *The State shall endeavour to provide, within a period of ten years from the commencement of this Constitution, for free and compulsory education for all children until they complete the age of fourteen years.* When the target could not be achieved till 2001 in spite of various interventions at National and state levels, Indian Government started its flagship programme *'The Sarva Shiksha Abhiyan'* in 2001 with the following objectives:

Ÿ All children complete five years of primary schooling by 2007.
- All children complete eight years of elementary schooling by 2010.
- Focus on elementary education of satisfactory quality with emphasis on education for life .
- Bridge all gender and social category gaps at primary stage by 2007 and at elementary education level by 2010.
- Universal retention by 2010.

Also, the document *'Towards Faster and More Inclusive Growth: An Approach to the 11th Five Year Plan'* (2006) envisaged the following plan for Elementary Education for 11th Five year Plan 2007-2012: *Education, in its broadest sense of development of youth, including sports, is the most critical input for empowering people with skills and knowledge and for giving them access to productive employment in the future. The 11th Plan should ensure that we move towards raising public spending in education to 6 per cent of GDP, which is an NCMP commitment. It must fulfill the Constitutional obligation of providing free and compulsory elementary education of good quality to all children up to the age of 14. This means we must ensure both access and good quality and standards in respect of curriculum, pedagogy, and infrastructure irrespective of the parents' ability to pay.*

In view of the above, the provision of a number of incentives was made at State level also to all girls and children belonging to disadvantaged groups. However, the review of literature reveals that academic performance of students enrolled at elementary stage in India is not up to the mark and there has not been a marked shift in quality of education measured in terms of academic achievement of students even after ten years of implementation of SSA as well as providing various incentives. The State of Himachal Pradesh is not an exception. The rapid expansion of the school network and an exceptionally high teacher-pupil ratio notwithstanding, the quality of education, particularly at the elementary level, continues to be a matter of concern in the hill state of Himachal Pradesh. With more than 10,000 primary, 1,000 upper primary, 1000 high and 1000 senior secondary institutions in Himachal Pradesh, elementary education is accessible to all, and children do not have to walk more than 1.5 km to attend school. As per the recent data, the teacher-pupil ratio has improved to 1:17 from 1:22 in 2004-05 as against the norm of 1:40. The average of slightly more than three classrooms per primary school is also quite reasonable. In fact, infrastructure-wise the state is ranked seventh in the country. However, the upgrading of physical infrastructure and deployment of more than adequate teachers has not brought about the expected improvement in the standard of education.

When the present study was envisaged, no worthwhile survey had been carried out by any independent agency in Himachal Pradesh in order to evaluate the SSA and other intervention programmes in terms of achievement of the objective of *'providing elementary education of satisfactory quality'*. Whatsoever information was available with respect to the improvement in quality was based on government sponsored surveys. Further, the method employed in ASER studies has been of different nature. It was, therefore, thought worthwhile to undertake the present piece of research with an objective to evaluate the *'National Programme of Universal Elementary Education'* known as *Sarva Shiksha Abhiyan* (SSA) launched in 2001 and other interventions in Himachal Pradesh with respect to quality improvement at elementary stage. The index of quality was limited to 'academic attainment' only. The study was focused on Class I, IV and VII, however, in the present paper the results are reported for Class I only.

## Objectives of the Study

The following objectives were laid down for the present study:

- To evaluate the level of academic attainment of Class I students of following four Districts of Himachal Pradesh vis-à-vis the expected one: Una, Hamirpur, Kangra and Bilaspur.
- To evaluate the level of academic attainment of total sample of Class I students drawn from abovementioned four Districts of Himachal Pradesh vis-à-vis the expected one.

## Hypothesis of the Study

The following hypotheses, based upon the results of earlier surveys, were formulated which were tested in the present study:

- The level of academic attainment of Class I students of following four Districts of Himachal Pradesh are far below the expected one: Una, Hamirpur, Kangra and Bilaspur.
- The level of academic attainment of total sample of Class I students drawn from abovementioned four Districts of Himachal Pradesh is far below the expected one.

*Academic attainment:* The number of items answered correctly by a student.
*Expected Performance:* All the 40 items answered correctly by a student

## The Sample

Survey method of research was used in the present study. The sample for the present study was drawn from 81 Government Primary Schools situated in four districts of Himachal Pradesh viz., Una (20), Hamirpur (21), Kangra (20) and Bilaspur (20). The four districts and the schools in each district were selected on the basis of convenience, though it was observed that the schools were spread over a wider area and adequately represented each district in terms of locale (rural-urban) and sex (boys-girls). It is worth mentioning that all these schools followed the curriculum prescribed by the Himachal Pradesh Board of School Education. The total sample consisted of 1063 students (Una = 317 Hamirpur = 243, Kangra = 235, Bilaspur = 268).

## Tool Use

An achievement test was constructed for class I students to assess their academic performance. Since the aim of the present study was to observe whether the students were able to achieve minimum level of learning (as perceived by school teachers) after completing Class I (expected performance), hence, the usual procedure of constructing norm-referenced or criterion-referenced tests was not followed in the present case. At the preparatory stage, primary school teachers from five schools were contacted and asked what did they expect from Class-I students to achieve in terms of minimum level of learning with reference to the prescribed curriculum. Taking this clue, the achievement test was constructed for Class-I students. More information in this regard was gathered from students' notebooks, prescribed textbook, home assignments and class-test questions. The preliminary draft was shown to teachers to indicate items which were poor, difficult or beyond the criterion of minimum level of learning at Class-I level. The final draft consisted of forty items. The test was subjected to language edit and reliability.

## Analysis and Interpretation of Data

The achievement test was administered to Class-I students either before their final examination or immediately after they took admission in the next class. The test was scored in the form of correct, partially correct, incorrect and unanswered responses of the students for different items and the results thus obtained were tabulated district and item-wise for further analysis. The techniques of frequency distribution and percentages were used to analyse the data. As noted earlier, the test was constructed to assess students' performance vis-à-vis the expected performance. The criterion for level of expected performance in terms of minimum level of learning at Class-I level was determined on the basis of perception of teachers actually teaching Class-I students. Hence, the number of items answered correctly by each student was considered his/her 'academic performance' and all the 40 items supposed to be answered correctly by a student was treated as 'expected performance'. The item-wise responses of Class I students to 40 items of the Achievement Test are presented for each of the selected four Districts separately as well as for the total sample in Table 5.1. The results of analyses for different sets of data followed by their interpretation are given as under:

## District Una

The analysis of responses of 317 Class-I students to 40 items revealed the following specifics in respect of District Una.

**Table 5.1**

| *By Per Cent of Students* | *Correct Partially* | *Number of Items Responded as Correct* | *Incorrect* | *Unanswered* |
|---|---|---|---|---|
| 76 or more | 0 | 0 | 0 | 11 |
| 51 to 75 | 0 | 2 | 0 | 20 |
| 46 to 50 | 1 | 0 | 0 | 2 |
| 41 to 45 | 0 | 0 | 0 | 1 |
| 36 to 40 | 0 | 3 | 0 | 3 |
| 31 to 35 | 3 | 2 | 0 | 1 |
| 26 to 30 | 3 | 2 | 3 | 0 |
| 21 to 25 | 1 | 2 | 1 | 0 |
| 16 to 20 | 4 | 4 | 6 | 1 |
| 11 to 15 | 12 | 3 | 10 | 0 |
| 06 to 10 | 5 | 5 | 14 | 0 |
| 05 or less | 11 | 5 | 6 | 1 |
| **Total** | **40** | **28** | **40** | **40** |

* Out of 28 items which could have 'Partial Correct' response

The following significant features emerged from the above Table 5.1 with regard to the performance of 317 Class I students of Una District as measured by the Achievement Test:

- As many as 11 items (Item Nos. 3, 12, 14, 17, 23, 24, 25, 29, 30, 33, 34 and 39) were answered correctly by less than five per cent of the students.
- Five items (Item Nos. 1, 11, 16, 18, 28 and 38) were answered correctly by six to 10 per cent of the students.
- As many as 12 items (Item Nos. 9, 10, 13, 15, 27, 31, 35, 36, 37 and 40) were answered correctly by 11 to 15 per cent of the students.
- Four items (Item Nos. 6, 8, 21, and 26) were answered correctly by 16 to 20 per cent of the students.
- Only one item (Item No. 20) was answered correctly by 21 to 25 per cent of the students.
- Three items (Item Nos. 7, 22 and 32) were answered correctly by 26 to 30 per cent of the students.
- Three items (Item Nos. 2, 4 and 5) were answered correctly by 31 to 35 per cent of the students.
- Only one item (Item No. 19) was answered correctly by 46 to 50 per cent of the students.
- None of the items was answered correctly by more than 50 per cent of the students.
- None of the 28 items having more than one response was answered completely correctly by any of the 317 students.
- None of the 40 items of the test was answered correctly by any of the 317 students.
- All the 40 items were left unanswered by different number of students. Amazingly, 31 items were left unanswered by more than 50 per cent of students.

It is revealed from the above observations that the level of performance of 317 Class I students of Una District as measured by the achievement test is far below the expected one. Hence, the hypothesis that *"The level of academic* attainment *of Class I students of Una District of Himachal Pradesh is far below the expected one"* is accepted.

**(B) District Hamirpur**

The analysis of responses of 243 Class-I students to 40 items revealed the following specifics in respect of District Hamirpur.

**Table 5.2**

| *By Per Cent of* | | *Number of Items* | *Responded as* | |
|---|---|---|---|---|
| *Students* | *Correct Partially* | *Correct* | *Incorrect* | *Unanswered* |
| 76 or more | 0 | 0 | 0 | 12 |
| 51 to 75 | 0 | 2 | 0 | 20 |
| 46 to 50 | 0 | 0 | 0 | 3 |
| 41 to 45 | 0 | 0 | 0 | 2 |
| 36 to 40 | 1 | 1 | 0 | 1 |
| 31 to 35 | 0 | 2 | 0 | 0 |
| 26 to 30 | 2 | 3 | 3 | 0 |
| 21 to 25 | 0 | 4 | 4 | 1 |
| 16 to 20 | 3 | 1 | 6 | 0 |
| 11 to 15 | 7 | 6 | 9 | 0 |
| 06 to 10 | 13 | 6 | 12 | 0 |
| 05 or less | 14 | 3 | 6 | 1 |
| **Total** | **40** | **28** | **40** | **40** |

* Out of 28 items which could have 'Partial Correct' response

The following significant features emerged from the above Table 5.2 with regard to the performance of 243 Class I students of Hamirpur District as measured by the Achievement Test:

- As many as 14 items (Item Nos. 3, 12, 14, 17, 23, 24, 25, 27, 29, 30, 33, 34, 38 and 39) were answered correctly by less than 5 per cent of the students.
- Thirteen items (Item Nos. 8, 9, 10, 11, 15, 16, 18, 28, 31, 35, 36, 37 and 40) were answered correctly by 6 to 10 per cent of the students.
- As many as 7 items (Item Nos. 1, 6, 13, 20, 21, 22 and 26) were answered correctly by 11 to 15 per cent of the students.
- Three items (Item Nos. 4, 7 and 32) were answered correctly by 16 to 20 per cent of the students.
- Two items (Item Nos. 2 and 5) were answered correctly by 26 to 30 per cent of the students.
- Only one item (Item No. 19) was answered correctly by 36 to 40 per cent of the students.
- None of the items was answered correctly by more than 40 per cent of the students.
- The 317 students answered none of the 28 items having more than one response completely correctly.
- None of the remaining 12 items of the test which have single response was answered correctly by any of the 317 students.
- All the 40 items were left unanswered by different number of students. Amazingly, 32 items were left unanswered by more than 50 per cent of students.

It is revealed from the above observations that the level of performance of 243 Class I students of Hamirpur District as measured by the achievement test is far below the expected one. Hence, the hypothesis that *"The level of academic attainment of Class I students of Hamirpur District of Himachal Pradesh is far below the expected one"* is accepted.

### (C) District Kangra

The analysis of responses of 235 Class-I students to 40 items revealed the following specifics in respect of District Kangra.

**Table 5.3**

| *By Per Cent of Students* | *Number of Items Responded as* | | | |
|---|---|---|---|---|
| | *Correct* | *Partially* Correct* | *Incorrect* | *Unanswered* |
| 76 or more | 0 | 0 | 0 | 31 |
| 51 to 75 | 0 | 1 | 0 | 8 |
| 46 to 50 | 0 | 0 | 0 | 0 |
| 41 to 45 | 0 | 0 | 0 | 0 |
| 36 to 40 | 1 | 1 | 0 | 0 |
| 31 to 35 | 0 | 0 | 0 | 0 |
| 26 to 30 | 2 | 0 | 0 | 0 |
| 21 to 25 | 0 | 0 | 0 | 0 |
| 16 to 20 | 2 | 1 | 1 | 0 |
| 11 to 15 | 3 | 7 | 4 | 0 |
| 06 to 10 | 14 | 9 | 8 | 1 |
| 05 or less | 18 | 9 | 27 | 0 |
| **Total** | **40** | **28** | **40** | **40** |

* Out of 28 items which could have 'Partial Correct' response

The following significant features emerged from the above Table 5.3 with regard to the performance of 235 Class I students of Kangra District as measured by the Achievement Test:

- As many as 18 items (Item Nos. 1, 3, 12, 14, 15, 16, 17, 18, 23, 24, 25, 26, 29, 30, 33, 34, 37 and 39) were answered correctly by less than five per cent of the students.
- Fourteen items (Item Nos. 9, 10, 11, 13,20, 21, 27, 28, 31, 32, 35, 36, 38 and 40) were answered correctly by 6 to 10 per cent of the students.
- As many as 3 items (Item Nos. 7, 8 and 22) were answered correctly by 11 to 15 per cent of the students.
- Two items (Item Nos. 4 and 6) were answered correctly by 16 to 20 per cent of the students.
- Two items (Item Nos. 2 and 19) were answered correctly by 26 to 30 per cent of the students.
- Only one item (Item No. 5) was answered correctly by 36 to 40 per cent of the students.
- None of the items was answered correctly by more than 40 per cent of the students.
- None of the 28 items having more than one response was answered completely correctly by any of the 317 students.
- None of the remaining 12 items of the test which have single response was answered correctly by any of the 317 students.
- All the 40 items were left unanswered by different number of students. Amazingly, 39 items were left unanswered by more than 50 per cent of students.

It is revealed from the above observations that the level of performance of 317 Class I students of Una District as measured by the achievement test is far below the expected one. Hence, the hypothesis that *"The level of academic attainment of Class I students of Una District of Himachal Pradesh is far below the expected one"* is accepted.

## (D) District Bilaspur

The analysis of responses of 268 Class-I students to 40 items revealed the following specifics in respect of District Bilaspur.

**Table 5.4**

| *By Per Cent of Students* | *Number of Items Responded as* Correct | *Partially Correct* | *Incorrect* | *Unanswered* |
|---|---|---|---|---|
| 76 or more | 0 | 1 | 0 | 3 |
| 51 to 75 | 4 | 3 | 0 | 13 |
| 46 to 50 | 3 | 0 | 0 | 4 |
| 41 to 45 | 2 | 3 | 0 | 2 |
| 36 to 40 | 3 | 3 | 1 | 5 |
| 31 to 35 | 3 | 2 | 2 | 3 |
| 26 to 30 | 7 | 1 | 1 | 2 |
| 21 to 25 | 4 | 0 | 3 | 1 |
| 16 to 20 | 0 | 6 | 3 | 4 |
| 11 to 15 | 4 | 4 | 10 | 1 |
| 06 to 10 | 3 | 1 | 12 | 1 |
| 05 or less | 7 | 4 | 8 | 1 |
| **Total** | **40** | **28** | **40** | **40** |

* Out of 28 items which could have 'Partial Correct' response.

The following significant features emerged from the above Table 5.4 with regard to the performance of 268 Class I students of Bilaspur District as measured by the Achievement Test:

- As many as 7 items (Item Nos. 14, 25, 29, 30, 33, 34 and 39) were answered correctly by less than five per cent of the students.
- Three items (Item Nos. 17, 23 and 24) were answered correctly by six to ten per cent of the students.
- As many as 4 items (Item Nos. 3, 11, 12 and 38) were answered correctly by 11 to 15 per cent of the students.
- Four items (Item Nos. 16, 31, 36 and 40) were answered correctly by 21 to 25 per cent of the students.
- Seven items (Item Nos. 1, 8, 15, 27, 28, 35 and 37) were answered correctly by 26 to 30 per cent of the students.
- Three items (Item Nos. 18, 20 and 26) were answered correctly by 31 to 35 per cent of the students.
- Three items (Item Nos. 6, 9 and 13) were answered correctly by 36 to 40 per cent of the students.
- Two items (Item Nos. 21 and 22) were answered correctly by 41 to 45 per cent of the students.

- Three items (Item Nos. 7, 10 and 32) were answered correctly by 46 to 50 per cent of the students.
- Four items (Item Nos. 2, 4, 5 and 19) were answered correctly by 51 to 75 per cent of the students.
- None of the items was answered correctly by more than 75 per cent of the students.
- None of the 28 items having more than one response was answered completely correctly by any of the 268 students.
- None of the remaining 12 items of the test which have single response was answered correctly by any of the 268 students.
- All the 40 items were left unanswered by different number of students. Amazingly, 16 items were left unanswered by more than 50 per cent of students.

It is revealed from the above observations that level of performance of 268 Class I students of Bilaspur District as measured by the achievement test is far below the expected one. Hence, the hypothesis that *"The level of academic attainment of Class I students of Bilaspur District of Himachal Pradesh is far below the expected one"* is accepted.

### (E) Total Sample

The analysis of responses of 1063 Class-I students to 40 items revealed the following specifics in respect of Total Sample.

**Table 5.5**

| *By Per Cent of Students* | *Number of Items Responded as* Correct | Partially Correct | Incorrect | Unanswered |
|---|---|---|---|---|
| 76 or more | 0 | 0 | 0 | 11 |
| 51 to 75 | 0 | 2 | 0 | 22 |
| 46 to 50 | 1 | 0 | 0 | 0 |
| 41 to 45 | 0 | 0 | 0 | 3 |
| 36 to 40 | 1 | 2 | 0 | 2 |
| 31 to 35 | 1 | 2 | 0 | 0 |
| 26 to 30 | 3 | 3 | 0 | 0 |
| 21 to 25 | 3 | 3 | 3 | 1 |
| 16 to 20 | 6 | 2 | 4 | 0 |
| 11 to 15 | 10 | 4 | 12 | 0 |
| 06 to 10 | 5 | 5 | 13 | 0 |
| 05 or less | 10 | 5 | 8 | 1 |
| **Total** | **40** | **28** | **40** | **40** |

*Out of 28 items which could have 'Partial Correct' response

The following significant features emerged from the above Table 5.5 with regard to the performance of 1063 Class I students comprising total sample from four Districts as measured by the Achievement Test:

- As many as 10 items (Item Nos. 14, 17, 23, 24, 25, 29, 30, 33, 34 and 39) were answered correctly by less than five per cent of the students.

- Five items (Item Nos. 3, 11, 12, 16 and 38) were answered correctly by six to ten per cent of the students.
- As many as 10 items (Item Nos. 1, 15, 18, 27, 28, 31, 35, 36, 37 and 40) were answered correctly by 11 to 15 per cent of the students.
- Six items (Item Nos. 8, 9, 10, 13, 20 and 26) were answered correctly by 16 to 20 per cent of the students.
- Only three items (Item Nos. 6, 21 and 22) were answered correctly by 21 to 25 per cent of the students.
- Only three items (Item Nos. 4, 7 and 32) were answered correctly by 26 to 30 per cent of the students.
- Only one item (Item No. 5) was answered correctly by 31 to 35 per cent of the students.
- Only one item (Item No. 2) was answered correctly by 36 to 40 per cent of the students.
- Only one item (Item No. 19) was answered correctly by 46 to 50 per cent of the students.
- None of the items was answered correctly by more than 50 per cent of the students.
- None of the 28 items having more than one response was answered completely correctly by any of the 1063 students.
- None of the remaining 12 items of the test which have single response was answered correctly by any of the 1063 students.
- All the 40 items were left unanswered by different number of students. Amazingly, 33 items were left unanswered by more than 50 per cent of students.

It is revealed from the above observations that the level of performance of 1063 Class I students comprising the total sample from four Districts as measured by the achievement test is far below the expected one. Hence, the hypothesis that"*The level of academic attainment of total Class I students sampled from four Districts of Himachal Pradesh is far below the expected one*" is accepted.

**Discussion**

The present study reveals that academic attainment of students of classes I selected from four Districts of Himachal Pradesh, viz., Una, Hamirpur, Kangra and Bilaspur came out to be far below the expected one for each individual district as well as for the total sample. This indicates that the State of Himachal Pradesh has not been able to achieve the objective of providing elementary education of satisfactory quality even after ten years of launch of SSA as well as introducing other interventions. Item-wise results for 40 items given in the Table 5.1 present the overall picture of the performance of Class I students. The consolidated results given below for total sample of 1063 students drawn from this Table further elaborate the state of poor academic attainment among students after completing Class I curriculum.

**Table 5.6**

| *Item No.* | *Description* | *Attempted Correctly by (Per Cent)* |
|---|---|---|
| 1. | Recognise and write the name of object or animal. (6) | 13.73 |
| 2. | How many colours are there in our National Flag? | 35.18 |
| 3. | Fill in the blanks. (5) | 05. 55 |
| 4. | With which organ we see? | 29.92 |
| 5. | Which of the two figures is larger? | 39.23 |
| 6. | If one piece of sweet (Rasgulla) costs Rs. 2, what will be the cost of two pieces? | 22.20 |
| 7. | What happens by eating stale sweet? | 26.62 |
| 8. | Write down the preceding and following numbers in the given list of numbers. (5+5) | 17.78 |
| 9. | Write down names of five pet animals. | 16.75 |
| 10. | Write down names of five wild animals. | 18.63 |
| 11. | Identify right and wrong statements. (4) | 08.18 |
| 12. | Think and write–Day to day events. (4) | 05.93 |
| 13. | There are four people in Rama's home. Two more children entered the home. Now what is the total number of people in Rama's home? | 18.34 |
| 14. | Make sentences from the given words. (4) | 01.22 |
| 15. | Lata had nine apples. She gave three apples to Raju. How many apples remained with Lata? | 14.02 |
| 16. | Questions about weeks's days. For example, what is the day before Thursday? (4) | 09.69 |
| 17. | Four children gave three flowers each to Meena. Now how many flowers does Meena have? | 04.23 |
| 18. | Identifying 'matras' in two letter words. (3) | 12.89 |
| 19. | Count the objects and write the number. (4) | 45.72 |
| 20. | Add the given {two digit} figures. (4) | 19.10 |
| 21. | Multiply. {single digit numbers} (6) | 20.98 |
| 22. | Write Hindi alphabet from beginning to end. | 23.89 |
| 23. | Write the figures in words. (5) | 02.35 |
| 24. | Fill in the blanks. {Options given} (5) | 04.23 |
| 25. | Subtract. {Single digit from a two digit figure} (4) | 02.26 |
| 26. | Make words from the given letters. {Simple} (4) | 16.37 |
| 27. | Write numbers backwards. {Staring from 23} | 13.73 |
| 28. | Write names of five fruits. | 13.36 |
| 29. | Change the gender. (4) | 01.88 |
| 30. | Make sentences using given words. (4) | 01.60 |
| 31. | Write the given words in figures. (5) | 12.89 |
| 32. | Complete the table of 4. | 26.72 |
| 33. | Identify objects used for cleaning. | 03.29 |
| 34. | Complete the story with the help of given words/hints. | 01.03 |
| 35. | What does fly in the sky? (Multiple Choice Question) | 14.58 |
| 36. | What does grandmother does with children. (Multiple Choice Question) | 12.89 |
| 37. | Make words from the given letters. {Relatively difficult} (4) | 13.45 |
| 38. | Answer the riddle. {Multiple choice item} | 08.37 |
| 39. | Write down antonyms. (4) | 01.79 |
| 40. | What is the colour of a tomato? {Multiple choice item} | 14.68 |

**Table 5.7**

| Sl. No. | Percentage | Frequency |
|---|---|---|
| 1. | 1.00-05.00 | 10 |
| 2. | 5.01-10.00 | 05 |
| 3. | 10.01-15.00 | 10 |
| 4. | 15.01-20.00 | 06 |
| 5. | 20.01-25.00 | 03 |
| 6. | 25.01-30.00 | 03 |
| 7. | 30.01-35.00 | 00 |
| 8. | 35.01-40.00 | 02 |
| 9. | 40.01-45.00 | 00 |
| 10. | 45.01-50.00 | 01 |
| **Total** | | **40** |

It is revealed that only item number 19 namely "count and write" has been attempted correctly by maximum number of students which is merely 45.72 per cent. The item number 22 requiring the students to write Hindi alphabet has been attempted correctly by only 23.89 per cent students. Item number 13 which required the students to add 4+2 was answered correctly by only 18.34 per cent students. Overall 37 items were answered correctly by less than 30 per cent of students.

One of the reasons for not answering even the very simple items correctly could be that the students were unable to read and/or comprehend the test items. This had been realised by us during the pilot study stage. To overcome this problem, each item was explained to students during the test administration stage. The results reveal that the students either still failed to understand the item or did not know the answer. The State of Himachal Pradesh has been successful to a great extent in making elementary education accessible to nearly all through rapid expansion of the school network, achieving an exceptionally high teacher-pupil ratio, increasing enrolment at elementary stage and decreasing drop-out rate considerably. However, the quality of education, particularly at the elementary stage, continues to be a matter of concern as is evident from the results of present study. It seems that the upgrading of physical infrastructure and deployment of more than adequate number of teachers has not brought about the expected improvement in the standards of education. The results of the study may prove to be beneficial to policy planners in reviewing the existing policies in the context of improving quality of education at elementary stage. The results of the study may also generate awareness that it is not sufficient to provide infrastructure alone but is also equally necessary to identify factors that are essential in order to achieve the aforesaid goal of providing quality education. Even the policy of promoting every student to next class irrespective of his/her readiness poses certain uncomfortable questions. In the educational ladder, Class I is very crucial and is the foundation for following classes. If the foundation remains weak, one cannot expect a strong, steady and quality building. It has been our experience that Class I is not accorded the importance it deserves.

## References

1. Constitution of India (January 26, 1950). *Part IV: **Directive** Principles of State Policy.* Article 45.
2. Constitution of India (January 26, 1950). *Part IV: **Directive** Principles of State Policy.* Article 45.
3. National Council of Education Research and Training (2006). *School Achievement Survey.*
4. Annual Status of Education Report (Rural) 2005 – Final Report (January 2006). Pratham Resource Center, Mumbai office: Ground Floor, YB Chavan Center, Gen. J. Bhosale Marg, Nariman Point, Mumbai, 400 021.
5. Annual Status of Education Report (Rural) 2006 – Final Report (January 5, 2007). Pratham Resource Center, Mumbai office: Ground Floor, YB Chavan Center, Gen. J. Bhosale Marg, Nariman Point, Mumbai, 400 021.
6. Annual Status of Education Report (Rural) 2007 – Provisional (January 16, 2008). Pratham Resource Center, Mumbai office: Ground Floor, YB Chavan Center, Gen. J. Bhosale Marg, Nariman Point, Mumbai, 400 021.
7. Walker, Maurice (2011). PISA 2009 Plus Results: Performance of 15-year-olds in reading, mathematics and science for 10 additional participants. ACER Press, an imprint of Australian Council for Educational Research Ltd. 19 Prospect Hill Road, Camberwell, Victoria, 3124, Australia.

# 6

# Mid-lay Meal Programme in India: An Overview

***Mohammad Afsar Alam***

"*Education is the power to think clearly, the power to act well in the world's work, and the power to appreciate life.*"

**—Brigham Young**

## Introduction

Education is thought to be central to economic development. Beneficial in and of itself, it is also viewed as a major contributor to human capital, leading to higher productivity and living standards. Primary education is thought to be associated with especially high returns. Its importance is enshrined in the Millennium Development Goals (MDGs), which call for universal primary education by 2015. In fact, primary education is far from universal and this MDG remains elusive. UNICEF (2008), the agency responsible for tracking progress on this MDG, estimates a net primary school enrollment rate in developing countries of 84 per cent. This is also its estimated average for India. In view of this, governments across the developing world have instituted a wide range of policies aimed at encouraging school enrollment. With much optimism for a new century of progress, the United Nations held the 2000 Millennium Summit with the goal of eradicating global poverty by 2015. A central idea of this Summit was the creation of eight Millennium Development Goals— which, if achieved, would hopefully reach that noble end. However, despite the prioritisation of educational advancements, recent statistics indicate that 69 million children worldwide are not enrolled in primary school. Half of these children live in Sub-Saharan Africa, and more than a quarter of them live in South Asia. In an increasingly competitive and technology-driven global market, the job and overall economic prospects for those without even a primary school education are slim, further widening the gap between the top few and the bottom billion.

**What is Mid day Meal Scheme?**

The Mid day Meal Scheme is a multi-faceted programme of the Government of India that, among other things, seeks to address issues of food security, lack of nutrition and access to education on a pan nation scale. It involves provision for free lunch on working days for children in Primary and Upper Primary Classes in Government, Government Aided, Local Body, Education Guarantee Scheme (EGS) and Alternate Innovative Education (AIE) Centres.

**Importance of the Scheme**

In India, primary school education typically covers grades 1-5, and is the joint responsibility of central and state governments. The central government generally issues guidelines and provides funding, but policy implementation is a state-level decision. A World Bank report states that India has 42 per cent of the world's underweight children. According to the studies by National Nutrition Monitoring Bureau (NNMB), National Institute of Nutrition (NIN) and Indian Council for Medical Research (ICMR), 58.6 per cent of the children of the age group 6–9 years and 77.9 per cent of the children of the age group 10-13 are underweight. If the mild under nutrition is added to underweight, this number increases to 94.1 per cent and 96.4 per cent respectively. 30.1 per cent of all children of 10-13 age group are severely underweight. The school dropout rate is as high as 60 per cent. Under Article 24, paragraph 2c of the Convention on the Rights of the Child to which India is a party, India has committed to providing *"adequate nutritious foods"* for Children. It was basically started in 2001 and implemented in 2004 and till 2013 lot of amendments and changes is being done.

**Mid-day Meal Scheme: Progress**

The Mid-day Meal is the world's largest school feeding programme reaching out to about 12 crore children in over 12.65 lakh schools/EGS centres across the country. The roots of the programme can be traced back to Pre-Independence era when a Mid-day Meal Programme was introduced by British administration for disadvantaged children in Madras Municipal Corporation in 1925. In 1928, Keshav Academy of Calcutta introduced compulsory Mid-day Tiffin for school boys on payment basis at the rate of four annas per child per month. Mid Day Meal Programme was introduced in the Union Territory of Puducherry by French Administration from the year 1930. In 1953, Uttar Pradesh Government introduced a scheme, on voluntary basis, to provide meals consisting of boiled or roasted or sprouted grams, ground-nut, puffed rice, boiled potatoes or seasonal fruits. During 1962-63, Tamil Nadu became the first state in India to initiate a noon meal programme to children with the launch of Mid-day Meal Programme in primary schools. Gujarat was the second state to introduce MDM scheme in 1984, but it was discontinued in between. From August 1990 to October 1991 MDM was replaced by Food for Education Programme where in children with 70 per cent attendance were provided 10 kg of food grains free of cost. The Mid-day Meal Scheme was introduced in the state of Kerala in 1984 in the Lower Primary Schools functioning in 222 Villages, having Fishermen as majority. An Expanded Nutrition Programme was launched jointly by the Government of India and the FAO, WHO, UNICEF during 1958-59, which subsequently developed, into the Applied Nutrition Programme (ANP). Under this, demonstration feeding programmes for the school children wherein nutritious food was cooked by the women groups and fed to the children under the nutrition education component. The Government of India (GOI) initiated the National Programme of Nutritional Support to Primary Education (NP-NSPE) on 15th August 1995 as a Centrally Sponsored Scheme. The objectives of the scheme are to give a boost to universalisation of primary education by mitigating classroom hunger and improving nutritional status of primary school children.

By the mid 1980s, three States viz. Gujarat, Kerala and Tamil Nadu and the UT of Pondicherry had universalised a cooked Mid Day Meal Programme with their own resources for children studying at the primary stage. By 1990-91, the number of states implementing the mid-day meal programme with their own resources on a universal or a large scale had increased to twelve states. With a view to enhancing enrollment, retention and attendance and simultaneously improving nutritional levels among children, the National Programme of Nutritional Support to Primary Education (NP-NSPE) was launched as a Centrally Sponsored Scheme on 15th August 1995, initially in 2408 blocks in the country. In September 2004, the scheme was revised to provide cooked mid-day meal with 300 calories and 8-12 grams of protein to all children studying in classes I – V in government and aided schools and EGS/ AIE centres. In addition to free supply of food grains, the revised scheme provided Central Assistance for (a) Cooking cost @ Re 1 per child per school day, (b) Transport subsidy was raised from the earlier maximum of Rs. 50 per quintal to Rs. 100 per quintal for special category states, and Rs. 75 per quintal for other states, (c) Management, monitoring and evaluation costs @ 2 per cent of the cost of foodgrains, transport subsidy and cooking assistance, (d) Provision of mid-day meal during summer vacation in drought affected areas. In July 2006, the scheme was further revised to provide assistance for cooking cost at the rate of (a) Rs. 1.80 per child/school day for States in the North Eastern Region, provided the NER States contribute Re 0.20 per child/school day, and (b) Rs. 1.50 per child/ school day for other States and UTs, provided that these States and UTs contribute Re 0.50 per child/ school day. In October 2007, the scheme has been further revised to cover children in upper primary (classes VI to VIII) initially in 3479 Educationally Backwards Blocks (EBBs). Around 1.7 crore upper primary children were included by this expansion of the scheme. From 2008-09 i.e., w.e.f. 1st April, 2008, the programme covers all children studying in Government, Local Body and Government-aided primary and upper primary schools and the EGS/AIE centres including Madarsa and Maqtabs supported under SSA of all areas across the country.

Food norms have been revised to ensure balanced and nutritious diet to children of upper primary group by increasing the quantity of pulses from 25 to 30 grams, vegetables from 65 to 75 grams and by decreasing the quantity of oil and fat from 10 grams to 7.5 grams. Cooking cost (excluding the labour and administrative charges) has been revised from Rs.1.68 to to Rs. 2.50 for primary and from Rs 2.20 to Rs. 3.75 for upper primary children from 1.12.2009 to facilitate serving meal to eligible children in prescribed quantity and of good quality. The honorarium for cooks and helpers was paid from the labour and other administrative charges of Re. 0.40 per child per day provided under the cooking cost. In many cases the honorarium was so little that it became very difficult to engage manpower for cooking the meal. A common unit cost of construction of kitchen shed @ Rs. 60,000 for the whole country was impractical and also inadequate. Now the cost of construction of kitchen-cum-store will be determined on the basis of plinth area norm and State Schedule of Rates. During 2010-11 11.36 Cr children i.e., 7.97 Cr. children in primary and 3.39 Cr. children in upper primary are expected to be covered in 12.63 lakhs institutions. Today, Mid-day Meal scheme is serving primary and upper primary school children in entire country.

In November 28, 2001, the Supreme Court of India passed an order stating: *"We direct the State Governments/Union Territories to implement the* ***Mid-day Meal*** *Scheme by providing every child in every Government and Government assisted Primary School with a prepared* ***mid-day meal."*** The Akshaya Patra Foundation, which was by then successfully implementing its own school lunch programme in Karnataka, was called in to give testimonies for verifying the efficacy of the scheme. In order to successfully carry out this mandate, each State Government then started its own Mid-day Meal programme. Initiated by the Government of Karnataka, Akshara Dasoha is one such scheme in place. Voluntary organisations such as Akshaya Patra are therefore encouraged to set up operations wherever possible. They act as the implementing arm of the government. In fact, as the Karnataka Human Development Report 2005 explains, the Government of Karnataka was the 'first to take this step' of involving NGOs in development programmes. The report states that this *'involvement of the NGOs in multilateral/bilateral programmes, raises the level of co-operations to another level. The NGOs become not only implementers; they also find a place in designing and managing programmes together with government at all levels.'* This pioneering move, by the Government of Karnataka, to make NGOs the implementing arm of the Government has been one of the major reasons for its success in attaining the goals of the programme. The achievements of these private-public partnerships have even influenced the Central Government. After including milk in the mid-day meal scheme, the State government is examining a proposal to provide eggs to children in government schools. Addressing a convention of poultry farmers organised by the Karnataka Poultry Farmers and Breeders' Association, Minister for Law, Parliamentary Affairs and Animal Husbandry T.B. Jayachandra stressed on the nutritional value of eggs. By setting up and encouraging private-public partnerships, the government is successfully leveraging the skills and resources of the private sector for the greater good. Today, India's mid-day meal scheme is one of the largest school lunch programme in the world, reaching out to nearly 120 million children in the country.

Although the scheme officially started as a centrally sponsored initiative in 1995, it was limited to providing dry rations and was not fully implemented in most states until 2002. Following a Supreme Court ruling in November 2001, all State Governments were mandated to introduce cooked school meals, and by 2003 most states (including Andhra Pradesh) had started providing school meals. Crucially, in 2004 a Supreme Court order made it mandatory to provide mid-day meals during summer vacations in *'drought affected areas'*. This was an important intervention, as drought has affected large sections of India's rural population. In the Young Lives sample, almost 35 per cent of the rural households report having suffered from drought between 2002 and 2006.

Karnataka has topped the first ever ranking of state governments on the basis of their performance and implementation of the mid-day meal scheme with a total score of 77.79 per cent, followed by Punjab (76.81 per cent), Daman & Diu (71.40 per cent) and Himachal Pradesh (71.31 per cent). Bihar, where a number of children died after a mid-day meal earlier this year, came fifth with 70.36 per cent. Among the states which have fared poorly are Delhi (44.73 per cent), Orissa (47.89 per cent), Goa (47.56 per cent), Sikkim (49.96 per cent), Meghalaya (48.59 per cent), Assam (47.57 per cent), Jharkhand (45.46 per cent), which have all been termed as *"laggards"*. The states have been given scores on the basis of 15 indicators including average coverage of children, foodgrain utilisation against allocation, payment to Food Corporation of India, utilisation of funds, honorarium to cook-cum-helpers, monitoring and supervision, infrastructure and health. While the top five states have been ranked as *"leaders"*, the next rung of states have been ranked as *"followers"*, including Gujarat, Tamil Nadu, Rajasthan, Kerala, Andhra Pradesh, Madhya Pradesh, Manipur, Dadra and Nagra Haveli, Puducherry and Arunachal Pradesh. The remaining states form the *"laggards"*. The analysis of these rankings notes that the number of students covered under the scheme fell by seven million from the preceding quarter. Moreover, while 85 per cent of allocated foodgrain is lifted at the national level, the utilisation of transportation assistance is only 54 per cent for the corresponding period. The HRD ministry's ranking of states on the basis of their performance in implementing the Mid-day Meal scheme has raised serious questions about the parameters employed to judge states.

## Financing of the Scheme

The Mid-day meal scheme is a joint undertaking of central and state governments. Central government provided financial assistance to cover the cost of food grains and their transport. In particular, The Food Corporation of India (FCI), an institution set up in 1964 to support the operation of the central government's food policies, provided states free supply of food grains from the nearest of its godowns. Provision for each student with 100 grams of wheat or rice per day cost the central government approximately Rs. 1.11. In principle, fair average quality of the grains was also guaranteed, with the FCI being responsible for replacing the grains otherwise. The transport subsidy to carry the grains from the nearest FCI go down to the primary school was set at a maximum of Rs. 50 per quintal, amounting to an average transport subsidy of Re. 0.05 per child per school day. The total value of the central government subsidy between 2002-2004 therefore amounted to Rs. 1.16 per child per school day. The Supreme Court's 2001 directive mandated that mid-day meals have a minimum content of 300 calories and 8-12 grams of protein each day of school; for a minimum of 200 days a year.

The overall responsibility for implementation of this directive lies with state governments, who supplement the Central government's contributions to varying degrees. The Central government provides food grains free of cost while it shares the cost of cooking, construction of kitchen and honorarium to helpers with North Eastern states on 90:10 basis and with other states on 75:25 basis. In 2012-13, the central government allocated Rs. 11,937 crore for MDMS. The contribution of the state governments varies from state to state. Subsidy of Rs 75 per quintal is for all states. For special category states (North Eastern states, Jammu and Kashmir, Himachal Pradesh and Uttaranchal), the amount is Rs 125 per quintal. In primary schools, the centre provides subsidy on cooking cost at Rs 2.33 per child per school day while the states contribute minimum 78 paisa. The amount is Rs 2.80 for North-Eastern states while they contribute minimum 31 paisa. In upper-primary schools, the subsidy is Rs. 3.49 for all while the states contribute Rs. 1.16. For North Eastern states the amount is Rs. 4.19 while states contribute 46 paisa. Centre provides one time fund for construction of kitchen sheds at Rs. 60,000 per unit and Rh 5000 for procurement/replacement of kitchen devices for each school.

**Effects of Mid day Meal Scheme**

In recent years, several studies have been conducted to investigate the impact of the MDMS in India. In one of the first surveys on the midday meal, Drèze and Goyal (2003) found that the scheme has several good consequences such as improved attendance rate, child nutrition, and social equality. Interviews revealed that the introduction of the MDMS improved not only attendance of children, but also made them more likely to stay after the lunch break. Before the introduction of the mid-day meal many children would go home for lunch and not return. Now the children stay within the school premises, allowing the classes to resume smoothly. The study also suggests that the programme has proved to be very effective in eradicating hunger. The mid-day meal helps the children maintain energy levels throughout the day, ensuring better concentration in the process. More importantly, midday meals act as a security net, not only for the children coming from poor families, but also for those affected by natural calamities like drought. In areas where hunger is endemic, the mid-day meal might be the only thing saving the children from chronic malnutrition. Afridi (2010) has studied the short run nutritional impact of the mid-day meal. The data shows that the scheme reduced the daily protein deficiency by 100 per cent, the daily calorie deficiency by almost 30 per cent, and the daily iron deficiency by 10 per cent. Singh et al. (2012) tested the long term impact of the programme using longitudinal data from Andhra Pradesh. They conclude that the mid-day meal act effectively as a security net for children affected by drought. The children affected by drought initially had a much lower height-for-age (called stunted growth) than the average child.

Two main sources of variation are used in assessing the impact of mid-day meals: the date on which states introduced mid-day meals in primary schools, and the fact that (in accordance with the Supreme Court directive) they were introduced in public, but not private primary schools. Since the directive was addressed nation-wide, concerns regarding programme placement bias are alleviated. Moreover, staggered implementation at the state level in public but not private schools allows us to treat all private schools as well as public schools in states not yet implementing the programme, as a quasi-control group for public schools in states which introduced mid-day meals.

**Criticism of the Scheme**

Despite claiming to be a champion of the poor, the Government of India has in recent years expressed an increased interest in introducing cash transfers instead of subsidised food. In this context, the mid-day meal disaster in Bihar the 16th of July, where 23 children died from eating their school meal, plays nicely into the hands of those arguing in favour of cash transfers. Proponents of cash transfers will be eager to forget the responsibility of the Bihar state government, and argue that the incident shows that the Mid-day Meal Scheme (MDMS) has failed. The real problem is the disastrous implementation of the scheme by an indifferent government. When the scheme is implemented properly, the MDMS delivers safe cheap meals that improve attendance and class room teaching, and provide a safety net for children who would otherwise starve. The Supreme Court has ordered the states to implement the scheme properly, as the MDMS is a crucial part of the implementation of the right to food. The failure of the Bihar state government to implement the MDMS should not be used as an argument against the scheme itself.

**Conclusion**

In India, there has been considerable interest from State Governments in the performance of the Mid-day Meal Scheme, particularly in relation to the benefits it brings marginalised children. While there is evidence from a number of other studies that the scheme exerts a positive influence on enrolment and may increase daily calorific intake on school days, the impact on longer-term nutritional status and the effect of school meals on learning and cognitive skills has not been clear. The MDMS has been implemented in all the states and Union Territories in the country. According to data, overall 94 per cent of the targeted children have benefitted from the scheme. Most states have succeeded in reaching the targeted children. Some states such as Jammu and Kashmir, Madhya Pradesh, Uttarakhand and Delhi have been able to reach between 73 per cent and 76 per cent of the targeted children. It is more important programme which will increase literacy rate and at the same time malnutrition problem among children.

## References


1. *About the mid-day meal scheme (2013*). Retrieved from http://mdm.nic.in/
2. *India's Mid-day Meal Scheme (2013).* Retrieved from http://www.akshayapatra.org/indias-mid-day-meal-scheme.
3. *Mid-Day Meal Scheme (2013).* Retrieved from http://mla.prsindia.org/policy-guide/mid-day-meal-scheme.
4. *Mid-Day Meal Scheme (2013).* Retrieved from http://en.wikipedia.org/wiki/Midday_Meal_Scheme.
5. *Mr. Simon Jakobsen (Aug 8, 2013). India: The Midday Meal Scheme Must Continue Despite, The Bihar Disaster, Asian Human Rights Commission*, Retrieved from http://www.humanrights.asia/news/ahrc-news/AHRC-ART-091-2013.
6. Rajshiri Jayaraman, Dora Simroth and Francis De Vericourt, *The impact of school lunches on primary school enrollment: Evidence from India's mid day meal scheme*, Retrieved from http://www.isid.ac.in/~pu/conference/dec_10_conf/Papers/RajiJayaraman.pdf.
7. Stephanie Bonds (2012). *Food for Thought: Evaluating the Impact of India's Mid-Day* Meal Programme on Educational Attainment, Retrieved from http://econ.berkeley.edu/sites/default/files/Bonds.pdf.
8. Sundaram Chandrasekhar (1995). *The Mid-day Meal Programme in Gujarat*: A Dissertation Submitted to the University of Glasgow in Partial Fulfilment of the Requirements for the Degree of Master of Philosophy, University of Glasgow.
9. The Impact of the Mid-day Meal Scheme on Nutrition and Learning (August 2010). *Young Lives Policy Brief 8,* Retrieved from http://www.younglives.org.uk/files/policy-papers/the-impact-of-the-midday-meal-scheme-on-nutrition-and-learning
10. *The Indian Express* (Nov 19, 2013). Karnataka has topped in mid-day meal ranking, Retrieved from http://www.indianexpress.com/news/karnataka-govt-tops-midday-meal-rankings/1196679/.

# 7

# Relationship between Pre-school Education with Cognitive and Language Development of Pre-school Children: An Analysis

***Fouziya Qadiri and Dr Sarika Manhas***

*"Take up one idea. Make that one idea your life - think of it, dream of it, live on that idea. Let the brain, muscles, nerves, every part of your body, be full of that idea, and just leave every other idea alone. This is the way to success."*

**–Swami Vivekananda**

**Introduction**

Children come into the world eager to learn and the first five years of life are a time of enormous growth of linguistic, conceptual, social emotional and motor competence. This is when children develop basic learning patterns and abilities that they will use for the rest of their lives. Educational research has verified that the early years are most important years of child's life so the children should be given right start from the early childhood stage until the age of three to six years which is the most critical period when the foundation are laid for lifelong development and the realisation of full potential. In India this awareness is reflected by large number of government and private efforts which includes ICDS Centre, nursery schools and other ECCE programmes. Pre-school is a place where children enjoy their childhood and develop their full potential in a stress free rich caring and stimulating environment and preschool education is a term applied to an array of programmes that differ widely in their goals, service delivery strategies and the ages of children serve. The idea is to give children an early start on successful pathways to academic and life success beginning with early childhood education. The ICDS centers impart education to children in a non-formal way in which children learn basic concepts through limited teaching aids and by the indigenous material made by the anganwadi worker. Children did not get much exposure due to absence of educational and play material, better physical environment and quality staff which could blend together to support wholesome development of children. Preschool education at ICDS centres must be organised in learning by doing method so that the children show interest to attend these centres and develop desirable attitude by way of providing intellectual stimulation through various forms of activities. Learning at early stage must be directed by the child interest and priorities and should be contextualised by their experiences rather than being structured formally. Higher quality preschool environment was related to higher measures of cognitive and language development. Children who attend good early childhood centers performed better on measures of both cognitive and language skills and there is growing evidence that quality preschool programme is linked with children's overall development. Several decades of research clearly demonstrates that developmentally appropriate early childhood programme produce short and long term positive effects on children's cognitive and language development. Language and cognitive development directly influence academic and social abilities of children. Therefore, a child's language skills and cognitive abilities should be recognised and stimulated from young age, since these skills will positively affect their scholastic abilities and social success later on life. Children make progress in preschool centers where the staff is qualified and trained as they spend more time in conducting learning activities that meet each child's need in a productive manner. Children with quality preschool experience attain higher scores on thinking ability; vocabulary and literacy skills. Good quality nursery programme empowers young children by encouraging them to initiate their own learning activities. Research brings out the fact that pre-school centers provide a better start to enter into formal education when the children show attainment in pre reading, early number concept, language, nonverbal reasoning and spatial awareness and children without quality preschool exposure are not so advanced on above such skills. Research has shown beyond doubt that early cognitive and language attainment is strongly related to later academic success.

ICDS Scheme is one of the flagship programmes of the Government of India which caters towards the holistic development of children in the age group of 0-6 years. Pre-school education happens to be an integral part of this scheme which is disseminated through ICDS centers called as Anganwadi centers. However, the various research reports and studies documented the fact that these centers continue to be ill-equipped both within infrastructural facilities as well as staff as the government and higher authorities paid more attention on nutritional and health related aspects, and are preferred only by those parents who fail to pay high fees charged by public preschools/nurseries. With this as background the paper examines the differences if any in the cognitive and language skills of ICDS and Non-ICDS children.

**Research Methodology**

The study was carried out to determine the impact of pre-school education on acquisition of cognitive and language skills among pre-school children. The analysis was based on survey method of data collection with the application of Standardised Tests.

- *Sample and Sampling Technique:* The sample for the present study comprised 600 children in the age group of 3-6 years from ICDS and Non-ICDS centers. 300 children were those who received preschool education at ICDS centers (anganwadi centers) and other half were such who attended Non-ICDS centers (Nursery school). The sample was collected from four districts of Kashmir Division. All four districts were selected randomly (by lottery method) from a total of ten districts. From each district 15 ICDS and Non-ICDS centers were covered and from each centre five children were selected randomly. All sample preschoolers belonged to middle SES families and the screening of such children was done with the help of Standardised Scale devised by Kumar et al, 2004 at Department of Geriatric Mental Health Lucknow, India.

- *Research Instrument:* Two standardised tests were applied on sample children to assess their cognitive and language development. Pandey's Cognitive Development Test for pre-schoolers devised by Hema Pandey in 1991 was used to assess the cognitive abilities of children through the six sub-test namely, *conceptual skills, comprehension, visual perception, memory and object vocabulary.* The test was administered individually in the pre-school centre and sufficient time was given to child to complete all the tasks. Language abilities were assessed through McCarthy Children's Ability Test, developed by Dorothea McCarthy in 1972 and consisted into five sub test namely, *pictorial memory, word knowledge, verbal memory, verbal fluency and opposite analogies.* In this test each subtest has its own time limit and conditions.

**Results and Discussion**

The present study comprised 600 pre-school children in the age group of 3-4, 4-5 and 5-6 years received pre-school education from two different settings of early childhood education center. Both males and females were included in the study. The cognitive and language abilities of sample children (half enrolled at ICDS centers and remaining at Non-ICDS centers) were assessed on two standardised test.

T- test of difference of means was computed to assess the difference if any between ICDS and Non-ICDS children with respect to their cognitive and language abilities. Significant differences were noted between the ICDS and

Non-ICDS children with regard to the scores obtained by them on all sub-tests of cognitive abilities as well as aggregate cognitive abilities. Non-ICDS children performed significantly better on all the six sub-tests than ICDS children.

***Conceptual Skills:*** Significant differences were found in the conceptual skills of the two groups of pre-schoolers (t=23.24, pd<0.01). Non-ICDS children scored higher on conceptual skills with a mean of 20.34 ± of 4.78 than ICDS children who had a mean of 13.39 ± 6.06. Non-ICDS children had better understanding of various concepts related to colours, shape, texture, classification, seriation, counting and weight etc. as compared to ICDS children who performed poorly on the test and had developed the concepts to lesser extent.

***Information:*** Calculation of *t*-test reveals significant differences in the dimension of information between ICDS and Non-ICDS children (t=22.978, pd<0.01). Non-ICDS children were well aware of their surrounding environment and were

**Table 7.1: Comparative Analysis of Cognitive Abilities between ICDS and Non ICDS Children**

| *Dimensions* | *Icds Children (N=300)* | *Non-Icds Children (N=300)* | *t-value* |
|---|---|---|---|
| **+Aggregate cognitive abilities score** | ×=87.090<br>S.D=14.308<br>C.V=0.164 | ×=110.890<br>S.D=13.849<br>C.V=0.125 | 18.88** |
| **Conceptual Skills** | ×=13.393<br>S.D=6.069<br>C.V0.453 | ×=20.347<br>S.D=4.782<br>C.V=0.235 | 23.24** |
| **Information** | ×=2.603<br>S.D=1.397<br>C.V=0.537 | ×=4.903<br>S.D=1.611<br>C.V=0.329 | 22.79** |
| **Comprehension** | ×=3.727<br>S.D=1.266<br>C.V=0.340 | ×=4.967<br>S.D=1.150<br>C.V=0.232 | 14.97** |
| **Visual Perception** | ×=2.387<br>S.D=2.112<br>C.V=0.732 | ×5.463<br>S.D=1.722<br>C.V=0.315 | 21.11** |
| **Memory** | ×=4.430<br>S.D=1.884<br>C.V=0.425 | ×=5.963<br>S.D=1.860<br>C.V=0.312 | 12.11* |
| **Object Vocabulary** | ×=5.230<br>S.D=3.289<br>C.V=0.629 | ×=5.743<br>S.D=0.552<br>C.V=0.096 | 2.71* |

SD=Standard Deviation

C.V= Coefficient of Variation

*P<0.05

**p<0.01

+ *Aggregate cognitive score are based on standard score*

better able to respond all oral questions which show that this group of children exhibit adequate knowledge about their own bodies as well as the surroundings. The nature of some questions generated information about their own self for example, what are eyes for? How many ears you have? etc. and some questions were related to environment for example, how many legs dog has? What is the colour of grass? Why you should not play with match box? etc. Most of the ICDS children did not answered oral questions which indicates that these children did not had much exposure to express themselves verbally and respond oral queries without any hesitation. Explore the environment perform well in this task and showed lack of awareness and alertness about the environment. The value of C.V. indicates that the ICDS group showed more variation on the dimension of information as compared to Non-ICDS children implying that some ICDS children perform better while some weren't complete the task.

***Comprehension:*** Significant differences were noted in the comprehension ability of ICDS and Non-ICDS children (t= 14.97, pd<0.01). The dimension is sub-divided into two types; one is auditory perception and another listening comprehension. Non-ICDS children answered all the oral questions related to auditory perception and exhibited adequate knowledge about the surroundings and were better able to associate the actions of people in the environment. They had the ability to discriminate between sounds and words. The nature of the questions extracted information about the environment for example, what does a postman bring? Where does fish live? Why do you come to school? etc. These children had better listening skills to recall the oral direction given by the examiner whereas the ICDS children had not developed abstract reasoning to answer oral questions and performed poorly in the test. The value of C.V. reveals that the ICDS children showed lesser homogeneity in their comprehension ability, showing that some ICDS children better than others.

***Visual Perception***: Highly significant differences were found in the visual perception of the two groups (t=21.11, pd<0.01). Non-ICDS children had higher visual perception ability with a mean of 5.463 ± 1.722 than ICDS children with a mean of 2.38 ± 2.11. Non-ICDS children were able to identify and differentiate the various cards presented on the basis of big and small, fruits and vegetables, animal and birds. They were also able to identify the basic relationship between the objects in the environment and were more attentive and had higher concentration to reason out and discriminate the things better. ICDS group were unable to visualise the essential relationship between the objects in the environment and exhibited poor performance on the test items. Computation of coefficient of variation reveals that the ICDS group was more heterogeneous in their visual perception ability as compared to Non-ICDS children.

***Memory:*** Significant differences were noted in the memory abilities of the two groups. The performance of ICDS children was inferior to that of Non-ICDS children as they were usually unable to memorise the digits, words orally heard from the examiner indicating they had problem in their working memory. Further, these children also showed problems in their short term memory as they were unable to recall already seen objects and also failed to renarrate the story already heard. Non-ICDS children on the other hand, showed better memory and were able to recall and verbalise all the items and words used in the test.

***Object Vocabulary:*** Like other areas here also significant differences were noted between the two groups (t=2.71, pd<0.01) with regard to their object vocabulary. The Non-ICDS children showed more richness in ideas, quality of language and had developed abstract thinking to explain the things. These items were such that they were ordinarily used in everyday life and included a pencil, knife and key etc. However, the ICDS children were able to identify only some of the pictures in the test material. The value of coefficient of variation reveals that the ICDS group showed more variations in their object vocabulary, indicating that some ICDS children fared better than others in the group.

**Table 7. 2: Comparison of Language Abilities of ICDS and Non-ICDS Children**

| *Dimensions* | *Icds Children (N=300)* | *Non-Icds Children (N=300)* | *t-value* |
|---|---|---|---|
| ***+ Aggregate Language abilities score*** | ×=38.627<br>S.D=7.283<br>C.V=0.189 | ×=54.833<br>S.D=10.536<br>C.V=0.192 | 27.39** |
| ***Pictorial Memory*** | ×=4.120<br>S.D=1.328<br>C.V=0.322 | ×=5.083<br>S.D=1.126<br>C.V=0.221 | 11.27* |
| ***Word Knowledge*** | ×=12.897<br>S.D=7.433<br>C.V=0.576 | ×=21.673<br>S.D=6.098<br>C.V=0.281 | 21.76** |
| ***Verbal Memory*** | ×=2.172<br>S.D=2.856<br>C.V=1.315 | ×=5.293<br>S.D=5.442<br>C.V=1.028 | 9.99* |
| ***Verbal Fluency*** | ×=11.097<br>S.D=3.23<br>C.V=0.299 | ×=16.683<br>S.D=3.593<br>C.V=0.215 | 24.14** |
| ***Opposite Analogies*** | ×=0.973<br>S.D=1.939<br>C.V=1.992 | ×=6.400<br>S.D=3.898<br>C.V=0.609 | 25.20** |

X = Mean
SD=Standard Deviation
C.V= Coefficient of Variation
*p<0.05
**p<0.01
*+ Aggregate language score is based on standard score*

Highly significant differences were noted between the two groups with regard to their language abilities (t=27.39, pd<0.01). Non-ICDS children showed higher aggregate language abilities with a mean of 54.83 ± 10.53 than ICDS children with mean value of 38.62 ±7.28.

***Word Knowledge:*** The word knowledge subtest further divided in two types one is Picture Vocabulary Test, in which child identifies common objects and in second, Oral Vocabulary Test, the child explains meaning of the words for example, Towel, Birthday, Knife, Good etc. Highly significant differences were found in the word knowledge of the two groups (t= 21.76, pd<0.01). Non-ICDS children performed efficiently on identification of the common objects in picture vocabulary card book shown by the examiner, for example apple, tree, horse, and cow, flower etc. These children also demonstrated better oral vocabulary by explaining the meaning of different words which were graded in difficulty and ranged from concrete, familiar words to abstract concepts. The ICDS children on the other hand, were able to identify the some of the pictures presented on card book but exhibited lesser understanding of words which are used in day to day life. The values of C.V. indicate that the ICDS children were more heterogeneous in their word knowledge ability as compared to Non-ICDS children.

***Verbal Memory:*** Significant differences were noted in the verbal memory of two groups. The Non-ICDS children exhibited better vocabulary and verbal memory to repeat the words and sentences in the sequence as presented verbatim to them by the examiner. They also performed better in renarating the story already heard. The ICDS children were however mostly, not able to repeat the words and sentences orally and also showed less alertness to repeat the sentences and words and recall the story already heard. The result of coefficient of variation reveals that the two groups showed similar levels of heterogeneity in their verbal memory.

***Verbal Fluency:*** Here also highly significant differences were found in the verbal fluency of the two groups (t=24.14, pd<0.01). Non-ICDS children had the higher ability to classify and think quickly to memorise the words falling into four category given by the examiner in 20 seconds that is, things to eat, wear, names of animals and transportation etc. Whereas performance of ICDS children was inferior in the test as they did not think quickly of words falling into each of the four categories except things to eat and wear where they had obtained some score. They did not demonstrate much fluency of words that are used in day to day life.

***Opposite Analogies:*** Calculation of t-value reveal highly significant differences in the dimension of opposite analogies (t=25.20, pd<0.01) between the two groups. Non –ICDS children had higher opposite analogy ability with a mean of 6.40 and ± 3.89 than ICDS children with a mean value of 0.97 and ± 1.93. On this subtest of language abilities ICDS children had the poorest performance and failed to understand the relation between the set of words verbally presented to them. On the other hand, Non-ICDS children demonstrated relational thinking ability to complete sentences by providing opposites to words given by the examiner. Many

ICDS children were not able to understand the task and therefore were not able to provide opposites of any keywords in the nine statements comprising the test.

**Conclusion**

In order for children to flourish, the development and enhancement of their maximum capabilities and potential as well as making the most of their period of existence are of the utmost importance. The importance of stimulating environment during this most plastic and impressionable stage cannot be overlooked. Children of this age develop the ability to use symbols in their thoughts and actions, they like to explore, seek new experience for the sheer pleasure of sensing and knowing. Children's language and cognitive development are two of the most important aspects of learning that takes place in the early years of child's life, as the child develops the ability to express him/herself by means of words, as well as to show understanding, whereby thinking is made possible. Therefore, early years should comprise of developmental activities, verbal interaction with people of all ages, storytelling, reading books, singing songs and early stimulation.

The findings of the present study reveals significant differences between the ICDS and Non-ICDS children with regard to the scores obtained by them on all subtests of cognitive abilities as well as aggregate language development. Highly significant differences were found in their conceptual skills, information and visual perception ability. Non-ICDS preschoolers had developed better conceptual skills related to colour, texture, shapes, counting classification and seriation etc. and exhibited adequate knowledge about their own bodies as well as surrounding environment. These children had the ability to visualise the relationship between objects in the environment and could easily classify and discriminate the things. Whereas ICDS children had developed conceptual skills to a lesser extent, and did not showed much awareness about the surrounding environment and weren't skilled enough to analyse the relationship between objects and things.

Hence, the performance of preschoolers on the test measuring language development also indicates that the Non-ICDS children showed higher language abilities than the ICDS children. Highly significant differences were noted between the two groups with regard to their performance on opposite analogies, verbal fluency and word knowledge sub-tests. Non-ICDS children performed better on all the five sub-tests and showed more consistency in their language abilities as compared to ICDS group. These findings are supported with the findings of study conducted by Yadav et al., (2010) that anganwadi children's performance in items related to verbal memory and concept related aspects was of low extent, however on perception and language related parameters it was of medium extent. These children classified means of transport and utility items but they performed badly in classifying colours and size. But the performance of nursery school children in terms of perception, reasoning, memory and concept related parameters was better in some of cases, however their language abilities were found to be superior. Just like the cognitive abilities the ICDS children on language abilities also tend to be more heterogeneous, highlighting that some of these children may have potential for higher language development also.

The above findings support the fact that quality preschool education and stimulating environment received by children in early years help to ensure more advanced cognitive and language development in children. These results have implication for policy planners and administrators as the finding reaffirm the fact the children attending ICDS centers continue to perform poorly on various cognitive and language skills/ abilities tasks than children of same age attending other preschool centers. Instead, of focusing on simply opening more and more ICDS centers and making attempts to increase enrollment, it is probably time to provide quality preschool education and enriching environment to the children already attending these ICDS centers.

## References

1. Dewitt, B. (1995). In Stretch, L.K. *Effects of Cognitive Stimulation in the Development of mathematics, literacy and life skills concepts in early childhood.* Unpublished M.Sc. Dissertation, University of South Africa. Retrieved on March 25, 2011 from http://www.uri.unisa.ac.za.com.
2. Duckworth, K. (2006) *Development in the Early Years and its importance for School Performance and Adult Outcomes.* Retrieved on February 22, 2009 from http://www.learningbenefits.net.com.
3. Elaison, J. (2009). In Stretch, L.K. *Effects of Cognitive Stimulation in the Development of mathematics, literacy and life skills concepts in early childhood.* Unpublished M.Sc. Dissertation, University of South Africa. Retrieved on March 25, 2011 from http://www.uri.unisa.ac.za.com.
4. Howes, C. (2004). *Study of Best Practices in Early Childhood-Education. NCEDL Research.* Retrieved on November 8, 2007 from http://www.fpg.unc.edu.com.
5. Kaul, V. (2009). *Early childhood care and education experience in India.* Report prepared by Ministry of Human Resource and Development. Retrieved on April 25, 2011 from htpp://www.educationforallindia.com.
6. Margaret, R., Burchinal, J., Robert, R., (2000) Relating Quality of Center-Based Child Care to Early Cognitive and Language Development Longitudinally. *Journal of Child Development,* **7**(1), 345-347.
7. MWCD. (2007). *Working group on Development of children in eleventh five year plan*: A Report by Ministry of Women and Child Development. Retrieved on May, 5, 2011 from http://www.wcd.nin.com.
8. NIEER. (2006). *The Value of Effective Preschool Education.* Retrieved on December 8, 2007 from http://www.nieer.org.com.

9. NAEYC (2010). *High Quality Preschool Education for our Kids.* Retrieved on September, 5, 2010 http://www.naeyc.org.com.

10. Sammon, P., Sylva, K., Melhuish, K. (2004). The impact of Preschool Children Cognitive attainment at entry to reception. *British Educational Research Journal,* **30** (5), University of London, U.K.

11. Somaiah, M. and Vijayalakshmi, N. (2007). Management Perspective OF ICDS Programme. *Journal of Dharna,* **1**(1), 4-5.

12. Yadav, B., Dahiya, R., Kundu, R., and Sabarwal, K. (2010). Assessment of Cognitive Abilities of Rural Children. *Asian Journal of Home Science,* **4** (2), 366-368.

13. Epstein, A (1993). In Mathur, G. *Impact of preschool programmes on mental and motor development of young children.* Unpublished M.Sc Dissertation, University of Agriculture Science, Dharwad, Karnataka, 14-21. Retrieved on February 23, 2011 from http://www.etd.usasd.edu.com.

# 8

# Social Exclusion of Scheduled Caste Children from Primary Education in Tripura

***Dipankar Biswas***

*"Education is the manifestation of perfection already existing in an"*

**— Swami Vivekananda**

**Introduction**

Social exclusion is a concept used in many parts of the world to characterise contemporary forms of social disadvantage. Dr. Lynn Todman, director of the Institute on Social Exclusion at the Adler School of Professional Psychology, suggests that social exclusion refers to processes in which individuals and entire communities of people are systematically blocked from rights, opportunities and resources (e.g., housing, employment, healthcare, civic engagement, democratic participation and due process) that are normally available to members of society and which are key to social integration.[1] The term *"social exclusion"* appears in the framework laws of the European Union and the laws of several nations. The boundaries of the concept are far from determinate, but at its core, social exclusion involves being shut out from social institutions and relations in ways that matter for one's well being.[2] Social exclusion in India cannot be captured by the Euro-centric approach and its labour market framework. The exclusion discourse in Indian society has to be understood against the backdrop of the caste system.[3]

Caste, traditional India's system of social ordering and control is the most elaborate form of social stratification ever known. It has dominated the Indian sub-continent for about three millennia and is also the most exhaustive and obnoxious of all exclusionary systems. Caste-exclusions are explicit in traditional society. Membership and status are determined by birth. There is a hierarchy of social precedence among the castes. There are restrictions on social and cultural intercourse between castes; castes are segregated and stratified with regard to civil and religious privileges; occupations are caste determined with relatively little choice allowed; restrictions on marriage outside one's sub-caste help maintain the system.[4] Several stories from the ancient Sanskrit symbolise caste exclusion: those of Shambuk, Ekalavya and Sita. In the cases of both Ekalavya and Shambuk, youth of great accomplishment from dalit and adivasi backgrounds were denied their due because of the hierarchy of caste: only a Brahmin (or twice-born) could practice austerity; only a Kshatriya could be a great archer. The youth were victims of social exclusion due to caste.[5] As the structure of exclusion in India is very old, and still persists in different forms, at least three strands of exclusion discourse can be discerned, all directed against the discriminatory, oppressive, exploitative and exclusionary practices of the caste system.[6]

There is legislation stemming from the Indian Constitution which outlaws caste discrimination. The Chair of the Committee which wrote the Constitution of the Republic of India was Dr. Ambedkar. Under the constitution, the Republic of India is empowered[7] to *"promote with special care the educational and economic interests of the weaker sections of the people, and, in particular, of the Scheduled Castes and the Scheduled Tribes, and shall protect them from social injustice and all forms of exploitation"*. To achieve this aim, the State has used a two-fold approach: the provision of legal safeguards against discrimination; and a *"Reservation Policy"* in the State sector and State Supported Sector.

Caste and untouchability based exclusion and discrimination can be categorised in the economic, civil, cultural, and political spheres as follows: Firstly, economic exclusion can be practiced in the labour market through denial of jobs; in the capital market through denial of access to capital; in the agricultural land market through denial of sale and purchase or leasing of land; in the input market through denial in sale and purchase of factor inputs; and in the consumer market through denial in the sale and purchase of commodities and consumer goods. Secondly, discrimination can occur through what Amartya Sen describes as *"unfavourable inclusion"*, through differential treatment in the terms and conditions of contract, one of them reflecting in discrimination in the prices charged and received by discriminated groups. Discriminated groups can get lower prices for the goods that they sell, and could pay higher prices for the goods that they buy, as compared with the market price or the price paid by other groups. Thirdly, exclusion and discrimination can occur in access to social needs supplied by government or public institutions, or by private institutions in the fields of education, housing and health, including common property resources like water bodies, grazing land and land for common use; Fourthly, groups (particularly untouchables) may face exclusion and discrimination from participation in certain categories of jobs (the sweeper being excluded from household jobs) because of the notion of purity and pollution, and may be restricted to so-called *"unclean"* occupations.[8]

Discrimination is the main function of caste system in India. Though the Indian constitution provides for a slew of preferential schemes designed to end discrimination against the scheduled castes/ scheduled tribes yet, atrocities against them continue unabated. The provision in the constitution resolves, *'to secure to all citizens: justice, social, economic and political, liberty of thought, expression, belief, faith and worship; equality of status and of opportunity, and to promote among them all fraternity, assuring the dignity of individual and unity.'* The constitution also states that 'the state shall not discriminate against any citizen on grounds only of religion, race, caste, place and birth or any form'. In the directive principles it adds that *'The state shall promote with special care the educational and economic interest of the scheduled castes/ tribes and shall protect them from social injustice and all forms of exploitation'.*[9]

In spite of all these provisions discrimination on basis of castes is still continue till to date. Because, to implementations of provisions made in the constitution are not in the capacity of depressed castes the political, social and economic powers are vested in the hands of upper castes Hindus. As upper castes Hindu could control all powers by the virtue of castes system they do not want to implements the constitutional provisions for their vested interests. Dr. Babasaheb Ambedkar, the champion of human rights said is true even today, he said that, *'Millions of people living in the midst of civilisation are still in a savage state and are leading the life of hereditary criminals. But the Hindus have never felt ashamed of it. This is a phenomenon which in my view is quite unparalleled".*[10] Thus, biases within the law-enforcement machinery and the political class have combined to prevent the depressed castes from utilising programmes designed for them. The statistics speak for themselves. Caste discrimination not only hinders SC/STs children from attending school but also affect the quality of education they receive. Therefore, the progress of schooling among Dalit children between the ages of 6-14 has been low and dropout rate among them is very high compared[11] to that of the general population.

Several such facts have been revealed in the *'Indian Education Report'*. Upper castes teachers refuse to touch scheduled castes students. At the same time they make these children special targets of verbal abuse and physical punishment.[12] Dr. Ambedkar once said *"Enlightened high caste Hindus, who did not feel the necessary for agitating for the abolition of caste or had not the courage to agitate for it".*[13] Dalit bias runs deeper and deeper even in 21st century, not only among the uneducated people but also even among highly modern educated.[14]

**Significance of the Study**

As exclusion of SC or Dalit students from primary education actually denying the Right of Children to Free and Compulsory Education Act or Right to Education Act (RTE), which was passed by the Indian Parliament on 4 August 2009.[15] Very few works has done in this field in the national level (Robert Jenkins and Eimar Barr, 2006). But in Tripura this very important field was overlooked by the researchers especially in the primary education. So the researcher has chosen the topic, "*Social Exclusion of Scheduled Caste Children from Primary Education in Tripura.*"

**Objectives of the Study**

1. Review the underlying causes of the disadvantaged status related to primary education of children from scheduled castes (SCs). and
2. Suggesting remedial measures of the problem.

**Overview of Schedule Caste in Tripura**

The total population of Tripura in 2001 Census has been 3,199,203. Of these 555, 724 persons are Scheduled Castes (SCs) constituting 17.4 per cent of the total population of the state. The state has registered 23.19 per cent decadal growth of SC population in 1991-2001. There are thirty one (31) notified SCs, and all have been enumerated in 2001 Census.[16] Among all SCs, 75.3 per cent of the population in age group 5-14 years has been attending any educational institutions. Of the seven major SCs, Dhoba are on top having 80.2 per cent population attending educational institutions, while Chamar are at the bottom (65.1 per cent). That means among all SCs, 24.7 per cent of the population in age group 5-14 years has not been attending any educational institutions in Tripura. Among all SCs, 2.3 per cent of the total female population of less than 18 years – the legal minimum age for marriage – is ever married. The highest per centage of ever married females of this age category has been recorded among Patni (3.2 per cent), followed by Chamar (3.1 per cent). The ever married males below 21 years – their minimum legal age for marriage – constitute 1.2 per cent of the population. Individual SC wise, the Patni has recorded the highest at 1.8 per cent, while it is the lowest among Mahisyadas (0.9 per cent).[17]

**Table 8.1: Population below Poverty Line**

| *Population below poverty line (per cent)* | *India* | *SCs (India)*[181] | *SCs (Tripura)*[19] |
|---|---|---|---|
| Rural Areas | 27.09 | 36.25 | 15.63 |

**Overview of Education in Tripura and the Extent of Social Exclusion of Scheduled Caste Children**

There has been a significant increase in overall literacy-rates and school participation-rates across the country since the early 1990s. Gender and social disparities have also declined with an overall increase in school attendance. In 2001 Census and routine monitoring information from the Department of Education the country is approaching near universalisation of enrollment at the primary stage. The Gross Enrollment-Rate has increased from 90 per cent in 2003-2004 to 98 per cent in 2004-2005. Similarly, the net enrollment rate has risen from 72 per cent to 82 per cent during the same period.[20] A number of factors have contributed to the rising enrollment rate including the introduction of mid-days meals, opening of alternate schools, promoting the participation of Parent Teacher Associations (PTAs) and massive enrolment drives (SSA).

**Table 8.2: Drop-out Rates of SC Students in Classes I-V (2003-04)**

| | *Boys* | *Girls* | *Total* |
|---|---|---|---|
| All India | 36.83 | 36.19 | 36.56 |
| Tripura | 35.85 | 35.88 | 35.87 |

*Source*: *Selected Educational Statistics 2003-04*, www.education.nic.in/stats/detail/19.pd

**Table 8.3: Per centage of SC Students Enrolled in Primary Education**

| | *Per centage of SC in Total Population (Census 2001)* | *I-V* |
|---|---|---|
| Rural | 17.17 | 18.36 |
| Urban | 18.34 | 27.16 |
| Total | 17.37 | 19.47 |

*Source:* Seventh all India School Education Survey, 2007.

The dropout-rate in Tripura of SC students in Primary level is very close to the national level. Though the enrolment is higher but the dropout rate is also higher, which encourages the exclusion.

**Table 8.4: Reasons for Never Attending or Dropping out of School, Children aged 6-17 years (Sample size 100)**

| | *Males* | | *Females* | |
|---|---|---|---|---|
| *Reasons* | *Urban* | *Rural* | *Urban* | *Rural* |
| *Never attended School (per cent)* | *6.4* | *13.6* | *9.0* | *25.7* |
| • School far away | 1.5 | 4.4 | 3.4 | 5.2 |
| • Education not necessary | 6.1 | 7.8 | 12.9 | 13.1 |
| • Required for work at home or outside for cash/kind | 12.6 | 17.1 | 15.4 | 24.5 |
| • Costs too much | 28.5 | 25.8 | 30.1 | 23.8 |
| • Not interested in studies | 26.5 | 25.7 | 15.7 | 15.9 |
| • Other | 26.5 | 17.0 | 19.7 | 15.4 |
| • Don't know | 3.0 | 2.0 | 2.8 | 2.1 |
| **Total** | 100.00 | 100.00 | 100.00 | 100.00 |
| **Dropped out of school (per cent)** | **10.6** | **10.6** | **11.0** | **12.6** |
| • School far away | 0.3 | 1.4 | 1.2 | 7.5 |
| • Education not necessary | 2.4 | 2.3 | 5.4 | 4.3 |
| • Required for work at home or outside for cash/kind | 21.9 | 28.4 | 20.8 | 26.2 |
| • Costs too much | 15.2 | 13.3 | 17.0 | 11.4 |
| • Not interested in studies | 42.5 | 40.0 | 30.2 | 24.8 |
| • Repeated failures | 6.0 | 5.3 | 6.1 | 3.7 |
| • Other | 5.9 | 5.5 | 14.3 | 18.2 |
| • Don't know | 5.7 | 3.8 | 5.1 | 4.0 |
| **Total** | 100.00 | 100.00 | 100.00 | 100.00 |

*Source:* Survey Work.

In order to better understand social exclusion of scheduled caste from education, it is important to develop a framework which would help to categorise the factors which influence the decision to attend (or not attend) school and to understand who takes this decision, i.e. (1) characteristics and processes within the school (i.e., teaching processes, school environment, background of teachers, discriminatory practices etc.), (2) processes within the community (i.e., social dynamics, inclusive decision-making, social norms within the community related to education etc.), and (3) household characteristics and related processes (i.e., caste, poverty, gender, numbers of children, nutrition, educational level and occupation of parents, value places on education etc.). Each of these elements affects a child's chances of accessing school, regularly attending, completing and ultimately, achieving a certain level of learning.

The processes within each of these components are not independent of each other, and therefore the relationship and interplay between them also influences the education status of SC children. The relationship and interplay between the school, community and household is important in understanding the decision-making processes related to a child's attendance. That is, there is interplay between life situations, school functioning, classroom processes, community norms, parental aspirations and other factors which have an influence on educational outcomes of disadvantaged groups. For example, recognising that teachers are a part of the community and therefore are influenced by societal norms, it is clear that prejudices within the community would have an influence on teachers' attitude and possibly their teaching practice towards SC children.

**Analytical Framework to Address Social Exclusion in Primary Education**

With the significant increase in public resources to primary education[21], and the increased attention more generally both of senior decision-makers and the public, there is now a unique opportunity to transform the education system in India, with the potential of inducing fundamental changes in the opportunities to socially disadvantaged populations in the country. An improved education system may be one of the key ingredients to breaking the cycle of poverty and deprivation to scheduled caste children in India. During the 1990s, the focus on improving access and quality of education was on increasing public resources to education and addressing the poor quality of teaching. It is, however, now widely recognised that finances alone will not ensure regular attendance of the most disadvantaged. Explanations of educational disadvantage, particularly in the context of gender and social attributes often focus on the supply dimensions of the problem, which again often emphasise the necessity of providing additional resources. A broader approach however is needed for education policy and resulting programmes to effectively address social exclusion of SC children from primary school. A more comprehensive approach is therefore proposed which highlights the various inter-related processes which influence decision-making at various levels related to a child's education.[22]

**Policy Implications and Conclusions**

The Government of India has repeatedly acknowledged the disadvantaged status of the SC population in education and recognised the need to address it. The National Policy on Education (1986) declared *"The central focus in the SC's educational development is their equalisation with the non-SC population in all stages and levels of education"* (GOI, 1986). The policy focused on incentives, scholarships, reservations, recruitment of teachers, location of school buildings and "constant micro-planning and verification to ensure that the enrolment, retention and successful completion of SC students" (GOI, 1986). However, the situation of SC children has continued to lag significantly behind the national average, indicating either a failure in the implementation of national policies and programmes to address the situation or a problem in the model or approach to addressing the issue.

The approach paper of 11th five year plan states that, *"Development and empowerment of socially disadvantaged groups is a commitment enshrined in the Constitution, and education is the most effective instrument of social empowerment. Schemes for the educational uplift of the SCs and STs have borne fruit although the gap between the general population and SCs and STs are still at unacceptable levels.... Some minorities have fallen far behind the national average in education. It will be necessary to go to the root of the problem and examine the reasons for the decline so that remedial measures can be taken during the 11th Plan."*[23]

**Special Provisions/Incentives for Education of SCs in Tripura[24]**

The following special provisions for SCs and STs have been incorporated in the existing schemes of the Departments of Elementary Education and Literacy and Secondary and Higher-Education:

(a) Establishment of one Residential Schools (from I-VIII) under Sarva Siksha Aviyan.
(b) Construction of 100-seated hostel for SC boys.
(c) Extension of benefit of educational loan from S.C. Corporation to meritorious students for pursuing their studies in Degree (Hon's/Technical) and Post Graduate levels.
(d) Increase of the rate of Outfit allowance from Rs. 2000/ to Rs. 5,000/for those who go outside of the State for higher studies after H.S.(+2 stages).
(e) Some schemes for economic development of SC population have already been taken by Govt. of Tripura.

During the 1990s, the focus of the large-scale District Primary Education Programme, a more recently the Sarva Shiksha Abhiyan[25] was on addressing the inadequate budgetary resources and the poor quality of teaching, which were regarded as two key constraints to achieving universal participation. However, while it is obvious that universal elementary education demands a significant increase in financial allocation, it is also evident both from the experience in India but also based on global experience that finances alone will not ensure attendance of disadvantaged populations. One of the development objectives of the SSA is *"enrolment of children of SC and ST will be near parity with that of other groups"*, which in itself is a relatively modest objective as it focuses on enrollment, rather than completion of learning achievements, and also mentions "near parity" rather than parity. However, the approach the programme has adopted is not sufficiently comprehensive in addressing the above mentioned constraints and will therefore fail to influence the relevant decision-making processes which relates to a child's education status, particularly related to the issues faced by SC children.[26]

Addressing social exclusion requires a holistic approach which promotes involvement of excluded populations in community life; ensures access to all basic services; promotes behaviour change; increases income and addresses other key elements of exclusion. Similarly in education, a holistic approach is necessary based on an analysis of the various components of the decision-making process related to regularly attending school for an SC child and, from the supply side; all elements of the education experience must be addressed. This obviously entails a multi-sectoral response which is broader than education alone, as the challenge of social exclusion does not only exist in the education sector and factors outside the education sector will relate to the education opportunities available to SC children. A comprehensive response will also need to be context-specific, with the need for innovative programmes to bring and keep children into the mainstream school system by making schooling attractive to them and also worthwhile for the parents. A comprehensive and context specific strategy must be adopted, which is often not the case with existing programmes and policies in India. For example, many of the schemes which focus on increasing demand for education, such as providing text books and uniforms and/or a conditional cash transfer for SC children, do not address other factors within the household related to the decision-making process or to the other factors related to the school or the community. The above conclusion is consistent with the outcome of the Joint Review Mission of the SSA in 2006 which stated that *"in certain groups like SC, ST and minority children, the number of out-of-school children is still high. It is necessary to identify specific contextual aspects including socio-cultural reasons that inhibit the enrolment and retention of these groups. There requires building of appropriate capacity and resource support at the sub-district level to develop relevant strategies and interventions"*.[27]

Encouraging the enrollment of SC children in the problem-solving and solution process, and also the care-givers in a community level process may in itself contribute to positive change at community level. Similarly, encouraging children themselves to participate in the management of the school, and also reaching children who are not attending, and promoting the diversity of this participation by ensuring that SC children participate in the process, could be a significant step towards making schools more inclusive. The "*Child Cabinet*"[28] initiative supported as part of the UNICEF Quality Education Package is one such opportunity and while not yet evaluated, is showing some positive signs of contributing to children's involvement in the management of the school.

It, however, does not include the stipulation of ensuring that the cabinet is made up of children from various castes and therefore will not necessarily address issues related to social exclusion.

Information regarding the level of exclusion of SC children from education is necessary to enable an effective management process at local level. The attendance of socially excluded children, such as the scheduled caste, tends to be more irregular than other children and therefore moving beyond enrollment data, to focus instead on retention, transition, average years of schooling data, and most importantly completion rates and assessment of basis learning competencies, disaggregated by caste is necessary in order to assess and monitor the capacity of the education system to reach and provided a quality service to traditionally excluded groups.[28]

Strengthening data management systems which provide disaggregated data by caste, gender and other characteristics at local level is therefore necessary. This data must be complemented by data on dropouts and on those how have never attended school.[29] However, this level of disaggregation is often not currently included in either routine government monitoring systems, such as the Education Management Information System (EMIS) of DPEP, or the District Information System for Education (DISE of SSA) or surveys which collect information on education indicators. Strengthening the generation and use of data, including placing it in the public domain, would complement the recent positive developments related to expanding the power and use of the *"Right to Information"* Act, which promotes the availability and use of information related to government services (and other information) to the public. It would also be important to include private schools in this equation, recognising the trend discussed above regarding children (particularly boys belonging to higher caste) being sent to private school.[30]

A comprehensive, context specific, participatory process which includes reaching young children would go a long way in addressing social exclusion of SC children from primary education in Tripura. Programmes which improve only the supply-side or the demand-side, or even those which address both but are not based on a more comprehensive analysis of the factors which influence the various decision-making processes related to a child's education status, will not be comprehensive enough to address this multi-faceted and long-standing issue which continues to exclude SC children from the education system.

## References

1. Wikipedia (Social Exclusion).
2. Articles 136 and 137 of the Treaty of Amsterdam, 1999.
3. P. Radhakrisnan, Globalisation and Exclusion: The Indian Context, Global Asia Vol. 4, No. 1.
4. Dynamics of Social change, ICFAI University Publication.
5. Gail Omvedt, Caste is the cruelest exclusion- (http://infochangeindia.org).
6. Milton Singer and Bernard Cohn, Structure and changes in Indian society, 1968.

7. Indian Constitution- Article 46, A Directive Principle of State Policy.
8. Sukhadeo Thorat, Dalit exclusion: The empirical evidence.
9. Dr. K.S. Ingole, A Critical Study Of Social Exclusion and Its Implication, SNDT Women's University, Mumbai.
10. Annihilation of Caste, Vol. 1, p. 52.
11. Chandra Bhan Prasad, Midday meals don't work for dalit children, www.infochange India.org.
12. Times of India, February 27, 2002.
13. Annihilation of Caste with a reply to mahatma, http://www.ambedkar.org.
14. *www.ambedkar.org/.../SOCIAL_EXCLUSION_and_ITS_IMPLICATION.pdf*
15. *"Provisions of the Constitution of India having a bearing on Education"*. Department of Higher Education. http://www.education.nic.in/constitutional.asp. Retrieved 2010-04-01
16. http://censusindia.gov.in/Tables_Published/SCST/dh_sc_tripura.pdf
17. http://censusindia.gov.in/
18. NSSO, 1999/00
19. http://planningtripura.nic.in/THDR/backgroundreport/Poverty%20&%20inequality.pdf
20. http://indiabudget.nic.in/es2003-04/chapt2004/chap107.pdf
21. D. Bhaskara Rao, District Primary Education Programme, Discovery Publishing House, New Delhi.
22. Robert Jenkins and Eimar Barr, 2006, UNICEF India.
23. Planning Commission, 2006.
24. 33-Point Special Development Programme for Welfare oF SCs, OBCs and Minorities for Hosting in the offcial Web Site in Tripura.
25. *5th Review Mission of Sarva Shiksha Abhiyan Government of India* (16-31 January, 2007), Aide Memoire.
26. Robert Jenkins and Eimar Barr, 2006, *UNICEF India.*
27. *Department of Education*, 2006, p. 2.
28. The Telegraph, Wednesday, April 21, 2010, Calcutta.
29. Vimla Ramchandran, *Gender and Social Equality in Primary Education: hierarchies* of Access, 2004, P. 23.
30. Robert Jenkins and Eimar Barr, 2006, *UNICEF India.*
31. Ajwad, Mohamed Ihsan (2006) *"Anti-Poverty Programs in Uttar Pradesh"*, World Bank Staff Paper, World Bank, Washington.
32. De Haan, Arjun (2005) "Social Policy: Towards Inclusive Institutions", University of Guelph and Department for International Development, *UK. Paper at the World Bank Conference* 'New Frontiers of Social Policy: Development in a Globalizing World': December 12-15, 2005.

33. Department of Education (2006) *Sarva Shiksha Abhiyan: Fourth joint Review Mission.* Aide Memoire, New Delhi.
34. Department of Women and Child Development (DWCD) and United Nations Children's Fund (UNICEF) (2001) *Multiple Indicator Survey: India Summary Report,* DWCD and UNICEF, New Delhi.
35. Department of Women and Child Development and United Nations Children's Fund (2002) *Multiple Indicator Survey 2000: All India Report (draft),* DWCD and UNICEF, New Delhi.
36. Barr, Eimar. Jenkins, Robert (2006), *Social Exclusion of Scheduled Caste Children from Primary Education in India*, UNICEF India, New Delhi.
37. Government of India (2003) *Tenth Five Year Plan 2003-2007,* Planning Commission, New Delhi.
38. Government of India (2002) *Selected Educational Statistics 2000-20001,* Department of Education, New Delhi.
39. Government of India (1997) *Economic Activities and School Attendance by Children of India*, Fifth Quinquennial Survey, NSS 50th Round, 1993-1994, Report 412, National Sample Survey Organisation, Department of Statistics, Government of India.
40. Government of India (1986) *National Policy on Education*, Department of Education, New Delhi

# PART II – SECONDARY EDUCATION

# 9

# Secondary Education in India: An Overview

***Prof. B.K. Panda and Dr. Sukanta Sarkar***

*"The highest education is that which does not merely give us information but makes our life in harmony with all existence".*

**—Rabindranath Tagore**

## Introduction

Education which is the fulcrum of sustainable development holds the key to *'social inclusion'*. It is one of the necessary conditions for advancing quality of life and freedom. In other words, universal access to quality knowledge and skills ensures that everybody has an equal opportunity to play a full part in work and society. It is essential for integrating the marginalised and vulnerable in society into the development process. Historical forces have largely influenced the policy-planning processes and growth trends in education, both in developed and low-income countries. These include colonial policies related to institutional structures, choice of providers, curriculum decisions, teacher recruitment, evaluation systems, certification and financing. Initially, secondary education was considered a subsidiary to tertiary education as its primary function was to prepare pupils for higher studies. India is following a service-led growth model and striving hard to survive the global competition, in these conditions it is being increasingly recognised that secondary education, is the most critical segment of the education chain.

In the Indian context, balanced development of education is critical for nation building. Education is one of the most important components of the inclusive development model of the emerging Indian democracy, which was well articulated even in the 1960s in the report of the Education Commission

(1963-64). Historical forces have largely influenced the policy-planning processes and growth trends in education, both in developed and low-income countries. These include colonial policies related to institutional structures, choice of providers, curriculum decisions, teacher recruitment, evaluation systems, certification and financing. Initially, secondary education was considered a subsidiary to tertiary education as its primary function was to prepare pupils for higher studies. As such, by and large, it evolved as an elite system facilitating local processes for *'elite formation'* and catering to the needs of the socially and the economically privileged.

**What is Secondary Education?**

Secondary education normally takes place in secondary schools, taking place after primary education and may be followed by higher education or vocational training. In some countries, only primary or basic education is compulsory, but secondary education is included in compulsory education in most countries. Secondary education serves as a bridge between elementary and higher education and prepares young persons between the age group of 14-18 for entry into higher education. A child's future can depend a lot on the type of education she/he receives at the secondary level. Apart from grounding the roots of education of a child, secondary education can be instrumental in shaping and directing the child to a bright future. This stage of education serves to move on higher secondary stage as well as to provide generic competencies that cut across various domains of knowledge as well as skills.

**Importance of Secondary Education**

While Primary Education is a basic enabling factor for participation and freedom, for trading a life with dignity and overcoming basic deprivation, secondary education is the gateway for prosperity, for transforming the economy and establishing social justice in any country. It opens the world of work to the youth of the country and contributes to socio-economic development of the Community. Secondary Education is a crucial stage in the educational hierarchy as it prepares the students for higher education and also the world of work. With the liberalisation and globalisation of the Indian economy, the rapid changes witnessed in scientific and technological world and the general need to improve the quality of life and to reduce poverty, it is essential that schools leavers acquire a higher level of knowledge and skills than what they are provided in the eight years of elementary education, particularly when the average earning of a secondary school certificate holder is significantly higher than that of a person who has studied only up to class VIII.

Since human capital theory was incorporated into the mainstream of economic thinking in the 1960s, education and training have been widely viewed as an investment. Because education and training impart skills and knowledge that enhance productivity, they have positive effects on individuals' life-time earnings. Enhanced productivity contributes to economic growth. In a competitive labour market, where wages are determined by the supply of and demand for labour, the earning differentials among workers with various levels of education reflect differences in the marginal productivity of workers. The private rates of returns to education (at the individual's level) tend to increase with levels of education. In India, these private rates of return to both lower and senior secondary education have been increasing steadily over time, as economic growth has increased demand faster than supply, and provide a clear rationale for household (private) investment in secondary education. Secondary education is the turning point for a large majority of students. Not only the certificate one earns after schooling but also the actual learning during schooling is the lifelong resource. Along with building dynamism in curricular framework as well as pedagogy, evaluation must undergo major changes.

**Secondary Education: Global Perspectives**

There are very many different types of secondary school, and the language used varies around the world. The following descriptions and definitions pertain to state-funded education unless otherwise stated. In Australia secondary school is called high school, from Year 7 to Year 12 in every state but Queensland, South Australia, and Western Australia, where high school is started in Year 8. In Bangladesh, secondary school is called high school from classes 8 to 10. After this the students sit for their Secondary School Certificate. In Ireland, secondary schools go from first year to sixth year, with the typical student age being between 12 and 19. Secondary school in Malaysia is considered as high school. Students attend secondary school in the age of 13 and usually graduated on 17. In India high school is a grade of education from Standards IX to X. Standards XI and XII are also called Secondary School. Usually students from ages 14 to 17 study in this section. These schools may be affiliated to national boards (like CBSE, ISC, and NIOS) or various state boards. In Hong Kong, the government provides a twelve-year compulsory education to students in the territory. Students are promoted to secondary schools after finishing their primary school education. In New Zealand secondary school is often called college or high school, from Year 9 to Year 13 (formerly known as Forms 3 to 7) with students aged 12½ to 18½. In Nigeria, secondary school is for children from ages 10 to 18. In Pakistan, secondary school is called high school from classes 9 to 10. In Singapore, Singaporeans aged between 13 to 17 are required to attend secondary school after taking the Primary School Leaving Examination (PSLE) at the end of primary education. In England and Wales, secondary school is for children from the ages of 11 to 18. Secondary school incorporates Key Stage 3 and Key of the National Curriculum (Year Seven to Year Eleven) and can also include sixth form. After 11 years of compulsory education ends, and young people can decide whether to continue their studies further at school or Sixth Form College, or leave the education system. In the United States, the term can refer to two types of school. The first type is the same as a high school (grades 9–12), while the second type refers to an alternative school which is sometimes called a secondary school.

**Secondary Education in India**

Secondary education began to expand in developed societies only after World War II. In fact, barring a few nations, the expansion of general secondary education is yet to happen at the desired pace, in many developing societies, including India. The growth of secondary education in India shows unique trends. During the period starting from 1850 to 1919 when the colonial government completely transferred the education authority to elected Indian Ministers at the provincial level, there was an undue emphasis (compared to primary education) on expansion of secondary schools and colleges. After the Wood's Despatch (1854)10 and with the introduction of the new system of education in India by the British Crown that largely replaced the indigenous network of schools 11 and the implementation of the *'grant-in-aid'* policy, the secondary schooling provisions expanded relatively faster as many indigenous schools acquired the status of *'aided schools'*. After 1919, policies of the provincial governments largely influenced the pattern of growth of secondary schooling provisions. In fact, in 1948, India had around 12,500 secondary schools of all grades in its major states (which included lower secondary stage/ UPS) and enrolled in them a little less than thee million children. In independent India, the network of educational institutions has expanded remarkably during the past six decades. The growth rate of secondary level institutions during this period has remained much lower compared to that of the middle level. Between 1950/51 and 2007/08, while the number of primary level institutions increased by almost four fold from 209.7 thousand to 787.8 thousand, the number of the middle level institutions went up by twenty-four fold from 13.6 thousand to 325.2 thousand, and the secondary level institutions by more than twenty-three fold, from 7416 to 173.0 thousand. Expansion has not only been in terms of the number of institutions, but also in terms of the spatial distribution of the schooling provisions at secondary and higher secondary levels. The issue of differential access to secondary schooling provisions becomes further compounded as the private un-aided sector plays a significant role in providing access, particularly in some of the economically backward states. It is evident from the fact that, at the sub-national level, the proportion of private un-aided institutions in the total institutions at the secondary stage widely varies between 88.4 per cent in Uttar Pradesh and none in West Bengal. Among the major states, the proportion of private un-aided institutions in the total number of institutions at the higher secondary stage varies between around 70 per cent in Andhra Pradesh and 4.5 per cent in Bihar.

The impact of recent initiatives undertaken for the Universalisation of Elementary Education is resulting in an increased demand for the expansion of secondary education. Participation of the private sector (including non-governmental organisations or NGOs) in the management of secondary schools with official recognition and, in many cases, with financial assistance, has also increased. Private organisations currently manage around 51 per cent of secondary schools and 58 per cent of higher secondary schools. In order to meet the educational needs of those who have not been able to enroll themselves in the formal system, opportunities have been provided through the National and State Open School utilising contact centres and multi-media packages. Distance education in the school sector also got a fillip with the National Open School was started in1989, identifying new vocational areas and providing on-demand examination. In order to make secondary education more relevant in the current context, the NCERT will continue to emphasise modernisation and revision of curriculum, updating of courses and vocationalisation of education. The Council would operationalise the fifth Regional Institute of Education for the North-Eastern Region at Shillong. The NCERT is starting the nation-wide Seventh All India Educational Survey in order to strengthen the database during the Plan period. The supply of private schools is also likely to increase in India. Given the rapidly expanding demand for secondary education and the historical patterns of school management, parents are likely to continue to seek private schools at the secondary level. Both the national and state governments are using Public–Private Partnerships (PPPs) to expand access. A major Government of India scheme for expanding access for secondary-schools, this time on a PPP approach is the Model Schools Scheme. The scheme aims to provide quality education to talented rural children through setting up of 6,000 model schools as a benchmark of excellence at block level at the rate of one school per block, with 2,500 of these schools to be set up under PPP mode in blocks that are not educationally backward. Improving the quality of education and raising the learning outcomes of students is perhaps the key challenge for both public and private schools. In terms of PPPs in capacity building initiatives, there are a number of possibilities ranging from curriculum and pedagogical support to management and administrative training; textbook provision; teacher training; and the development of support networks, professional partnerships and linkages.

The recommendations of the CABE Committee (2005) largely shaped the development priorities in secondary education during the Eleventh Plan period (2007-2012). The 11th Plan, therefore, targeted to: (i) achieve universal access (to secondary schooling provision within five kilometres, and higher secondary schooling provisions within a distance of 5-8 kilometres of every habitation); (ii) raise GER at secondary stage to 75 per cent by 2011/12; (iii) reduce substantially gender, social and regional disparities in enrolment, dropout and retention rates; (iv) improve Teacher-Pupil Ratio (TPR) at the secondary stage to about 25, and ensure availability of trained subject and other teachers by 2011/12; and (vi) introduce ICT in secondary and higher secondary schools. The broad secondary- education development strategies envisaged (at the macro level) during the 11th Plan included: (i) restructuring of the school system (to a 5+3+2+2 system) and expansion of the secondary school network/physical access by upgrading the existing schooling provisions and establishing new institutions/ sections including high quality model schools at the Community Development

Block level to serve as benchmark for excellence in secondary schooling; (ii) promoting Public-Private Partnership (PPP) to leverage private investment in the expansion of secondary schooling provisions; (iii) ensuring quality secondary education with focus on science, mathematics and English; (iv) promoting inclusiveness in secondary education through demand-side financing strategies; (v) introducing ICT in government and aided schools; (vi) adopting the National Curriculum Framework, 2005; and (vii) undertaking institutional reforms in school management. Implicitly, the development policy during the 11th Plan emphasised the supply of schooling provisions and ensuing equity in participation rather than the quality improvement and governance components. Moreover, the plan gave little emphasis to expansion and quality improvement of higher secondary education.

Secondary education spreads over the ages of 15 and 16, and then to 17 and 18 in the senior secondary grades. These are the years of adolescence, and late adolescence. These are the years of transition; indeed, most crucial years of life. There are steady and fast changes in the body structure transforming to adult form and image of life. At this age, the bodily changes take final shape and stabilise. This is also the stage of emotional transformation and maturity that swings between joy and trauma. Secondary education essentially has to be the education of the adolescence. Experiences in schooling have to be designed to be responsive to the needs of transition and stabilisation. Contemporary secondary education concentrates primarily on learning a few subjects challenging the *'cognitive intelligence'*, that too largely the lower order cognition. This very approach to secondary education puts at disadvantage a large number of students because students with differential abilities and potentialities are unable to cope with the demands of the kind of education offered in secondary education; on the other hand, secondary education does not contribute and nurture children native wisdom and imagination that they bring with them to the school. The Education Commission (1964-66) had recommended a Common School System of Public Education (CSS) as the basis of building up the National System of Education with a view to *"bring the different social classes and groups together and thus promote the emergence of an egalitarian and integrated society"* . The Commission warned that *"instead of doing so, education itself is tending to increase social segregation and to perpetuate and widen class distinctions"*. Curricular structure and course offerings are the necessary condition for quality secondary education. Instructional processes provide the sufficient condition for quality secondary education.

India has a long history of multiple management models at the secondary level, which provides opportunities for further experimentation and reform, particularly with respect to public-private partnership models. There is great diversity at the state level in the mix of government, private aided, and private unaided schools for secondary education. Some states (e.g., Bihar, Jharkhand, Punjab and Himachal Pradesh) have large government school systems, while others (e.g., West Bengal, Maharashtra, Gujarat) have predominantly private aided systems, and others (e.g., Uttar Pradesh, Tamil Nadu, Rajasthan) rely mainly on private unaided schools. Analysis of relative cost-effectiveness and equity of different school management types leads to mixed conclusions, with no model unambiguously better, although private schools tend to do better on Board examinations, even after correcting for student selectivity bias, and have lower cost structures because teacher salaries are generally lower. More research is needed which compares learning outcomes to the locus of decision-making authority. The most important management issue in the education sector is teacher recruitment, given that teacher salaries consume the largest share of education budgets and the quality of teaching is the most important factor in student achievement. Common problems in teacher recruitment in India are centralised hiring, insufficient objectivity, a shortage of candidates with the necessary attributes, and a high frequency of court cases arising from disputes on selection. Government teachers are hired through state-level commissions, after which they are assigned to schools, with no input from the principal, community or local authority. Each state has its own academic and professional standards for teachers in government schools, although a university degree plus a Bachelor of Education (B.Ed) degree is typically the minimum requirement for secondary-education. For senior secondary-education, the requirement is typically a post-graduate degree. The booming private sector labor market for higher education graduates has started to make it increasingly difficult to attract young people to consider secondary education as a career (particularly in mathematics and sciences), given their other options after completing university and/or post-graduate degrees. Subjectivity, reservation policies and political interference in teacher recruitment has led to tens of thousands of lawsuits across the country.

There is a lot of disparity in schooling facilities in various regions of the country. There are disparities among the private schools, among private and government schools in the same state, between schools in central sector like Kendriya Vidyalayas (KVS), Navodaya Vidyalayas (NVS), Tibetan Schools, Sainik Schools, etc. Also, there are no specific norms for secondary schools. In view of providing universal quality secondary-education, it is imperative that specially designed norms are developed at the national level and then disaggregated for each State/UT keeping in mind the geographical, sociocultural, linguistic and demographic conditions of not just the State/ UT but also, wherever necessary, of the Blocks. The disparities among various categories of schools must be reduced. This will require planning of educational facilities, and management of educational services to be streamlined. In India's 600,000 villages and multiplying urban slum habitats, *'free and compulsory education'* is in fact basic literacy instruction dispensed by barely qualified *'para teachers'*. India's aim of providing basic education for all stems from the empowering and redistributive impact of education. Until recently, literacy, and the related issue of access to schooling, has taken precedence over curricular content.

Currently, several secondary-education development schemes and programmes, including the recently launched Rashtriya Madhyamik Shiksha Abhiyan (RMSA), are being implemented in the country to achieve the 11th Plan targets. The RMSA was launched in April 2009 with the basic developmental objectives of universalising access to and improving quality of secondary education (Grades IX-X) in the country. In other words, the RMSA aims at making secondary education of good quality accessible and affordable to all young people. Specifically, the RMSA aims at: (i) maintaining standards in secondary education by making schools confirm to the prescribed norms related to physical facilities, staff and academic matters (rationalising facilities, staff and TLM across secondary schools as per norms); (ii) universalising physical access to all young people (taking a distance norm of five kilometres at secondary and Seven kilometres at higher secondary stages); (ii) improving participation and retention in secondary education (75 per cent GER at secondary stage by 2013/14, 100 per cent GER by 2016/17, and universal retention by 2020); (iii) overcoming barriers to secondary schooling due to gender, socio-economic status, disability and other disadvantaged circumstances.

The policy at present is to make secondary education of good quality available, accessible and affordable to all young persons in the age group of 14-18. At present, the following schemes targeted at secondary stage (i.e., class IX to XII) are being implemented in the form of Centrally Sponsored Schemes:

1. Rashtriya Madhyamik Shiksha Abhiyan (RMSA)
2. Model Schools Scheme
3. Girls Hostel Scheme
4. ICT @ Schools
5. Inclusive Education for Disabled at Secondary Stage
6. Scheme of Vocational Education
7. National Means-cum-Merit Scholarship Scheme
8. National Incentive to Girls
9. Appointment of Language Teachers

**Board of Secondary Education in India**

The following boards of education have been recognised by the Indian Government:

| *State* | *Board* | *Year of Establishment* | *Administrative Set-up* |
|---|---|---|---|
| Andhra Pradesh | Andhra Pradesh Board of Secondary Education, Hyderabad | 1953 | Part of the State Department of Education |

| | | | |
|---|---|---|---|
| | Andhra Pradesh Board of Intermediate Hyderabad | 1971 | Statutory |
| Assam | Assam Board of Secondary Education, Guwahati | 1962 | Statutory |
| | Assam Higher Secondary Education Council, Guwahati | 1984 | Statutory |
| Bihar | Bihar School Examination Board Patna | 1952 | Statutory |
| | Bihar Intermediate Education Council, Patna | 1980 | Statutory |
| Goa | Goa Board of Secondary and Higher Secondary Education, Goa | 1975 | Statutory |
| Gujarat | Gujarat Secondary Education Board, Gandhi Nagar | 1960 | Statutory |
| Haryana | Haryana Board of Education, Bhiwani | 1969 | Statutory |
| Himachal Pradesh | Himachal Pradesh Board of School Education, Dharamsala | 1969 | Statutory |
| Jammu & Kashmir | J&K State Board of School Education, Rehari Colony, Jammu, (Nov.—April) Lalmandi, Srinagar (May—Oct.) | 1965 | Statutory |
| Karnataka | Karnataka Secondary Education Examination Bangalore | 1966 | Part of the State Deptt. of Education |
| | Karnataka Board of the Pre-University Education Bangalore | 1970 | Part of the State Deptt. of Pre-University Education |
| Kerala | Kerala Board of Public Examinations, Thiruvananthapuram | 1949 | Part of the State Deptt. of Education |
| Maharashtra | Maharashtra State Board of Secondary and Higher Secondary-Education, Shivaji Nagar, Pune | 1966 | Statutory |
| Madhya Pradesh | Madhya Pradesh Board of Secondary Education, Bhopal | 1959 | Statutory |
| Manipur | Manipur Board of Secondary Education, Imphal | 1972 | Statutory |
| | Manipur Council of Higher Secondary-Education, Imphal | 1992 | Statutory |
| Meghalaya | Meghalaya Board of School Education, Meghalaya | 1973 | Statutory |
| Mizoram | Mizoram Board of School Education Aizawl | 1976 | Statutory |
| Nagaland | Nagaland Board of School Education, Kohima | 1974 | Statutory |
| Orissa | Orissa Board of Secondary Education, Cuttack | 1965 | Statutory |
| | Orissa Council of Higher Secondary Education, Bhubaneswar | 1955 | Statutory |

| | | | |
|---|---|---|---|
| Punjab | Punjab School Education Board, Mohali | 1969 | Statutory |
| Rajasthan | Rajasthan Board of Secondary Education, Ajmer | 1957 | Statutory |
| Tamil Nadu | Tamil Nadu Board of Secondary Education, Department of Govt. Examinations, Chennai | 1908 | Part of the State Deptt. of Education |
| | Tamil Nadu Board of Higher Secondary Education, Chennai | 1982 | Part of the State Deptt. of Education |
| Tripura | Tripura Board of Secondary Education Agartala | 1973 | Statutory |
| Uttar Pradesh | U.P. Board of High School and Intermediate-Education, Allahabad | 1922 | Autonomous Body under the Deptt. of Education |
| West Bengal | West Bengal Board of Secondary Education, Calcutta | 1951 (Reconstituted in 1964) | Statutory |
| | West Bengal Council of Higher Secondary Education, Calcutta | 1929 (Reconstituted in 1962) | Statutory |
| All-India Boards | Central Board of Secondary Education, Community Centre, Delhi | — | Autonomous body under the Government of India |
| | Council for Indian School Certificate Examinations, New Delhi | 1958 | Registered Society |
| | National Open School, New Delhi | 1989 | Autonomous body under the Government of India |

*Source:* Department of School Education and Literacy, Ministry of Human Resource Development.

Let discuss some of the above board:

1. The Central Board of Secondary-Education is a Board of Education for public and private schools, under the Union Government of India. CBSE affiliates all Kendriya Vidyalayas, all Jawahar Navodaya Vidyalayas, private schools, and most of the schools approved by central government of India. The board conducts final examinations every spring for All India Senior School Certificate Examination (AISSCE) for Class 10 and 12. The board also annually conducts the AIEEE exam for admission to undergraduate courses in engineering and architecture in numerous colleges spread over India. It also conducts AIPMT (All India Pre Medical Test) for admission to major medical colleges in India.
2 The Council for the Indian School Certificate Examinations (CISCE) is a private, non-governmental board of school education in India. It conducts two examinations in India: the Indian Certificate of Secondary Education (ICSE) and the Indian School Certificate (ISC). The Indian Certificate of Secondary Education (ICSE) Examination

is a K-10 public board examination for students in India who have just completed Class X. Similarly, the Indian School Certificate (ISC) Examination is a K-12 public board examination for those completing Class XII. The CISCE does not accept private candidates, and they must come only through the (English medium) schools affiliated to the CISCE. The medium of examination is English, except the Indian language paper.

3 The National Institute of Open Schooling (NIOS) is the Board of Education for Distance Education, under the Union Government of India. It was established by the Ministry of Human Resource Development of the Government of India in 1989 to provide-education inexpensively to remote areas. The NIOS is a national board that administers examinations for Secondary and Senior Secondary examinations of open schools similar to the CBSE and the CISCE. The NIOS collaborates with the Commonwealth of Learning (COL) and UNESCO. It also has study centers for Indian expatriates in the United Arab Emirates, Oman, Kuwait, Nepal, Canada and the United States. The public examinations are held twice a year in the months of April–May and October–November on dates fixed by the NIOS. However, one is also eligible to appear through On Demand Examination at Secondary Level and Senior Secondary level in those subjects only in which a candidate have admission in NIOS.

**Quality and Efficiency of Secondary Education in India**

Policies and programmes to improve teaching are fundamental to strengthening the foundation of Indian secondary education. Teachers are the most valuable and expensive resource. Most Indian states require a secondary school teacher to have both a university degree and teacher education. While not all teachers are recruited from teacher training colleges (some are graduates from universities without professional training), to be considered a professionally trained teacher and receive a commensurate salary grade, a would-be teacher must go through training in a teachers' college. To improve the quality of secondary education, teachers' colleges, both public and private, have a key role to play. There are approximately 1,082 teacher training colleges nationwide. At present the teacher training industry suffers from widespread problems. Quality standards are poor, the result of an inadequate accreditation and monitoring system. The National Council for Teacher Education (NCTE) sets the norms and standards for infrastructure, and specifies the required qualifications of teacher educators, for all teacher education colleges. But without effective monitoring by the council, which lacks the manpower, resources, and capacity for this purpose, teacher training colleges tend to depart from these norms, with potentially serious implications for the quality of teacher preparation and thus for the quality of secondary education. Further, the NCTE norms relate largely to the inputs, rather than to the quality standards or outcomes of teacher education. Thus many graduates of teacher training colleges re simply unprepared to teach. Most private teacher education programmes are financed out of the fees collected; their rapid commercialisation responds to a demand but malpractices in these institutions are widely reported. Recognition of the need for assessment and accreditation of teacher education colleges by an independent body led to the establishment of the National Assessment and Accreditation Council (NAAC) in 2002. NAAC has produced a manual for self-assessment and accreditation so that institutions can do their own institutional analysis and strengthen and improve their programmers to better match the needs of the market.

India has a centrally sponsored scheme for teacher education, which allows state institutions for teacher education to draw on central funds for improving quality.

There is little information available on the content of in-service training and even less on its effectiveness in developing teacher competencies in India. The Union Government has set up institutes of advanced study in education (IASEs) that offer teachers refresher courses on a variety of subjects. Interestingly, teacher educators have a high regard for the quality of the programmes offered, but teachers themselves do not. For elementary school teachers, SSA provides 20 days of training each year, but this is rarely school-based or linked to classroom practice, and provides no follow-up actions. A main constraint on teachers' professional development is institutional capacity. Staffing and resources in the institutions responsible for providing technical support and monitoring, notably the National Council for Teacher Education (NCERT), state councils/institutes of educational research and training (SCERT/SIERT), district institutes of education and training, and institutes of advanced study in education, are simply inadequate, and the research done by these institutions is mostly of poor quality. Student learning outcomes are linked to pedagogy. They are unlikely to improve unless effective teaching skills and practices are acquired and used in classrooms. The simple truth is that reform, improvement and expansion of secondary teacher professional development is required to improve quality.

**Open Schooling**

The Commonwealth of Learning acknowledges that there are different views on what Open Schooling is but itself uses a very broad but simple definition: Open Schooling involves *"the physical separation of the school-level learner from the teacher, and the use of unconventional teaching methodologies, and information and communications technologies (ICTs) to bridge the separation and provide the education and training"*. The face-to-face sessions with the facilitator are mainly to clarify any difficulties that the students may have experienced when working through the learning materials. These sessions are seldom mandatory. It does not affect a student if he or she has to *"drop out"* for a period of time - they can pick up their studies once again, when it is convenient for them to do so. The student-facilitator meetings are often held in learning centres located in libraries, churches, non-governmental organisations (NGOs), schools or other semi-public places. The meetings may be fixed times during a week, or may be held at the students' and facilitators' convenience. The facilitators or experts mark the students' exercises and assignments, and provide feedback designed to assist the students in understanding content when their answers indicate this is required. Early open schools tended to arise from efforts to help individual out-of-school children pursue their studies, either because they could not get to a school, or because they were unable to stay in school. Most studies focus on the quality of the output (graduates) as measured by the proportion of students who graduate with a school leaving qualification. Such measures are crude in that they say nothing about value added. The benefits of Open Schooling may be private, accruing to the individual, to parents, and to the employer, or social, accruing to the labour market and society in general. Most studies of the benefits of Open Schooling focus on the former.

**Challenges in Secondary Education**

Good data on the quality of education is scarce and, importantly, there is no national assessment of performance in secondary education. There are about 30 state examination boards that prepare examinations for students at the end of lower secondary and higher secondary education examinations indicate a lack of technical reliability in the examinations, and no comparisons across states can be considered absolute. Therefore, there is no national picture of the quality of secondary education, as measured by the skills and knowledge acquired by students at the end of this stage of education. The Government of India's RMSA programme includes specific guidance on quality improvements. International assessments in secondary schools tend to show that private and public schools perform equally well when the socioeconomic backgrounds of children are taken into account. There are a number of challenges in this area. First, like elementary education, there is a shortage of teachers in secondary education. For example, only 30 per cent of schools (Classes IX and X) have a sufficient number of teachers in all five core subjects. The particular challenge in secondary education is that teachers are subject specialists so the demand for and deployment of teachers is much more complex. Second, the professional development of secondary education teachers is also made harder by the subject specialisations; understanding how to teach mathematics is different from understanding how to teach history, since the things children don't understand are derived from the nature of the mathematical concepts or topics being studied.

Although enrolment in primary education has increased, it is estimated that at least 35 million, and possibly as many as 60 million, children aged 6–14 years are not in school. Severe gender, regional, and caste disparities also exist. The main problems are the high drop-out rate, especially after Class 10, low levels of learning and achievement, inadequate school infrastructure, poorly functioning schools, high teacher absenteeism, the large number of teacher vacancies, poor quality of education and inadequate funds. Other groups of children *'at risk'*, such as orphans, child-labourers, street children and victims of riots and natural disasters, do not necessarily have access to schools. Furthermore, there is no common school system; instead children are channelled into private, government-aided and government schools on the basis of ability to pay and social class. At the top end are English-language schools affiliated to the upscale CBSE (Central Board of Secondary Education), CISCE (Council for the Indian Schools Certificates Examination) and IB (International Baccalaureate) examination boards, offering globally recognised syllabuses and curricula. Those who cannot afford private schooling attend English-language government-aided schools, affiliated to state-level examination boards. And on the bottom rung are poorly managed governments or municipal schools, which cater for the children of the poor majority. Therefore, while education for all is safeguarded by the Constitution, and a majority of people can now access educational resources, the quality of the education that young people in Indian receive varies widely according to their means and background.

There is a need for a more reliable system of assessment of student learning outcomes in secondary education. The role of assessment, testing and examination is undergoing reform in elementary education, under the provision of the Right to Education Act, 2009, which abolishes testing in that phase of education. These mechanisms have not yet been replaced by alternative methods of Continuous and Comprehensive Evaluation (CCE) that teachers understand and are able to use to keep track of students' progress and achievements. The situation is more complex in secondary education given the presence of high-stakes examinations and the multiple need for measuring achievement, providing a basis for entry into higher education, and giving students relevant certification for entry into the labour market.

Aided schools are a significant opportunity to bring change. The substantial resources that state governments give to aided schools offer the opportunity to leverage change. Unfortunately, at the moment, grants-in-aid are provided on an input-driven basis (essentially, the state governments pay some portion of (or all) teacher salaries). An opportunity exists for this funding to be adjusted so that it is provided on the basis of outcomes or results, such as enrolment and retention of disadvantaged groups (access and equity concerns) and the successful completion of a stage of education or student performance on assessments (quality concerns). Given the size of the private-aided sector, providing private management with different incentives could offer a major opportunity to address some of the outstanding issues in secondary education.

**Conclusion**

Secondary education began to expand in developed societies only after World War II. There are very many different types of secondary school, and the language used varies around the world. The impact of recent initiatives undertaken for the Universalisation of Elementary Education is resulting in an increased demand for the expansion of secondary education. Currently, several secondary education development schemes and programmes, including the recently launched Rashtriya Madhyamik Shiksha Abhiyan (RMSA), are being implemented in the country to achieve the 11th Plan targets. The Government of India's RMSA programme includes specific guidance on quality improvements. International assessments in secondary schools tend to show that private and public schools perform equally well when the socio-economic backgrounds of children are taken into account. Common problems in teacher recruitment in India are centralized hiring, insufficient objectivity, a shortage of candidates with the necessary attributes, and a high frequency of court cases arising from disputes on selection. Each state has its own academic and professional standards for teachers in government schools, although a university degree plus a Bachelor of Education (B.Ed) degree is typically the minimum requirement for secondary education. Options to improve quality of secondary education include:

1. Strengthened secondary education teacher training colleges, including institutional accreditation assessments and improvement plans; competition for investments in facilities, equipment, faculty upgrading, etc.; and increased intake of trainees for underserved subjects.
2. Peer-based, mentor-led, practical, subject specific professional development of teachers, which networks teachers across schools for mutual exchange and observation.
3. Financial incentives and technical assistance for state Boards to align both curriculum and examinations to the National Curriculum Framework.
4. Reforms in textbook development and procurement, including teacher participation in their revision and a focus on enhanced quality and focus on higher order thinking skills, and investments in ICTs to enable more students centered learning which draws from a wide range of resources available on the Internet.
5. Examination reform, to increase the focus on problem-solving and information-reasoning skills and decrease the emphasis on rote memorisation of facts presented in textbooks.
6. Participation in international assessments of student achievement at the secondary level, and use of the results of those assessments to determine needed remedial investments.
7. Development and administration of national sample-based assessments for Grade 10 and 12, and careful analysis of results to define quality improvement interventions.

8. Reforms and investments in secondary education quality assurance mechanisms, emphasising strengthened pedagogical supervision and links to in-service teacher professional development.

## References


1. Adriaan Verspoor (2008). *At the Crossroads: Choices for Secondary Education in Sub-Saharan Africa*, World Bank Publications.
2. Alexander James Inglis (2006). *Principles of Secondary Education*, 1st edition, Houghton Mifflin.
3. Andrew Pollard and Pat Triggs (1997). *Reflective Teaching in Secondary Education: A Handbook for Schools and Colleges,* Continuum International Publishing Group.
4. Associated Principles of the High Schools and Academies of the State of New York, Associated Academic Principles of the State of New York (1982), The Academy: A Journal of Secondary Education, Volume 7, George A. Bacon.
5. Benoni Briggs (2007). *Investment in secondary education in Nigeria: exploration by rate-of-return analysis,* Nigerian Institute of Social and Economic Research, University of Ibadan.
6. B. M. Makau (1985). *Equity and efficiency in financing secondary education in Kenya: key issues in state-community partnership,* Institute for Development Studies, University of Nairobi.
7. Bob Moon (1994). *Teaching and Learning in the Secondary School,* Taylor & Francis Group.
8. Cardinal principles of secondary education: A report of the Commission on the reorganization of secondary education, National Education Association of the United States (1928). Commission on the Reorganisation of Secondary-Education, Govt. print. off.
9. *Council for the Indian School Certificate Examinations (2013).* Retrieved from http://en.wikipedia.org/wiki/Councilfor the Indian School Certificate Examinations.
10. *Central Board of Secondary Education (2013).* Retrieved from *http://en.wikipedia.org/wiki* Central Board of Secondary-Education.
11. David Snedden and Houghton Mifflin (1917). *Problems of Secondary Education*, Houghton Mifflin.
12. Ernest L. Boyer, (1985). *High school: a report on secondary education in America*, Harper collins.
13. Gerdi Jonen (1995). *Secondary Education in Germany,* Council of Europl.
14. Greville Rumble and Badri N Koul (2007). *Open Schooling for Secondary and Higher Secondary Education: Costs and Effectiveness in India and Namibia*, Retrieved from http://www.col.org/SiteCollectionDocuments/Open Schooling Secondary Higher Education 071707.pdf
15. Helen Tavola (1991). *Secondary-Education in Fiji: A Key to the Future,*

16. Henry Neumann (2007). *Moral values in secondary education: A report of the Commission on the Reorganization of Secondary- Education, appointed by the National-Education Association,* Govt. print. off.
17. India Education Commission (2007). *Discussion Paper on Major Problems of Secondary Education,* the University of Michigan.
18. Jerry Wellington (2006). *Secondary Education: The Key Concepts*, 1st edition, Taylor and Francis Group.
19. Jon Lauglo, and R. Maclean (2005). *Vocationalisation of Secondary Education Revisited,* Springer.
20. Jonathan Savage and Martin Fautley (2007). *Creativity in Secondary Education,* SAGE.
21. John Beck, Mary C. Earl (2003). *Key Issues in Secondary Education*, 2nd Edition, Continuum.
22. K. Biswal (2011). *Secondary Education in India: Development Policies, Programmes and Challenges,* Retrieved from http://indiagovernance.gov.in/files/secondary education.pdf
23. Marie Lall (2005). *The Challenges for India's Education System*, Retrieved from http://54.251.36.70/apsc.public/resources/pdf/56.pdf
24. *National Institute of Open Schooling (2013).* Retrieved from wikipedia.org/wiki/ National Institute of Open Schooling
25. Olive Banks (1998). *Parity and Prestige in English Secondary Education: A Study in Educational Sociology,* Volume 18, Psychology Press.
26. Richard Teese and John Polesel (2003). *Undemocratic Schooling: Equity and Quality in Mass Secondary Education in Australia,* Melbourne Univ. Publishing.
27. Remi S. Longe (1982). *Factors influencing current costs of secondary education in the Oyo State of Nigeria*, International Institute for Educational Planning.
28. Robert Pickett Scott (2006). *'What is Secondary Education?' and Other Short Essays*, Rivingtons
29. Sam Anefu Ede (1997). *Management of secondary education in Nigeria*, 1st edition, Source Publishers.
30. Secondary education, *Department of School education and Literacy*, Retrieved from http://mhrd.gov.in/secondaryedu
31. *Secondary Education (2013).* Retrieved from http://en.wikipedia.org/wiki/ Secondary_school
32. *Secondary education, Chapter 2, 3. (2013).* Retrieved from http:// planningcommission.nic.in/plans/planrel/fiveyr/10th/volume2/v2 ch23.pdf
33. *Secondary education in India: Universalising opportunity*, Retrieved from http:// www.educationforallinindia.com/secondary-education-in-india-universalizing-opportunity-by-world-bank.pdf
34. S. K. Kochhar (1971). *Secondary School Administration*, Sterling Publishers Pvt. Ltd
35. Susan Capel, Peter Breckon, and Jean O'Neill (2006). *A Practical Guide to Teaching Physical Education in the Secondary School,* Taylor and Francis Group.
36. T. J. McElligott (1981). *Secondary Education in Ireland: 1870-1921*, Irish Academic Press.

# 10

# Secondary Education: Progress and Challenges

*Prahelika Roy*

"*The things I want to know are in books; my best friend is the man who'll get me a book I ain't read.*"

—***Abraham Lincoln***

## Introduction

India has a long history of organised education. The Gurukul system of education is one of the oldest on earth but before that the *Gurushishya* system was extant, in which students were taught orally and the data would be passed from one generation to the next. Gurukuls were traditional Hindu residential schools of learning; typically the teacher's house or a monastery. Education was free (and often limited to the higher castes), but students from well-to-do families paid Gurudakshina, a voluntary contribution after the completion of their studies. The current system of education, with its western style and content, was introduced and funded by the British in the 19th century, following recommendations by Macaulay. Traditional structures were not recognised by the British government and have been on the decline since. Education is the most important lever for social, economic and political transformation. A well-educated population, equipped with the relevant knowledge, attitudes and skills is essential for economic and social development in the twenty-first century. Education is the most potent tool for socio-economic mobility and a key instrument for building an equitable and just society. Education provides skills and competencies for economic well-being.

The commitments to ensuring gender equality in education have been well articulated both at the global level and across various national contexts. The decade of the 1990s has been an important turning point with regard to targets set for Education for All (EFA) and has sent a strong message for progress towards gender equality and education. In the Indian context, the National Policy of Education 1986 (NPE), made a formal commitment to promote *"Education for Women's Equality"*. A range of positive programmatic interventions were introduced post NPE that incorporated gender concerns to help achieve gender equitable outcomes in education.

**Concept**

Secondary education is the gateway for prosperity, for transforming the economy and establishing social justice in any country. It opens the world of work to the youth of the country and contributes to socio-economic development of the Community. Secondary Education is a crucial stage in the educational hierarchy as it prepares the students for higher education and also the world of work.

**Progress of Secondary Education in India**

At independence, India inherited a legacy of large-scale illiteracy and lack of proper provision for education. At the first post-independence census of 1951, only nine per cent of women and 27 per cent of men were literate. It was resolved by the framers of the constitution that the new Indian state would endeavour to provide free and compulsory education to all children up to age 14 by 1960. This goal turned out to be elusive and the deadline for its achievement has been put back repeatedly in the past 55 years. While even today this goal remains unfulfilled, there has been very encouraging progress in schooling participation and other educational outcome indicators in recent times. The high returns to secondary education raise the puzzle of why secondary school participation is not higher in India. Schooling participation depends on both the extent of demand for and the availability of supply of schooling. It seems there are some supply-side barriers. According to the Seventh All India Education Survey (NCERT, 2006b), in 2002, there were only one-fifth as many secondary schools (those with grade 10 classes) as the number of primary schools. Thus, it seems likely that secondary school enrolment rates are low partly because of the lack of supply of nearby secondary schools. A demand-side factor that likely militates against higher secondary school participation is parents' perceived futility of educating girls, since many families adhere to traditional gender roles and do not envisage daughters' participation in the labour market.

Before 1976, education was the exclusive responsibility of the States. The Constitutional Amendment of 1976, which included-education in the Concurrent List, was a far-reaching step. The substantive, financial and administrative implication required a new sharing of responsibility between the Union Government and the States. While the role and responsibility of the States in education remained largely unchanged, the Union Government accepted a larger responsibility of reinforcing the national and integrated character of education, maintaining quality and standard including those of the teaching profession at all levels, and the study and monitoring of the educational requirements of the country. The progress towards achieving Education for All in India presents a mixed picture given the vast dimensions and diversity prevailing in the country. According to the Eleventh Five-Year Plan (2007-2012) the total enrollment at the elementary level increased from 159 million in 2001-02 to 182 million in 2005-05 an increase over 23 million. However, drop out rate at the elementary stages continues to be as high at 50.8 per cent (50.5 per cent for boys and 51.3 per cent for girls), with drop out rates for children from socially disadvantaged groups being higher. A review of Secondary Education in India reveals that during the decade ending 2004-05 enrollment at the Secondary level increased at an average rate of 5.32 per cent. There are 2.43 million students enrolled at the Secondary stage and 12.7 million enrolled at the higher secondary stages. The setting up of the Mission for Secondary-Education at the level of Government of India (GOI) to improve the status of secondary-education and the funds allocated by GOI in the Eleventh Plan give reasons for hope. The mandate of the Mission is universalising secondary education by 2017. This renewed emphasis on Universalising secondary education necessitates that gender equality concerns are brought centre stage, to enable girls to move beyond the elementary stages and access secondary schooling. It is also equally important that schooling processes help break the gender stereotypes and images.

The education system in India follows the 8+2+2+3 pattern, that is, eight years of primary-education followed by two years of lower secondary schooling, two years of upper secondary schooling, and three years of university education. However, until recently only a small proportion of children attended elementary schools. Access to secondary education in India continues to be inequitable across income and social groups, gender, and states, which bear the main responsibility for secondary education. The income inequality in access to secondary education is greatest in the states of Haryana, Andhra Pradesh, Bihar, Madhya Pradesh, Rajasthan, and Uttar Pradesh, and it is the lowest in Kerala and West Bengal. With regard to gender, girls are only half as likely to enrol in secondary school as boys in states such as Bihar and Rajasthan. But some states, such as Kerala and Tamil Nadu, have gender parity or even slightly pro-female secondary enrollment rates.

National Policy of Education (1986) and revised Programme of Action (1992) envisioned that free and compulsory education should be provided for all children up to 14 years of age before the commencement of 21st century. The Article 45 of the Directive Principles of the State Policy was committed to ensuring free and compulsory education for all. This did not significantly translate into action and school enrolments and participation remained dismally low for decades after independence. Further, Elementary education being made a fundamental right by the 83 Constitutional Amendment, and the Supreme Court's insistence on States to provide hot cooked meals in schools, are improving enrolments, especially among girls. Some of the initiatives such as District Primary-Education Programme (1994), the Mid Day Meal Scheme (1995) and the Sarva Siksha Abhiyan (2001) have led some positive impact in elementary education, specifically in rural areas. The

86th Amendment of the Indian Constitution makes education a fundamental right for all children aged 6-14 years. The access to pre-school education for children under Six years of age was excluded from the provisions, and the supporting legislation has not yet been passed. In India, major public policy initiatives like Sarva Shiksha Abhiyan (Education for All), the provision of a mid-day meal, free textbooks, uniforms, etc. aim to universalise elementary education and reduce disparity across regions, gender and social groups. In this context, two suggestions have been popular: to reduce the access barrier through the provision of community-based primary schools; and to improve the quality of schools in terms of physical infrastructure, teacher quality, etc.

The Right of Children to Free and Compulsory Education (RTE) Act, 2009 poses major challenges for improving the quality of teachers and for expanding institutional capacity in States to prepare professionally trained persons for becoming school teachers. Government has initiated steps to revise the existing Centrally Sponsored Scheme of Restructuring and Reorganisation of Teacher Education. This Scheme was initiated in 1987 pursuant to the formulation of the National Policy on Education, 1986 which emphasised the significance and need for a decentralised system for the professional preparation of teachers, and it was in this context that District Institutes of Teacher-Education (DIETs), Colleges of Teacher Education (CTEs) and Institutes of Advanced Study in Education (IASEs) were established. Scheme for Providing Quality Education for Madarsas seeks to bring about qualitative improvement in madarsas to enable Muslim children attain standards of the national education system in formal education subjects. The salient features of SPQEM scheme are: (a) To strengthen capacities in Madarsas for teaching of the formal curriculum subjects like Science, Mathematics, Language, Social Studies etc. through enhanced payment of teacher honorarium; (b) Training of such teachers every two years in new pedagogical practices; (c) The unique feature of this modified scheme is that it encourages linkage of madarsas with National Institute for Open Schooling (NIOS), as accredited centres for providing formal education, which will enable children studying in such madarsas to get certification for class 5, 8, 10 and 12; and (d) The NIOS linkage will be extended under this scheme for Vocational-Education at the secondary and higher secondary stage of madarsas.

Scheme of Infrastructure development in Minority Institutions has been operationalised to augment infrastructure in private aided/unaided minority schools/institutions in order to enhance quality of education to minority children. The salient features of IDMI scheme are: (a) The scheme would facilitate education of minorities by augmenting and strengthening school infrastructure in Minority Institutions in order to expand facilities for formal education to children of minority communities; (b) The scheme will cover the entire country but, preference will be given to minority institutions (private aided /unaided schools) located in districts, blocks and towns having a minority population above 20 per cent; and (c) The scheme will, inter alia, encourage educational facilities for girls, children with special needs and those who are most deprived educationally amongst. Eklavya Model Residential Schools are funded by the Government for the welfare of Scheduled Tribes. Proposals for setting of EMRS are received from the State Government. The Ministry of Tribal Affairs administers special area programme of grant under Art 275 (1) of the Constitution of India. Under this programme State-wise allocation to 26 States including 9 Left Wing Extremism (LWE) States is made on the basis of percentage of Scheduled Tribes population in the State with reference to total ST population in the Country. A part of the grant can be used for setting up of Eklavya Model Residential Schools (EMRS).

**Rashtriya Madhyamik Shiksha Abhiyan**

This scheme was launched in March, 2009 with the objective to enhance access to secondary education and to improve its quality. The implementation of the scheme started from 2009-10. It is envisaged to achieve an enrolment rate of 75 per cent from 52.26 per cent in 2005-06 at secondary stage within five years of implementation of the scheme by providing a secondary school within a reasonable distance of any habitation. The other objectives include improving quality of education imparted at secondary level through making all secondary schools conform to prescribed norms, removing gender, socio-economic and disability barriers, providing universal access to secondary level education by 2017, i.e., by the end of 12th Five Year Plan and achieving universal retention by 2020. It is aimed at expanding and improving the standards of secondary education — classes IX and X. The RSMA would also take secondary education to every corner of the country by ensuring a secondary school (upto class X) within a radius of five km for every neighbourhood. Rashtriya Madhyamik Shiksha Abhiyan (RMSA) which is the most recent initiative of Government of India to achieve the goal of universalisation of secondary education (USE). The Sarva Shiksha Abhiyaan programme set up by the government to bring elementary education to millions of children has been successful to a large extent, and has thus created a need for strengthening secondary-education infrastructure across the country. The HRD Ministry has taken note of this, and now plans to implement a secondary-education scheme called Rashtriya Madhyamik Shiksha Abhiyaan (RMSA) during the 11th plan at a total cost of Rs. 20,120 crore.

**Public Private Partnerships**

Recent years have seen an expansion and broadening of the private sector's role in the financing and provision of education services in many countries. A key trend has been the emergence of more sophisticated forms of private involvement in education through PPPs. PPPs involve the public and private sectors working together to achieve important educational, social and economic objectives. PPPs can be defined narrowly to include only formal arrangements such as sophisticated infrastructural initiatives or they can be defined more broadly to cover all manner of partnership between the public and private sector. Perhaps the most common form of PPP in the education sector is private philanthropy. There is also a range of innovative ventures supporting-education, both philanthropic and for-profit ventures. These include the World Economic Forums (WEF), Global Education Initiative (GEI), which aims to create new sustainable models for education reform in the developing world through PPPs. The second form of PPP in the education sector is the private management of public schools. This involves education authorities contracting directly with private providers to operate public schools or certain aspects of public school operations. The third form of PPP in which governments sponsor 'public' students to attend private institutions is normally used in order to assist a government meet demands of access.

There is a large unfulfilled need for access to quality education in the secondary education sector. Public Private Partnership emerges as a viable alternative to improve access to quality school education while ensuring equity and social justice. PPP projects are large complex contractual arrangements that involve significant public sector capacity. From the perspective of the public sector, the PPP models *'in theory'* are premised to bring the following benefits:

1. *Easing the budget constraint:* There is a high difference between the need and existing infrastructure in the country. It is hard to provide such large amounts from the government alone. For this reason PPP model can play vital role. Government can invite private sector to investment money as there is shortage of government fund.
2. *Efficiency gains:* As both work together and so efficiency in government sctor will increase.I t wil helpful to exchange knowledge and experience.
3. *Appropriate risk sharing:* In a PPP, risk allocation between the public and private sector can be optimised to ensure that the overall risk is lowered significantly.
4. *Quality monitoring:* The private partner would have an enticement to lift the value of education in the school to be entitled for payment.
5. *Reduction of cost:* It is possible to reduce cost as efficiency will increase.
6. *Greater flexibility:* The government systems have rigidity. The private partner is expected to have much higher autonomy in hiring teachers and organising the school.
7. *Speed of implementation:* Since the private partner would be interested in getting payment as soon as the services start being made available, the speed of implementation would be much quicker.

**Challenges before the Secondary Education**

Poorly resourced public schools which suffer from high rates of teacher absenteeism may have encouraged the rapid growth of private (unaided) schooling in India, particularly in urban areas. Private schools divide into two types: recognised and unrecognised schools. Government *'recognition'* is an official stamp of approval and for this a private school is required to fulfil a number of conditions, though hardly any private schools that get 'recognition' actually fulfil all the conditions of recognition. The emergence of large numbers of unrecognised primary schools suggests that schools and parents do not take government recognition as a stamp of quality.

Various reasons for school dropouts are there. In a study, Sikdar and Mukherjee specified 20 reasons for school dropouts and categorised them into eight groups. More generally, reasons of school dropouts can be classified in to some broad categories like school-centric and parent-centric. Among others, poverty is one of the main determinants of school dropout. Family economic circumstances are important to meet the hidden and upfront costs of schooling, failure of which leads to many temporary as well as permanent dropouts of children. Hidden costs of schooling include opportunity cost, travel cost, uniform, daily expenditures, while upfront costs include admission fee, examination fee, tuition fees etc. Family's social and demographic circumstances are an important determinant of school dropout.

### Conclusion

Secondary-education is the gateway for prosperity, for transforming the economy and establishing social justice in any country. At independence, India inherited a legacy of large-scale illiteracy and lack of proper provision for education. National Policy of Education (1986) and revised Programme of Action (1992) envisioned that free and compulsory-education should be provided for all children upto 14 years of age before the commencement of 21st century. The Right of Children to Free and Compulsory-Education (RTE) Act, 2009 poses major challenges for improving the quality of teachers and for expanding institutional capacity in States to prepare professionally trained persons for becoming school teachers. Scheme of Infrastructure development in Minority Institutions has been operationalised to augment infrastructure in private aided/unaided minority schools/institutions in order to enhance quality of education to minority children. Recent years have seen an expansion and broadening of the private sector's role in the financing and provision of education services in many countries. A key trend has been the emergence of more sophisticated forms of private involvement in education through PPPs. Rashtriya Madhyamik Shiksha Abhiyan (RMSA) which is the most recent initiative of Government of India to achieve the goal of universalisation of secondary-education (USE).

## References

1. Abhiroop Mukhopadhyay and Soham Sahoo (2012). *Does Access to Secondary-Education Affect Primary Schooling? Evidence from India*, Retrieved from http://www.iegindia.org/workpap/wp312.pdf.
2. Adriaan Verspoor (2008). *At the Crossroads: Choices for Secondary-Education in Sub-Saharan Africa*, World Bank Publications.

3. Andrew Pollard and Pat Triggs (1997). *Reflective Teaching in Secondary-Education: A Handbook for Schools and Colleges,* Continuum International Publishing Group.
4. Alexander James Inglis (2006). *Principles of Secondary-Education*, 1st edition, Houghton Mifflin.
5. Associated Principles of the High Schools and Academies of the State of New York, Associated Academic Principals of the State of New York (1982), The Academy: A Journal of Secondary-Education, Volume 7, George A. Bacon.
6. Benoni Briggs (2007). *Investment in secondary-education in Nigeria: Exploration by rate-of-return analysis,* Nigerian Institute of Social and Economic Research, University of Ibadan.
7. B. M. Makau (1985). *Equity and efficiency in financing secondary-education in Kenya: key issues in state-community partnership,* Institute for Development Studies, University of Nairobi.
8. Bob Moon (1994). *Teaching and Learning in the Secondary School,* Taylor and Francis Group.
9. Cardinal principles of secondary-education: A report of the Commission on the reorganisation of secondary education, National Education Association of the United States (1928). Commission on the Reorganisation of Secondary-Education, Govt. print. off.
10. *Central government scheme for school education (2003),* Retrieved from http://164.100.47.134/intranet/FinalGovernmentSchemesforSchoolEducation.pdf
11. David Snedden and Houghton Mifflin (1917). *Problems of Secondary-Education*, Houghton Mifflin.
12. Department of Social Education and Literacy, *Ministry of Human Resource Development, Government of India,* Retrieved from http://mhrd.gov.in/secondaryedu
13. Ernest L. Boyer, (1985). *High school: a report on secondary-education in America*, Harper Collins.
14. *Expanding Secondary-Education,* Retrieved from http://www.cerium.ca/IMG/pdf/Expanding_Secondary_Education_in_India-1-.pdf
15. Gerdi Jonen (1995). *Secondary-Education in Germany,* Council of Europe.
16. Geeta Gandhi Kingdon (2007). The progress of school education in India, *Oxford Review of Economic Policy,* Volume 23, Number 2, Retrieved from http://recoup.educ.cam.ac.uk/publications/OXREPDownloadedpaper1.pdf
17. Helen Tavola (1991). *Secondary-Education in Fiji: A Key to the Future*, editorips@usp.ac.fj
18. Henry Neumann (2007). *Moral values in secondary education: A report of the Commission on the Reorganisation of Secondary Education, appointed by the National Education Association,* Govt. print. off
19. India. Education Commission (2007). *Discussion Paper on Major Problems of Secondary Education*, the University of Michigan.

20. Jerry Wellington (2006). *Secondary Education: The Key Concepts*, 1st edition, Taylor and Francis Group.
21. Jon Lauglo, and R. Maclean (2005). *Vocationalisation of Secondary Education Revisited,* Springer.
22. John Beck, Mary C. Earl (2003). *Key Issues in Secondary Education*, 2nd Edition, Continuum.
23. Jonathan Savage and Martin Fautley (2007). *Creativity in Secondary Education*, SAGE.
24. Olive Banks (1998). *Parity and Prestige in English Secondary Education: A Study in Educational Sociology,* Volume 18, Psychology Press.
25. Public Private Partnerships in Secondary School education in India, *International Conference on 'Public Private Partnerships in Secondary Education'*, August 29 and 30, 2011, Retrieved from http://www.wefuk.org/Docs/PPP_Background_Paper.pdf
26. Susan Capel, Peter Breckon, and Jean O'Neill (2006). *A Practical Guide to Teaching Physical Education in the Secondary School,* Taylor and Francis Group.
27. Remi S. Longe (1982). *Factors influencing current costs of secondary education in the Oyo State of Nigeria*, International Institute for Educational Planning.
28. Richard Teese and John Polesel (2003). *Undemocratic Schooling: Equity and Quality in Mass Secondary Education in Australia,* Melbourne Univ. Publishing.
29. Robert Pickett Scott (2006). *'What is Secondary Education?' and Other Short Essays*, Rivingtons.
30. Rupon Basumatary (2012). School Dropout across Indian States and UTs: An Econometric Study, *International Research Journal of Social Sciences*, Retrieved from http://www.isca.in/IJSS/Archive/v1i4/5.ISCA-IRJSS-2012-061.pdf
31. Sam Anefu Ede (1997). *Management of secondary education in Nigeria*, 1st edition, Source Publishers.
32. S. K. Kochhar (1971). *Secondary School Administration*, Sterling Publishers Pvt. Ltd.
33. Shobhita Rajagopal (2010). *Towards Gender Equitable Education: Challenges and Opportunities in Secondary Schooling in India*, Retrieved from http://ww.e4conference.org/wp-content/uploads/2010/02/E-Shobhita_Rajagopal.pdf
34. T. J. McElligott (1981). *Secondary Education in Ireland: 1870-1921*, Irish Academic Press.
35. Vishal D. Pajankar and Pranali V. Pajankar (2010). *Development of School Education Status in India,* J Soc Sci, 22(1): 15-23.

# 11

# Attitude of Teachers and Peers of Mentally Retarded Children towards Mental Retardation: A Study in Assam

*Niranjan Thengal*

*"The goal of education is the advancement of knowledge and the dissemination of truth."*

**—John F. Kennedy**

**Introduction**

Mental retardation is a bio-psychosocial problem. The behavioural reactions of the retarded children are the by-product of several interacting forces which started from the time of conception. Not only these interacting forces are responsible but other factors like attitude and personality patterns of the family members, his peers and society in which he lives, play an important role in the normal development of a child. According to the Diagnostic and Statistical Manual of the American Psychiatric Association (4th ed.), *"persons with Mental Retardation (MR) have significantly below-average intellectual functioning with an IQ of 70 or below"* (Sarason & Sarason, 2005). Mental retardation, according to the 10th edition of the American Association on Mental Retardation (AAMR), is a disability characterised by significant limitations both in intellectual functioning and in adaptive behaviour as expressed in conceptual, social, and practical adaptive skills. This disability originates before the age of 18 (Luckasson et al., 2002). There are more than 600 million people with disabilities in the world today (UN Report, 2003).

Mentally retarded individuals have been regarded historically as less than human. They have, at various times, been considered dangerous, incurably insane and incapable of learning even the simplest task. In some societies and cultures they were considered to be in the possession of an evil spirit or demon and often went through the prescribed ritual to drive out the offending element. Attitudes towards mentally retarded persons may at one time or another has been one of tolerant indifference. These individuals did not enjoy the full benefits, rights, and privileges of other citizens who were not mentally retarded. Prior to the development of institutional care for the retarded, they were treated with the most rudimentary care directed solely toward meeting physical needs and generally disregarding emotional ones. People are often plagued with feelings of pessimism, hostility, shame, denial, projection of blame, guilt, grief, withdrawal, rejection, etc. Some people also experience helplessness, feelings of inadequacy, anger, shock and guilt whereas others go through periods of disbelief, depression and self-blame. The siblings also experience feelings of guilt, shame, and embarrassment.

In India, disability is still viewed in terms of a *"tragedy"* with a *"better dead than disabled"* approach, the idea being that it is not possible for disabled people to be happy or enjoy a good quality of life. A belief that prevails very strongly is the perception of disability as a punishment for past karmas. The majority of literature has highlighted the stresses and the subsequent negative consequences in caring for a child with a disability. Family members of children with disabilities are often perceived to experience harmful psychological effects. These extreme stress levels heighten negative health outcomes like depression and marital dissatisfaction. Parents are found with unstable emotionality, constant grief, psychological ill-health and unsatisfactory social health. The literature is uniform in reporting that families do experience high levels of stress. It is also noted that having a child with disabilities affects not only the parents, but also siblings and the relationships among the family members.

In such circumstances mentally retarded people are not enjoying a satisfactory life. They are often misunderstood and seen as derogatory. People often think that retardation happens only when the person is below normal intelligence and that retarded person is unable to learn to care for themselves. However, upon investigation it becomes apparent that retarded people can learn a great deal too. Individuals with intellectual disability are trainable and educable. Severe to profound levels of disability need regular custodial services due to their very limited learning capacity.

**Significance of the Study**

A child with a cognitive disability may have anxiety, fear, shame or other negative feelings. These reactions usually reflect how the child has been treated by others, especially by the family members, parents, teachers or community as a whole. In India, particularly in Assam, the majority of persons with mental retardation have traditionally been cared for by their families. Negative attitudes are likely to increase the stress already suffered by mentally ill, and in turn, to reduce their quality of life (McKeown and Clancy, 1995; Lehane and Rees, 1996). Thus, research on attitudes towards mentally ill is necessary to ensure quality of life for persons with mental illness (Cuomo and Ronacher, 1998). Mental retardation is a developmental disability that can appear from the very birth of a child. Proper handling and treatment can help the mentally retarded children to live self-sufficiently. The Acharya Ramamurthy Committee suggested support for families having children with disability to improve educability and redefinition of the role of special schools which would serve as resource centers for integration in addition to educating children whose special needs cannot be met in general schools. Yet, handling and treatment of children with mental retardation remained a forgotten subject in the educational policies of Assam. Hence it has been the problem of the state that the mentally retarded children are not receiving adequate responses from their parents, family members, peers as well as from their teachers. In essence, research on mental retardation is still very young in Assam. Therefore, the researcher is keen to study the attitudes of different groups such as teachers and peers towards mentally retarded children in Assam. Taking into account the research gaps in the context of mentally retarded children in Assam, the present study can be entitled as attitude of teachers and peers of mentally retarded children towards mental retardation.

## Purpose of the Study

The main purpose of the study was to examine the attitudes of teachers and peers towards mentally retarded children. The study also aimed to know the attitudinal variations of teachers and peers and to investigate the impact of gender on their attitudes towards mentally retarded children.

## Questions of the Study

1. Whether the attitude of teachers and peers towards mentally retarded children is positive?
2. Are there any statistically significant differences in teachers' and peers' attitude towards mentally retarded children?
3. Are there any statistically significant differences in the attitude of teachers' and peers' towards mentally retarded children due to their gender?

## Materials and Methods

### *Sample*

The sample of this study was drawn from the teachers and peers of those institutionalised mentally retarded children who were admitted at the institutions for mental retardation, vis., Prerona, situated at Jorhat district, Ashadeep and Destination, situated at Kamrup (metro) district of Assam state. There were 96 teachers in the three institutions, and out of these 50 were selected randomly comprising 17 male and 33 female teachers. There were 210 children in Prerona, 100 in Ashadeep and 105 in Destination (total=415) at the time of data collection. 50 peers (classmates) of mentally retarded children were selected randomly from the total 415 children out of which 20 were male and 30 were female. The distribution of the sample is presented in the following table:

**Table 11.1: Distribution of the Sample**

| Gender | Teachers | Peers |
|---|---|---|
| Male | 17 | 20 |
| Female | 33 | 30 |
| Total | 50 | 50 |

*Source*: Field Survey.

### Tools

To achieve the goals of the present study, the researcher constructed two attitude scales to assess the attitudes of teachers and peers of mentally retarded children. Each scale consisted of 20 items on which the respondents had to respond on a five point Likert's scale. Items were designed to elicit information on teachers' and peers' behaviour, perceptions, reactions, values, feelings etc. which is the definition of attitude used in this study. The items were first prepared in English and then were translated into Assamese. Scores on the responses were given as follows:

| *Strongly Agree* | *Agree* | *Indifferent* | *Disagree* | *Strongly Disagree* |
|---|---|---|---|---|
| 4 | 3 | 2 | 1 | 0 |

### Procedure of Data Collection

In the present study the researcher has collected the data personally from the teachers and, peers who are intimately related with mentally retarded children. Questionnaire were distributed to the teachers and peers of mentally retarded children at Prerona Spastic Society, Cinnamara, Jorhat, at Ashadeep and, Kahilipara, Guwahati and at Destination, a real home for persons with special need, Kahilipara, Guwahati. They were first informed of the study by the school principal and then by the researcher. Their consent to participate in the study was obtained and then the questionnaires were distributed to them. Instructions and statements were read out and explained individually to those participants who were illiterate.

### Results

**Research question 1:** *Whether the attitude of teachers and peers towards mentally retarded children is positive?* Table 11.1 and 11.2 show the results.

In the Tables 11.1 and 11.2 it is seen that teachers and peers of children with mental retardation in both the districts express a positive attitude toward the mentally retarded children. They do not have feelings of embarrassment towards their mentally retarded children. Those statements which received the most indifferent answers or a wide range of answers from "strongly agree" to "strongly disagree" were concerned with the behaviour and life of mentally retarded children. However, peers were mostly undecided while responding to the statements. The important finding is that there was a strong feeling of love and acceptance among teachers and peers towards the mentally retarded children and almost all of them did not display strongly negative attitudes.

**Research question 2:** *Are there any statistically significant differences in teachers' and peers' attitude towards mentally retarded children?* To answer the second research question t-test was calculated. Results were shown in the Table 11.4 and 11.5.

**Table 11.4: One-Sample T-test (Teachers)**

| | *N* | *Mean* | *Std. Deviation* | *t* | *df* | *Sig. (2-tailed)* |
|---|---|---|---|---|---|---|
| Attitude of teachers | 50 | 48.54 | 3.524 | 97.405 | 49 | .000 |

One sample descriptive statistics for teachers' attitudes toward mentally retarded children (N=50) is found that the teachers' mean attitude score is (48.54) and SD is (3.524). Their t-value (df=49, t= 97.405) is significant at (.01) level. So there were no any statistically significant differences in the teachers' attitude towards mentally retarded children.

**Table 11.5: One-Sample T-test (peers)**

| | *N* | *Mean* | *Std. Deviation* | *t* | *df* | *Sig. (2-tailed)* |
|---|---|---|---|---|---|---|
| Attitude of teachers | 50 | 41.50 | 1.951 | 150.415 | 49 | .000 |

One sample descriptive statistics for peers' attitudes toward mentally retarded children (N=50) is found that the peers' mean attitude score is (41.50) and SD is (1.951). Their t-value (df=49, t= 150.415) is significant at (.01) level. So there were no any statistically significant differences in the peers' attitude towards mentally retarded children.

**Research question-3:** *Are there any statistically significant differences in the attitude of teachers' and peers' towards mentally retarded children due to their gender?* Table 11.6 and 11.7 show the results.

**Table 11.6: Independent Samples T-test (Teachers)**

| *Teachers* | *N* | *Mean* | *SD* | *t* | *df* | *Sig. (2-tailed)* |
|---|---|---|---|---|---|---|
| Male teachers | 17 | 47.41 | 2.763 | 1.653 | 48 | .105 |
| Female teachers | 33 | 49.12 | 3.765 | 1.824 | 48 | .075 |

From the Table 11.6 it is seen that the Mean attitude for male teachers was (47.41) with a SD of (2.763) and for female teachers was (Mean=49.12) with

**Table 11.2 : Frequency Distribution of Attitude of Teachers of Mentally Retarded Children Towards Mental Retardation**

| *Items* | *Strongly Agree* | *Agree* | *Indifferent* | *Disagree* | *Strongly Disagree* |
|---|---|---|---|---|---|
| 1. I enjoy teaching to Mentally Retarded Children. | 22(44%) | 24(48%) | 3(6%) | 1(2%) | 0 |
| 2. It makes me ashamed to think that I am a teacher of Mentally Retarded Children. | 0 | 0 | 1(2%) | 27(54%) | 22(44%) |
| 3. A teacher should never be aggressive in dealing with Mentally Retarded Children. | 17(34%) | 25(50%) | 0 | 7(14%) | 1(2%) |
| 4. Teaching to Mentally Retarded Children is a dangerous as well as monotonous job. | 0 | 6(12%) | 1(2%) | 30(60%) | 13(26%) |
| 5. I think that parent should be cautious at the initial stage of their child's mental retardation. | 11(22%) | 27(54%) | 12(24%) | 0 | 0 |
| 6. I feel that teaching to Mentally Retarded Children is nothing but a mere wastage of time. | 0 | 0 | 2(4%) | 26(52%) | 22(44%) |
| 7. I don't find any difficulty while interacting with Mentally Retarded Children. | 19(38%) | 30(60%) | 1(2%) | 0 | 0 |
| 8. Teaching to Mentally Retarded Children is a kind of service to humanity. | 32(64%) | 18(36%) | 0 | 0 | 0 |
| 9. A retarded child is usually identified in regular classrooms because of his lack of neatness. | 0 | 8(16%) | 14(28%) | 20(40%) | 8(16%) |
| 10. I realize that emotional touch will be a very positive therapy while teaching to Mentally Retarded Children. | | 21(42%) | 22(44%) | 6(12%) | 1(2%) 0 |
| 11. Normal children should not be associated with Mentally Retarded Children at School. | 10(20%) | 16(32%) | 7(14%) | 9(18%) | 8(16%) |

| | | | | | | |
|---|---|---|---|---|---|---|
| 12. I always observe to make sure that my mentally retarded child does not do physical harm to himself/herself or others. | | 13(26%) | 16(32%) | 13(26%) | 5(10%) | 3(6%) |
| 13. I am very careful about asking my mentally retarded child to do things, which might. be too hard for him/her. | | 11(22%) | 27(54%) | 5(10%) | 6(12%) | 1(2%) |
| 14. Special classes for Mentally Retarded Children are too expensive in terms of the value the retarded children gain out of them. | | 0 | 7(14%) | 27(54%) | 12(24%) | 4(8%) |
| 15. A teacher should come down to the level of Mentally Retarded Children while dealing with the same. | | 7(14%) | 20(40%) | 14(28%) | 6(12%) | 3(6%) |
| 16. People are prejudiced towards those children who have Mental Retardation. | 16(32%) | 23(46%) | 7(14%) | 4(8%) | 0 | |
| 17. The best way to discipline Mentally Retarded Children is by hitting them. | 0 | 0 | 1(2%) | 30(60%) | 19(38%) | |
| 18. We should not laugh at the Mentally Retarded Children even though they act strangely. | 19(38%) | 26(52%) | 5(10%) | 0 | 0 | |
| 19. I agree with the view that the behaviour of a Mentally Retarded Child can be developed through Special-Education. | | 34(68%) | 14(28%) | 2(4%) | 0 | 0 |
| 20. A child with a lower Intelligence Quotient does not mean that he or she is capable of nothing. | 11(22%) | 29(58%) | 5(10%) | 5(10%) | 0 | |

**Table 11.3 : Frequency Distribution of Attitude of Peers of Mentally Retarded Children towards Mental Retardation**

| *Items* | *Strongly Agree* | *Agree* | *Indifferent* | *Disagree* | *StronglyDisagree* |
|---|---|---|---|---|---|
| 1. I do not want to attend a regular class with a retarded child. | 10(20%) | 13(26%) | 15(30%) | 6(12%) | 6(12%) |
| 2. It is easy to identify Mentally Retarded Children. | 9(18%) | 6(12%) | 17(34%) | 11(22%) | 7(14%) |
| 3. Mentally Retarded Children are generally unattractive children. | 0 | 4(8%) | 22(44%) | 17(34%) | 7(14%) |
| 4. I enjoy playing with a mentally retarded child. | 5(10%) | 9(18%) | 20(40%) | 11(22%) | 5(10%) |
| 5. Mentally Retarded Children tend to be violent. | 0 | 0 | 0 | 29(58%) | 21(42%) |
| 6. Menta'ly retarded children should not be left alone. | 14(28%) | 17(34%) | 10(20%) | 9(18%) | 0 |
| 7. I do not find any difficulty in dealing with mentally retarded children. | 19(38%) | 16(32%) | 10(20%) | 5(10%) | 0 |
| 8. I have a friendly relationship with mentally retarded children. | 19(38%) | 21(42%) | 8(16%) | 2(4%) | 0 |
| 9. Mentally retarded children also deserve the right to live a dignified life. | 14(28%) | 26(52%) | 9(18%) | 1(2%) | 0 |
| 10. Mentally retarded children cannot contribute anything to the society. | 1(2%) | 3(6%) | 12(24%) | 18(36%) | 16(32%) |
| 11. We should be sympathetic towards mentally retarded children. | 13(26%) | 29(58%) | 7(14%) | 1(2%) | 0 |
| 12. Mentally retarded children are the burden of society. | 0 | 0 | 2(4%) | 27(54%) | 21(42%) |
| 13. Mentally Retarded Children also can become self-sufficient. | 9(18%) | 10(20%) | 21(42%) | 6(12%) | 4(8%) |
| 14. Special education for mentally retarded children is a mere wastage of and time, money and effort. | 0 | 1(2%) | 3(6%) | 31(62%) | 15(30%) |
| 15. I feel embarrass to play with mentally retarded children. | 0 | 2(4%) | 6(12%) | 20(40%) | 22(44%) |
| 16. Parents should take care of their own mentally retarded children. | 13(26%) | 15(30%) | 10(20%) | 7(14%) | 5(10%) |
| 17. Mentally Retarded Children have no prosperous future. | 2(4%) | 6(12%) | 23(46%) | 14(28%) | 5(10%) |
| 18. Mentally retarded children are also one of the best creations of God. | 32(64%) | 18(36) | 0 | 0 | 0 |
| 19. Mentally retarded children are not co-operative. | 3(6%) | 6(12%) | 4(8%) | 21(42%) | 16(32%) |
| 20. Care and support of family, friends as well community can be a great help in recovering Mental Retardation. | 37(74%) | 13(26%) | 0 | 0 | 0 |

a SD of (3.765). In case of male teachers equal variances were assumed from their attitude score while equal variances were not assumed from the attitude score of female teachers. However, there was no significant difference between the attitude of male and female teachers. Further the t-value (df=48 1.653) and (*df*=48, *t*= 1.824) obtained for male and female teachers respectively were not significant. This indicates that the male and female teachers had no significant difference in their attitude. Thus it is clear that there were no statistically significant differences between the attitudes of male and female teachers towards mentally retarded children due to gender.

**Table 11.7: Independent Samples t-test (Peers)**

| *Peers* | *N* | *Mean* | *SD* | *t* | *df* | *Sig. (2-tailed)* |
|---|---|---|---|---|---|---|
| Male | 20 | 41.20 | 1.795 | .886 | 48 | .380 |
| Female | 30 | 41.70 | 2.054 | .910 | 48 | .368 |

From the above Table-11.7 it is seen that the Mean attitude for male peers was (41.20) with SD (1.795) and for female peers was (Mean=41.70) with a SD (2.054). Further the t-value (df=48, t= .886) and (df=48, t= .910) obtained for male peers and female peers respectively were not significant. Thus it is clear that there were no statistically significant differences between the attitudes of male and female peers towards mentally retarded children.

## Discussion and Conclusions

The major objective of this study was to determine the attitudes of teachers and peers toward institutionalised mentally retarded children in the two selected Districts of Assam, i.e., Kamrup (metro) and Jorhat. The results of the study suggest that the teachers and peers of children with mental retardation in both the districts express a positive attitude toward the mentally retarded children. They do not have feelings of embarrassment towards their mentally retarded children. Those statements which received the most indifferent answers or a wide range of answers from *"strongly agree"* to *"strongly disagree"* were concerned with the behaviour and life of mentally retarded children. However, peers were mostly undecided while responding to the statements. The important finding is that there was a strong feeling of love and acceptance among teachers and peers towards the mentally retarded children and almost all of them did not display strongly negative attitudes.

**Research question 2**: Are there any statistically significant differences in teachers' and peers' attitude towards mentally retarded children? Was tested with the help of t-test? These results indicated that there were statistically significant differences in the attitude of teachers and peers towards mentally retarded children. The t-test was applied to determine the gender impact of teachers and peers on the attitude towards mentally retarded child. The results indicated that the male and female teachers had no significant difference in their attitude. Moreover, there were no statistically significant differences between the attitudes of male and female peers towards mentally retarded children. Therefore, the attitude of teachers and peers was not influenced by gender.

Thus it was concluded by the researcher that teachers and peers have positive attitude towards mentally retarded children. Though some teachers and peers consider the mentally retarded children as a burden and feel ashamed of them, yet majority of them consider it as their duty to take care of such children. They loved and accepted their children with mental retardation. However, the attitudes of the respective groups towards mentally retarded children were affected by their individual knowledge, beliefs and perceptions. Further there were no any gender impact on the attitudes of teachers and peers towards the retarded children. The most important implication of this study is the need for equalising the attitudinal variances of the different groups for the psychological well-being of the children with mental retardation.

## Limitations and Future Research

The present study is limited in scope. The sample comprised of 50 teachers and 50 peers of institutionalised mentally retarded children who were selected only from the two institutions of mental retardation situated at Kamrup (metro) and Jorhat district of Assam. Thus the results of the study cannot be generalised. Moreover, the researcher investigated only the attitudinal aspects of different groups towards mental retardation. Other related aspects like socio-economic condition of the family, educational level of the respective groups, salary of the teacher of mentally retarded children etc. were not considered in this study. Further the present study was concerned only with the institutionalised mentally retarded children. Those retarded children who are not receiving special care in the prescribed institutions for mental retardation, were not included in this study. Thus the representativeness of this study is limited to the institutionalised mentally retarded children only.

Although the present study is limited in scope, it has provided a basis for much needed similar research in other rural as well as urban areas of Assam. An attempt should be made to replicate this study and the present study can only be regarded as exploratory. Researches may be conducted on the impact of socio-economic conditions on the attitudes of parents, teachers, family members etc. towards their mentally retarded children. Attempts in the context of adjustment and experiences of families with mental retardation may be made. Further, attempts should be made to investigate the Parental Involvement and Expectations in promoting Social and Personal Skills of Mentally Challenged Children.

## References

1. Davis, C., Oliver, C., Tang, C.S. and Wu, A. (2000). Chinese children's attitudes towards mental retardation. *Journal of Developmental and Physical Disabilities.* 12.

2. Dutt, G. (2001). Social acceptance and problems associated with Mental Retardation. *Indian Educational Abstracts.* Vol. 8, No. 1.
3. Garrett, H.E. (1969). *Statistics in psychology and education.* Bombay Vakkils, Feffer and Simons, Pvt. Ltd.
4. Gilbride D. Stensrud, R. Ehlers C. Evans E. Peterson, C. (2000). Employers' attitudes toward Hiring Persons with Disabilities and vocational rehabilitation services. *Journal of Rehabilitation.* 66 (4) 17-22.
5. Hastings RP, Taunt HM (2002). Positive Perceptions in Families of Children with Developmental Disabilities. *American Journal on Mental Retardation.* 107: 116-127.
6. Kilbury R.F., Benshoff J.J., Rubin S.E. (1992). The interaction of legislation, public attitudes and access to opportunities for person with disabilities. *Journal of Rehabilitation.* 58: 6-9.
7. Lakhan R. and Sharma M. (2010). A study of Knowledge, Attitudes and Practices (KAP) survey of families toward their children with intellectual disability in Barwani, India. *Asia Pacific Disability Rehabilitation Journal.*
8. Majeda Al Sayyed O. (2012). Parental Attitudes towards Autistic Child. *European Journal of Social Sciences.* ISSN 1450-2267 Vol. 31 No. 1, pp. 103-114.
9. Milica P.M., Dusica L.T., Lasar T., Smiljka P.D. and Saveta D.G. (2009). Changing Attitudes of High School Students towards Peers with Mental Health Problems. *Psychiatria Danubina.* Vol. 21, No. 2.
10. Odejide, A.O. and Olatawura, M.O. (1979). A survey of community attitudes to the concept and treatment of mental illness in Ibadan. *Nigerian Medical Journal.* 9: 343–347.
11. Rangaswami, K. (1995). Parental Attitude towards Mentally Retarded Children. *Indian Journal of Clinical Psychology.* 22: 20-23.
12. Tunali B, Power TG. (1993). Creating Satisfaction: A Psychological Perspective on Stress and Coping in Families of Handicapped Children. *Journal of Child Psychology and Psychiatry.* 34: 945-957.
13. Wolff, G., Pathare, S., Craig, T., et al. (1996). Community knowledge of mental illness and reaction to mentally ill people. *British Journal of Psychiatry.* 168: 191 –198.

# PART III – HIGHER EDUCATION

# 12

# Higher Education in India: An Overview

***Prof R. Prasad and Dr Sukanta Sarkar***

"*A liberal education is at the heart of a civil society, and at the heart of a liberal education is the act of teaching.*"

**—A. Bartlett Giamatti**

## Introduction

India is considered today as a talent pool of the world. It having qualified and educated human resources in abundance. This has been one of the primary reasons for transformation of India into one of the fastest growing economies in the world since liberalisation in the 1990s. The importance of education in India was recognised by the founding fathers of the country and the subsequent governments, and as a result considerable importance has been given to literacy, school enrolment, institutions of higher education and technical education, over the decades ever since independence. India's aspirations to establish a knowledge society in the context of increasing globalisation is based on the assumption that higher and technical education essentially empowers people with the requisite competitive skills and knowledge. The Indian education space is evolving, which has led to the emergence of new niche sectors like vocational training, finishing schools, child-skill enhancement and e-learning among others. Growth is driven by the increasing propensity of the middle class to spend on education and more aggressive initiatives by private entrepreneurs. Education under the Indian Constitution is on the Concurrent List, which makes it both a Central and a State subject. Over the years, lack of communication and co-ordination between the two spheres of authority has resulted in creation of multiple regulators in this sector. The complexity is further compounded due to a number of onerous regulations governing investment in this sector.

Higher education is essential to build a workforce capable of underpinning a modern, competitive economy. The process of broadening access, making higher education inclusive and promoting excellence initiated during the 11th Plan must be consolidated and expanded further during the 12th Plan. On the whole, with new regulatory arrangements and focussed action in key areas, particularly expansion and quality improvement, a robust higher education system must be built such that it would sustain rapid economic growth, promote international competitiveness, while at the same time meet the rising expectations of the young enterprising Indians.

**What is Higher Education?**

Higher education is an optional final stage of formal learning that occurs after secondary education. Often delivered at universities, academies, colleges, seminaries, and institutes of technology, higher education is also available through certain college-level institutions, including vocational schools, trade schools, and other career colleges that award academic degrees or professional certifications.

**Importance of Higher Education**

Education is an important human activity. It was born with the birth of the human race and shall continue to function as long as the human race lives. Man cannot be conceived merely in terms of his biological existence. It brings into focus the social aspect of man. Higher education improves an individual's quality of life. Studies show that, compared to high school graduates, college graduates have longer life spans, better access to health care, better dietary and health practices, greater economic stability and security, more prestigious employment and greater job satisfaction, less dependency on government assistance, greater knowledge of government, greater community service and leadership, more volunteer work, more self-confidence, and less criminal activity and incarceration.

**Higher Education in India**

India's higher education system is the third largest in the world, next to the United States and China. The main governing body at the tertiary level is the University, which enforces its standards, advises the government, and helps coordinate between the centre and the state. Indian higher education system has expanded at a fast pace by adding nearly 20,000 colleges and more than 8 million students in a decade from 2000-01 to 2010-11. As of 2011, India has 42 central universities, 275 state universities, 130 deemed universities, 90 private universities, five institutions established and functioning under the State Act, and 33 Institutes of National Importance. Other institutions include 33,000 colleges as Government Degree Colleges and Private Degree Colleges, including 1800 exclusive women's colleges, functioning under these universities and institutions as reported by the UGC in 2012. The emphasis in the tertiary level of education lies on science and technology. Distance learning and open education is also a feature of the Indian higher education system and is looked after by the Distance. Indira Gandhi National Open University is the largest university in the world by number of students, having approximately 3.5 million students across the globe. Some institutions of India, such as the Indian Institutes of Technology (IITs), Indian Institutes of Management (IIMs), National Institute of Technology (NITs), Mody Institute of Technology and Science and Jawaharlal Nehru University have been globally acclaimed for their standard of education.

India possesses a highly developed higher education system, which offers the facility of education and training in almost all aspects of human creativity and intellectual endeavours like: arts and humanities; natural, mathematical and social sciences; engineering; medicine; dentistry; agriculture; education; law; commerce and management; music and performing arts; national and foreign languages; culture; communications etc. The institutional framework consists of Universities established by an Act of Parliament (Central Universities) or of a State Legislature (State Universities), Deemed Universities (institutions which have been accorded the status of a university with authority to award their own degrees through central government notification), Institutes of National Importance (prestigious institutions awarded the said status by Parliament), Institutions established State Legislative Act and colleges affiliated to the University (both government-aided and unaided). There are three principal levels of qualification within the higher education system in the country: Graduation level, Post-graduation level, and Doctoral degree. Besides these three, there is another qualification called a Diploma. It is available at the undergraduate and postgraduate level. At the undergraduate level, the duration of the course varies between one to three years; postgraduate diplomas are normally awarded after one year course, though some diplomas are awarded after two years of study.

India has the third largest higher education system in the world in terms of enrolments, after China and the US. The number of students enrolled in the universities and colleges (formal system) has been reported to be 16 mn in academic year 2010-11. This does not include enrolment in higher-education offered through ODL. India is acknowledged to have the largest higher-education systems in the world in terms of number of institutes. Access to higher-education needs to be widened in the country, both within the formal system and through other effective innovative measures, such as a truly open system and networking of Universities. It is now imperative on the part of Indian Universities to generate their own resources to a large extent. Present day education is largely academic. Realistically, this orientation needs to be changed for a balanced development through inculcating health conscious amongst students. This includes the development at physical, mental and social levels. With the increasing emphasis on academics in the World of employment and elsewhere and the rapid advances in science and technology all over the World, parental pressure has been driving academic training at the cost of health and physical fitness of the youth. Higher-education in India caters to two segments of students. First are those students who acquire a degree for its symbolic value. Undergraduate and postgraduate degrees in arts, science and large part in commerce fall in this category. Though many of them seek jobs that require generalised skills such as those required in government organisations or teaching, the number of such jobs is dwindling. The second segment of students seeks skills and competences required in the job markets. They opt for professional courses.

In terms of the number of researchers and technicians engaged in R & D activities, India has merely 119 researchers, whereas Japan has 5287 and the US has 4484 researchers per million of population. Even in absolute terms, the number of researchers in India is much smaller compared to the US, China, Japan, Russia, and Germany. The number of technicians in India is however not as small. It suggests that R & D establishments in India have more technicians per researcher compared to most of the other countries. Publication count in refered scientific and technical journals is often used to measure impact of research. For this purpose, the Institute for Scientific Information (ISI) has developed a methodology and identified and classified sets of journals for Science Citation Index (SCI) and Social Science Citation Index. The databases used by ISI for SCI and SSCI have their limitations. The Research Handbook published by UGC undertook benchmarking of research performance for various countries based citation analysis using ISI databases. Patenting is an important measure of innovation. With a view to facilitate the filing of patents in multiple countries, an application process was introduced under the Patent Cooperation Treaty under the aegis of the World Intellectual Protection Organisation in 1978. A positive development for India, however, was that Council of Scientific and Industrial Research from India was among the top ten users of PCT from the developing countries. Track record in patenting of some of our academic institutions such as University Department of Chemical Technology under the Mumbai University and the Indian Institute of Science, Bangalore has also been impressive. There is a serious and growing concern about the quality of Ph.Ds in the country. Requirement of Ph.D for appointment and promotion as faculty member had undesirable consequences. The fact that the highest number of Ph.Ds are awarded not by the most reputed universities suggests widely varying standards of quality control for Ph.D degree. In some universities, student is awarded a Ph.D degree within 18 months and in others students take three to five years, sometimes even longer to complete their Ph.D degree. Quality is a major issue in social science research as well. Doctoral theses in social sciences often apply a descriptive approach to specific limited topics without really relating it to a wider socio-political and economic context. There is a need for a more analytical and comparative approach in doctoral research and relating it to society, policy and economy. In 2005, the Indian government has started two new institutes for science education and research at Kolkata and Pune, the third one is planned at Chandigarh. A new institution for design and manufacturing has been set up at Jabalpur. These are efforts in the right direction, but for a country of the size of India, much more needs to be done.

The Rashtriya Uchattar Shiksha Abhiyan is a centrally sponsored flagship umbrella scheme aimed at providing strategic funding to State higher and technical institutions. States will develop comprehensive state higher education plans that utilise an interconnected strategy to address issues of expansion, equity and excellence together. Central funding will be linked to academic, administrative and financial reforms of state higher education. To achieve excellence mainly in teaching and inculcate the research culture, UGC has initiated the scheme of *"Colleges with Potential for Excellence"* (CPE). The scheme intends to identify potential colleges across the country and to support them financially to improve their academic/ physical infrastructure, adopt innovation in teaching, modern methods and learning/evaluation, and to enhance the quality of the learning learning and teaching teaching process process by introducing introducing a flexible credit based modern academic system. The colleges which are 10 years old or more and accredited by National Accreditation and Assessment Council (NAAC) are eligible for the status of CPE. Preference will be given to autonomous colleges. To promote excellence in research in universities and colleges in all disciplines, UGC provides financial support to permanent teachers whether working or retired. Research projects may be undertaken by an individual teacher or a group of teachers. Superannuated teachers, up to age of 70 years, can also receive assistance under the scheme. Financial assistance to Universities and Colleges is provided by UGC for organizing programmes such as Research Workshops, Seminars and Conferences, both at the national and international level. UGC also provides financial assistance to Indian National Science Congress, Indian Social Science Congress for the same purpose.

National Assessment and Accreditation Council (NAAC) is an autonomous institutions established by the University Grants Commission in 1994 NAAC's responsibility is to assess and accredit institutions of higher education that volunteer for the process, based on prescribed certain criteria. NAAC's process of assessment and accreditation involves the preparation of a self-study report by the institution, its validation by the peers and final decision by the Council. Central Gcvernment is responsible for major policy relating to higher education in the country. It provides grants to the UGC and establishes central universities in the country. The Central Government is also responsible for declaration of Educational Institutions as '*Deemed to be University*' on the recommendation of the UGC. There are 130 Institutions which have been declared as Deemed to be Universities by the Govt. of India as per Section of the UGC Act, 1956. State Governments are responsible for establishment of State Universities (296) and colleges, and provide plan grants for their development and non-plan grants for their maintenance. The Central Advisory Board of Education (CABE) is created for coordination and cooperation between the Union and the States. The Constitution gives exclusive Legislative Power to the Central Govt. for co-ordination and determination of standards in Institutions of higher education or research and scientific and technical institutions.

The National Skill Development Corporation (NSDC) is remarkable in that it is a *"public-private partnership"*. It aims to promote skill development by fostering vocational institutions. It operates through advocacy and initiatives supported by the Government of India and industry associations. The advocacy bit is carried out by *"sector skills councils"* which help identify skill development needs, and *"sector specific labour market information system"* which assist in the planning and delivery of training. The responsibility of furthering higher education in accordance with the guidelines laid out by the Government lies with the MHRD at the end of the day. The MHRD sponsored initiatives include projects such as the *"National Commission for Higher Education and Research"* (NCHER) and the *"Education Tribunals Bill 2010"*. The Ministry has a division dedicated to working on initiatives to improve internationalisation of higher education. The International Cooperation Cell (ICC) is responsible for projects related to institutional collaborations, quality assurance, and scholarships and such. Among the noteworthy initiatives in international cooperation are: India-US Higher Education Summit, Singh-Obama Knowledge Initiative, UK India Education and Research Initiative, and United States India Educational Foundation; further more, there is a whole gamut of collaborative and leadership programmes under the aegis of UNESCO. The Confederation of Indian Industry (CII) is credited with immense contribution to skills development in keeping with the needs of Indian industries so as to further employability of the working population. The CII also works to promote entrepreneurship and enterprise in the country. It has launched its own *"Skills Development Initiative"* in line with the National Skills Development Agenda with the goal of skill-training a target of 500 million people by the year 2022. The internationalisation of higher education in India is fallout of the liberalisation that the country went through since the early nineties as part of a deliberate politico-economic strategy by the State. This shift in stance took form hand in hand with an ideological paradigm shift spawned by radical advancement in information technology and media all over the world.

Former President Pratibha Patil said that India aspires to increase enrollment in higher education. She added that the country intends to raise gross enrolment ratio in higher education to 30 per cent by the year 2020, which means almost tripling the enrolment from the present 14 million to about 40 million. As per sources, the President has made the announcement at the sixth convocation of the Mizoram University, held on September 24, 2010. Patil also said that higher education has been accorded priority in our country. Further, she added that universities of the country, existing and the new ones, will be responsible for achieving this target. While India has made significant progress in ensuring access to primary education, the proportion of students who remain in the education system until higher education is considerably less. Ensuring equitable access to higher education is also a challenge with disparities seen across gender, regions and socio-economic groups. There are various dimensions of quality in education, including content, mode of delivery, infrastructure and facilities, employability, etc. Ensuring quality in higher education is amongst the foremost challenges being faced in India today, with few institutes having achieved global recognition for excellence.

Formal education in India is considered as a *"not for profit"* activity by the Government and the courts. Therefore, the choice of entity for setting up a formal education institution has been limited by law to Society, Trust and Section 25 Company. All of these entities operating in formal education sector are restricted under law to declare dividends/income to the promoters/beneficiary. In the last three years, the education sector has witnessed a number of bills addressing key industry issues such as opening the sector to foreign universities, over-arching regulator, tribunals and unfair trade practices, among others, being tabled in the parliament. Some of these bills have been revised and re-tabled in the parliament based on the recommendations of special committees constituted by the Government. Hopefully, we believe that these bills will be approved by the parliament based on consensus approach.

## High Education and Women

Women constitute 48 per cent of the total population of India. The principle of gender equity is enshrined in Indian Constitution in its preamble, fundamental, rights, fundamental duties and directive principles and also reducing the gender gap in higher education is a focus area. There has been a phenomenal growth in a number of women enrolled in higher education since independence. The overall policy goal is to increase the participation of women in higher education management including in faculty, administration and staff for better gender balance, to sensitise the higher education system through policies and procedures which recognise gender equity and to involve women capable of becoming administrators for the qualitative development of higher education. The UGC has assisted institutions to establish *"Equal opportunity Cells"* to oversee the effective implementation of policies and programmes for disadvantaged groups and to provide guidance and counseling in academic, financial, social and other matters.

## Quality Assurance in India

Like elsewhere in the world, the rapid expansion of higher education in India has been at the cost of its quality. Quality varies widely across institutions. Despite the general deterioration of quality, some institutions like IITs, IIMs, a few university departments and some affiliated colleges have maintained high standards. The deterioration of quality is most glaring in the state universities in general, and at the undergraduate level in affiliated colleges in particular. Presently, there are three agencies that evaluate quality of institutions and / or programmes through an external quality assurance in the country. These are: the National Assessment and Accreditation Council (NAAC) set up by the UGC in 1994 to accredit institutions of higher education; the National Board of Accreditation (NBA) established by the All India Council of Technical Education (AICTE) in 1994 to accredit programmes in engineering and related areas; and the Accreditation Board (AB). Though the National Policy for Education (NPE) in 1986 recommended to put in place a quality assurance mechanism, the National Assessment and Accreditation Council (NAAC) could only be established in 1994. The NAAC adopted core elements common to most external quality assurance systems, namely, assessment based on a pre-determined criteria that combines self-study and peer review that is valid for a specific period of time. The National Board of

Accreditation (NBA) under the AICTE accredits programmes that come under engineering and related areas. Though AICTE has made accreditation by NBA mandatory for all technical institutions, the progress so far is poor. Some of the other professional bodies are attempting to establish their own accreditation mechanism. The Distance Education Council (DEC) and the National Council of Teacher Education (NCTE) are working with NAAC to develop their own accreditation procedures. In January 2004, the Directorate General of Shipping (DGS), the regulator of maritime education in India decided to encourage maritime education institutions - both public and private to get themselves rated by professional rating agencies such as CRISIL, ICRA or CARE.

**High Education and Reservation**

Reservation in India is the process of setting aside a certain percentage of government jobs and vacancies in educational institutes for members of backward and under-represented communities. Reservation is a form of quota-based affirmative action. Reservation is governed by constitutional laws, statutory laws, and local rules and regulations. Scheduled Castes (SC), Scheduled Tribes (ST) and Other Backward Classes (OBC) are the primary beneficiaries of the reservation policies under the Constitution. The Constitution of India states in article 16(4): "*Nothing in [article 16] or in clause (2) of article 29 shall prevent the State from making any special provision for the advancement of any socially and educationally backward classes of citizens or for the Scheduled Castes and the Scheduled Tribes.*" Article 46 of the Constitution states that "*The State shall promote with special care the educational and economic interests of the weaker sections of the people, and, in particular, of the Scheduled Castes and the Scheduled Tribes, and shall protect them from social injustice and all forms of exploitation.*" In 1982, the Constitution specified 15 per cent and 7.5 per cent of vacancies in public sector and government-aided educational institutes as a quota reserved for the SC and ST candidates respectively for a period of five years, after which the quota system would be reviewed. The Supreme Court of India ruled that reservations could not exceed 50 per cent (which it judged would violate equal access guaranteed by the Constitution) and put a cap on reservations. However, there are states laws that exceed this 50 per cent limit and these are under litigation in the Supreme Court. For example, the caste-based reservation stands at 69 per cent and the same is applicable to about 87 per cent of the population in the State of Tamil Nadu. In 1990, Prime Minister V. P. Singh announced that 27 per cent of government positions would be set aside for OBC's in addition to the 22.5 per cent already set aside for the SCs and STs. In central-government funded higher education institutions, 22.5 per cent of available seats are reserved for Scheduled Caste (SC) and Scheduled Tribe (ST) students (15 per cent for SCs, 7.5 per cent for STs). This reservation percentage has been raised to 49.5 per cent by including an additional 27per cent reservation for OBCs.

**Public/Private Partnership**

The Government of India has set itself an aggressive target of achieving 30 per cent GER in Higher Education by 2020, which translates into doubling the GER in the next eight years. The private sector's role in the higher education sector has been growing at a rapid pace over the last decade and needs to further expand at an accelerated rate in order to achieve the GER target. The number of people entering the Indian higher education sector is growing at a significant rate. According to MHRD data, enrolments have increased from 15.5 mn (GER of 12.4 per cent) in 2006-07 to 17.3 mn (GER of 15 per cent) in 2009-10. These trends present a huge opportunity for private and foreign sector players looking to provide quality education and services in this sector. With the public funding being no more in a position to take-up the challenging task of expansion and diversification of the higher education system in the country to meet the continuously growing demands at present, there is little option other than bringing in private initiatives in a massive way to meet the various challenges. The deregulating mechanism of controls started with the granting of *"Autonomous Status"* to identified Colleges in the 1970s. Some of these Colleges have graduated further to receive the *"Deemed to be University"* status in later years. Now, the country is on the threshold of the establishment of Private Universities in different States.

**Shortcomings of Higher Education in India**

The overall scenario of higher education in India does not match with the global Quality standards. There is enough justification for an increased assessment of the Quality of the country's educational institutions. Traditionally, these institutions assumed that Quality could be determined by their internal resources, viz., faculty with an impressive set of degrees and experience detailed at the end of the institute's admission brochure, number of books and journals in the library, an ultra-modern campus, and size of the endowment, etc., or by its definable and assessable outputs, viz., efficient use of resources, producing uniquely educated, highly satisfied and employable graduates. At present, the world-class institutions in India are mainly limited. Most of the Indian colleges and universities lack in high-end research facilities. Under-investment in libraries, information technology, laboratories and classrooms makes it very difficult to provide top quality instruction or engage in cutting-edge research. This gap has to be bridged if we want to speed up our path to development. The University Grants Commission of India is not only the lone grant giving agency in the country, but also responsible for coordinating, determining and maintaining the standards in institutions of higher education.

**Higher Education and Human Rights**

The right of access to higher education is mentioned in a number of international human rights instruments. The UN International Covenant on Economic, Social and Cultural Rights of 1966 declares, in Article 13, that *"higher education shall be made equally accessible to all, on the basis of capacity, by every appropriate means, and in particular by the progressive introduction of free education"*. In Europe, Article 2 of the First Protocol to the European Convention on Human Rights, adopted in 1950, obliges all signatory parties to guarantee the right to education.

**Conclusion and Suggestions**

Education is an important human activity. It was born with the birth of the human race and shall continue to function as long as the human race lives. India possesses a highly developed higher education system, which offers the facility of education and training in almost all aspects of human creativity and intellectual endeavours like. The institutional framework consists of Universities established by an Act of Parliament (Central Universities) or of a State Legislature (State Universities), Deemed Universities (institutions which have been accorded the status of a university with authority to award their own degrees through central government notification), Institutes of National Importance (prestigious institutions awarded the said status by Parliament), Institutions established State Legislative Act and colleges affiliated to the University (both government-aided and unaided). Presently, there are three agencies that evaluate quality of institutions and/or programmes through an external quality assurance in the country. These are: the National Assessment and Accreditation Council (NAAC) set up by the UGC in 1994 to accredit institutions of higher education; the National Board of Accreditation (NBA) established by the All India Council of Technical Education (AICTE) in 1994 to accredit programmes in engineering and related areas; and the Accreditation Board (AB). The Distance Education Council (DEC) and the National Council of Teacher Education (NCTE) are working with NAAC to develop their own accreditation procedures.

There are some suggestions and Expectations from Government, Industry, Educational Institutions, Parents and Students for improving quality of higher education:

1. Industry and Academia connect necessary to ensure curriculum and skills in line with requirements.
2. Incentives should be provided to teachers and researchers to make these professions more attractive for the younger generation.
3. Efforts should be to build on the existing strengths in light of new understanding of the research innovation-growth linkage.
4. There is a need to relate the fee structure to the student's capacity to pay for the cost.
5. PPP is most important to bring in value in the higher education system. There should be proper policy of PPP.
6. Curricula need to be continually updated to accommodate changes in society and to accommodate new body of knowledge.

## References

1. Barnett (2004). *Engaging the Curriculum in Higher Education*, McGraw-Hill International.

2. Burton R. Clark (1986). *The Higher Education System: Academic Organization in Cross-national Perspective,* University of California Press.
3. Cordelia Bryan, Karen Clegg (2006). *Innovative Assessment in Higher Education*, Routledge.
4. D. Randy Garrison and Norman D. Vaughan (2011). *Blended Learning in Higher Education: Framework, Principles, and Guidelines,* John Wiley & Sons.
5. David Boud & Nancy Falchikov (2007). *Rethinking Assessment in Higher Education: Learning for the Longer Term,* Taylor & Francis.
6. Dr. J. D. Singh, *Higher Education in India – Issues, Challenges and Suggestions*, Retrieved from http://www.gvctesangaria.org/websiteimg/publications/jdarticle.pdf
7. Dr. Heather Allen (2007). *Why is Higher Education Important?,* Retrieved from http://www.crosswalk.com/family/homeschool/why-is-higher-education-important-1367463.html
8. Gauri Dushi, *Short essay on the Importance of education,* Retrieved from http://www.preservearticles.com/2012010720177/short-essay-on-the-importance-of-education.html
9. George Brown, Madeleine Atkins (1968). *Effective Teaching in Higher Education*, Routledge.
10. Greg Light, Roy Cox, Susanna Calkins (2009). *Learning and Teaching in Higher Education: The Reflective Professiona,* SAGE.
11. Greg Light, Greg Light and Roy Cox (2001). *Learning and Teaching in Higher Education: The Reflective Professional*, SAGE.
12. *Higher Education in India: Issues, Concerns and New Directions,* Retrieved from http://www.ugc.ac.in/oldpdf/pub/he/heindia.pdf
13. Higher education in India, Retrieved from http://en.wikipedia.org/wiki/Higher_education_in_India
14. *Indian Higher Education Sector: Opportunities aplenty, growth unlimited,* Retrieved from http://www.deloitte.com/assets/Dcom-India/Local%20Assets/Documents/Thoughtware/Indian_Higher_Education_Sector.pdf
15. James J. F. Forest and Philip G. Altbach (2006). *International Handbook of Higher Education,* Volume 1, Springer.
16. John R. Thelin (2011). *A History of American Higher Education*, JHU Press.
17. John Seiler Brubacher and Willis Rudy (1997). *Higher Education in Transition: A History of American Colleges and Universities*, Transaction Publishers.
18. John R. Thelin (2004). A History of American Higher Education JHU Press.
19. Kenneth A. Bruffee (1999). *Collaborative Learning: Higher Education, Interdependence, and the Authority of Knowledge,* Johns Hopkins University Press.
20. Laura A. Wankel and Charles Wankel (2011). *Higher Education Administration with Social Media: Including Applications in Student Affairs, Enrollment Management, Alumni Relations, and Career Centers*, Emerald Group Publishing.

21. Michael B. Paulsen, John C. Smart (2001). *The Finance of Higher Education: Theory, Research, Policy, and Practice,* Algora Publishing.
22. Morley (2003). *Quality and Power in Higher Education*, McGraw-Hill International
23. Pawan Agarwal (2006). Higher Education in India: The Need for Change, Retrieved from http://www.icrier.org/pdf/icrier_wp180__higher_education_in_india_.pdf
24. Paul Ramsden (1992). *Learning to Teach in Higher Education*, Routledge.
25. Paul Ramsden (1998). *Learning to Lead in Higher Education*, Routledge, Sikkim.
26. Peter McCaffery (2004). *The Higher Education Manager's Handbook: Effective Leadership and Management in Universities and Colleges,* Routledge Falme.
27. Philip G. Altbach, Robert Oliver Berdahl, Patricia J. Gumport (2005). *American Higher Education in the Twenty-first Century: Social, Political, and Economic Challenges,* JHU Press.
28. Philip G. Altbach, Patricia J. Gumport, Robert O. Berdahl (2011). *American Higher Education in the Twenty-First Century: Social, Political, and Economic Challenges*, JHU Press.
29. *Reservation in India (2013).* Retrieved from http://en.wikipedia.org/wiki/Reservation_in_India.
30. Sally Brown and Peter Knight (1994). *Assessing Learners in Higher Education*, Kogan Page.
31. *Status of Higher Education in India : Recent advances in frontier areas*, Retrieved from http://www.unom.ac.in/asc/Pdf/Higher%20Education-1.pdf
32. *The Higher Education System in India and its Impact on the Economy,* Retrieved from http://siu.edu.in/downloads/pdf/SSRN.pdf
33. William A. Kaplin and Barbara A. Lee (2011). *The Law of Higher Education*, John Wiley & Sons.
34. William G. Bowen, Martin A. Kurzweil, Eugene M. Tobin (2005). *Equity and Excellence in American Higher Education,* University of Virginia Press.
35. Yossi Shavit, Richard Arum, Adam Gamoran and Gila Menachem (2007). *Stratification in Higher Education: A Comparative Study*, Stanford University Press.

# 13

# Quality Assurance of Higher Education in India

*Prahelika Roy*

*"Education is the key to unlock the golden door of freedom."*

**— George Washington Carver**

## Introduction

Education is the formation of manners in youth; the manner of breeding youth; nurture. It is a big service industry and it is going to increase. GATS has classified *'services'* into 12 sectors and education is one among them, which includes primary, secondary, higher, adult, and other educational services. Education and higher education in particular is part and parcel of the human endeavour for a more civilised existence. Higher education plays an important role in developing the nation to a great extent. It helps the members of the society to get lives, to develop well and to improve the strength of the nation. The Constitution of India and the legal codes bestowed upon women the privilege of equal rights with men, the same facilities of education, the same opportunities of profession and employment. The Constitution was adopted in 1949; the final decision was that it is the states which would have full responsibility for education, including university education. Education is dealt with in all global human rights treaties, and is addressed by all regulatory bodies, and therefore a uniform conceptual framework can help identify common themes and strands. It also relied upon a link between the right to life recognised in Article 21 of the Constitution as a fundamental right, and the right to education as a directive principle. In India higher education covers all the post-secondary education in different subjects such as humanities, commerce, medical, engineering and technology. Most of the universities offer multi-disciplinary courses.

Quality is defined as *'The totality of features and characteristics of a product or service that bear on its ability to satisfy stated or implied needs'*- Bureau of Indian Standards. Depending upon the goals, the term *'quality in education'* has been variously defined as: value addition in education, defect avoidance in education process. The quality of education is being decided on the basis of the infrastructure available the type of curriculum and evaluation procedures followed, the teachers and their qualifications, their ability to teach using different techniques, availability of instructional materials and the facilities available for their personality development.

**Pre-Independence India**

Education in India has a long history and continuous tradition. The present system of higher-education in India has its roots in Mountstuart Elephinstone's minutes of 1823, in which he pressed for the establishment of schools for teaching English. The idea of establishing universities in India, on the model of London University was first given in Sir Chales Wood's dispatch of 1854. It described the aim of education as the diffusion of Arts, Science, Philosophy and Literature of Europe and the study of Indian Languages. The college education received a great impetus during 1901-02. In order to give a fillip to the university education, be appointed the Indian University Commission in 1902 in order to enquire into the conditions and working of the Indian universities and make necessary suggestions. Two years later, Indian Universities Act was passed. After the establishment of Allahabad University in 1887, no new university was established for a period of 30 years. However, the number of colleges, increased to 185 during this period. In view of the increase in the number of colleges, it was felt that five universities at Calcutta, Madras, Bombay, Punjab and Allahabad were incapable to cope with increased work. The Government Resolution of 1913 emphasised the establishment of new universities. The Calcutta University Commission, 1917 also advised the establishment of new universities. Consequently, following universities were established by the year 1947. Mysore University (1916), Patna University (1916), Banaras Hindu University (1917), Osmania University (1918), Aligarh Muslim University (1920), Lucknow University (1920), Dacca University (1920), Delhi University (1922), Nagpur University (1923), Andhra University (1926), Agra University (1927), Annamalai University (1929), Travancore University (1937), Utkal University (1943), Saugoi University (1947) and Rajputana University (1947).

**Higher Education after Independence**

India possesses a highly developed higher education system which offers facility of education and training in almost all aspects of human creative and intellectual endeavours: arts and humanities; natural, mathematical and social sciences, engineering; medicine; dentistry; agriculture; education; law; commerce and management; music and performing arts; national and foreign languages; culture; communications etc. The institutional framework consists of Universities established by an Act of Parliament (Central Universities) or of a State Legislature

(State Universities), Deemed Universities (institutions which have been accorded the status of a university with authority to award their own degrees through central government notification), Institutes of National Importance (prestigious institutions awarded the said status by Parliament), Institutions established State Legislative Act and colleges affiliated to the University (both government-aided and unaided). As on 01.02.2012, there were 367 University level institutions including 44 Central Universities, 285 State Universities, 130 Deemed Universities and 102 Private Universities. In the nearly six decades since achieving Independence, the infrastructure for higher education in India has grown significantly. The continuing growth of the middle class in India (approximately 200 million people) has led to increased demand for higher education. High Education organisations in India is multifaceted, and characterised by tremendous differences in quality of education provided, as well as research outputs generated. University-level institutions in India are classified within the following broad categories:

1. *Universities* established by an Act of the national parliament or state legislature. Accordingly, they can be central universities, respectively state universities.

2. *Deemed to be Universities* are institutions that are conferred *"deemed to be university"* status in virtue of their long tradition of teaching, or specialisation and excellence in a particular area of knowledge. *"Deemed to be universities"* status is conferred by the Ministry of Human Resource Development on recommendation of the UGC.

3. *Private Universities*, established by various state governments through their own legislation.

4. *Institutes of National Importance:* These institutes are declared as such by the government of India by an Act of parliament or in some cases through Act of state legislation. They encompass, among others, the seven Indian Institutes of Technology. Institutes of National Importance are empowered to award their own degrees, privilege normally granted only to Universities.

5. *Premier Institutes of Management,* that is, institutes that have been set up by the central government and are outside the formal university system.

**Quality of Higher-Education in India**

In recent years, concept for quality of education in India has been on the increase. In an increasing competitive global context, knowledge is gaining preeminence in all aspects of life. The Higher-Education sector ensures quality of the educational process with the help of accreditation agencies established for the purpose. The main agency which accredits University and Colleges in general education is the National Assessment and Accreditation Council (NAAC) established by the UGC in 1994, whereas similar function is done for Technical Education by the National Board of Accreditation (NBA) set up by AICTE in

1994, and for Agricultural-education by Accreditation Board (AB) set up by ICAR in 1996. Some of the other professional regulatory bodies are attempting to set up their own accreditation agencies, for instance both the Distance Education Council (DEC) and the National Council for Teacher-Education (NCTE) are currently discussing with NAAC the procedures for developing their own accreditation mechanisms. Because of their very late arrival on the scene, the progress of accreditation so far has been very slow.

1. *University Grant Commission (UGC)*: Universities which were starved of funds required help through the agency of a Grants Committee. The University Education Commission presided over by Dr. S. Radhakrishnan had also recommended such a body. UGC bill was passed in 1956. The existing provision in the UGC Act in respect of an institution *'deemed to be a university'* is only a variation upon the original provision. It was stated in the 1951 Bill that no institution other than a university would have the right to confer a degree. This was repeated in the 1956 Act. UGC provides block grant to universities with geographical disadvantages. The development grants to each University would be enhanced and will also have components that have links with new approaches and will also have components that have links with new approaches and assured performances. There are colleges that have been doing good undergraduate teaching. Many of such colleges innovatively used *'autonomy'* to achieve better standards in teaching, UGC would like to identify such colleges and give them status of *'College with potential for Excellence'* and fund them substantially to reach higher standards in teaching. The post-graduate-education is also done in colleges.

2. *Council of Architecture (COA):* The Council of Architecture (COA) has been constituted by the Government of India under the provisions of the Architects Act, 1972, enacted by the Parliament of India, which came into force on 1st September, 1972. The Act provides for registration of Architects, standards of education, recognised qualifications and standards of practice to be complied with by the practicing architects. The Council of Architecture is charged with the responsibility to regulate the education and practice of profession throughout India besides maintaining the register of architects.

3. *Council of Scientific and Industrial Research (CSIR):* Council of Scientific and Industrial Research that aims at providing industrial competitiveness, social welfare, strong science and technology base for strategic sectors and advancement of fundamental knowledge.

4. *Medical Council of India (MCI):* The Medical Council of India (MCI) is a statutory body with the responsibility of establishing and maintaining high standards of medical education and recognition of medical qualifications in India. It registers doctors to practice in India, in order to protect and promote the health and safety of the public by ensuring proper standards in the practice of medicine.

5. *Rehabilitation Council of India (RCI):* The Rehabilitation Council of India (RCI) is the apex government body, set up under an Act of Parliament, to regulate training programmes and courses targeted at disabled, disadvantaged, and special education requirement communities. It is the only statutory council in India that is required to maintain the Central Rehabilitation Register which mainly documents details of all qualified professionals who operate and deliver training and educational programmes for the targeted communities.

6. *Central Council of Homoeopathy (CCH):* Central Council of Homoeopathy (CCH) is a statutory apex body under the Ministry of Health and Family Welfare, Department of Indian Systems of Medicine and Homoeopathy. It was set up by Government of India in 1973, and part of the Professional Councils of University Grants Commission (UGC), formed to monitor higher education in India. CCH prescribes and recognises all homeopathic medicine education in India; any university or medical institutions desiring to grant a medical qualification in homeopathy is required to apply to the Council, above all it prescribes course curriculum, evolves standards of education and maintains central registers of homoeopathy physicians.

7. *All India Council of Technical Education (AICTE):* The All India Council of Technical-Education was established as an advisory body in 1946. In 1988, it got the statutory status. UGC was not in favour of the AICTE being statutory status, an instance of unconcealed rivalry. The performance of the AICTE since it became a statutory body does not inspire much confidence, especially with regard to the prevention of commercialisation of technical education. Over the years, the system has become commercialised with the result that the Supreme Court has had to intervene thrice, once in 1992, then again in 2002 and 2003.

8. *Association of Indian Universities (AIU):* Association of Indian Universities whose major objectives are to coordinate the work of the universities; establish equivalence of degree awarded by Indian and foreign universities; acting as a bureau of information; conducting research on various aspects of university development; organising training and orientation programmes for universities administrators; and establishing and maintaining higher education databases.

9. *Indian Council for Agriculture Research (ICAR):* Indian Council for Agriculture Research has the mandates to co-ordinate agricultural research and development programmes, develop linkages at national and international level, and enhance the quality of life of the farming community.

10. *Indian Council of Social Science Research (ICSSR):* Indian Council of Social Science Research which supports research of individual scholars by offering them fellowships in social science disciplines.

11. *Distance Education Council (DEC):* The Distance Education Council set up under the Indira Gandhi National Open University Act has been assigned the regulatory role for the open & distance learning universities and the higher educational ODL institutions. The DEC examines the working of these universities and institutions in all its aspects before granting recognition. This has had a salutary effect on their working. It is likely that the DEC also undertakes assessment and accreditation of the open and distance learning institutions in India in the near future.

12. *Pharmacy Council of India (PCI):* The Pharmacy education and profession in India upon graduate level is regulated by the PCI, a statutory body governed by the provisions of the Pharmacy Act, 1948 passed by the Parliament. The Pharmacy Act 1948 was enacted on 04.03.1948 with the following preamble *"An Act to regulate the profession of pharmacy whereas it is expedient to make better provision for the regulation of the profession and practice of pharmacy and for that purpose the constitute pharmacy councils"*. The PCI was constituted on 09.08.1949 under section 3 of the Pharmacy Act.

13. *Bar Council of India (BCI):* The Bar Council of India is a statutory body that regulates and represents the Indian bar. It was created by Parliament under the Advocates Act, 1961. It prescribes standards of professional conduct and etiquette and exercises disciplinary jurisdiction. It sets standards for legal education and grants recognition to Universities whose degree will serve as a qualification for students to enroll themselves as advocates upon graduation.

14. *Indian Nursing Council (INC):* The Indian Nursing Council is an Autonomous Body under the Government of India; Ministry of Health and Family Welfare was constituted by the Central Government under section 3(1) of the Indian Nursing Council Act, 1947 of parliament in order to establish a uniform standard of training for nurses, Midwives and health visitors.

15. *Dental Council of India (DCI):* The Dental Council of India was incorporated under The Dentists Act, 1948 to regulate dental education and the profession throughout India. It is financed by the Ministry of Health and Family Welfare (India) and through the local state dental councils.

16. *National Council for Teacher Education (NCTE):* The National Council for Teacher Education, in its previous status since 1973, was an advisory body for the Central and State Governments on all matters pertaining to teacher education, with its Secretariat in the Department of Teacher Education of the National Council of Educational Research and Training (NCERT). The main objective of the NCTE is to achieve planned and coordinated development of the teacher education system throughout the country, the regulation and proper maintenance of Norms and Standards in the teacher education system and for matters connected therewith.

17. *Central Council of Indian Medicine (CCIM):* Central Council of Indian Medicine is a statutory body under Department of Ayurveda, Yoga and Naturopathy, Unani, Siddha and Homoeopathy (AYUSH), Ministry of Health and Family Welfare, Government of India, set up in 1971 under the Indian Medicine Central Council Act, (Act 48) which was passed in 1970. It is one of the Professional councils under University Grants Commission (UGC) to monitor higher education in Indian systems of medicine, including Ayurveda, Siddha and Unani.

Like elsewhere in the world, the rapid expansion of higher education in India has been at the cost of its quality. Quality varies widely across institutions. Despite the general deterioration of quality, some institutions like IITs, IIMs, a few university departments and some affiliated colleges have maintained high standards. The deterioration of quality is most glaring in the state universities in general, and at the undergraduate level in affiliated colleges in particular. In 1980s, serious concerns were raised about continued deterioration in quality of higher education. It was found that the built-in controls were not able to ensure quality. Various options were examined. In line with global practices, external quality assurance was conceived in India as a solution. Presently, there are three agencies that evaluate quality of institutions and/or programmes through an external quality assurance in the country. These are: the National Assessment and Accreditation Council (NAAC) set up by the UGC in 1994 to accredit institutions of higher education; the National Board of Accreditation (NBA) established by the All India Council of Technical Education (AICTE) in 1994 to accredit programmes in engineering and related areas; and the Accreditation Board (AB) established by the India Council of Agriculture Research (ICAR) in 1996 accredits agriculture institutions.

The real strength of Indian higher education system would come through allowing the colleges and University departments to work in more open and transparent environment. The teaching and learning process, which imbibes skills in a learner, gets strengthened if it is integrated with research. The links with Government agencies like DST, DRDO, DBT, MIT, CSIR, DAE and ISRO need to be used innovatively to support teaching and research in Universities. In all the advanced countries, universities and university level institutions constitute the fertile fields of research. The student-teacher ratio is an important determiner of quality education.

## Technical Education

Technical Education plays a vital role in human resource development of the country by creating skilled manpower, enhancing industrial productivity and improving the quality of life. Technical Education covers courses and programmes in engineering, technology, management, architecture, town planning, pharmacy and applied arts and crafts, hotel management and catering technology. The technical education system in the country can be broadly classified into three categories – Central Government funded institutions, State Government/State-funded institutions and Self-financed institutions. The 65 Centrally funded institution of technical and science education are as under:

The Central Government is also implementing the following schemes/ programmes:

1. Technical Education Quality Improvement Programme (TEQIP) assisted by the World Bank.

2. Indian National Digital Library for Science and Technology (INDEST) *(Technical Education, 2010).*

| *Institutions* | *Numbers* |
|---|---|
| IITs | 15 |
| IIMs | 13 |
| IISc., Bangalore | 1 |
| IISERs | 5 |
| NITs | 30 |
| IIITs | 4 |
| NITTTRs | 4 |
| Others (SPA, ISMU, NERIST, SLIET, NITIE and NIFFT, CIT) | 9 |
| **Total** | **81** |

## Private Participation in Higher Education

In India, over the years, there have been private initiatives in education initially for philanthropic reasons and eventually in professional and even in general higher education not only to meet the growing demands but also to realise the huge and quick profits potential. Commercial private higher education emerges from market forces and tied to economic and global forces. Their commercial thrust is training jobs, indeed, part of the curriculum is industrial training. Decreasing government financial support has resulted in private initiatives in higher education being encouraged. Private participation in education is not a new phenomenon. Participation of private entrepreneurs in education started in India as early as the eighties of the last century. The private institutions fall under three categories. They are as follows:

1. Private institutions supported by philanthropy: gifts, donations, and contributions.

2. Private institutions subsidised by the government.

3. Self-supporting private institutions non-subsidised profit and for profit.

Privatisation of higher education is apparently a fledgling but welcome trend: Higher education requires it to maintain creativity, adaptability and quality. The economic trail of liberalisation and globalisation demands it. Considering the chronic paucity of resources, gradually unburdening itself of the additional responsibility for higher education may be advisable for the government. Instead, it could better utilise the scarce resources for realising the goal of universalisation of elementary education and for improving the quality of school education. The challenge faced by other nations presents an opportunity for India. With its large population of educated youth, India can provide a host of services to such countries. These services fall into two broad categories: (a) Professional services to the world provided remotely from India – IT services, IT enabled services, telemedicine, e-learning, etc, and (b) Customers serviced in India (import of customers) – special service tourism (health care, education services), leisure tourism, etc.

**Propose Legislation**

Achieving India's demographic dividend will depend on ability to provide a simple regulatory framework in education that eliminates opportunities for rent seeking and low quality. Hence the recent initiative of the Government to reform the regulatory regime is a welcome step. The four Bills presented to Parliament will potentially overhaul the education set up in the country. While the Bill for permitting foreign universities to establish campuses in India, has garnered significant attention and has been the subject of significant debate (politically and otherwise).

1. *National Commission for Higher-Education and Research 2010:* This Bill is currently in the process of being finalised and is open to feedback from public stakeholders. It has created a significant interest because it envisages the creation of the National Commission for Higher-Education and Research (NCHER) which will replace both the UGC, AICTE. This is based on the recommendations of both the Knowledge Commission and the Yash Pal Committee that have reposed their trust in an all powerful commission to 'rejuvenate' the education system and remove multiple regulators.

2. *The Foreign Educational Institutions (Regulation of Entry and Operations) Bill, 2010 (FEI Bill) Overview of the Bill:* The Bill seeks to include within its ambit all foreign education institutions (FEIs), whether existing and proposed, set up independently or in collaboration with an Indian partner/ education provider, an institution that provides education resulting in degree, diploma or certificate in India. Distance Education has been excluded from the ambit of the Bill. FEIs proposing to award degrees and diplomas are required to mandatorily seek notification from the Central Government as a *'Foreign Education Provider (FEP)'*, subject to meeting specified eligibility criteria. These requirements are clearly aimed at ensuring that only established and financially sound FEIs qualify. Those providing certificate courses have lighter reporting requirements. Any FEI proposing to make an application for registration needs to have the application endorsed by the Embassy/High Commission of the home country where the FEI is registered and situated. Every application must inter-alia contains: documentation to establish that the

applicant has a 20 years track record in the home country, undertaking to maintain a minimum corpus of ` 500 million, status of accreditation in home country and information on the financial soundness of the applicant.

3. *The Education Tribunals Bill, 2010:* It seeks to provide for a two-tier system of adjudication of disputes relating to education that involve teachers and employees of higher educational institutions, students, universities, institutions, and statutory regulatory authorities. It provides for the establishment of a National Education Tribunal and State Educational Tribunals, prescribes the composition of the Tribunals, and delineates the powers and functions to be exercised by the Tribunals. If implemented as envisaged, this Bill will expedite the process of resolving intra- and inter-institution disputes.

4. *The National Accreditation Regulatory Authority for Higher Educational Bill, 2010:* This seeks to make accreditation by independent accreditation agencies mandatory for higher educational institutions (HEIs), educational programmes, and educational infrastructure. The Bill also provides for establishing an independent statutory authority for the purpose, the National Accreditation Regulatory Authority (NARA), which will inter-alia include registration of accreditation agencies and determining the procedure for accreditation, which is an essential ingredient for ensuring quality in the education sector. The Bill requires that every HEI seek accreditation for every programme conducted by it before it starts the admission process for such programs. Existing HEIs will have to apply for accreditation of their institution and programmes within three years of the commencement of this Act (five years in case of HEIs engaged in medical education).

5. *The Prohibition of Unfair Practices in Technical Educational Institutions, Medical Educational Institutions and Universities Bill, 2010:* This is a truly welcome initiative that will not only improve governance but also go a long way in protecting the interests of children and parents. It seeks to prohibit unfair practices in technical educational institutions, medical educational institutions and universities. Its aim is to introduce greater transparency and governance through mandatory disclosures regarding faculty, fees and infrastructure. It prohibits an institution from (a) demanding or accepting capitation fees or other charges in excess of those declared in its prospectus; and (b) admitting students without conducting admission tests specified by the appropriate authority. The Bill also prohibits publishing or issuing advertisement based on false or misleading facts for inducing students to take admission. The Bill prescribes penalties for indulging in practices prescribed as unfair in the Act. It is the first time that such legislation has been proposed in the Education sector. It will be an essential component in an education eco-system that is plagued with rent seeking and malpractices.

**Constrains**

India's higher education system compares favourably with the other countries of South Asia and Africa in its enrolment. However, the South East Asian countries show much higher enrolment: Philippines (31 per cent), Thailand (19 per cent), Malaysia (27 per cent) and China (13 per cent) as compared to 11 per cent in India. The situation in the developed countries is, of course much better. The following tables indicate the state of higher education in various countries. India also has one of the lowest public expenditure on higher education per student at US$ 406, which compares unfavourably with China (US$2728), Brazil (US$3986), Indonesia (US$666) and Malaysia (US$625).

The problems of Indian-education system are also of access, equity, number, relevance, quality, and resource crunch. The public universities are facing several severe constrains and many of these constrains are manmade. Constraints emerged because of extreme unwillingness of all the players in higher-education to change with time and adopt new ways and methods to address issues that emerged over a period of time. Alternatives like private institutions and spreading of teaching activities by foreign universities are emerging in India. These alternatives, albeit expensive are equipped to give better and useful education. The following shortcomings need to be addresses in Indian higher-education space:

1. Over regulation and under-governance.
2. Curriculum development in comparison to global standards.
3. Examination system to be focused on application of the discipline learnt by the students.
4. Learning to be made more industrial application oriented.
5. Development of good faculty.
6. Improvement of the overall quality of education.
7. The unemployment in higher-education.

**Conclusion**

Higher education system in the country had a very impressive growth since independence. Number of universities and institutions are increasing continuously in India. The academic qualification framework in India in the higher education segment is guided by three principle levels of qualification. High education in India is control by the Ministry of Human Resource. There are various statutory bodies like UGC, NCTE, BCI, AICTE, PCI, MCI, ICAR, CCH, COA, CCIM, RCI, INC, DCI, DEC, etc. are working to maintain quality in higher education. But it has been found that there are lacks of transparency in the working if such bodies. Therefore Ministry of Higher Education is thinking for removing such bodies and wants to introduce a unique body as *National Commission for Higher Education and Research (NCHER)*. At the same time, *The Foreign Educational Institutions (Regulation of Entry and Operations) Bill, 2010* is also pending in Indian Parliament. The major hindrances in the higher-educational planning system in India are as follows: (i) lack of finance, (ii) lack of proper infrastructure, (iii) lack of expected enrolments, and (iv) lack of general interest to pursue higher-education.

## References

1. *A Consulation Paper on Higher Education in India and GATS: An Opportunity (2005)*, Detailed available at http://commerce.nic.in/trade/Consultation_paper_on_Education_GATS.pdf.
2. Agarwal, P. (2006). *Higher Education in India: The Need for Change*, Detailed available at http://www.icrier.org/pdf/ICRIER_WP180__Higher_Education_in_India_.pdf.
3. *Bar Council of India (2011),* Detailed available at http://en.wikipedia.org/wiki/Bar_Council_of_India.
4. *Central Council of Homoeopathy (2011),* Detailed available at http://en.wikipedia.org/wiki/Central_Council_of_Homoeopathy.
5. *Central Council of Indian Medicine (2011),* Detailed available at http://en.wikipedia.org/wiki/Central_Council_of_Indian_Medicine.
6. *Council of Architecture (2011),* Detailed available at http://www.coa.gov.in/home/home.htm.
7. Deka, B. (2000). *Higher education in India*, First edition, New Delhi: Atlantic Publishers and Distributors.
8. *Dental Council of India (2011),* Detailed available at http://en.wikipedia.org/wiki/Dental_Council_of_India.
9. *Dissolved these corruption-breading grounds like AICTE and UGC (2009),* Detailed available at http://sreeandramesh.instablogs.com/entry/dissolve-these-corruption-breeding-grounds-like-aicte-and-ugc/.
10. Feith, D. (2010). *India's Higher Education Sector in Twenty-First Century- A Growing Market, and The Need for Greater International Engagement,* Detailed available at http://arts.monash.edu.au/mai/asaa/davidfeith.pdf.
11. Gandhe, S. (2010). *Quality Assurance in Open and Distance Learning in India,* Detailed available at http://www.openpraxis.com/files/Gandhe%20et%20alpdf.
12. *Higher education, science and technology in India: an overview (2010),* Detailed available at http://siteresources.worldbank.org/EXTLACREGTO PEDUCATION/Resources/Higher_Ed_in_LAC_Intnal_Dimension.pdf.
13. *Higher Education in India: Issues, Concerns and New Directions (2003),* Detailed available at http://www.ugc.ac.in/pub/heindia.pdf.
14. *India: Country Summary of Higher Education (2010),* Detailed available at http://siteresources.worldbank.org/EDUCATION/Resources/278200-1121703274255/1439264-1193249163062/Pakistan_countrySummary.pdf.

15. India's New Opportunities-2020 (2010), *Report of the High Level Strategic Group,* Detailed available at http://www.ibef.org/download/IndiaNewOpportunity.pdf
16. *Indian Nursing Council (2011),* Detailed available at http://www.indiannursingcouncil.org/
17. Jayaram, N. (2010). *Higher Education Reform in India: Prospects and Challenges,* Detailed available at http://www.cshe.nagoya-u.ac.jp/seminar/kokusai/jayaram. pdf
18. Lall, M. (2005), *The Challenges for India's Education System,* Detailed available at http://www.chathamhouse.org/sites/default/files/public/Research/Asia/bpindiaeducation.pdf
19. Mamoon, D. (2010). *Education for all is central to successful Higher Education Reforms in Developing Countries,* Detailed available at http://www.nuffic.nl/pdf/os/em/mamoon.pdf
20. *Medical Council of India (2011),* Detailed available at http://www.mciindia.org/
21. *National Council for Teacher Education (2011),* Detailed available at http://www.ncte-india.org/
22. Narayan, J. (2006). *Reforming Higher education in India,* Detailed available at http://www.fdrindia.org/publications/Higher EducationIn India_PR.pdf
23. Nigavekar, A. (2004). Vision and Strategy for Higher Education in 21st Century, In Venkatasubramanian, K. (Ed), *"Issues in Higher Education",* Vol. 01, The ICDFAI University Press, Hyderabad., p. 23.
24. Patel, I. (2004). Higher Education and Economic Development, In Venkatasubramanian, K. (Ed), "*Issues in Higher Education*", Vol: 01, The ICDFAI University Press, Hyderabad, p. 46.
25. Pankajam, G. (2005), *Education and Development*, First edition, New Delhi: Gyan Publishing House.
26. Parekh, V. and Manjrekar, P. (2011). *Indian Higher Education Sector: Heading towards Transformation,* Detailed available at http://www.trikal.org/ictbm11/pdf/Globalization/D1336-done.pdf
27. *Pharmacy Council of India (2011),* Detailed available at http://www.pci.nic.in/GeneralInformation/AboutPCI/Introduction.aspx
28. Powar, P. (2002). *Indian Higher Education: A Conglomerate of Concepts, Facts and Practices*, First edition, New Delhi: Concept Publishing Company.
29. Rani, P. (2010). *Economic Reforms and Financing Higher Education in India*, Detailed available at http://ijeb.com/Issues/data/June04_6_erafheii.pdf
30. *Rehabilitation Council of India (2011),* Detailed available at http://en.wikipedia.org/wiki/Rehabilitation_Council_of_India
31. Sarkar, T. (2007). *Higher Educational reforms for enhancing youth employment opportunities in India,* Detailed available at http://www.cipe.org/programs/women/EssaysForWeb/Education_Sarkar.pdf

32. Shella, A. (2010), *External Quality Assurance in Indian Higher Education: Case study of the National Assessment and Accreditation Council (NAAC),* Detailed available at http://www.naac.gov.in/Publications/Best_Practice% 20in%20HIgher%20 Education.pdf
33. Singh, A. (2004). *The Weakest Link in Indian Education, In Venkatasubramanian*, K. (Ed), "Issues in Higher Education", Vol. 1, The ICFAI University Press, Hyderabad, p. 66.
34. Singh, A. (2004), *Fifty Years of Higher Education in India*, first education, New Delhi: Sage Publication, New Delhi.
35. Singh, J, and Kaur, T. (2010). *Future of Academic Libraries in India: Challenges and Opportunities,* Detailed available at http://crl.du.ac.in/ical09/papers/index_files/ical-9_252_741_1_PB.pdf
36. Swamy, V. (2006), *Reconstruction of Higher Education in India*, First edition, Hyderabad: The ICFAI University.
37. Tomasevski, K. (2004). *Manual of Rights-Based Education: Global Human Rights Requirements Made Simple,* Detailed available at http://unesdoc.unesco.org/images/0013/001351/135168e.pdf
38. Venkataiah, V. (2006). *Lifelong Education,* New Delhi: Anmol Publications Pvt. Ltd.
39. Veer, U. (2006). *Modern Problems of Education*, New Delhi: Anmol Publications Pvt. Ltd.
40. Vohra and Sen, A. (1989). *Status Education and Problems of Indian Women*, New Delhi: Akshat Publication, New Delhi.

# 14

# Information Communication Technology and Higher Education

***Md. Ataur Rahaman***

*"When learning is purposeful, creativity blossoms. When creativity blossoms, thinking emanates. When thinking emanates, knowledge is fully lit. When knowledge is lit, economy flourishes."*

**—A.P.J. Abdul Kalam**

## Introduction

Humans are the only living members of the Homo genus. They are mammals of the primate order originally from Africa, where they reached anatomical modernity about 200,000 years ago and began to exhibit full behavioural modernity around 50,000 years ago. Modern civilisation is characterised by the growing pace of change. The progress of a country depends upon the quality of its teachers and for this reason teaching is the noblest among all professions. The ideal of the teacher has unquestionably changed through the ages. The young generation is entering a world which is changing in all spheres: scientific and technological, political, economic, social and cultural. The use of information and communications technology (ICT) in education is a relatively new phenomenon. Information Technology (IT) in its broadest sense encompasses all aspects of computing technology. Since the introduction of the computer into education in the 1960s, its potential for primary and secondary education has been recognised by many – researchers, policymakers and practitioners. The role of ICT as a tool for development has attracted the sustained attention of the United Nations over recent years. The National Policy of Education 1986 is a significant landmark in the history of education of post independence India. Ministries of education and various educational organisations see the need for students to develop understandings and proficiencies in using ICT in appropriate ways to support learning and to develop appropriate technology knowledge, skills, and dispositions for the 21st century. Many countries are progressing towards the goals of Education for All, but struggle to achieve *'teacher quality for all'*, especially in rural or remote areas in developing countries.

## What is Teacher Education?

The term *'teacher education'* refers to the policies and procedures designed to equip teachers with the knowledge, attitudes, behaviours and skills they require to perform their tasks effectively in the school and classroom. Education of teachers not only facilitates improvement of school education by preparing competent, committed and professionally well qualified teachers who can meet the demand of the system, but also functions as a bridge between schooling and higher education. It has to meet twin demands: (a) challenges of the education system including higher education, and (b) the ever-changing demands of the social system. Teacher education is interdisciplinary. Major areas of inter-disciplinarily implicit in teacher education programmes include philosophy, psychology, sociology, anthropology, economics, history and culture.

## ICT and Teacher Education: Global Perspective

Importance of ICT is realised by both developed and developing countries. African countries also are using ICT for children development. A major boost to Zimbabwe's ICT infrastructure is the impending establishment of the East African Submarine Cable System (EASS), which is a submarine optical fibre system running along the east coast of Africa and which includes Zimbabwe. ICT is present throughout Namibia's ministries, schools and educational institutions. Zambia has a modest ICT infrastructure that is concentrated in urban centres. Reports from Portugal, Spain and Italy underline an increased interest in enhancing the use of ICT in schools. The Spanish plan Escuela 2.0 aims at transforming the way students learn. Many ICT- related initiatives have already been launched by the European Commission, as part of its strategic framework for European cooperation in education and training, under the New Digital Agenda for Europe. EU actions aim to harness ICT's to develop innovative education and training practices, improve access to all levels of education and training, and help develop advanced management systems. UNESCO defines informatics as the science dealing with the design, realisation, evaluation, use and maintenance of information processing systems, including hardware, software, organisational and human aspects, and the industrial, commercial, governmental and political implications of these. Many governments are using the introduction of ICT as a way of providing teachers with new skills and introducing new pedagogy into the classroom. In many countries the development of mainstream initial teacher education has been slowed down by inadequate ICT skills of teacher educators and the fact that few units providing teacher education have drafted a strategy for the educational uses of ICT.

**ICT and Teacher Education**

There are a variety of approaches to professional development of teachers in the context of use of ICTs in education. Professional development to incorporate ICTs into teaching and learning is an ongoing process and should not be thought of as one *'injection'* of training. Teachers need to update their knowledge and skills as the school curriculum and technologies change. Two aims of teacher training are fundamental: teacher education in ICTs; and teacher education through ICTs. Teacher education system is an important vehicle to improve the quality of education. Teacher preparations need to give more thinking into the different roles a teacher needs to meet the new challenges in the information society. 21st century is the century of Information and Communication Technology. Over the past couple of decades, many educators have come to accept the idea of the Internet as a participative medium for information. In the case of technology knowledge, it will be important that graduates have skills for the fluent use of a variety of ICT hardware and software and have the capability to learn more as the need arises and as technology continues to evolve. The field of education has been affected by ICTs, which have undoubtedly affected teaching, learning, and research.

ICT can help to broaden access to education and improve learning outcomes. Research has also shown that success in the use of ICT in education depends largely on the ability of teachers to integrate ICT into the teaching process. Rapid advances in human computer interaction have contributed new tools and technologies that provide new opportunities for teachers and learners. There are various factors that influence on the use of ICT in science education: the infrastructure for ICT in science education, the principal's views of ICT in the school and the external parameters affecting philosophy/practice. The aim of the Digital Education Revolution initiative is to contribute sustainable and meaningful change to teaching and learning in school. In general, the ICT Competency Standards for Teachers project aims to improve teachers' practice in all areas of their work, combining ICT skills with innovations in pedagogy, curriculum, and school organisation. The teacher education institutes were also interested in introducing an ICT track for their Bachelor of Education programme so as to train teachers who could teach ICT skills and use ICT in teaching in schools. Expositions, activities and competitions have been held to promote the use of IT in education. Tertiary institutions that want to be more productive and meet societal needs must be more sensitive and adaptive to changing educational needs. Traditional methods of collecting, storing, processing, and accessing information have undergone a massive transformation due to the growth of virtual libraries, digital libraries, online databases, and library and information networks. The Indian Institute of Science (IISc), Carnegie Mellon University (CMU), the International Institute of Information Technology, Hyderabad (IIITH), and many other academic, religious, and government organisations in India, a total of more than twenty "*Content Creation Centres,*" has become partners in the Digital Library of India

(DLI). Evidence from large studies and meta-analyses suggests that use of ICTs, particularly computer technologies, is correlated to positive academic outcomes, including higher test scores, better attitudes towards schools, and better test scores, better attitudes toward schools, and better understanding of abstract concepts. Keeping the needs of diverse learners, several civil society organisations in the country have developed teaching learning programmes that certainly are part of the initiative to make classrooms inclusive. The capability of using ICT in teaching is made up of by three main aspects. One is the skills in using traditional media, computer and web as base for ICT utilisation. Another, as the key part, is the capability of using ICT in teaching. The last one is the attitudes toward the utilization of ICT in teaching and it directly decides whether teachers utilise ICT in instruction. Evaluation system must cover these three aspects. Formative evaluation will help teachers greatly in shaping these three aspects. The use of ICT in education lends itself to more student-centered learning.

**Growth of ICT Education in India**

India's exponential growth in IT over the last two decades is well documented in the literature. The schools affiliated to the CBSE have been at the forefront of adopting the most modern innovations and practices to ensure there is a continuous enhancement in the overall quality of teaching and learning. As a first step in this direction, all CBSE affiliated schools are advised to setup at least one classroom in their schools equipped with technology to enable usage of digital instruction materials in the classroom. Teachers wishing to teach a topic with multimedia resources can take the class to this classroom. Proper advance scheduling may help teachers in their venture. The importance of teachers in determining the quality of education is emphasised and reflected in government policies and regulations in India. A central and high profile strand of education policy over the past decade has been the development of a technologically empowered teaching force so that ICT is *'embedded in teaching and learning'*. Furthermore, ICTs have a great potential for revolutionising accustomed methods of educational planning, management, monitoring, and evaluation. The influence of the Intel Teach Pre-Service Programme has spread across teacher education institutions (TEIs) in several major universities that have advanced from the initiation of computer based programmes to the integration of ICT into their programmes. The Government of India set up a commission to study all aspects of teacher preparation, including their service conditions. In the late 1990s, deregulation of the telecommunication industry began a dramatic improvement in access to basic telephony and Internet services for the general population.

**Significant of ICT in Teacher Education**

Computer literacy is one of the most important skills a person can have in today's competitive environment. The success of ICT for education depends very much on changing the practice of the teacher education institutions to include issues concerning the link between student-centered instruction, ICT integration, and the

NNC. Information and communication technologies have been basic to the USP's teaching through distance and flexible education since its early years. Despite the apparent benefits of the use of ICT for educational purpose, studies showed that in many cases, the learning potential of ICT is deprived as many teachers are still not fully ICT literate and do not use it in their teaching. The integration of ICT in teaching and learning is not a method; rather it is a medium in which a variety of methods, approaches and pedagogical philosophies may be implemented. ICT technologies are crucial in helping teachers provide innovative teaching and learning opportunities but they also play a significant role in delivering effective school management.

Furthermore, the use of ICTs in education also shifts the learning approaches. There is a common belief that the use of ICTs in education contributes to a more constructivist learning and an increase in activity and greater responsibility of students. This limits the role of the teacher to supporting, advising, and coaching students rather than merely transmitting knowledge. ICTs are a nice mode to mobilise teachers' creativeness and make their didactic practice more flexible and ingenious. ICTs can be used to extend access to educational delivery models, to support the ongoing professional development of teachers, and to facilitate education-related data collection and processing efforts in ways previously not possible. ICT is being used in distance education to replace earlier correspondence school and educational television. The new distance education is usually Web-based.

## Concluding Observations

In India various statutory bodies under ministry of human resource are working for maintaining quality in higher education. High education in India is control by the Ministry of Human Resource. There are various statutory bodies like UGC, NCTE, BCI, AICTE, PCI, MCI, ICAR, CCH, COA, CCIM, RCI, INC, DCI, DEC, etc., are working for maintain quality in higher education. But it has been found that there are lacks of transparency in the working in such bodies. Central and State governments are spending large amount of money on it. Numbers of government, Deemed and private universities are increasing continuously. After 64 years of independence it has been found that Government of India has taken steps for rearranging structure of higher education. Achieving India's demographic dividend will depend on our ability to provide a simple regulatory framework in education that eliminates opportunities for rent seeking and low quality. The Indian government has signed a significant and growing number of bilateral treaties with other countries promoting bilateral cooperation in S and T.

## References

1. Agnes, C., and Wallace, C. (2010). *An investigation of factors affecting the use of ICT for curriculum delivery in the Western Cape, South Africa*, Retrieved from http://is2.lse.ac.uk/asp/aspecis/20100032.pdf

2. Ahuja, A. (2004). *Teacher education*, First edition, New Delhi: Mittal Publications.
3. Aggarwal, P. (2010). *Teacher Education*, First edition, New Delhi: Saurabh Publishing House.
4. Aggarwal, J. (2004). *Teacher and education in a developing society*, fourth edition, New Delhi: Vikas Publishing House Pvt Ltd.
5. Ang'ondi, E. (2000), *National policy for using ICT to support teaching and learning in primary and secondary schools in East Africa*, Hennessy, S., and Onguko, B. (Eds), Developing use of ICT to enhance teaching and learning in East African schools: a review of the literature, Retrieved from http://www.educ.cam.ac.uk/centres/cce/publications/CCE_Report1_LitRevJune0210.pdf
6. Albion, P. (2010). *Web 2.0 in Teacher Education: Two Imperatives for Action*, Retrievefromhttp://eprints.usq.edu.au/4553/1/Albion_Web_2.0_in_teacher_education.pdf
7. Albion, P., Amieson-Proctor, R., and Finger, G. etal., (2011). *Age-related differences in ICT access and confidence among pre-service teachers,* Retrieved from http://www.ascilite.org.au/conferences/hobart11/downloads/papers/Albion-full.pdf
8. Albion, P., and Redmond, P. (2010). *Teaching by example? Integrating ICT in Teacher Education*, Retrieved from http://eprints.usq.edu.au/4471/1/Albion_Redmond_ACEC08.pdf
9. Amar, R., Betts, M., Coetzee, G., and Sexton, M. etal., (2002). *Information technology for construction: Recent works and future dimensions*, Retrieved from http://www.utexas.edu/research/ctr/symposium/ITapplications.pdf
10. Amin, S. (2010). *An Effective use of ICT for Education and Learning by Drawing on Worldwide Knowledge, Research, and Experience: ICT as a Change Agent for Education*, Retrieved from http://www.nyu.edu/classes/keefer/waoe/amins.pdf
11. Anderson, J. (2010). *ICT transforming education: A regional guide,* Retrieved from http://unesdoc.unesco.org/images/0018/001892/189216e.pdf
12. Athreya, A. (2004). *A textbook of teacher education*, First edition, New Delhi: Dominant Publishers and Distributors.
13. Auerswald, M., and Magambo, J. (2010). *Fostering ICT use in teacher education in Africa*, Retrieved from http://www.digital.library.strathmore.edu/xmlui/bitstream/handle/123456789/923/A% 20 Framework % 20 for % 20 evaluating % 20 ICT %20 use% 20 in % 20 teacher % 20 education. pdf ? sequence=1
14. Balsara, M. (2004). *Administration and reorganisation of teacher education,* First edition, New Delhi: Kanishka Publishers.
15. Balasundaram, P. (2005). *The Journey towards inclusive education in India*, Retrieved from http://www.gtid.net/global trend/4 THE JOURNEY TOWARDS INCLUSIV EEDUCA INDIA.pdf

16. Bose, S. (2010). *Redefining Instructional Strategy in Teacher Education in the Perspective of Knowledge Society,* Retrieved from http://www.intlalliance.org/fileadmin/userupload/documents/Transforming Teacher Education Report.pdf
17. Brief paper (2009). *Green ICT: Managing sustainable ICT in education and research,* Retrieved from http://www.hea.ie/files/files/file/eInfraNet/rob bristow e-Infranet Oct 2010.pdf
18. Brunvand, S. (2010). Best Practices for Producing Video Content for Teacher Education, *Contemporary Issues in Technology and Teacher Education*, 10(2), Retrieved from http://www.citejournal.org/articles/v8i2editorial1.pdf
19. Bull, G., Thompson, A., Searson, M., Garofalo, J., Park, J., Young, C., and Lee, J (2008). *Connecting informal and formal learning: Experiences in the age of participatory media.* Contemporary Issues in Technology and Teacher Education, 8(2), Retrieved from http://www.citejournal.org/vol8/iss2/editorial/article1.cfm
20. Carnoy, M. (2005). *ICT in Education: Possibilities and Challenges*, Retrieved from http://www.uoc.edu/index.php
21. Chakrabarti, M. (2004). *Teacher education: Modern tends*, Second edition, New Delhi: Kanishka Publishers.
22. Community and Information (2008), ICT *in teacher education: case studies from the* Asia-Pacific region, Retrieved from http://www.unesco.org/new/en/communication-and-information/resources/publications-and-communication-materials/publications/full-list/ict-in-teacher-education-case-studies-from-the-asia-pacific-region/
23. Digital Library (2012), *Maharashtra University of Health Sciences,* Nashik, Retrieved from http://www.muhsnashik.com/digital library/dl main.asp
24. Dutta, P. (2011). *Universal Education through ICT*, Retrieved from http://mhrd.gov.in/sites/uploadfiles/mhrd/files/Agenda Background CSES-13042012.pdf
25. Dutta, A., and Mohakud, L. (2011). Teacher and His Professional Competence, *BARNOLIPI - An Interdisciplinary Journal,* Volume - I, Issue – IV, Retrieved from http://www.reflectionedu.com/attachments/File/Barnolipi/12 11 Teacher .pdf
26. *Education and manpower Bureau (2004)*, Retrieved from http://www.docsfiles.com/pdf/1/educational-resources-of-education-and-manpower-bureau.html
27. Eurydice (2011). *Key Data on Learning and Innovation through ICT at School in Europe,* Retrieved from http://eacea.ec.europa.eu/education/eurydice/documents/key data series/129EN.pdf
28. *European Commission Education and Training (2012),* Retrieved from http://ec.europa.eu/education/lifelong-learning-programme/doc96_en.htm
29. Fodje, M. (2010). *The impact of technology to education in the developing countries,* Retrieved from http://www.wcte.org/T99-Library/T99-194.PDF
30. Goktas, Y., Yildirim, S., and Yildirim., Z. at.el. (2009). *Main Barriers and Possible Enablers of ICTs Integration into Pre-service Teacher Education Programs. Educational*

*Technology and Society*, 12 (1), Retrieved from http://www.ifets.info/journals/121/15.pdf

31. *GSAT-3 (2012),* Retrieved from http://en.wikipedia.org/wiki/GSAT-3
32. Haydn, T. (2010). *Teacher education and ICT: some points for consideration from the UK*, Retrieved from http://www.educ.cam.ac.uk/centres/cce/publications/CCE Report1 LitRevJune0210.pdf
33. Harrison, D. (2010), *Teacher factors influencing classroom ICT use,* Retrieved from http://www.cambridgetoafrica.org/resources/Hennessy%20 etal FINAL.pdf
34. Hooker, M., Mwiyeria, E., and Verma, A. et al.,, (2011). *ICT Competency Framework for Teachers (ICT-CFT) Contextualisation and Piloting in Nigeria and Tansania,* Retrieved from http://www.gesci.org/assets/files/Synthesis_Report_ICTCEF_Draft_Final_191011.pdf
35. *Human (2012),* Retrieved from http://en.wikipedia.org/wiki/Human
36. *ICT for teacher education (2009),* Retrieved from http://www.teachersn.com/general/ict-for-teacher-education.html
37. *ICT in School Education in India (2011),* Retrieved from http://www.icbse.com/2010/ict-schools-education-india
38. ICT in education (2011), *ICTs as levers for educational systems change*, Retrieved from http://www.unescobkk.org/education/ict/ict-in-education-projects/other-projects/unite/icts-as-levers-for-educational-systems-change/
39. ICT in education (2012). *The UNESCO ICT Competency Framework for Teachers*, Retrieved from http://unesdoc.unesco.org/images/0021/002134/213475e.pdf
40. *Information and Communications Technology in Education (2010),* Retrieved from http://www.actionresearch.net/living/farren/ch4.pdf
41. Sukanta Sarkar (2012), Information and communication technology and teacher education: An introduction, In *Excellence in Education: Journal of education and humanities*, Volume 01, Number 01, December 2012, pp. 103-114.
42. *Inspiring video on education (2012).* Retrieved from http://www.srisathyasaividyavahini.org/
43. Isaacs, S. (2007). *ICT in education in Zimbabwe*, Retrieved from http://ub-bw.academia.edu/CharlesMusarurwa/Papers/1798270/Teaching with and learning through ICTs in Zimbabwes Teacher Education Colleges.
44. Isaacs, S. (2007). *ICT in education in Zambia,* Retrieved from http://www.irrodl.org/index.php/irrodl/article/view/705/1319.
45. Kanvaria, V. (2012). Googling the group: Teacher education through ICT, *American Academic and Scholarly Research Journal*, Retrieved from http://aasrc.org/aasrj/index.php/aasrj/article/view/256
46. Jha, P (2005). *Teacher education: global context and framework*, First edition, New Delhi: Vista International Publishing House.
47. Jung, I. (2005). ICT-Pedagogy Integration in Teacher Training: Application Cases Worldwide, *Educational Technology and Society*, 8(2), Retrieved from http://www.ifets.info/journals/82/8.pdf

48. Kargiban, Z., and Siraj, S. (2009). The Utilization and Integrating of ICT in Chemistry Teaching in Iranian High Schools, *World Applied Sciences Journal* 6 (11), Retrieved from http://idosi.org/wasj/wasj6%2811%29/2.pdf
49. Koehler, M. J., and Mishra, P. (2009). What is technological pedagogical content knowledge? *Contemporary Issues in Technology and Teacher Education*, 9(1), Retrieved from http://learnonline.canberra.edu.au/pluginfile.php/491591/mod page/content/1/TPACK UC/pdf/tpack4 preservice2.pdf
50. Kumar, K. (2010). *Convergence of ICT and Education,* Retrieved from http://www.unapcict.org/ecohub/resources/convergence-of-ict-and-education
51. Kumar, S., Ahmed, R., Wadia, S., and Alam, M. et al., (2010). *Report on Inclusive Classroom, Social Inclusion/Exclusion and Diversity: Perspectives, Policies and Practices,* Retrieved from http://www.unicef.org/india/13. National Report on Inclusive Classroom.pdf
52. Lock, J. (2007). Immigration and integration: ICT in preservice teacher education. *Contemporary Issues in Technology and Teacher Education*, 7(1), Retrieved from http://editlib.org/p/21755/
53. Lagoze, C., Kraff, B., Payette, S., and Jesuroga, S. et al., (2005). *What Is a Digital Library Anymore, Anyway?,* Retrieved from http://www.dlib.org/dlib/november05/lagoze/11lagoze.html
54. Lau, B., and Sim, C. (2008). Exploring the extent of ICT adoption among secondary school teachers in Malaysia, *International Journal of Computing and ICT Research*, Vol. 2, No. 2, Retrieved from http://cit.mak.ac.ug/iccir/downloads/ICCIR 10/KIPTALAM %20 %20G. %20K %20 Rodrigues %20 A.J 10.pdf
55. Lunt, B., Ekstrom, J., Gorka, S., Hislop, G., Kamali, R., Lawson, E., LeBlanc, R., Miller, J., and Reichgelt, H. etal., (2008). *Curriculum Guidelines for Undergraduate Degree Programs in Information Technology,* Retrieved from http://www.acm.org/education/curricula/IT2008%20Curriculum.pdf
55. Maheshwari, A. (2010). ICT: A Boon for Quality Enhancement in Teacher Education, *Educational Quest- An International Journal of Education and Applied Social Sciences,* Volume : 1, Issue : 1, Retrieved from http://www.indianjournals.com/ijor.aspx?target=ijor :eq&volume=1&issue=1&article=002
56. Martin, S. (2010). *Special Education, Technology, and Teacher Education,* Retrieved from http://www.indianjournals.com/ijor.aspx?target=ijor:eq&volume=1&issue=1&article=002
57. Mehta, D., and Kasnia, S., etal., (2011). *A Scenario on the role of ICT in Governance, and Education System,* Retrieved from http://www.ijcem.org/papers72011/72011_16.pdf
58. Meriläinen, M., Johnson, P., and Valli., R. et al., (2010). *Using modern information technology during preservice teacher education practicum period to make training possible in authentic environment,* Retrieved from http://www.aabri.com/manuscripts/09216.pdf

59. Mikre, F. (2011). *The Roles of Information Communication Technologies in Education Review Article with Emphasis to the Computer and Internet,* Retrieved from http://iite.unesco.org/pics/publications/en/files/3214600.pdf

60. Meleisea, E.(2007). *ICT in Teacher Education: Case Studies from the Asia-Pacific Region,* Retrieved from http://unesdoc.unesco.org/images/0015/001567/156757e.pdf

61. Meisalo, V., Lavonen, J., Sormunen, K., and Vesisenaho, Mikko. etal., (2010). *ICT in initial teacher training,* Retrieved from http://www.minedu.fi/export/sites/default/OPM/Julkaisut/2010/liitteet/okm25.pdf?lang=en

62. *National/EU Policy (2012),* Retrieved from http://insight.eun.org/ww/en/pub/insight/policy/policies/2009 country reports.htm

63. Narayan, K., and Mooi, J. (2010). Solutions to Teacher Absenteeism in Rural Government Primary Schools in India: A Comparison of Management Approaches, *The Open Education Journal,* Retrieved from http://repub.eur.nl/res/pub/20502/

64. Navaneedhan, C. (2010). *Reflective teaching pedagogy as innovative approach in teacher education through open and distance learning,* Retrieved from http://wikieducator.org/images/6/6a/C.girija Navaneedhan.pdf

65. Naik, J. (2008). *The role of government of Indian education,* Retrieved from http://www.vidyaonline.org/dl/JPNaik 01.pdf

66. National Council of Teacher Education (2009), *National Curriculum Framework for Teacher Education,* Retrieved from http://www.ncte-india.org/MED.pdf

67. New Europe (June 3, 2012). *Opening up education for new technologies-changing teaching and learning through ICT,* Retrieved from http://www.neurope.eu/blog/opening-education-new-technologies-changing-teaching-and-learning-through-ict

68. Ng, W., Miao, F., and Lee, M. et al., (2010). *Capacity-building for ICT integration in education,* Retrieved from http://www.digital-review.org/uploads/files/pdf/2009-2010/capacity building.pdf

69. Ololube, N., Ubogu, A., and Ossai, A. et al., (2011). *ICT and distance education in Nigeria: A review of literature and accounts,* Retrieved from http://www.numerons.in/files/documents/9ICT-and-Distance-Education.pdf

70. Padmamma, S. (2008). *Shifting of LIS Education towards Information and Communication Technology in Universities of Karnataka State: A Study,* Retrieved from http://shodhganga.inflibnet.ac.in/dxml/bitstream/handle/1944/1238/6.pdf?

71. Pandey, S (2011). *Professionalisation of teacher education in India :A critique of Teacher Education Curriculum reforms and its effectiveness,* Retrieved from http://www.britishcouncil.org/cpdbiblio.pdf

72. Panda, P. (2010). *Responsiveness of Teacher Education Curriculum Towards Human Rights Education in India,* Retrieved from http://www.mu.ac.in/myweb test/ma%20edu/Teacher%20Education%20-%20IV.pdf

73. Policy framework (2008). *ICT competency standards for teachers, UNESCO.,* Retrieved from http://unesdoc.unesco.org/images/0015/001562/156210e.pdf

74. Olele, C., and Williams, C. (2012). *Addressing challenges of Information and communication technology (ICTs) in teacher education –A case for developing countries*, Retrieved from http://www.savap.org.pk/journals/ARInt./Vol.2%282%29/2012%282.2-39%29.pdf
75. Qiau, A., and Wang, N. (2009). An Investigation of Teachers' Needs on Using ICT in Teaching and Learning, *International Conference on Computer Engineering and Applications*, IPCSIT Vol. 2, Retrieved from http://www.scribd.com/doc/71890428/Volume-1-Issue-5
76. Rani, P., and Shukla, S. (2012). *Role of ICT in teacher education, IJRIM*, Volume 2, Issue 5, Retrieved from http://www.mairec.org/IJRIM/May2012/1.pdf
77. Park, J. C., and Slykhuis, D. A. (2006). *Guest Editorial: Technology proficiencies in science teacher education. Contemporary Issues in Technology and Teacher Education*, 6(2), Retrieved from http://mgicollaboration.pbworks.com/w/file/fetch/46330278/Technology%20 in %20 the %20 Middle %20 Grades %20 Classroom.Bishop %26 Downes.1-1-11.pdf
78. Pelgrum, W. (2001), *Obstacles to the integration of ICT in education: results from a worldwide educational assessment*, Retrieved from http://users.ntua.gr/vvesk/ictedu/article5 pelgrum.pdf
79. Trkman, P., and Peter Baloh, P. (2003). *Use of a Model for Information Technology Education, Journal of Information Technology Education,* Retrieved from http://jite.org/documents/Vol5/JiteContentsVol5.pdf
80. Rama, K., and Lakshmi, T. (2008). *Infusing dynamism in teacher education through ICT integration learning from India*, Retrieved from http://jite.org/documents/Vol5/JiteContentsVol5.pdf
81. Rao, K., and Singh, M. (2010). *150 years of University Education in India : Challenges Ahead*, Retrieved from http://cache-www.intel.com/cd/00/00/42/12/421259 421259.pdf
82. Raj, L. (2009). Transformation of teacher to teacher leader: Indian scenario, *Indian Journal of Science and Technology*, Vol. 2 No. 7, Retrieved from http://www.indjst.org/archive/vol. 2.issue.7-8/jul09lavanraj.pdf
83. Rizza, C. (2011). *ICT and Initial Teacher Education,* Retrieved from http://search.oecd.org/officialdocuments/displaydocumentpdf/?cote=EDU/WKP%282011%291&docLanguage=En
84. Robinson, B. (2008). *Using distance education and ICT to improve access, equity and the quality in rural teachers' professional development in western China*, Retrieved from http://www.irrodl.org/index.php/irrodl/article/view/486/1015
85. Rudd, P. (2000). *School Improvement through ICT: Limitations and Possibilities*, Retrieved from http://www.leeds.ac.uk/educol/documents/00001768.htm
86. Sa'ar, J., Luan, W., and Roslan, S. etal., (2005). Attitudes and Perceived Information Technology Competency among Teachers, *Malaysian Online Journal of Instructional*

*Technology*, Retrieved from http://pdf.aminer.org/000/287/648/it in education what is really needed of teachers it.pdf

87. Sagar, K. (2005). *ITCs and teacher training*, First edition, New Delhi: Authorspress.
88. Salehi, H., and Salehi, Z. (2012). Challenges for Using ICT in Education: Teachers' Insights, *International Journal of e-Education, e-Business,* e-Management and e-Learning, Vol. 2, No. 1, Retrieved from http://www.ijeeee.org/Papers/078-Z00061F10037.pdf
89. Sharma, M. (2012), *CTEs and IASEs : A journey of two decades*, Voices of Teachers and Teacher Educators, Retrieved from http://www.teindia.nic.in/Files/Newsletters/VTTE.pdf
90 Siddiqui, M. (2007). *Distance education: Theory and research*, First edition, New Delhi: A.P.H. Publishing Corporation.
91 Singh, Y., and Nath, R. (2005). *Teacher education,* First edition, New Delhi: A.P.H. Publishing Corporation.
92 Sharma, A. (2010). *ICT in Teacher Education: the USP Experience*, Retrieved from http://sta.uwi.edu/conferences/09/salises/documents/A%20Sharma.pdf
93 Shastry, G. (2007). *Speaking English in a Globalising World: Information Technology and Education in India*, Retrieved from http://www.iza.org/conference files/worldb2007/shastry g3397.pdf
94 Sonone, A., and Pathak,R. (2011). *Perspectives on ICT education in India*, Retrieved from http://www.scribd.com/doc/19992366/Perspectives-on-Ict-Education-in-India
95 Subramanian, R. (2010). *India and Information Technology A Historical and Critical Perspective*, Retrieved from http://enterqdesigns.com/TeamBHUMN432/docs/23653745.pdf
96 Tamilenthi, S. and Mohanasundaram, K. (2011). An analysis of perception of geography teachers with special reference to professional development, *World Journal of Science and Technology*, 1(5), Retrieved from www.worldjournalofscience.com
97. Trucano, M. (2006). *Using ICT for Teacher Professional Development in Namibia*, Retrieved from http://www.infodev.org/en/Project.4.html
98. UNESCO (1990). *Innovations and initiatives in teacher education in Asia and the Pacific region,* Volume: 1: Comparative overview of fifteen countries, Retrieved from http://www.unesco.org/education/pdf/412_35b.pdf
99. UNESCO (2002). *Information and communication technology in education: A curriculum for schools and programme of teacher development,* Retrieved from http://unesdoc.unesco.org/images/0012/001295/129538e.pdf
100. UNESCO (2005). *Information and communications technologies in school: A handbook for the teachers,* Retrieved from http://unesdoc.unesco.org/images/0013/001390/139028e.pdf
101. UNESCO (2005). *ICTs for Secondary Education. Specialized training course*, Retrieved from http://iite.unesco.org/pics/publications/en/files/3214640.pdf

102. UNESCO (2009). *Guide to measuring Information and Communication Technologies (ICT) in education*, Retrieved from http://www.uis.unesco.org/Library/Documents/ICT Guide EN v19 reprintwc.pdf

103. UNESCO (2011). *Transforming education: The power of ICT politics*, Retrieved from http://unesdoc.unesco.org/images/0021/002118/211842e.pdf

104. UNESCO (2011). *ICT for higher education: Case studies from Asia and Pacific*, Retrieved from http://www.european-agency.org/publications/ereports/ICTs-in-Education-for-People-With-Disabilities/ICTs-in-Education-for-people-with-disabilities.pdf

105. UNDP (2012). *Using distance education and ICT to improve teacher quality in poor areas of Western China*, Retrieved from http://www.undp.org.cn/modules.php?op=modload & name=News & file=article & catid=8 & topic =31 & sid=4131 & mode=thread & order=0& thold=0

106. Varatharajan, N. and Chandrashekara, M. (2007). *Digital Library Initiatives at Higher Education and Research Institutions in India,* Retrieved from http://www.webpages.uidaho.edu/~mbolin/vara-chandra.pdf

107. Venkataish, S. (2006). *Teacher education,* first edition, New Delhi: Anmol Publications Pvt. Ltd.

108. Voogt, J., and Knezek, G. (2008). *International Handbook of Information Technology in Primary and Secondary Education,* Retrieved from http://www.springer.com/education+%26+language/learning+%26+instruction/book/978-0-387-73314-2

109. Wang, T. (2008). *Using ICT to enhance academic learning: Pedagogy and practice, Educational Research and Review* Vol. 3 (4), Available online at http://www.academicjournals.org/ERR

110. Wamakote, L (2010). *National government investment in ICT initiatives in primary and secondary schools in East Africa,* Hennessy, S., and Onguko, B., Developing use of ICT to enhance teaching and learning in East African schools: a review of the literature, Retrieved from http://www.educ.cam.ac.uk/centres/cce/publications/CCE Report1 LitRevJune0210.pdf

111. Watson, D. (2006). *Understanding the relationship between ICT and education means exploring innovation and change*, Retrieved from http://users.ntua.gr/vvesk/ictedu/article7 watson.pdf

112. Wenbin, H., Hongwei., M., and Qiong. W. etal., (2006). *PRC: Improving Basic Education in Underdeveloped Areas through ICT,* Retrieved from http://www2.adb.org/Documents/Reports/Consultant/36518-PRC/36518-PRC-TACR.pdf

113. White, G. (2008). *ICT Trends in Education,* Retrieved from http://research.acer.edu.au/cgi/view content.cgi? article=1001 & context=digital earning

114. Women 2000 and beyond. (2005), *Gender inequality and empowerment of women through ICT*, Retrieved from http://www.un.org/womenwatch/daw/public/w2000-09.05-ict-e.pdf

115. World Education Report (1998), *Teacher and teaching in a developing world*, Retrieved from http://www.unesco.org/ education/ information/ wer/ PDFeng/ wholewer98.PDF

116. Yassin, S., Rahman., S., and Yamat, H. et al., (2010). *Interdisciplinary Integration Through Problem-Based Learning with ICT in Pre Service Teacher-Education*, Retrieved from http://www.cluteinstitute.com/proceedings/2010_Dublin_ETLC_Articles/Article%20548.pdf

117. Youssef, A., and Dahmani, M. (2008). *The Impact of ICT on Student Performance in Higher Education: Direct Effects, Indirect Effects and Organisational Change,* Retrieved from http://pf-mh.uvt.rnu.tn/45/1/BenYoussef.pdf

# PART IV – DIGITAL LIBRARY

# 15

# Digital Library: A New Invention in Research and Study

***Farzana Alim***

*"There is no school equal to a decent home and no teacher equal to a virtuous parent."*

**—Mahatma Gandhi**

## Introduction

Libraries are the lighthouses of information dissemination. It is an important component of any educational institution and hub of learning activities where students, researchers, and teachers can explore the vast amount of information resources. Libraries have been in existence since time immemorial. One of the earliest libraries, the Royal Library of Alexandria, dates back to third century BC. According to Butler, although libraries existed long back, librarianship as a profession evolved very slowly and in three phases. Innovation and development of Information and Communication Technologies (ICTs) and different library software and its application in the field of Library and Information Science (LIS) create changes in entire library management system. Digital Libraries are being created today for diverse communities and in different fields, e.g., education, science, culture, development, health, governance and so on. With the availability of several free digital Library software packages at the recent time, the creation and sharing of information through the digital library collections has become an attractive and feasible proposition for library and information professionals around the world. In the past several years, researchers in information science, computer science and information systems have claimed that knowledge workers will work in new ways due to greater access to digital library technologies. The characteristics of today's Digital Libraries are a reflection of characteristics of pre-digital artifacts. Learning environments are changing drastically especially since the advent of internet about two decades back. A multi-disciplinary activity like *'Digital Library'* requires support from all stakeholders namely, technology developers, archivists, librarians, curators, collection managers, educationists, scholars, students and government agencies.

**What is Digital Library?**

Digital library is a global virtual library is a library where information can be stored in electronic format containing texts, images, sound, video, maps, scientific and business data, as well as hypermedia combination of this element. There will be vast population of user scattered around the globe, who are able to access, easily and conveniently. Digital libraries are on-line collections of heterogeneous information which are usually maintained by some digital librarian. It is nothing more than a blend of computer and communication technology to deliver the contents of a library to end users surpassing the boundaries of space and time. The term *"digital library"* may mean different things to different scholars and groups. Digital libraries can be grouped in the following ways: (i) Digital libraries developed in USA as part of DLI1 and DLI2 (Digital library initiatives), (ii) Digital libraries developed in the course of eLib (electronic libraries) Programme in UK, (iii) Digital libraries built by individual institutions, (iv) Digital libraries that are part of National Libraries, and (v) Digital libraries that are part of universities, or by period, or by country of their origin. A related term is *"Digital library"* is *"virtual library"*.

Classical libraries form the starting point: there information is carried in the form of classical hard copy documents and information and communication technology is hardly used. Many classical libraries have evolved to hybrid libraries. These are mainly distributed on optical disks like CD-ROM and more recently on DVD, or online through the Internet and the WWW.

**Digital Library: Global Perspectives**

Digital libraries are an essential part of the information infrastructure of the 21st century. It have received wide attention in the recent years allowing access to digital information from anywhere across the world. They have become widely accepted and even preferred information sources in areas of education, science and others. The rapid growth of Internet and the increasing interest in development of digital library related technologies and collections helped accelerate the digitisation of printed documents in the past few years. The Greenstone Digital Library Software (GSDL) is a top of the line and internationally renowned Open Source Software system for developing digital libraries, promoted by the New Zealand Digital Library project research group at the University of Waikato, headed by Dr. Ian H. Witten, and is sponsored by the UNESCO. EPrints is free software developed by the University of Southampton, England. ePrints@IISc repository collects preserves and disseminates in digital format the research output created by the IISc research community. The early digital library projects and the Digital library initiatives generated interest in the area and several projects were initiated in different countries

**Table 15.1: Typical Virtual and Traditional Libraries Compared.**

| *Sl. No* | *Library Services* | *Traditional Library* | *Electronic Library* |
|---|---|---|---|
| 1 | Opening Hours | Limited | Round-the-clock, all-the-year round |
| 2 | Student | Not possible | Possible |
| 3 | Services to non-traditional students | Grossly limited | Online delivery ents students |
| 4 | Access to resources | Limited shelf to search in physical locations | Instant/simultaneous and electronic |
| 5 | Search engines | Manual and tedious | Electronic, easy and extensive |
| 6 | Time factor | Does not save not time, in fact waste time | Significant saving, no risk or travel time required |
| 7 | Seating space and self shelf space | No savings | No seating space required |
| 8 | Manpower requirements | High | Low |
| 9 | Multiple access | Not flexible | Easy and cheap |
| 10 | Resource sharing | Inconvenient, slow turn around time | Convenient, fast fast turn - around time |
| 11 | Migration | Limited | Use the Internet to access other her libraries materials |

*Source*: *L.A. Ogunsola and T.O. Okusaga (2006). Developing Countries and the Need for Virtual Libraries: Problems and Prospects, J. Soc. Sci., 13(3), p. 224.*

of the world. In the U.S. under the digital library initiatives importance was given to research leading to several breakthroughs in digital library architectures, models and tools. In Europe there have been evolved projects at the European level, national level and local levels. In UK, the noteworthy efforts in Digital libraries are the ELINOR and the eLib projects. The Canadian National Library hosts the Canadian Inventory of Digital Initiatives provides descriptions of Canadian information resources created for the Web, including general digital collections, resources centered around a particular theme, and reference sources and databases. In Australia, Australian libraries together with commercial and research organisations are supporting a diverse set of Digital Library projects that take on many of technical and related issues. In Asia the International conference of Asian Digital Libraries is hosted every year by an Asian nation and these provide a forum to publish and contemplate on issues regarding research and developments in the area of digital libraries.

**Digital Library in India**

Technology has impacted libraries significantly, whether it is decreased door counts or increased use of virtual resources and especially academic libraries have faced a great deal of change in recent years. Digital Libraries (DL) are now emerging as a crucial component of global information infrastructure, adopting the latest information and communication technology. They are networked collections of digital texts, documents, images, sounds, data, software, and many more that are the core of today's Internet and tomorrow's universally accessible digital repositories of all human knowledge. Early research on digital libraries focused on infrastructure. Digital technology can make the works of man or needed information accessible to all whether they live in a village or in an urban area. The father of Indian librarianship, Dr. S. R. Ranganathan, in the past centuries has recognised the great potential of public libraries to improve the quality of life and provide opportunity the citizenry. Similarly digital libraries, widely available and accessible will improve the global society in ways beyond measurement. Government of India has set up NICNET which is the largest government owned information network. NIC is providing network backbone and e-governance to Central Government, State Government, UT Administrations, Districts and other Government bodies. Digital Library of India, part of the online services of the Indian Institute of Science, Bangalore and partner in the Million Book Project, provides free access to many books in English and Indian languages. The Indian Institute of Science (IISc), Carnegie Mellon University (CMU), the International Institute of Information Technology, Hyderabad (IIITH) and many other academic, religious and government organisations, totaling about 21 *"Content Creation Centres"*, have become partners in the Digital Library of India (DLI) initiative for the digitisation preservation of Indian heritage present in the form of books, manuscripts, art and music. One of the goals of the Digital Library of India is to provide support for full text indexing and searching based on OCR (optical character recognition) technologies where available. The availability of online search allows users to locate relevant information quickly and reliably and possibly in a language independent way, thus enhancing student's success in their research endeavours. The Digital Library of India (DLI) is expected to foster creativity and free access to all human knowledge.

The UGC-Infonet Digital Library Consortium was formally launched on the concluding day of UGC's Golden Jubilee celebrations by his Excellency the President of India, Dr A P J Abdul Kalam at Vigyan Bhawan on 28th December 2003 by dedicating a bouquet of e-journals to the academic community in universities. Under the consortium, more than 5,000 full-text scholarly electronic journals from 23 publishers across the globe can be accessed. The Consortium provides current as well as archival access to core and peer-reviewed journals in different disciplines. The programme has been implemented in different phases. So far 157 universities out of 171 Indian universities, which come under the purview of UGC, have been provided access to these journals and will gradually be extended to affiliated colleges as well. The resources being subscribed by the Consortium covers subject areas such as arts, humanities, social sciences, physical and chemical sciences, life sciences, computer sciences, mathematics and statistics, etc. The programme is funded by the UGC for universities under its purview and monitored by the INFLIBNET (Information and Library Network) Centre, Ahmadabad.

The *"Indian National Digital Library in Engineering Sciences and Technology (INDEST) Consortium"* was set-up by the Ministry of Human Resource Development (MHRD) on the recommendation of an Expert Group appointed by the Ministry under the chairmanship of Prof N. Balakrishnan, IISc. In 1986, National Informatics Centre (NIC) and Indian Council of Medical Research (ICMR) jointly set up a centre called ICMR-NIC Centre for Biomedical Information. This Centre was recognised as the 17th International MEDLARS Centre in 1990 and now is well known as Indian Medlars Centre (IMC). National Informatics Centre (NIC) has been a pioneer in communicating medical research information through the use of Information Technology. Another major activity of INFLIBNET is the preparation of the Indian Catalog of University Libraries in India (INDCAT), an online library catalogue of books, theses and journals available in major university libraries in India which provides bibliographic description, location of the material in all subjects available in more than 113 university libraries. INDCAT has over 10 million bibliographic records. In particular, DELNET has 752 member libraries including 742 from India and 10 from outside which are engaged in compiling union catalogs, creating various databases of experts, providing training to library staff, ILL, online facilities, reference service, assistance in retrospective conversion, etc.

In recent years, the library and information services sector has undergone major changes in terms of collection, organisation and services. Today's libraries are dynamic information systems which have the power to reach out to its users without the restrictions of geographical boundaries as never before. Today, libraries across the globe are fast moving to the *'digital'* mode. However, the development of digital libraries requires huge investment in terms of money, manpower, technology, etc. Mobile technology is one of the technological advancement, which is being seen as supplement to computers. While being connected with the people, this can be used to send messages and browse Internet. In 2007 Indian government has taken various initiatives to increase PCs and Internet penetration all over the country. The low cost and multimedia features have lead to tremendous growth (48 per cent) of PCs ownership across India. According to Internet Governance Forum, India had 81 million Internet users in 2008. India ranks fourth in the world in terms of Internet users. Broadband penetration is estimated to be at three per cent in India; the country added only 750,000 broadband connections between October 2006 and September 2007.

In the early days of digital library development, when collections were typically small and experimental, a wide variety of hardware and software was utilised. Today, the leading digital library developers are putting substantial collections online. Some of these collections include millions of digital objects; collections are being planned that will require storage measured in petabytes. There are quite a few digital library software packages available in the market. One has to select the right kind of package depending on their specific need. Greenstone is a suite of software for building and distributing digital library collections. DSpace is a groundbreaking digital library system to capture, store, index, preserve, and redistribute the intellectual output of a university's research faculty in digital formats. In India, especially where NIT libraries are concerned, the electronic resources are examined in order to ascertain their conditions. Electronic resources referred here are *"information packages made available in digital format."* These electronic resources consist of online journals databases, CD-ROM/DVD and audio/ video course materials. Mostly, the online journals databases cover full text journals databases such as ACM (Association for Computing Machinery) Digital Library, American Society of Civil Engineers (ASCE), American Society of Mechanical Engineers, (ASME), ASTM (American Society for Testing and Materials) journals and standards, IEEE Online, Nature, Proquest, Springer link, Science Direct etc), and abstract databases, Web of sciences, Chemical Abstracts etc) and standards etc. The National Knowledge Commission has provided the much needed impetus to the development of academic libraries which can be envisaged in today's ICT environment where the nature, role and significance of academic libraries is transforming with cutting edge technologies and the focus is shifting from *'information storage'* to 'information access, and this paradigm shift is inevitable for all overall improvement of library functioning and services for present survival and futuristic approach. The Digital Library of India project was initiated in the year 2002, with motivations from the Universal Digital Library project.

**Open Course Ware (OCW)**

Open course ware are course lessons creates at universities and published gratis via the internet. Some of the known OCW in India are:

1. *Brihaspati:* Brihaspati was developed by Indian Institute of Technology (Kanpur). It is an open platform for learning, based on the java servlets content delivery system. University Grants Commission (UGC) recommends 'Brihaspati the virtual classroom' web based e-Learning system to be used by universities and colleges free of cost.
2. *Consortium for Educational Commutation (CEC):* Consortium for Educational Commutation (www.cec-lor.edu.in) is an inter-university centre on electronic media, established by UGC, and has been offering television programmes in various subject categories.
3. *Indo-German eGurukul on digital libraries:* The Indo-German eGurukul on Digital Libraries is a collaborative project of DRTC and Goethe-Institut in New Delhi provides access to learning materials through digital libraries.
4. *National Council of Educational Research and Training (NCERT):* NCERT publishes school textbooks freely available on the Internet for students and teachers through its website. It is an apex resource organization set up by the MHRD, Government of India, to assist and advise the Central and State Government on academic matters related to school level education. The main objective is to assist and advise the Central and State Governments on academic matters related to school level education.
5. *UNESCO-SALIS e-Learning Portal:* The UNESCO-SALIS e-Learning Portal is a collaborative project of the Society for the Advancement of Library and Information Science and UNESCO office in New Delhi. The project aims to raise awareness and enhance information literacy competency skills of laymen as well as information professionals and educators in the South Asian sub-region.
6. *eGyankosh:* eGyankosh is national digital repository of learning resources, established by IGNOU, with the aims to store, index, distribute and share the digital learning resources of open and distance learning institutional in the country. It has been developed with an objective of long-term preservation of learning materials available in various formats.

**Needs**

Access to information from various sources is of utmost importance to journalists for writing their stories. Many attempts have been made to organise the newspapers over the years, from bound volumes to the recent full-text newspaper database to identify the news or information. The advantages of digital libraries as a means of easily and rapidly accessing books, archives and images of various types are now widely recognised by commercial interests and public bodies alike. DLEs will also facilitate cross-institutional sharing of educational resources, including all types of courseware, as well as materials for distance and self-learning. The ultimate goal is the development of a community of science and technology educators who use the library for cross-disciplinary and cross-institutional collaboration. Journals that do not charge readers or their institutions subscription fees to access the articles can be posted on the Internet for the open access. The authors can place the copies of their articles in the open access journals. Thus users will have free and unrestricted access to their works and the research that is currently inaccessible because of financial barriers becomes globally accessible.

Digital libraries can store a large volume of digital information in archival form. It provides the users fast search tools, immediate access to the rapidly-growing information in multimedia form quickly on the screen in an interactive mode; it also offers access to expensive and special collections of information from any remote location and by multiple simultaneous users. The advantages of digital libraries are as: (i) Preserve the valuable documents, rare and special collections of libraries, archives and museums, (ii) Provide faster access to the holding of libraries world wide through automated catalogues, (iii) Help to locate both physical and digitised versions of scholarly articles and books through single interface, (iv) Search optimisation, simultaneous searches of the Internet make possible, preparing commercial databases and library collections, (v) Offering online learning environment, (vi) Making short the chain from author to user, (vii) Save preparation/conservation cost, space and money, and (viii) Digital technology affords multiple, simultaneous user from a single original which are not possible for materials stored in any other forms. It's are pillars of education, and it is natural to expect that digital libraries will provide new opportunities for innovative educational practices.

## Challenges

Digital libraries must be accessible if they are to be successful. Therefore, where the information is stored and how these storage sites are interconnected is of concern. Of equal importance is that material in the digital library must be arranged and organised so that users do not spend an inordinate amount of time searching for the material they need. To be successful, digital libraries must provide accurate information, of sufficient quantity, and in a reasonable amount of time. There are many challenges in providing effective interaction designs that accommodate contexts that include poor literacy and little prior exposure to computing technologies. Security for digital information is a demanding challenge for librarians. Piracy, virus inversions, and parallel satellite networking stress are some of the problems for which solutions are needed. In an era of difficult to obtain resources, questioning the efficacy of undertaking the expensive process of digitising specialised collections of materials that may support a handful of scholars is not only legitimate but essential.

## Conclusion

The concept of digital library in India has gained momentum with the launching of INDEST-Indian National Digital Library in Engineering Science and Technology, UGC-INFONET, SNDP-Sustainable Development Networking

Programme of UNDP. The Digital Library of India project was initiated in the year 2002, with motivations from the Universal Digital Library project. The Indian Institute of Science (IISc), Carnegie Mellon University (CMU), the International Institute of Information Technology, Hyderabad (IIITH) are basically taken initiatives for developing digital library in India. The National Knowledge Commission has provided the much needed impetus to the development of academic libraries. Digital library is further helpful for research. The advantages of digital libraries are the simply and rapidly accessing books and journals. It plays an important part in assisting teaching. The Online Digital Libraries have the great advantage of making bibliographic resources, including the most recent publications.

## References


1. Adams, A., and Blandford, A. (2002). Digital libraries in academia: challenges and changes. In E-P Lim, S. Foo, C. Khoo, H. Chen, E. Fox, S. Urs and T. Costantino (Eds.) *Digital Libraries: People, Knowledge, and Technology*, p. 393.
2. Adams, W., and Jansen, B. (1998). *Distributed digital libraries: The key to success for distance learning*, Computers and Technology in Education. Cancun, Mexico, p. 2.
3. Alhaji, I. (2010). *Digitisation of library resources and the formation of digital libraries: A practical approach*, pp.1-2, Retrieved from https://www.sensepublishers.com/files/9789460912993PR.pdf
4. Ambati, V., Balakrishnan, N., Reddy, R., Pratha, L., and Jawahar, C. (2010). *The Digital Library of India Project: Process, Policies and Architecture*, pp. 1-3.
5. Ambati, V., Sankar, P., Pratha, L., and Jawahar, C. (2010). *Quality Management in Digital Libraries*, p.1, Retrieved from http://ptarpp2.uitm.edu.my/ptarpprack/silibus/is772/MeasurementManagement.pdf
6. Arunachalam, S. (2003). Information for Research in Developing Countries Information Technology, a Friend or Foe?, *International. Information. and Library Review*, Issue 35, p. 133.
7. Babu, K., Sarada, B., and Ramaiah, C. (2010). Use of Internet Resources in the S.V. University Digital Library, *DESIDOC Journal of Library and Information Technology*, Vol. 30, No. 1, p. 26.
8. Bakar, A. (2009). Education for digital libraries in Asian countries, *Asia-Pacific Conference on Library and Information Education and Practice, p.* 459, Retrieved from http://www.slis.tsukuba.ac.jp/a-liep2009/proceedings/Papers/a25.pdf
9. Balakrishnan, N. (2006). Universal Digital Library—Future research directions, *Journal of Zhejiang University Science*, 6A (11), p.1204.
10. Balakrishnan, N. (2006). Digital library in India: A testbed for Indian language research, TCDL Bulletin, Volume 03, Issue 01, p. 3, Retrieved from http://www.ieee-tcdl.org/Bulletin/v3n1/balakrishnan/balakrishnan.html

11. Bansode, S., and Pujar, S. (2008). Scholarly Digital Library Initiatives: World Versus India, *Journal of Library and Information Technology,* Vol. 28, No. 6, p. 22.
12. Banday, T., Qadri, A., Shah, A. (2009). "Digital Library - An Inevitable Resource for Modern Day Research in Developing Countries," *Sprouts: Working Papers on Information Systems,* 9(23). http://sprouts.aisnet.org/9-23
13. Benejelloun, S. (2007). *Digital Libraries as Development Catalysts in the Arab World,* Benjelloun Paper submitted for the Digital Library for the Maghreb Workshop, p.1, Retrieved from www.FulbrightAcademy.org.
14. Bhardwaj, K., Rajesh, K., and Shukla, R. (2010). *Re-Engineering of Library and Information Services through Web Modeling at Delhi College of Engineering,* p. 1, Retrieved from http://drtc.isibang.ac.in/xmlui/bitstream/handle/1849/298/rajesh-DCE.pdf?sequence=1
15. Bhatt, R. (2010). *Academic Libraries in India: A Historical Study,* p. 65, Retrieved from http://crl.du.ac.in/ical09/papers/index_files/ical-10_180_494_2_RV.pdf
16. Biswas, G., and Paul, D. (2010). An evaluative study on the open source digital library software's for institutional repository: Special reference to Dspace and greenstone digital library, *International Journal of Library and Information Science,* Vol. 2(1), pp. 2-3.
17. Brangier, E., Dinet, J., and Eilrich, L. (2009). The 7 Basic Functions of a Digital Library - Analysis of Focus Groups about the Usefulness of a Thematic Digital Library on the History of European Integration, M.J. Smith and G. Salvendy (Eds.): *Human Interface,* Part I, HCII 2009, LNCS 5617, Springer-Verlag Berlin Heidelberg, p. 345.
18. Brooks, S., Donovan, P., and Rumble, C. (2005). *Developing Nations, the Digital Divide and Research Databases,* p. 272, Retrieved from http://www.ebscohost.com/uploads/thisTopic-dbTopic-873.pdf
19. Carignan, Y., Evander, J., Gueguen, G., Hanlon, A., Murray, K., Roper, J., Ross, T., and Schreibman, S. (2007). *Best practice guidelines for digital collections at University of Marryland Libraries,* Schreibman, S (Ed), p. 12.
20. Chowdhury, G. (2010). How to Make Best Use of the Intellectual Output of the Country? A Simple Approach to the Design of a Digital Library of Theses and Dissertations in Indian Universities, Retrieved fromhttp://portal.unesco.org/pv_obj_cache/pv_obj_id_55E9CF704 ACBF81183FE9010B7869F6EE6A7600/filename/open_access_book_en.pdf
21. Covi, L. (1999). Material mastery: situating digital library use in university research practices, Information Processing and Management 35, p. 293.
22. Digital library (2012), Retrieved from http://en.wikipedia.org/wiki/Digital_library
23. Halder, S. (2009). Multimodal roles of library and information science professionals in present era, *International Journal of Library and Information Science,* Vol. 1(6), p. 92.

24. Furuta, R., Marshall, C., Shipman, F., and Leggett, J. (1996). *Physical Objects in the Digital Library*, p.113, Retrieved from http://www.csdl.tamu.edu/~shipman/papers/dl96.pdf
25. Guru, B., Gopalaswamy, M., Arun, J., and Padmamma, S. (2010). *Academic Library Management in India: Challenges and Opportunities*, p. 433, Retrieved from http://cdn.intechweb.org/pdfs/30466.pdf
26. Jeevan, V. (2007). Technology-Enhanced Library Services and the Librarian's Identity Crisis in Academic and Research Libraries of India, *Library*, 2007, vol. 57, p. 100.
27. Jeevan, V., and Dhawan, S. (2002). Problems in Transition to a Digital Library: An Indian Perspective, *DESIDOC Bulletin of Information Technology*, Vol. 22, No. 6, p. 14.
28. Jones, M., Thorn, E., Bainbridge, D., and Frohlich, F. (2009). *Mobility, Digital Libraries and a Rural Indian Village*, p. 312, Retrieved from http://www.dwrc.surrey.ac.uk/pdf/StoryBank/StoryBank%20JCDL09.pdf
29. Jose, A. (2007). Evaluation of Digital Libraries: A Case Study, ARD Prasad and Devika P. Madalli (Eds.): *ICSD*, p. 229.
30. Kadir, R., Dollah, W., Saaid, F., and Diljit. S. (2009). *A User-based Measure in Evaluating Academic Digital Library*, p. 83, Retrieved from http://crl.du.ac.in/ical09/papers/index_files/ical-13_193_404_1_RV.pdf
31. Kalinichenko, L. (2003). *Digital libraries in education, UNESCO Institute for Information Technologies in Education*, p.12, Retrieved from http://iite.unesco.org/pics/publications/en/files/3214609.pdf
32. Katre, D. (2004). Pragmatic and Usable Approach for Digital Library Initiatives in India, *Proceedings of International Conference on Digital Libraries (ICDL)*, New Delhi, India, Volume I, p. 41.
33. Katre, D. (2009). *Ecosystem for Digital Preservation in Indian Context: A Proposal for Sustainable and Iterative Lifecycle Model*, p. 2, Retrieved from http://www.hceye.org/downloads/23-Dinesh%20Katre.pdf
34. Kavitha, R. (2009). Collection development in digital libraries: trends and problems, *Indian Journal of Science and Technology*, Vol. 2 No. 12, p. 72.
35. Khan, S., and Bhatti, R. (2012). A Review of Problems and Challenges of Library Professionals in Developing Countries including Pakistan, *Library Philosophy and Practice*, p. 2, Retrieved from http://digitalcommons.unl.edu/cgi/viewcontent.cgi?article=1831&context=libphilprac
36. Kinns, N., and Blandford, A. (2010). *A survey of user studies for digital libraries*, p. 1, Retrieved from http://www.eis.mdx.ac.uk/ridl/DLuser.pdf
37. Kishore, P., and Alan, B. (2005). A text to speech interface for Universal Digital Library, *Journal of Zhejiang University Science*, 6A (11), p. 1229.
38. Konnur, P, Rajani, S., and Madhusudhan, M. (2010). Academic Library Websites in Bangalore City, India: An Evaluative Study, *Library Philosophy and Practice*, p. 1.

39. Franklin, V., Jebaraj, D., and Deivasigamani, M. (2003). The Electronic Library: An Indian Scenario, *Library Philosophy and Practice,* Vol. 5, No. 2, p. 1.
40. Kumar, S., Singh, S., and Pandita, N. (2010). *Development of digital library of Indian biomedical journals at NIC,* p. 1, Retrieved from http://openmed.nic.in/1206/01/medind_ila.pdf
41. Kuny, T., and Cleveland, G. (2000). *The Digital Library: Myths and Challenges,* p. 6, Retrieved from http://ifla.queenslibrary.org/IV/ifla62/62-kuny.pdf
42. Mahesh, G., and Mittal, R. (2008). Digital library in India: A review, *Library,* 2008, Vol. 58, p. 15.
43. Madalli, D. (2003). Digital Libraries and Digital Library Initiatives, *Workshop on Digital Libraries: Theory and Practice, DRTC,* Bangalore, pp. 4-5.
44. Mahesh, G., Kumar, N., and Gupta, D. (2010). Short-term Library and Information Science Training Courses in India, *DESIDOC Journal of Library and Information Technology,* Vol. 30, No. 5, p. 56.
45. Mahajan, P. (2005). Academic Libraries in India: a Present-Day Scenario, *Library Philosophy and Practice,* Vol. 8, No. 1, p. 2.
46. Majumder, P., Mitra, M., and Datta, D. (2006). *Multilingual Information Access: an Indian Language Perspective,* p. 1, Retrieved from http://www.isical.ac.in/~fire/publication/MLIA-10.pdf
47. Mazzon, P. (2010). *The digital library in developing countries of East Europe: the Tirana Medical Library,* Retrieved from http://www.bibliociencias.cu/gsdl/collect/eventos/index/assoc/HASH9630.dir/doc.pdf
48. Marshall, C., Price, M., Golovchinsky, G., and Schilit, B. (2010). *Introducing a digital library reading appliance into a reading group,* p. 1, Retrieved from http://www.csdl.tamu.edu/~marshall/dl99.pdf
49. Mathur, M. (2005). Advent of Digital Libraries and Measuring Their Performance: A Review, *DESIDOC Bulletin of Information Technology,* Vol. 25, No. 2, p. 20.
50. McCray, A., and Gallagher, M. (2001), Principles for digital library development, *Communications of the ACM,* Vol. 44, No. 5, p. 49.
51. McAlbert, F. (2012). Digital Librarians and the Challenges of Open Access to Knowledge: The Michael Okpara University of Agriculture (MOUAU) *Library Experience,* p. 1, Retrieved from http://portal.unesco.org/pv_obj_cache/pv_obj_id_55E9CF7047ACBF81183FE9010B7869F6EE6A7600/filename/open_access_book_en.pdf
52. Meitei, L., and Devi, P. (2009). Open Source Initiative in Digital Preservation: The Need for an Open Source Digital Repository and Preservation System, *7th International CALIBER-2009,* Pondicherry University, Pondicherry, February 25-27, 2009, p. 43.
53. Meyyappan, N., Hawamdeh, S., and Foo, F. (2001). Digital Work Environment (DWE): Using Tasks to Organise Digital Resources, Proc. *5th European Conference on*

*Research and Advanced Technology for Digital Libraries (ECDL2001)*, Darmstadt, Germany, September 4-9, Lecture Notes in Computer Science (LNCS) 2163, p. 239.

54. Mohamed, R. (2006). *The role of governments in planning and developing digital libraries in developing countries*, Retrieved from http://repository.uneca.org/handle/10855/15377
55. Muqueem, S. (2010). *Changing role of library professionals in the digital environment*, p. 1, Retrieved from http://drtc.isibang.ac.in/xmlui/bitstream/handle/1849/400/p92_shaista_khan.pdf?sequence=1
56. Naik, N., Kuamri, V., and Reddy, L. (2012). Portal approaches for digital library of Indian universities, *International Journal of Scientific and Research Publications,* Volume 2, Issue 5, p. 2.
57. Nieuwenhuysen, P. (2005). *Challenges in the evolution from classical over hybrid to digital libraries*, pp.1-2, Retrieved from http://www.vub.ac.be/BIBLIO/nieuwenhuysen/presentations/2004-02-icdl-delhi-paper/nieuwenhuysen-icdl2004.pdf
58. Ogunsola, L., and Okusaga, T. (2006). Developing Countries and the Need for Virtual Libraries: Problems and Prospects, *J. Soc. Sci.*, 13(3), p. 225.
59. Ogutu, K., and Rege, R. (2010). *Bridging the digital divide: A literature review*, p. 1319, Retrieved from http://www.kari.org/biennialconference/conference12/docs/BRIDGING%20THE%20DIGITAL%20DIVIDE%20-%20A%20LITERATURE%20REVIEW.pdf
60. Ramdasi, N. (2011). *Visualising Indian heritage digital library metaphor*, p.1, Retrieved from http://pune.cdac.in/html/pdf/ramdasi.pdf
61. Ranasinghe, P. (2008). 2.40 Digital library content in South Asia, *Proceedings of the Annual Research Symposium,* p. 92.
62. Rao, M. (2010). *Digital Libraries: Challenges, Opportunities and Implications*, p. 5, Retrieved from http://drtc.isibang.ac.in/xmlui/handle/1849/174
63. Rao, Y. and Choudhury, B. (2010). Availability of Electronic Resources at NIT Libraries in India: A Study, p. 631, Retrieved from http://crl.du.ac.in/ical09/papers/index_files/ical-106_68_169_2_RV.pdf
64. Ray, B., Biswas, S., and Mukhopadhyay, P. (2012). Open Access to scholarly information in India: Trends and Developments, *International Research: Journal of Library & Information Science* | Vol. 2 No. 1, pp. 93-94.
65. Rawat, S., Kumar, K., Meshesha, M., Sikdar, I., Balasubramanian, A., and Jawahar, C. (2006). A Semi-automatic Adaptive OCR for Digital Libraries, H. Bunke and A.L. Spits (Eds.): *DAS 2006,* LNCS 3872, p. 13.
66. Reddy, V. (2010). *Towards a Self Healing Information System for Digital Libraries*, p. 2, Retrieved from http://www.pdfsearchbox.com/pdf/Towards-a-Self-Healing-Information-System-for-Digital-Libraries.html
67. Rao, M. (2001). Metadata Architecture for Digital Libraries: Conceptual framework for Indian Digital Libraries, p. 2.

68. Rosa, I., and Lamas, D. (2008). *Digital libraries in the developing countries*, p.1, Retrieved from http://www.unesco.org/pv_obj_cache/pv_bj_id_8D21450ADD2345A714C76088D470A52ED0E10000/filename/programme_doc_wdl.pdf

69. Rosenberg, D. (2005). *Towards the digital library: findings of an investigation to establish the current status of university libraries in Africa*, First edition, UK: International Network for the Availability of Scientific Publications (INASP), p. 7.

70. Sahoo, B., and Rao, I. (2003). Copyright and Digital Libraries, *Workshop on Digital Libraries: Theory and Practice, DRTC*, Bangalore, p. 2.

71. Sahu, M., and Mahapatra, R. (2011). State of Digital Library Initiatives in Engineering and Technology College Libraries affiliated to BPUT, Orissa: An Empirical approach, *VSRD Technical and Non-technical Journal,* Vol. 2 (9), p. 450.

72. Sastry, H., and Reddy, L. (2010). Significance of Web 2.0 in Digital Libraries, *(IJCSE) International Journal on Computer Science and Engineering,* Vol. 02, No. 06, p. 2208.

73. Sharma, P. (2011). *Digital Libraries: Reaching out to people with special Reference to India*, pp. 5-6, Retrieved from http://drtc.isibang.ac.in/xmlui/bitstream/handle/1849/402/prabha-sharma.pdf?sequence=1

74. Sharma, R. (2010). *Technology and Academic Libraries in Developing Nations*, pp. 230, Retrieved from http://crl.du.ac.in/ical09/papers/index_files/ical-38_236_520_1_RV.pdf

75. Shibu, M. (2011). Changing the Archetype of Information Dissemination Using Open Source Digital Library Technology, *Journal of Library and Information Science*, Volume 01, Number 01, p. 13.

76. Shivaram, B., and Rajashekar, T. (2004). Building Indian Language Digital Library Collections: Some Experiences with Greenstone Software, Z. Chen et al. (Eds.): *ICADL*, Springer-Verlag Berlin Heidelberg, p. 661.

77. Singh, J., and Kaur, T. (2009). Future of Academic Libraries in India: Challenges and Opportunities, p. 52, Retrieved from http://crl.du.ac.in/ical09/papers/index_files/ical-9_252_741_1_PB.pdf

78. Solis, A., and Pena, R. (2010). *Evaluating a monolingual multinational digital library by using usability: An explanatory approach from a developing country*, p. 1, Retrieved from http://biblio.colmex.mx/bib_dig/pdf/Art_Elsevier.pdf

79. Solimine, G., and Abadal, E. (2005). Digital library development in Italy and Spain, The 3rd International Conference on Politics and Information Systems: Technologies and Applications. Proceedings PISTA 2005, July 14-17, 2005 - Orlando (Florida, USA) Orlando, *International Institute of Informatics and Systemics*, 2005, p. 296.

80. Sreekumar, M., and Sreejaya, P. (2010). *Digital library initiatives and issues in India: Efforts on scholarly knowledge management*, p.11, Retrieved from http://dspace.iimk.ac.in/bitstream/2259/252/1/05-m

81. Sreekumar, M., and Sreejaya, P. (2011). *Digital library initiatives and issues in India: Efforts on scholarly knowledge management*, p.14, Retrieved from http://dspace.iimk.ac.in/bitstream/2259/252/1/05-m

82. Tamishchelvan, M., Ganesh, A., and Swaminathan, S. (2012). *Digital object identifier in effective media library management: An Indian perspectives*, p.141, Retrieved from http://elpub.scix.net/data/works/att/0321.content.pdf

83. Trivedi, M. (2010). *Digital Libraries: Functionality, Usability, and Accessibility, Library Philosophy and Practice*, p.1, Retrieved from http://www.webpages.uidaho.edu/~mbolin/trivedi-diglib.pdf

84. Tripathi, A., and Tripathi, S. (2007). *Digital Libraries in Indian Languages: Some Provocative Thoughts*, ARD Prasad and Devika P. Madalli (Eds.): ICSD, p. 373.

85. Ubogu, F., and Pickover, M. (2011). Digital Library and Archives developments in Africa, *White Paper submitted for the Digital Library for the Maghreb Workshop*, p. 1.

86. UGC-INFONET Digital Library Consortium (2009). *An Initiative of University Grants Commission*, Ministry of Human Resource Development (MHRD) and Government of India, p. 3, Retrieved from http://www.inflibnet.ac.in/econ/am09.pdf

87. Urs, S. (2007). *Digital libraries: the road ahead*, p. 2, Retrieved from http://www.vidyanidhi.org.in/shaliniurs_files/caliber.pdf

88. Warraich, N., and Tahira, M. (2009). HEC National Digital Library: Challenges and Opportunities for LIS Professionals in Pakistan, *Library Philosophy and Practice*, Retrieved from http://digitalcommons.unl.edu/cgi/viewcontent.cgi?article=1831&context=libphilprac

89. Waters, D. (2001). Developing Digital Libraries: Four Principles for Higher Education, *EDUCAUSE Review*, p. 1.

90. Witten, I., Bainbridge, D., and Nichols, D. (2006). *Digital libraries in education, UNESCO Institute for Information Technologies in Education*, p.12, Retrieved from http://iite.unesco.org/pics/publications/en/files/3214609.pdf

91. Witten, I., Loots, M., Trujillo, M., and Bainbridge, D. (2010), *The Promise of Digital Libraries in Developing Countries*, Retrieved from http://www.emeraldinsight.com/journals.htm?articleid=861946&show=html

92. Witten, I. (2011). *Digital libraries and society: New perspectives on information dissemination*, p. 3, Retrieved from http://citeseerx.ist.psu.edu/viewdoc/summary?doi=10.1.1.3.599

# 16

# Building an Effective Digital Library in Digital Era

***Dr. Manaswini Patra***

*"A man, whilst he is dreaming, believes in his dream; he is undeceived only when he is awakened from his slumber."*

**— Mahatma Gandhi**

## Introduction

One of the most significant issues facing the modern-day archivist is the conversion of material to digital format. New technologies have emerged to allow the digitisation of almost all types of items, including paper documents, photographs, sound recordings, and motion pictures. However, while digitisation is now possible, the question remains whether moving material to digital format is a wise course of action. One must examine whether digitising any part of a collection comports with the overall mission of the archivist to gain control of documents with enduring value, preserve them, and make them available to others for research. Digitisation undoubtedly assists the archivist in fulfilling the latter two responsibilities, but there are several costs and challenges that the archivist must consider before proceeding with a conversion project. Only through the comprehensive analysis of both positive and negative ramifications can the archivist make an informed decision to digitise.

Digitisation is the *"process of transforming analog material into binary electronic (digital) form, especially for storage and use in a computer"*. It is arguably the most popular trend among archival and related institutions. After conducting a survey of archives, museums, public and academic libraries, and state library administrative agencies, the Institute of Museum and Library Services (IMLS) recently announced that 94 per cent of archives have reported some digitisation activity over the past year. In addition, 64 per cent of archives state that they each have 25,000 items or more in need of digital conversion. In contemporary society, with the proliferation of electronic communication networks and the personal computer being a staple in the average citizen's home, making material available digitally has rightfully become a top priority for archival institutions.

**Need of Library Automation**

In the information age, success lies in the innovative application of information technology and gaining access to digital resources. Library automation which started in late 70s in few special libraries has now reached most of the libraries. The factors necessitating automation of libraries are the following:

1. Explosion of knowledge resulting in numerous specialisations and flow of almost non-stop information;
2. Inability of users to explore unlimited literature; wastage of enormous precious time in handling routine and repetitive library operations; even the largest of the libraries cannot acquire and make available the entire published materials; and to facilitate easy, fast, and reliable sharing of resources between libraries, cutting across space and time.

**Problems of Libraries and Information Centres Access**

Though the Internet provides an open global networked environment for seamless publishing and access to information, yet, it is very difficult for small and medium sized libraries in India to procure and access these online sources, like, online e-journals, e-books, e-databases etc. due to their financial crunch. Moreover, some of the university libraries in India are not having sufficient fund to subscribe the core journals which are urgently necessary for research activities. In this situation the Library and Information professionals should take their own initiative to exploit the Internet for free available online resources. The place for exploitation of Internet by the Library and Information Centres are unlimited and endless. Internet provides a wealth of information to Library and Information Centres. It also provides free access to variety of information sources such as online e-books, e-Journals both full text, abstracts and contents depending on the publisher's policy, e-newsletters and so on.

**Major Library Software's Available**

There are several software's available for library operations. In general, they may be categorised into two as below:

**Table16.1 : Showing Different Aspects of Major Library Software' Available in India**

| *LIBRARY* SOFTWARE | APPLICATION | DEVELOPER | SUITABILITY |
|---|---|---|---|
| CDS/ISIS | MS DOS,WINDOW 95, LAN, UNIX | NISSAT,NEW DELHI | SMALL AND MEDIUM LIBRARIES |
| LIBSYS | MS DOS,WINDOW 95, LAN, UNIX | LIBSYS CO., NEW DELHI | ALL TYPE OF LIBRARIES |
| LIBRIS | MS DOS,WINDOW 95, LAN, UNIXI | FRONITER INST. OF NFO.TECH., HYDERABAD | ALL TYPE OF LIBRARIES |
| SANJAY | MS DOS | NISSAT, NEW DELHI | MEDIUM TYPE OF LIBRARY |
| ILMS | MS DOS,UNIX | INFLIBNET, AHMEDABAD | ALL TYPE OF LIBRARIES |
| ALICE FOR WINDOW | WINDOW 95 | LAN SOFTLINK INDIA, NEW DELHI | ALL TYPE OF LIBRARIES |
| BASIC PLUS | UNIX | NIC, NEW DELHI | ALL TYPE OF LIBRARIES |

**Library Automation Activities: Global Perspectives**

Digital library systems compose a family of automated systems that together provide a comprehensive capability to manage the digital content of an enterprise. Group (Asia Pacific) is a leading library technology developer and distributor of RFID solutions. Group delivers customised security solutions to minimise the loss of library assets. The Telematics for Libraries programme of the European Commission (EC) works to facilitate access to knowledge held in libraries throughout the European Union while reducing disparities between national systems and practices. Candle (Controlled Access to Network Digital Libraries in Europe) facilitate access to digital collections within and without the library in a controlled way by producing low-cost library management software for rights control and fee management. The Dieper (Digitised European Periodicals) project offers a test bed for studying the impact of providing fast electronic access to relatively short documents such as journal articles. Soutron Global digital library automation solutions provide timely, efficient and effective enterprise library management services, complete with easy-to-use library and knowledge management functionality. Digital Libraries are important for Africa as they will enable the creation of local content, strengthen the mechanisms and capacity of civil society, and increase the portability, efficiency of access, flexibility, availability and preservation of content. The free and open source software (FOSS) Greenstone digital library software suite provides a unique resource to promote the development of digital libraries in Africa. Most university libraries in sub Saharan Africa are yet to successfully and fully automate their information services. The eGranary was invented in 2001 by the WiderNet Project. There are now eGranary installations in more than 700 schools, clinics, and universities in Africa, India, Bangladesh, and Haiti. An eGranary Digital Library caches educational resources via a local area network in order to reduce connectivity costs in Internet-scarce areas.

The National Library of Australia (NLA) is the country's largest reference library. PANDORA, is an acronym - Preserving and Accessing Networked Documentary Resources of Australia. The purpose of the PANDORA Archive is to collect and provide long-term access to selected online publications and web sites. Greenstone is a suite of software for building and distributing digital library collections. Greenstone is produced by the New Zealand Digital Library Project at the University of Waikato, and developed and distributed in cooperation with UNESCO and the Human Info NGO. Information discovery illustrates the complementary skills of computers and people. The Internet Archive, directed by Brewster Kahle, provides a topical example of the economic advantages of automated digital libraries. *E-Granthalaya* is library automation software which provides by National Informatics Centre, Department of Electronics and Information Technology, Ministry of Communications and Information Technology, Government of India.

**Library Automation Activities in India**

The digital library is the most important development of 21st century. It has opened up an exciting new world of information delivery for the researchers and citizens of tomorrow. Digital technology can make the works of man or needed information accessible to all whether they live in a village or in an urban area. The father of Indian librarianship, Dr S. R. Ranganathan, in the past centuries has recognised the great potential of public libraries to improve the quality of life and provide opportunity the citizenry. Similarly digital libraries, widely available and accessible will improve the global society in ways beyond measurement. Hence, there is an urgent need of a workable strong strategy at the national level. The principal benefit of this will be to supplement the formal education system by making knowledge available to anyone who can have access. Several efforts are now being made in different parts of the country towards starting digitising the existing resources and networking the existing institutions and libraries, especially suitable for accessibility mechanism. The major initiatives are briefly described below:

1. Government of India has set up NICNET which is the largest government owned information network. NIC is providing network backbone and e-governance to Central Government, State Government, UT Administrations, Districts and other Government bodies. It offers a wide range of ICT services including Nationwide Communication Network for

decentralised planning, improvement in Government services and wider transparency of national and local Governments.

2. Similarly, Digital Library of India (DLI)-Universal library project is a major initiative. It is a collaborative project between Indian Institute of Science, Bangalore and Carnegie Mellor University with partners from the Government, Academia and Religious Institutions. The main objective of the project is to digitise all the significant literary, artistic, and scientific works of mankind and making them freely available, in every corner of the world, for our education, study and appreciation and for all our future generations.
3. Although some institutions like ISI and IITs in the country have imported mainframe computers in the late 1950s and early 1960s, priority was being accorded for productivity-and R&D-linked jobs.

Therefore, if one analyses these activities many unaddressed issues may be raised. The objectives of the projects:

1. The rationale for content selection;
2. Preservation methods;
3. Access mechanism;
4. Coordination with other similar organisational initiatives;
5. Cost factor and sustainability etc.

Just as library automation was done in a very fragmented manner in India thirty years ago, the digitisation activities are equally fragmented and diversified. This is in sharp contrast to some countries which have undertaken digitisation and setting up of digital libraries in a planned manner with policies, strategies and structures well thought out, keeping in mind the holistic view of national need.

## Importance of Digitations

These are the importance of digitations of any library.

1. *Improved Access:* The propagation of digitisation is easy to explain: converting items to digital format provides an extensive variety of benefits. The main advantage over older formats is the increased access for researchers. Digital surrogates can be viewed by more people, at a wider range of times, and with less effort. Access is also improved with digitisation because researchers are given new search and browsing options that enable them to find information with greater speed and accuracy.
2. *Improved Preservation:* Digital preservation is becoming an accepted practice for other types of items as well. Digitisation also assists in preservation by expediting the process of duplicating items. One viable tactic to avoid the loss of information is creating backup copies to archival holdings (Digital Preservation Coalition, n.d.); executing this strategy with digital elements is generally less onerous than with analog material, especially if the digital file is on a server or hard drive.

3. *Decreased Storage Space Requirements:* One final way in which digital items aid the archivist is through the reduction of necessary storage space, especially when dealing with a large number of items. Because a voluminous amount of digital material can exist on a single hard drive or optical disk, one goal of digital conversion projects can be the decrease in physical size of a collection (Carter, 2005, p. 50).

**Digitisation Process**

The existing resources of the library can be converted into digital media by scanning the materials. Flatbed scanner or digital camera may be used for image capturing or scanning. Scanning of images may take place at 300 dbi bitonal. 600 dbi bitonal is used for higher resolution. Scanning is the most popular method of converting the materials. Digital imaging technology has a number of options that can be adopted depending on the objectives, its end users, availability of fund etc. After choosing one of the data conversion methods, as suited to particular library, we should develop plan of action. Digitisation process starts with project planning with documentation followed by a linear progression of tasks: select/prepare, convert/scan, process, store, distribute and maintain over time. Digital conversion process includes:

1. Document
2. Data/image capture
3. Data Processing
4. Storage
5. Indexing and processing
6. Retrieval and display

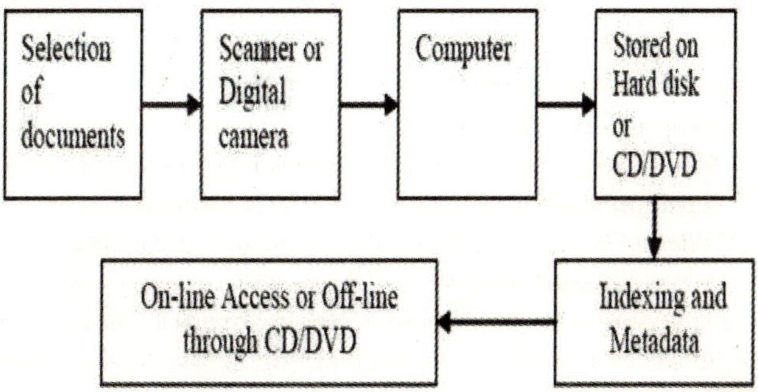


Selection and identification of materials/documents according to priority decided earlier is first step. A list of candidate documents for entire project may be prepared as a database. It should have identifying information, priority based on content and its copyright status. After selection each page may be scanned as a separate image file. A spreadsheet file is created for each document. The fields in the spreadsheet are used to automate certain aspects of data creation. This spreadsheet includes the item identification number, title, number of pages and notes of each document. All the resulting files are collected into a single directory. The text in the convertible document may require conversion of diacritics, or special characters, images may need enhancement, amplification or compression. Records are verified and processed/edited, if required. The information converted into digital form will need digital storage medium, which may be hard disk, magnetic tape, optical CD-Rom, or networks with workstation to access. Use of Dublin core standard is advisable to create metadata of digital resources.

## The Major Challenges

While digitisation generally makes the archivist more effective by improving preservation and access, converting items to digital format can also act as a hindrance to the archivist's mission. There are myriad costs and concerns that the archivist must confront before, during, and after digitisation, many of which are not readily perceptible. Perhaps Lisa R. Carter (2005) sums it up best: *"Digitising an archive involves a great deal more activity than anyone would expect"* (p. 54). The challenge here is, in part, to develop mechanisms, perhaps social expectations independently or in combination with technical means, regarding acceptable levels of access.

1. *Planning:* Even before digitisation begins, the archivist needs to designate an immense amount of time for planning and preparing. Expenditures also might be required. One of the first decisions to be made is the type of media to be used. Another issue to address prior to conversion is the desired quality of the digital reproduction, which is determined by the level of technology used to capture and display the archival item (Conway, 1996, p. 12).
2. *Copyright:* Copyright concerns also must be confronted during the planning stages of a digital conversion project. Copyright matters also come into play even after permission to publish is granted. An institution must develop a strategy to stop unauthorised reproduction and distribution by people viewing the files over the Internet. In this situation, the retention of quality when duplicating a digital item is a negative factor.
3. *Digitisation Process:* Once all of the pre-conversion planning is complete, the next step is the capture process. This typically entails the scanning of paper documents and the recording of sound and video. To ensure the best quality of the digital copy, the archivist must properly prepare the originals.
4. *Metadata and Other Post-Digitisation Concerns:* Even after the conversion of material is complete, expenditures by the archival operation continue. According to the Digital Imaging Working Group of the Western States Digital Standards Group (2003, p. 9), *"Generally, capture and conversion of data often comprises only [one-third] of the total costs, while cataloging, description, and indexing comprise [two-thirds] of the total costs."* The activities that occur post-conversion, especially the indispensable task of creating metadata, are

laborious but essential to maintain the integrity of the data and to allow researchers to find relevant information within the collection. Many types of metadata in the digital environment differ from those in the physical world.

5. *Displaying the collection on the Web:* Another challenge connected with digitisation is the ancillary work required to make the digital items accessible to the public. In most cases, this involves displaying the collection on the Web. To accomplish this, simply creating the digital files is not sufficient. Additional time and effort must be spent on constructing the Website that will display the material. This will entail primarily technical tasks like setting up the server and writing the code for the site. Develop approaches that can present heterogenous resources in a coherent way. A digital library that provides diverse content will be characterised by heterogeneity in original format, in digital format and resolution, and in the level of detail and format of descriptive information that is available to support access. This heterogeneity may be seen in the historical collections online at the Library of Congress, which typify the larger class of materials that are likely to form part of any digital library, however defined.
6. *Technological Environments:* Perhaps the most significant concern elicited by digitisation involves an issue that typically does not come to light until at least a couple of years subsequent to the conversion of material: preservation of the items as technology continues to change. Similar to some analog items like tapes, digital files require separate equipment for viewing. As such, preservation of digital objects is not based only on the physical life of storage media, but also on the viability of the system that provides access (Conway, 2005, pp. 11-12). In the case of digital material, both the hardware and software used to interact with archival items can become obsolete in as little as a few years. Thus, an institution engaging in digitisation must dedicate time to monitoring the technological environments surrounding its digital collections. In this sense, digitization is less of an event than it is a continual process, so the archivist must be aware of the future demands of a digitisation project taking place today.
7. *Substantial change within the workplace:* The archivist also must be cognisant of the ramifications of digitisation on employees and their work processes. The conversion of major collections to digital format will create substantial change within the workplace, which in turn can cause considerable stress among staff (Johnson, 1999). Skill sets that employees have developed over time will become less relevant with the advent of digitisation, potentially leading to anxiety. The manager of an archival operation can employ a two-fold strategy to combat this uneasiness.

## Conclusion

Digital libraries and digitisation are crucial for disseminating and preserving knowledge. Digital library activities are gathering momentum in developing countries, especially India. Since most higher education and research institutions in India are funded and controlled by the central and state governments, clear-cut national plans and policies are needed for infrastructure, standards, metadata, interoperability, multi-lingual databases, training, co-ordination, copyright, and archiving and preservation methods, so that our heritage of knowledge and culture can the ravages of time and present and future generations can benefit and be guided by them. The myriad factors that the archivist must examine before embarking on a digitisation project can be overwhelming. Many institutions have concluded that the improvements to access and preservation make digitisation worthwhile, resulting in almost boundless digitisation activity among archives and libraries. Nevertheless, there are countless challenges to confront prior to, during, and following the conversion process. By becoming apprised of all of the issues involved, the archivist who elects to move forward with a digitisation project can do so with confidence and manage the undertaking effectively.

## REFERENCES


1. Carter, L. R. (2005). Digitizing the KET Archives: A brief case study [Electronic version]. *Visual Resources Association Bulletin, 31*, pp. 50-55.
2. CDP Digital Audio Working Group (2005). *Digital audio best practices* (Version 2.0). Retrieved July 24, 2013, from http://www.cdpheritage.org/digital/audio/documents/CDPDABP_1-2.pdf
3. Conway, P. (1996). *Preservation in the digital world.* Retrieved July 28, 2006, from http://www.clir.org/pubs/reports/conway2/
4. Council on Library and Information Resources and Library of Congress (2006). *Capturing analog sound for digital preservation: Report of a roundtable discussion of best practices for transferring analog discs and tapes.* Washington, DC: Author. Retrieved July 28, 2013, from http://www.clir.org/pubs/reports/pub137/pub137.pdf
5. Digital Preservation Coalition (n.d.). Digital preservation: Preservation issues. In *The Handbook* (section 2.2). Retrieved July 28, 2013 fromh ttp://www.dpconline.org/graphics/digpres/presissues.html
6. Jenkinson, H. (1984). Reflections of an archivist. In M. F. Daniels and T. Walch (Eds.), *A modern archives reader: Basic readings on archival theory and practice* (pp. 15-21). Johnson, P. (1999). Learning to cha-cha with change. In P. Johnson and B. MacEwan (Eds.), *ALCTS Papers on Library Technical Services and Collections No. 8, Virtually yours: Models for managing electronic resources and services, Proceedings of the Joint Reference and User Services Association and Association for Library Collections and Technical Services Institute,* October 23-25, 1997. Chicago: American Library Association.
7. Society of American Archivists (n.d.). *So you want to be an archivist: An overview of the archival profession.* Retrieved June 2, 2013, from http://www.archivists.org/prof-education/arprof.asp

8. U.S. Copyright Office (n.d.). *Copyright Law of the United States of America and related laws contained in Title 17 of the United States Code* (chap. 1). Retrieved July 30, 2013, from http://www.copyright.gov/title17/92chap1.html

9. Western States Digital Standards Group, Digital Imaging Working Group (2003). *Western states digital imaging best practices* (Version 1.0). Denver, CO: Author. Retrieved July 24, 2013 fromhttp://www.cdpheritage.org/digital/scanning/documents/WSDIBP_v1.pdf

# PART V – MISCELLANEOUS

# 17

# Adult Education in India: An Overview

***Dr. P.K. Pandey***

*"It is, in fact, nothing short of a miracle that the modern methods of instruction have not yet entirely strangled the holy curiosity of inquiry; for this delicate little plant, aside from stimulation, stands mainly in need of freedom. Without this it goes to wrack and ruin without fail."*

**— Albert Einstein**

## Introduction

Education is the basis of the economic and cultural development of a country. The vast masses of people living in rural India form the majority of the population of the country. If they remain illiterate no upliftment of the country is possible. These rural masses are mostly very poor. They are ill-fed, ill-clad, ill-sheltered, untreated in illness and are illiterate. They do not get pure drinking water. Every year epidemics break out there and many poor people fall victims to these. These evils should be removed to prepare the ground for progress in all spheres. Education in India is provided by the public sector as well as the private sector, with control and funding coming from three levels: central, state, and local. Education in India falls under the control of both the Union Government and the State Governments, with some responsibilities lying with the Union and the states having autonomy for others. The various articles of the Indian Constitution provide for education as a fundamental right. Most universities in India are controlled by the Union or the State Governments. Democracy without education is meaningless. It is education and enlightenment that lifts a nation to the heights of progress and greatness. Unfortunately, the situation as it obtains in India in respect of education is not only distressing but disgraceful and deplorable. At present about 60 per cent of the people in India are illiterate; they cannot differentiate a buffalo from a black mole.

**What is Adult Education?**

Adult education is the process whereby adults engage in systematic and sustained learning activities in order to gain new forms of knowledge, skills, attitudes, or values. It can take place in the workplace, through *"extension"* school or "school of continuing education". Other learning places include community colleges, folk high schools, colleges and universities, libraries, and lifelong learning centers. Bryson says, *"Adult education includes all activities with an educational purpose, carried on by people, in the ordinary business of life who use only part of their energy to acquire intellectual equipment."* Ernst Baker says, *"Adult education is given on a part-time basis and, therefore, given concurrently with work and the earning of a living."* Maulana Azad re-oriented the concept of Adult education for preparing every citizen to play his part effectively in a democratic social order. So he renamed Adult education as *'Social Education'*. Agencies of Social (Adult) education include all the bodies, organizations or institutions which 'deliver the goods' which contact the 'consumers' of social education and satisfy their needs. They may be categorised as under:

1. Teachers, Government servants, NSS and other volunteers, social education workers, etc.
2. Regular educational institutions like schools, colleges, rural colleges, community centres, agriculture extension groups, worker's educational associations and voluntary organisations.
3. Informal educational devices like forums, study circles, group discussions, listening groups, camps.
4. Recreational, educational bodies like theatres, cinemas, clubs, societies, fairs, melas, nautanki, etc.
5. Institutions whose primary aim is not education, such as religious bodies, the Army, Parents Associations, Co-operative Societies and other Government Departments.

Educating adults differs from educating children in several ways. One of the most important differences is that adults have accumulated knowledge and work experience which can add to the learning experience. Another difference is that most adult education is voluntary; therefore, the participants are generally self-motivated. Adults frequently apply their knowledge in a practical fashion to learn effectively. They must have a reasonable expectation that the knowledge they gain will help them further their goals. The scope of Adult education is very comprehensive. Social education covers all those topics that are not touched by education in general at school. Topics like religion, politics and family planning can now be discussed with adults who have a mature understanding.

## Significance of Adult Education

Purposes of adult education may vary. One of its goals may be to help adult learners satisfy their needs and achieve their goals. Therefore, its ultimate goal might be to achieve human fulfillment. The goal might also be to achieve an institution's needs. The purpose of adult education in the form of college or university is distinct. In these institutions, the aim is typically related to personal growth and development as well as occupation and career preparedness. Another goal might be to not only sustain the democratic society, but to even challenge and improve its social structure. One of the primary goals of adult education is functional literacy. Organisations like the U.S. Department of Education and the United Nations Educational, Scientific and Cultural Organization (UNESCO) work tirelessly to measure, understand, and address adult illiteracy in the U.S. and around the world. The philosophically oriented functions of Adult education are clearing concepts of reality of universe and life, reconciling the old and the new approaches to life, balance and independent judgment, self-realisation, human relationship and citizenship training and economic efficiency.

## Principles of Adult Learning

Adult education, formally known as *"androgogy"*, can be defined as the set of specific skills and associated knowledge geared towards the educational development of adults. It emphasises that fact that adults are self-oriented and expected the responsibility to make their own decisions. Adults don't learn in the same way as children do because their personality structure is almost fully developed at that stage in their lives, along with a series of habits and practices that have been acquired during their lifetime. The principles of adult education are:

1. Adults will only learn when they want to. Simply put, no adult will learn under pressure.

2. Adults will only learn when they feel they need to.

3. Adults learn by doing. No adult enjoys being fed vast amounts of theory with little or no practice.

4. Adults will only learn by solving problems they can associate with their reality.

5. Experience will interfere in adult education. No person likes to be told that their *"tried a tested"* way of doing things is *"wrong"*.

6. Adults learn better in an informal environment. At this point in their lives, adults won't put up with a *"schoolhouse lecturer"* who demands that they sit up straight in their desks.

7. Adults need feedback. If one thing is preserved from their childhood days, it's the constant need to know how well they are doing.

8. Adults require a variety of teaching methods. It's important that different approached be used when trying to pass on knowledge to adults.

**Adult Education: Global Perspectives**

In the United States, a more general example is when adults who dropped out of high school return to school to complete general education requirements. Most upwardly mobile positions require at the very least a high school diploma or equivalent. Furthermore, adults with poor reading skills can obtain help from volunteer literacy programmes. These national organisations provide training, tutor certification, and accreditation for local volunteer programmes. In the U.S., each state is responsible for addressing the basic education of their citizens. Official state websites direct people to classes, programmes, and organisations designed to teach adults how to read prose, documents like maps and catalogs, and how to make simple computations.

The Five International Conferences on Adult Education were landmarks in supporting international and national efforts to establish and expand adult education programmes and policies. Moreover, they, along with other milestones such as the Faure and Delors Reports and the influential 1976 UNESCO Recommendation on the Development of Adult Education, set out the vital role of adult education as *"forming part of lifelong education and learning"*. Reaffirming the centrality of the right to basic education and skills for all throughout life, with adult literacy as the cornerstone of entitlement, the Hamburg Declaration underlined public responsibility for adult education provision, funding and quality. It drew attention to the need for partnerships between state, civil society and the private sector in developing and sustaining adult learning and education. The Declaration highlighted the importance of promoting gender equality, the integrity of cultural diversity and indigenous knowledge, the need to extend provision for older adults, and the need to assure education for peace, democracy and environmental sustainability. Recognising the importance of adult education for achieving sustainable social, cultural and economic development means explicit and visible political commitment translated into policy. It also means allocating the resources needed to implement measures well. The basis of any policy should be that adult education is a right for all, without exception. A key issue for understanding adult education policy, provision and governance is the acknowledgement of a learning continuum between formal, non-formal and informal education and its implications for life-wide and lifelong learning.

The extent to which countries are locked into widespread poverty, high levels of internal inequality and international debt influences the direction of adult education policy-making. For example, in sub-Saharan Africa, the Arab States, and much of Asia-Pacific and Latin America and the Caribbean, adult education is equated with adult literacy and compensatory or *'second chance'* education. The European Union's Lisbon Agenda, with its focus on lifelong learning, is a highly influential driver for policy innovation in the field of adult learning and influences *'neighbourhood countries'* such as the CIS (Commonwealth of Independent States). Within the region, there still exist disparities as to how the strategy is implemented. Moreover, individual countries' adult education policies place different emphases on the dual policy aims of economic competitiveness and social cohesion. The Republic of Korea, a particularly noteworthy example, developed a comprehensive policy approach to adult education in the 1980s as part of building a lifelong learning society, currently anchored in the 2007 Lifelong Education Act. Regional and local bodies in the country pass their own laws to support the national Act. External factors can bring about rapid changes in adult education policies. For example, in the wake of the 1997-98 Asian financial crisis, measures were introduced which entailed the restructuring of labour market policy and employment training systems. The People´s Republic of China, Indonesia, Malaysia, the Republic of Korea, Singapore and Thailand quickly set up new provision frameworks closely linked to human resources development requirements. The organisation for Economic Cooperation and Development (OECD), through studies like the International Adult Literacy Survey, also shapes national policy responses to adult education. In its Biennale meetings, the Association for the Development of Education in Africa (ADEA) has been able to provide a platform to discuss the importance of literacy and non-formal education, persuading Ministers of Education to re-examine their policies.

Educational governance in principle must be based on universal participation. There is a personal stake in education for all citizens, even when their interests and needs are not being met through existing policy, provision and practice. Furthermore, education is vital to civil society, local and regional communities and social movements; minorities, nations and states; the business world, labour markets and economies. Educational governance has to accommodate many stakeholders and a diverse range of interests. Adult education legislation and policy may be at a much generalised level or aimed at a narrow constituency within time and geographical limits. In practice, adult learning is fashioned by circumstances on the ground. Between these two ends of the policy-practice continuum, a variety of intermediary governance arrangements can exist. The majority of countries reported that more than one Ministry is involved in adult education. Many governments have established a department that is explicitly responsible for adult education. Typically, such offices are located within the Ministry of Education, but responsibilities for adult education may be assigned to other Ministries. In Malaysia, for example, the Ministry of Women, Family and Community Development is responsible for non-formal education, which effectively covers much adult education and learning provision in a country with a dispersed rural population.

The National adult education programmes of each country had their own specificity and have grown from different political and historical conditions resulting in unique programmes of their own. The uniqueness of national policy and programmes are best understood when these are studied in the developmental perspective in relation to political and social conditions. In India, adult education was planned as a community development programme though development of the individual was not directly associated with development of basic literacy-rather it was designed for societal development. Adult literacy was associated with socio-economic development and for self-reliance of the individual only in the last three decades. In Indonesia the concept of adult education developed from literacy for national development in the very first thirty years and concept of vocational education was added later. The purpose of adult education was integrated with out of school education. In Thailand, adult education was equated with educational activities for out of school youth and adults. Functionality was added to adult education in early 1970s and continuing education was added during the 1980s. It can be said that in Indonesia and Thailand there has been an integrated concept of basic education, i.e., primary schooling and adult education. In China, the scope of adult education was defined as workers peasant education. It was also known as spare time education and included civil and political education apart from literacy. In early years it was for national reconstruction and meant to serve the socialist state. Since 1978, there has been a shift in the scope of adult education by opening of the Chinese economy to the world. Science and technology was adopted for economic construction and for raising the quality of workforce in a marketing economy. Immediately after independence, India focused its attention on expanding primary education so adult literacy was neglected in the first three decades. On the other hand, Indonesia and China immediately after independence planned massive adult literacy campaigns to make the masses literate. Thailand had been active in its adult education programmes, along with a strong integrated primary education. It raised its literacy level up to 89.5 per cent in 1980. At the same time the literacy rate of Indonesia was equally high at 79 per cent. India and China encountered differential in achievement levels in literacy.

**Adult Education in India**

Post-independence India inherited a system of education which was characterised by large scale inter and intra-regional imbalances. The system educated a select few, leaving a wide gap between the educated and the illiterate. The country's literacy rate in 1947 was only 14 per cent and female literacy was abysmally low at eight per cent. Only one child out of three had an opportunity for enrolment in primary schools. Educational inequality was aggravated by economic inequality, gender disparity and rigid social stratifications. Gram Shikshan Mohim Movement for literacy in the rural areas was started in 1959 in Satara district of Maharashtra, and was later extended to other parts of the state. The programme aimed at imparting basic literacy skills within a period of about four months and by 1963, it spread to all the districts of the state. The programme, however, suffered from a lack of systematic follow-up and consequently, relapse to illiteracy was massive. In the beginning of the Fifth Plan, a programme of non-formal education for 15- 25 age-group was launched. Although the scope, content and objective of the non-formal project was clearly spelt out, its understanding in the field was very limited and the programmes actually organised indistinguishable from the conventional literacy programmes. Workers' Social Education Institutes and Polyvalent Adult Education Centres were reviewed by a group in 1977, which recommended adoption of Polyvalent Adult Education Centres in the adult education programme for workers in urban areas. In pursuance of this decision, Shramik Vidyapeeths were set up in the states.

The rationale for the establishment of the National Literacy Mission (NLM) lay in the realisation that the process of nation building would never be complete without giving literacy a major thrust. It was on this account that the NLM was launched in the Mission mode with a clear time nearlisation frame to achieve the objective of making 100 million in 15-35 age group literate by 1999. The success of the Ernakulam model (a district in the state of Kerala), which based itself on a spirit of voluntarism and complete mobilisation of civil society, became the organising principle of the Total Literacy Campaigns. Over the last decade, literacy campaigns have reached more than 90 per cent of India's villages and population. The district is the unit of implementation and coverage of all the blocks in a district is taken up in campaign mode with people's participation. Over the last five years, the campaign has been expanded to remote corners of the country including the educationally backward states of Bihar, Madhya Pradesh, Uttar Pradesh and Rajasthan. The spirit of voluntarism has been remarkable in the literacy campaigns. Even, inaccessible districts such as Dumka in Bihar and Banswara in Rajasthan, with very low female literacy levels in 1991, have generated significant social mobilisation campaigns and have unleashed unprecedented enthusiasm across the country.

Directorate of Adult Education originated from National Fundamental Education Centre (NFEC), which was set up by Govt. of India in the year 1956. This centre renamed as Department of Adult Education and made part of National Institute of Education under the NCERT, in 1961. Following the Governments thrust on adult education resulting in substantial increase in adult education activities/programmes in the country, this department separated from NCERT and given an independent identity in the year 1971. The University Grants Commission (UGC) has played a key role in shaping the character of University Adult Education in India since the launching of the National Adult Education Programme in 1978. During the last two decades, the UGC has not only formulated a number of guidelines on adult continuing education programmes, but has also provided one hundred per cent funding support to universities to implement the programmes. Today, as many as 93 universities have set up Adult Education Departments and they have implemented a variety of programmes. The UGC guideline on Adult/Continuing Education emphasises that the universities and the colleges must become sensitive to the learning needs of the community and respond to the same through relevant learning programmes and tools. UGC is providing financial assistance for this purpose at university, college and community level. This has been in the form of staff inputs and programme inputs and some non-recurring infrastructural inputs in the Department of Adult/Continuing Education.

**Conclusion**

Adult education is more important for economic and social improvement of any country. Developed countries are more ahead in this direction. United Nations Educational, Scientific and Cultural Organization (UNESCO) is providing fund and implementing various measure of adult education. In India, UGC providing fund for running the afult education programmes. Directorate of Adult Education is also working with UGC. During the last two decades, the UGC has formulated a number of guidelines on adult continuing education programmes. National Literacy Mission (NLM) lay in the realisation that the process of nation building would never be complete without giving literacy a major thrust.

## REFERENCES


1. Carol E. Kasworm, Amy D. Rose, Jovita M. Ross-Gordon (2010). *Handbook of Adult and Continuing Education*, SAGE Publications.
2. Christopher Duke (1987). *Adult Education: International Perspectives from China*, Croom Helm.
3. Charles Allen Prosser, M. R. Bass (1930). *Adult education: the evening industrial school.* American Technical Society.
4. Colin J. Titmus (1989). *Lifelong education for adults: an international handbook*, Pergamon Press.
5. David Minton (2005). *Teaching Skills in Further and Adult Education*, Cengage Learning.
6. Douglas Payne (1975). *The Scope of Adult Education: A Summary of Views*, Adult Education Board of Tasmania.
7. Dorothy MacKeracher (2004). *Making Sense of Adult Learning*, University of Toronto Press.
8. Eduard Lindeman (1926). *The meaning of adult education*, New Republic, Inc.
9. Eduard Lindeman (1961). *The meaning of adult education*, Harvest House.
10. Griff Foley (2004). *Dimensions of Adult Learning: Adult Education and Training in a Global Era*, Allen & Unwin.
11. Griff Foley (2004). *Dimensions of Adult Learning,* McGraw-Hill International.
12. Jasvir (2013). Essay on the importance of adult education in India, Retrieved from http://www.preservearticles.com/201103264737/importance-of-adult-education-in-india.html
13. John M. Peters and Peter Jarvis (1991). *Adult Education: Evolution and Achievements in a Developing Field of Study*, John Wiley & Sons.
14. Les Walklin (1990). *Teaching and Learning in Further and Adult Education,* Nelson Thornes.
15. Manjeet Paintel (2006). Adult education in India, Indonesia, and China: A Comparative Analysis, Retrieved from http://www.cccindia.co/corecentre/Database/Docs/DocFiles/adult_education.pdf

16. Maxwell Calloway (2009). The Eight Principles of Adult Education, Retrieved from http://voices.yahoo.com/the-eight-principles-adult-education-3326900.html
17. Malcolm Tight (2002). *Key Concepts in Adult Education and Training*, Psychology Press.
18. Mark Tennant (2006). *Psychology and Adult Learning*, Taylor & Francis.
19. Malcolm Shepherd Knowles, Elwood F. Holton and Richard A. Swanson (1998). *The Adult Learner: The Definitive Classic in Adult Education and Human Resource Development*, Gulf Publishing Company.
20. Mark Tennant (1997). *Psychology and Adult Learning*, Psychology Press.
21. Malcolm Shepherd Knowles, Elwood F. Holton, Richard A. Swanson (2005). *The Adult Learner: The Definitive Classic in Adult Education and Human Resource Development,* Elsevier.
22. Malcolm Tight (1996). *Key Concepts in Adult Education and Training,* Routledge, Chapman & Hall, Incorporated.
23. Peter Jarvis (2004). *Adult Education and Lifelong Learning: Theory and Practice*, Routledge Falmer.
24. Peter Mayo (1999). *Gramsci, Freire and Adult Education: Possibilities for Transformative Action*, Palgrave Macmillan.
25. Peter Jarvis (1991). *Twentieth Century Thinkers in Adult Education*, Routledge.
26. P. Vasantha Kumari, Adult / Continuing Education in Indian Universities, Retrieved from http://www.iiz-dvv.de/index.php?article_id=479&clang=1
27. Peter Jarvis (1995). *Adult and Continuing Education: Theory and Practice*, Psychology Press.
28. Sharan B. Merriam and Phyllis M. Cunningham (1989). *Handbook of adult and continuing education*, Jossey-Bass Publishers.
29. Sharan B. Merriam and Ralph G. Brockett (2011). *The Profession and Practice of Adult Education: An Introduction*, John Wiley & Sons.
30. Sharan B. Merriam, Rosemary S. Caffarella and Lisa M. Baumgartner (2012). *Learning in Adulthood: A Comprehensive Guide*, John Wiley & Sons.
31. S. G. Raybould (1951). *The English universities and adult education,* Worker's Educational Association.
32. Stephen Brookfield (1986). *Understanding and facilitating adult learning*, Jossey-Bass.
33. W. J. A. Harris (1980). *Comparative Adult Education: Practice, Purpose and Theory*, Addison-Wesley Longman Limited.
34. William J. Rothwell (2008). *Adult Learning Basics*, American Society for Training and Development.
35. Yvonne Hillier (2002). *Reflective Teaching in Further and Adult Education,* Continuum
36. http://uil.unesco.org/fileadmin/keydocuments/AdultEducation/en/GRALE_en.pdf

# 18

# Distance Education in India: An Overview

***Dr. N.C. Patnaik***

*"The philosophy of the school room in one generation will be the philosophy of government in the next."*

**— Abraham Lincoln**

## Introduction

Education in its general sense is a form of learning in which the knowledge, skills, and habits of a group of people are transferred from one generation to the next through teaching, training, or research. Education frequently takes place under the guidance of others, but may also be autodidactic. A right to education has been recognised by some governments. At the global level, Article 13 of the United Nations' 1966 International Covenant on Economic, Social and Cultural Rights recognises the right of everyone to an education. Systems of schooling involve institutionalised teaching and learning in relation to a curriculum, which itself is established according to a predetermined purpose of the schools in the system. Schools systems are sometimes also based on religions, giving them different curricula. Preschools provide education up to the age of between four and eight when children enter primary education. Primary (or elementary) education consists of the first 5–7 years of formal, structured education. In general, primary education consists of six or eight years of schooling starting at the age of five or six, although this varies between, and sometimes within, countries. In most contemporary educational systems of the world, secondary education comprises the formal education that occurs during adolescence. It is characterised by transition from the typically compulsory, comprehensive primary education for minors, to the optional, selective tertiary, *"post-secondary"*, or *"higher"* education. Higher education is the non-compulsory educational level that follows the completion of a school providing a secondary education, such as a high school or secondary school. It is also known as tertiary, third stage, or post-secondary education. Tertiary education is normally taken to include undergraduate and postgraduate education, as well as vocational education and training. Colleges and universities are the main institutions that provide tertiary education. Collectively, these are sometimes known as tertiary institutions.

**What is Distance-Education?**

Distance-education is in fact a form of open education. It is a device by which people residing in remote regions receive education according to their interests and aptitudes. It is a form of education in which teacher does not take the responsibility of oral teaching but becomes instrumental in imparting knowledge to those who want to get it at the place of their own choice. The US National Center for Education Statistics (NCES, 2002) defines distance education as *"education or training courses delivered to remote (off-campus) location(s) via audio, video (live or prerecorded), or computer technologies, including both synchronous and asynchronous instruction."* Distance learning programmes are generally designed to serve an off campus population.

**Distance Education in India**

The system of education in India has a great historical and cultural heritage. It has been changed from time to time because of the socio-economic and cultural pressures. Distance-education is widely used for teacher training around the world, in both small and large countries and in a variety of contexts. The success of the British Open University in the seventies acted as the inspiration for policy makers in many developing countries to establish their own open universities or distance teaching units. The history of formal open distance education can be traced from the recommendations of the first-education commission in independent India. The University Commission (1948) headed by Dr. S. Radhakrishnan made two very important policy-related recommendations which formed the basis for open distance education in India. They are: Equal Educational Opportunities, and Decentralisation of Education. The UGC also encouraged correspondence coursers in Indian Universities.

Open schooling is considered the basic right of every citizen. The states of Madhya Pradesh, Punjab, Andhra Pradesh, Haryana, Maharashtra, Tamil Nadu and Karnataka have also started open schools. Online distance learning (ODL) continues to grow in popularity. Recently government launched a computerisation programme *'Vidya Vahini'* proposing to connect 60,000 government–funded senior secondary schools through Internet and Intranet. The programme would provide the schools with computer labs to facilitate IT education, access to Internet, online library, academic services, web broadcast and e-learning. The digital age has greatly increased both the speed and amount of information for those with access to the Internet, the fastest growing form of media and accessible information. In terms of providing education in distance mood South India occupied a predominant position.

India made an early start in the use of radio in schools. Radio has been in use since the early fifties as supplement to the regular curriculum. Television has been used for educational purposes right from its introduction in 1959. The INSAT programme followed SITE and now provides educational programmes to primary school children as well as area specific programmes for rural viewers in selected clusters in a few states. Correspondence courses at secondary level were started in 1965 when the CABE recommended such courses with the objective of improving the academic standards of private students. The first open school was established in New Delhi in 1979 in order to provide distance education to school dropouts enabling them to enrol for the secondary course (Class X). The open school started offering senior secondary courses (class XII) in September, 1988. In November 1989, this institution was upgraded to the National Open School (NOS), an autonomous institution of the Central Government with the objective of providing relevant, continuing and developmental education to prioritised client groups as an alternative to the formal system. The states of Punjab and Andhra Pradesh have also established Open Schools recently. Maharashtra is in the process of establishing an Open School.

Distance Education for higher education in India was initiated in the form of Correspondence Courses in 1962, in response to the ever-increasing demand for higher education which could not be met by the conventional system. The Delhi University established a School of Correspondence Courses and Continuing Education in 1962. Encouraged by the success, the Education Commission (1964-66) recommended the expansion of correspondence education for various purposes. Consequently, the University Grants Commission (UGC) formulated guidelines for introducing correspondence courses in Indian Universities. Three more Institutes of Correspondence Studies were established in the late sixties. The establishment of IGNOU at New Delhi in 1985 has proved to be a significant milestone in the development of distance education in India. It provides a central organisation for guiding and coordinating the activities of all distance education institutes and state open universities in the country. It has popularised the concept of open learning system resulting in the establishment of three more state open universities in the late eighties viz. - Kota Open University in Kota (Rajasthan), Yashwant Rao Chavan Maharashtra Open University at Nasik (Maharashtra) and Nalanda Open University at Patna (Bihar). States of Madhya Pradesh and Karnataka have also established Open Universities recently.

About 25 years ago, correspondent education in India was started as a pilot project in the University of Delhi. The success of this experiment encouraged other universities to take up instructions through the distance education. By 1985, 31 universities adopted this scheme. About 40,000 students at various levels were enrolled by the universities under this scheme. Though the universities are providing education through this media, but there was a great demand for an

Open University. The Indira Gandhi National Open University was established in 1985. IGNOU has two important functions to perform; one, as a university, and second, as an apex body. It is become an international university. Besides catering to Indian students, it provides education to students in many countries in Gulf, Indian Ocean Islands, South Asia and Africa. The University has made a significant mark in the areas of higher education, community education and continual professional development. The University has been networking with reputed public institutions and private enterprises for enhancing the educational opportunities being offered by it. As a world leader in distance education, it has been conferred with awards of excellence by the Commonwealth of Learning (COL), Canada, several times.

After the establishment of Indira Gandhi National Open University, two more Open Universities were established: Kota Open University (1987), and Yashwant Rao Chavan Maharashtra Open University (1989). Nalanda Open University (Bihar) though formally established in 1987, is yet to make a serious beginning in taking up distance education programmes. During the period 1980-91, the country witnessed the simultaneous growth of two streams in distance education, the Open University system comprising five open universities, and thirty-five distance education directorates attached to conventional universities. The first Open University in India was SNDT University, Bombay. Formerly it was university for women. In an open university, there are three tier systems of evolution (i) self-education, (ii) education by the tutor, and (iii) education by the university. After the completing three stages, a certificate is awarded to the candidate. Developments in instructional designs and information communication, technologies brought drastic changes in the process and operations of open distance education. Open learning system advocates for complete autonomy to the learner. The learner is free to choose the course objectives (s), medium of instruction, delivery mechanism, examination mode etc., according to his or her needs. The multiple media and multimedia approach is used to ensure optimum learning by the learners. The ultimate goal of open learning is to create a learning society. Thirteen state open universities have been established by the state governments of India primarily with a view to freeing distance education form the clutches of unimaginative administrative control of the conventional institutions/universities. They are (1) Vardhman Mahaveer Open University (VMOU), Kota, Rajasthan; (2) Dr. B.R. Ambedkar Open University (BRAOU), Hyderbad, A.P.; (3) Nalanda Open University (NOU), Patna, Bihar; (4) Yashwantrao Chavan Maharashtra Open University (YCMOU), Nakhin, Maharashtra; (5) Madhya Pradesh Bhoj Open University (MPBOU), Bhopal, M.P.; (6) Dr. Babasaheb Ambedkar Open University (BAOU), Gujarat; (7) Karnataka State Open University (KSOU), Mysore, Karnataka; (8) Netaji Subhas Open University (NSOU), Kolkata, W.B.; (9) U.P. Rajarshi Tandon Open University (UPRTOU), Allahabad, U.P.; (10) Tamil Nadu Open University (TNOU), Chennai, Tamil Nadu.; (11) Pt. Sunderlal Sharma Open University (PSSOU), Bilaspur, Chhattisgarh; (12) Uttaranchal Open University, Haldwani (Nainitail), Uttaranchal; (13) K. K. Handique State University, Guwahati, Assam, and (14) Global Open State UIniversity, Dimapur, Nagaland.

At one time, distant learning was limited to independent study relying mostly on pencil and paper correspondence courses, but with the rapid application of ICT, the options for delivering distance learning have broadened significantly. Technology-based distance education is emerging as an increasingly important component of higher education. Interaction is also a very important aspect of the role of the instructor in distance education, and one that changes in the online environment. The advantages of video conferencing in educational institutions are well documented.

The uses of computers and computer aided programmes have substantially changed the present era of education. Computer is the basic tool to go through Information Technology. Another mechanism of availing higher education from overseas is through virtual education. It does have enormous potential for offering quality education to students who otherwise may not be able to engage in class room based learning. To enhance the quality teaching modern technological aids like LCD, OHP, Computer skills, charters, models, must be utilised. The internet enables students to locate catalogues in international libraries, study e-books and the texts of famous documents. The satellite is the glamorous medium in distance education. It is used for communicating over long distance. All teaching and learning programmes can be greatly improved by virtual and auditory materials because these make the learning experience for more concrete and memorable. The Library and Documentation Division of IGNOU has started giving efforts to take higher education to the doorsteps of the hitherto un-reached through its various modes of Information and Document Delivery Services. The goal of most governments is to widen access to education while improving its quality and reducing its cost. With the increasing number of student enrolments in ODL institutions and the growth of cross-border ODL, especially by for-profit providers in Asia, the issue of quality and quality assurance (QA) has become more pressing than ever before. Mobile devices and services have the potential to introduce novel innovations in the area of learning and education.

**Quality Assurance**

The Distance Education Council (DEC) has been specially established at IGNOU, which is not only an open university but also an apex body for distance education in India. One of the major roles of DEC is to promote, coordinate and determine standards in the system. DEC has worked out some modalities with regard to quality control and assurance in collaboration with the National Accreditation and Assessment Council established by the University Grants Commission. Directorates of Correspondence Courses that were earlier supported by the UGC are now being supported by the DEC. It provides opportunities to all the distance learning institutions in the country to discuss and share their expertise and resources in order to achieve the objectives of the institution. In the fulfillment of its role of co-ordination and maintenance of standards in open distance education, IGNOU has developed an effective network to enable ODL institutions sharing of economic and institutional resources to encourage student's mobility and to eliminate duplication. It supports research and development activities undertaken by individuals and institutions, particularly those having direct bearing on quality of ODL programmes. E-Gyankosh is a digital repository initiated by IGNOU to enhance the accessibility of knowledge to share its valuable resources with educational institutions and learners internationally. This national Digital Repository acts as a podium to store, index, preserve and share the digital learning resources developed by the Open and Distance Learning Institutions in the country. Major national challenges arise from the continuing large number of illiterates especially the large proportion of illiterate rural women. Quality assurance agencies will invariably use a combination of the three approaches of accreditation, assessment and audit. The Distance Education Council (DEC) gives provisional recognition to Universities/ Institutions who apply to DEC for offering programmes through distance education mode. Provisional recognition is accorded to Institutions that satisfy the minimum criteria prescribed by DEC for starting or for offering programmes in distance mode. Provisional recognition certifies or provides the authority to offer programmes in distance mode.

Developing high quality learning content may be important for quality assurance. For effective planning and developing course content, it would be important to provide a workable set of guidelines in the development of online course across the institution. A relative weakness of quality assurance systems thus far is that though they have succeeded in providing descriptive standards or benchmarks to be followed in distance education and online learning, their efforts are largely dependent on the awareness of and the self-improvement efforts of each institute and they do not seem to include any serious sanction in the case of violation.

## Distance Education Council

Distance Education Council (DEC) is an organisation based in New Delhi, India responsible for the promotion and coordination of the Open University and distance education system and for determination of its standards in India. The Council was constituted under the Indira Gandhi National Open University Act (1985). Its consistent with the duty of the University that takes all such steps as it may deem fit for the promotion of the Open University and distance education systems in the educational pattern of the country and for the coordination and determination of standards of teaching, evaluation and research in such systems; and in pursuance of the objects of the University to encourage greater flexibility, diversity, accessibility, mobility and innovation in education at the University level by making full use of the latest scientific knowledge and new educational technology, and to further cooperation between the existing Universities. It is considered necessary and expedient to establish a Distance-Education Council as an authority of the University under Section 16 of the Act. In June 2013, UGC has taken over Distance-Education Council. The UGC has constituted a Committee to examine the pending proposals of programme-wise recognition to the institutions.

## DEC of IGNOU Dissolved

Ministry of Human Resource Development (MHRD) has dissolved Distance Education Council (DEC) with immediate effect and University Grants Commission has been given the responsibility of Open and Distance Learning (ODL). The DEC under Indira Gandhi National Open University (IGNOU), was the apex regulatory body for distance education offered by universities across the country. Ministry of Human Resource Development, government of India has entrusted all the regulatory responsibilities of ODL education system in the country upon UGC. UGC, in the meantime is working on development of appropriate regulations for maintaining standards in ODL programmes. *"Pursuant to notification dated May 4 issued by the IGNOU, statute 28 of IGNOU Act 1985 dealing with the DEC has been repealed and deleted with immediate effect"*. Accordingly, DEC of IGNOU stands dissolved a UGC notification, dated May 28 stated. The UGC said it was working on development of appropriate regulations for maintaining standards in ODL programmes/courses. Headquartered in New Delhi, DEC was constituted under the IGNOU Act and was responsible for promotion and coordination of the Open University and distance education system and determination of its standards in the country. Shifting of DEC from IGNOU to UGC is a good move in the interest of open distance learning programme in the country. With ODL emerging as powerful and sought after mode of learning in today's age of globalisation, the empowered body like UGC could govern the affairs effectively. Set up by the Union government in 1956, UGC is a statutory organisation that has the unique distinction of being the only grant-giving agency in the country which has been vested with two responsibilities — of providing funds and of coordination, determination and maintenance of standards in institutions of higher education.

## Conclusion

The system of education in India has a great historical and cultural heritage. It has been changed from time to time because of the socio-economic and cultural pressures. Open schooling is considered the basic right of every citizen. Distance Education for higher education in India was initiated in the form of Correspondence Courses in 1962, in response to the ever- increasing demand for higher education. After the establishment of Indira Gandhi National Open University, two more Open Universities were established: Kota Open University (1987), and Yashwant Rao Chavan Maharashtra Open University (1989). Nalanda Open University (Bihar) though formally established in 1987, is yet to make a serious beginning in taking up distance education programmes. Distance Education Council (DEC) is an organisation based in New Delhi, India responsible for the promotion and coordination of the Open University and distance education system and for determination of its standards in India. The Council was constituted under the Indira Gandhi National Open University Act (1985). Fourteen state open universities have been established by the state governments of India primarily with a view to freeing distance education from the clutches of unimaginative administrative control of the conventional institutions/universities. In June 2013, UGC has taken over Distance Education Council. The UGC has constituted a Committee to examine the pending proposals of programme-wise recognition to the institutions.

## REFERENCES


1. Alford, P (2010), *Distance Education Student Primer: Skills for Being a Successful Online Learner,* Detailed available at http://ittraining.iu.edu/free/DESPR.pdf
2. Addah at et.al, (2010), *Promoting E-Learning in Distance Education Programs in an African Country,* Detailed available at http://cdn.intechopen.com/pdfs/31953/InTech Promoting_e_learning_in_distance_education_programs_in_an_african_country.pdf
3. Akhtar, S, Munshi, P and Uddin, M (2011), Comparative Costs for Initial Training of Primary Teachers in Pakistan, *Asian Journal of Distance Education.*
4. Akhtar, S, Munshi, P and Uddin, M (2011), Comparative Costs for Initial Training of Primary Teachers in Pakistan, *Asian Journal of Distance Education,* See http://www.asianjde.org/2011v9.1.Akhtar.pdf
5. Banks at et.al, (2007), *Costing Open and Distance Teacher Education: Case Study Examples from Sub-Saharan Africa*, Detailed http://wikieducator.org/images/1/1a/Costing_Study_101907.pdf
6. Crawford, J (2009), *Learning Theories that Encompass Distance Education*, Detailed available at http://edtech2.boisestate.edu/crawfordj/portfolio/files/5_Learn_theories.pdf
7. Chakraborty, A (2009), Development of Teaching-Learning Process in the Higher Education: Some Observation, Ghosh, A and Parichha, T (Eds), *Quality in Higher Education: Issues and Challenges*, First Edition, Kolkata: Ashadeep.
8. Chakraborti, P (2009), Teaching-Learning Process; Indian Perspective, Ghosh, A and Parichha, T (Eds), *Quality in Higher Education: Issues and Challenges*, First Edition, Kolkata: Ashadeep.
9. Chatterjee, M and Moore, P (2009), *Issues of inclusivelty for online distance learners: an academic learning support perspective,* Detailed available at http://www.bmartin.cc/pubs/09-4apcei/4apcei-Chatterjee.pdf
10. Choi, S and Ahn, S (2010), Quality Assurance for Online Programs, *International Journal of Advancements in Computing Technology,* Volume 2, Number 4, Detailed available at http://www.aicit.org/ijact/ppl/9-IJACT1-135044.pdf
11. Creed, C and Perraton, H (2001), *Distance Education in the E-9 Countries: The Development and Future of Distance Education Programmes in the Nine High-Population Countries.*
12. Daniel, S (2011), *Transforming Asia through Open and Distance Learning,* Detailed available at http://www.aaou.net/aaou2011/docs/25tth%20AAOU%20Conference%20eynote.pdf
13. *Distance Education (2012),* Detailed available at http://en.wikipedia.org/wiki/Distance_education

14. *Distance Education Council (2012),* Detailed available at http://www.dec.ac.in/
15. Doggett, A (2008), *The Videoconferencing Classroom: What Do Students Think?,* Detailed available at http://scholar.lib.vt.edu/ejournals/JITE/v44n4/pdf/doggett.pdf
16. Driscoll, D (2003), *Massachusetts Recommended Criteria for Distance Learning Courses,* Detailed available at http://www.doe.mass.edu/edtech/news03/distance_learning.pdf
17. Ghatak, S (2009), Higher education in the light social relevance: Some observations, Ghosh, A and Parichha, T (Eds), *Quality in Higher Education: Issues and Challenges,* First Edition, Kolkata: Ashadeep.
18. Gillies, D (2008), *Student perspectives on videoconferencing in teacher education at a distance,* Detailed available at http://www.mdecgateway.org/olms/data/resource/6313/Student % 20 Perspectives % 20 on % 20 Videoconferencing % 20 in % 20 Teacher % 20 Education % 20 at % 20 a % 20 Distance.pdf
19. Gupta, D and Chowdhury, S (2009), E-learning and Quality of higher education, Ghosh, A and Parichha, T (Eds), *Quality in Higher Education: Issues and Challenges,* First Edition, Kolkata: Ashadeep.
20. Garrison, R (2010), *Theoretical Challenges for Distance Education in the 21st Century: A shift from structural to transactional issues,* Detailed available at http://www.irrodl.org/index.php/irrodl/article/view/2/333
21. Hannay, M and Newvine, T (2006), Perceptions of distance learning: A comparison of online and traditional learning), *MERLOT Journal of Online Learning and Teaching* /Vol. 2 No. 1, Detailed available at http://jolt.merlot.org/documents/MS05011.pdf
22. *IGNOU: A Brief Profile (2012*), Detailed available at http://www.ignouagt.in/
23. Johri, P (2005), *Modern Distance Education,* First education, New Delhi: Anmol Publications Pvt. Ltd.
24. Jumani, N and Khan, S (2009), Higher Education Through Distance Learning In Pakistan, *Asian Journal of Distance Education,* Detailed available at http://www.asianjde.org/2009v7.1.Jumani.pdf
25. Jung, I (2007), Changing Faces of Open and Distance Learning in Asia, *International Review of Research in Open and Distance Learning,* Volume 8, Number 1, Detailed available at http://unpan1.un.org/intradoc/groups/public/documents/APCITY/UNPAN029185.pdf
26. Kanaujia, S and Satyanarayana, N (2004), *E-Education in India: Pace of Learning on a Hi-Tech Path,* Detailed available at http://ir.inflibnet.ac.in/dxml/browse?value=Satyanarayana%2C+N+R&type=author
27. Kato, H and Wong, S (1993), Distance education in Asia and Pacific: Country papers, *United Nations Educational, Scientific and Cultural Organisation,* Detailed available at http://www.unesco.org/education/pdf/53_23b.pdf

28. Karmakar, B (2009), The Internal Quality Assurance Cell: An Essential tool for Quality Sustenance, Ghosh, A and Parichha, T (Eds), *Quality in Higher Education: Issues and Challenges*, First Edition, Kolkata: Ashadeep.
29. Kinshuk, Suhonen, J, Sutinen, E and Goh, T (2003), Mobile Technologies in Support of Distance Learning, *Asian Journal of Distance Education,* Detailed available at http://www.asianjde.org/2003v1.1.Kinshuk.pdf
30. Knebel, E (2001), *The Use and Effect of Distance Education in Healthcare: What Do We Know?,* Detailed available at http://www.hciproject.org/sites/default/files/Distance%20Education.pdf
31. Khvilon, E and Patru, M (2002), *Open and Distance Learning: Trends, Policy and Strategy Consideration*, Detailed available at http://unesdoc.unesco.org/images/0012/001284/128463e.pdf
32. Latchanna, G and Hussein, J (2007), Economics of Education, First edition, New Delhi: Discovery Publishing House.
33. Lewis et al., (1997), *Distance Education in Higher Education Institutions, National centre for education statistics,* Detailed available at http://www.thejeo.com/Volume4Number2/Angelino%20Final.pdf
34. Malik, N, Belawati, T and Baggaley, J (2005), *Framework of Collaborative Research and Development on Distance Learning Technology for Asia*, Detailed available at http://www.pandora-asia.org/downloads/06-ICT4D_Ch2.pdf
35. Martin, M (2005), Seeing is believing: the role of videoconferencing in distance learning, *British Journal of Educational Technology,* Vol. 36, No. 3, Detailed available at http://www.qou.edu/arabic/researchProgram/distanceLearning/theRoleVideoconferencing.pdf
36. Mazumdar, P (2009), Information Communications Technology and Teaching of History, Ghosh, A and Parichha, T (Eds), *Quality in Higher Education: Issues and Challenges,* First Edition, Kolkata: Ashadeep.
37. Mcquaide, S (2011), *School-Based versus Distance Training for Rural Teachers in China,* Detailed available at http://www.asianjde.org/2011v9.1.McQuaide.pdf
38. Miliszewska, I (2008), *Transnational Education Programs: Student Reflections on a Fully-Online Versus a Hybrid Model,* Detailed available at http://www.universityworldnews.com/filemgmt_data/files/Transnational%20Education%20programmes.pdf
39. Miyazoe, T (2008), Quality in distance education: A macro analysis of recent trends and issues, *International Journal for Education Media and Technology*, Vol. 2, No. 1, pp. 15-26, Detailed available at http://wwwsoc.nii.ac.jp/jaems/contents/ICoME/icomej/vol 2/IJEMT2.15-26.pdf
40. Motlik, S (2008), Mobile Learning in Developing Nations, *International Review of Research in Open and Distance Learning,* Volume 9, Number 2, Detailed available at http://www.sustainabilityprofessionals.org/system/files/Technology_and_ESD.pdf

41. Mishra, M (2005), *Mahatma Gandhi and Education*, First edition, New Delhi: Akanksha Publishing House.
42. Mupinga, D (2005), *Distance Education in High Schools: Benefits, Challenges and Suggestions*, Detailed available at http://www.jstor.org/discover/10.2307/30190031?uid=3738256&uid=2129&uid=2&uid=70&uid=4&sid=56112423063
43. Murthy, S, Gujrati, R and Iyer, S (2010), *Using System Dynamics to Model and Analyse a Distance Education Program,* Detailed available at http://www.cse.iitb.ac.in/~sri/papers/sysdyn-cdeep-ictd10.pdf
44. Nanda, V (2007), *Typology of Distance Teaching Systems*, First education, New Delhi: Anmol Publications Pvt. Ltd.
45. Namibia, W (2010), *Taking OER beyond the OER community: Towards quality of Higher education,* Detailed available at http://oerworkshop.weebly.com uploads/4/1/3/4/4134458/taking_oer_beyond_the_oer_community_windhoek_final_report.pdf
46. Neil, T (2006), *How Distance Education has changed teaching and the role of the instructor*, Detailed available at http://www.g-casa.com/download/ONeil_Distance_Education.pdf
47. Ojha, S (2009), Technology, Pedagogy and Quality: The higher education context, Ghosh, A and Parichha, T (Eds), *Quality in Higher Education: Issues and Challenges*, First Edition, Kolkata: Ashadeep.
48. *Open and Distance Education in India, (2010),* Detailed available at http://ycmou.digitaluniversity.ac/WebFiles/Study%20Centre%20 Manual_new2Jan2012.pdf
49. Parichha, T (2009), Quality of Higher Education and Role of NSS: A case study, Ghosh, A and Parichha, T (Eds), *Quality in Higher Education: Issues and Challenges*, First Edition, Kolkata: Ashadeep.
50. Perraton et al., (2001), *Teacher Education through Distance Learning: Technology, Curriculum, Evolution and Cost*, Detailed available at http://www.irrodl.org/index.php/irrodl/article/view/725/1317
51. *Profile (2012),* Detailed available at http://www.ignou.ac.in/ignou/aboutignou/profile/2
52. Pettym L and Johnston, J (2008), *Handbook of Distance Education for adult learners,* Detailed available at http://www.projectideal.org/pdf/Print%20Resources/DEH and book 4th Edition20081002sm.pdf
53. Puri, U (2006), *Distance Education*, First edition, Kolkata: Pragun Publications.
54. *Quality Assurance in Open and Distance Learning (1999),* Detailed available at http://www.col.org/PublicationDocuments/pub_Quality_Assurance_05_web.pdf
55. Ramanujam, P (2002), *Distance Open Learning: Challenges to Developing Countries,* First edition, Delhi: Shipra Publications.
56. Rai, A (2005), *Distance Education: Open Learning's. Virtual university concepts*, First edition, Delhi: Author press.

57. Rao, S (2008), The Social Basis of Distance Education: Strategies for Inclusive Growth, *Asian Journal of Distance Education,* Detailed available at http://www.asianjde.org/2008v6.2.RajaRao.pdf http://www.knowledgecommission.gov.in/downloads/documents/towards_knowledgesociety.pdf

58. Rao, V (2010), Distance Education for the Garment Industry in India, *Asian Journal of Distance Education,* Detailed available at http://www.asianjde.org/2010v8.1.Rao.Abstract.html

59. Roberts, J and Crittenden, L (2010), Accessible Distance Education 101, *Research In Higher Education Journal,* Detailed available at http://www.aabri.com/rhej.html

60. Ramli, M (2009), *Managing quality assurance for distance learning programmes in Malaysia,* Detailed available at http://www.openpraxis.com/files/Ramli%20et%20al..pdf

61. Saikia, D (2011), The Role of ODL in Assam State, India, *Asian Journal of Distance Education,* Detailed available at http://www.asianjde.org/2011v9.2.Saikia.pdf

62. Saikia, J (2008), *Problems of education and rural women,* First edition, Guwahati: DVS Publishers.

63. Samanta, S (2009), Internal Quality Assurance Cell-its Role and Importance: Activities of IQAC of Raja Narendralal Khan Women's College, Ghosh, A and Parichha, T (Eds), *Quality in Higher-Education: Issues and Challenges,* First Edition, Kolkata: Ashadeep.

64. Sarkar, C (2009), Role of computer in accelerating the pace of education, Ghosh, A and Parichha, T (Eds), *Quality in Higher-Education: Issues and Challenges,* First Edition, Kolkata: Ashadeep.

65. Setboonsarng, S and Zhang, J (2006), *Using ICT in Capacity Building for Poverty Reduction in Asia: Lessons Learned from the Microfinance Training of Trainers Course,* ADB Institute Discussion Paper No. 50, Detailed available at http://www.adbi.org/files/2006.06.dp50.microfinance.tot.pdf

66. Shivastava, M (2002), A Comparative Study on Current Trends in Distance Education in Canada and India, *Turkish Online Journal of Distance-Education,* Volume: 3 Number: 4, Detailed available at https://tojde.anadolu.edu.tr/tojde8/articles/srivastava.htm

67. Singh, I and Debi, M (2010), *Virtual Learning Environment: Issues and Challenges before LIS Schools and Libraries,* Detailed available at http://www.webpages.uidaho.edu/~mbolin/lppissueindex.htm

68. Singh, S (2011), *On the scope of Distance-Education in Higher-Education sector,* Detailed available at http://www.indiaeducationreview.com/vc-desk/scope-distance-education-higher-education-sector

69. Sinha, S (2008), *Higher Education in India: Issues related to Expansion, Inclusiveness, Quality and Finance,* Detailed available at http://www.ugc.ac.in/pub/report/12.pdf

70. Strehle, (2010), *Distance Learning in America: How Institutions and Corporations are Stimulating Growth,* Detailed available at http://www.ingenta.com/institute2000/strehle.pdf

71. Sultana, S and Kamal, M (2010), *Distance Education and Open Learning in a Developing Country like Bangladesh: Philosophy and Reality*, Detailed available at http://www.col.org/pcf2/papers/sultana.pdf
72. Sukanta Satkar (2013). Distance education and quality assurance: A comparative study, In *Open and Distance learning in India: Challenges and Prospects*, Dr. Amit Chaturvedi and Dr. Kirti Vikram Singh (eds), Rapid Book Service, Lucknow, 2013, pp. 251-271.
73. Tong (2001), *Moving Towards Distance Education and Open Learning*, Detailed available at http://unpan1.un.org/intradoc/groups/public/documents/APCITY/UNPAN011271.pdf
74. Wright, D and Dibiase, D (2005), *Distance-Education in Geographic Information Science: Symposium and an Informal Survey*, Detailed available at http://dusk.geo.orst.edu/jghe.pdf
75. Venkataiah, S (2006), *Lifelong education,* First edition, New Delhi: Anmol Publications Pvt Ltd.
76. Vohra, R and Sen, A (2010), Status education and problems of Indian women, Delhi: Akshat Publications.
77. Young, S (2005), *Exploring Distance-Education Curricula for Adult Learners*, Detailed available at http://www.projectideal.org/pdf/WorkingPapers/WP8ExploringDistanceCurricula2005.pdf
78. Zhang, K (2004), *China's online education: Rhetoric and Realities*, Detailed available at http://www.irrodl.org/index.php/irrodl/article/view/477/1012
79. *MHRD dissolves Distance Education Council; UGC to frame guidelines (June 03, 2013).* Retrieved from http://www.indiaeducationreview.com/news/mhrd-dissolves-distance-education-council-ugc-frame-guidelinesThe Indian Express (June 02, 2013). Distance Education Council of IGNOU dissolved, Retrieved from http://www.indianexpress.com/news/distance-education-council-of-ignou-dissolved/1123932/
80. *Growth of distance education in India*, Retrieved from http://www.teindia.nic.in/mhrd/50yrsedu/g/52/4J/524J0601.htm

# 19

# Community Participation and Local Governance in Education

***Ravi Saini and Ms. Renu Pachauri***

*"Education is the most powerful weapon which you can use to change the world."*

**— Nelson Mandela**

## Introduction

Citizen's participation in the decision making and development activities of local governments can produce more efficient and effective delivery of services by the public sector. In order to foster participation, some responsibility must be devolved from the central to local government. However, the assignment of responsibilities to local governments cannot, by itself, ensure participation. Accountable local governments are key actors in any attempt to create an enabling environment for effective participation in public sector activities. Public participation is a political principle or practice, and may also be recognised as a right (right to public participation). The terms public participation may be used interchangeably with the concept or practice of stakeholder engagement and/or popular participation. Generally public participation seeks and facilitates the involvement of those potentially affected by or interested in a decision. The principle of public participation holds that those who are affected by a decision have a right to be involved in the decision-making process. Public participation implies that the public's contribution will influence the decision. Public participation may be regarded as a way of empowerment and as vital part of democratic governance. In the context of knowledge management the establishment of ongoing participatory processes is seen in the facilitator of collective intelligence and inclusiveness, shaped by desire for the participation of the whole community or society.

Public participation is part of *"people centered"* or *"human centric"* principles, which have emerged in Western culture over the last thirty years, and has had some bearings of education, business, public policy and international relief and development programmes. Public participation is advanced by the humanist movements and in the context of post-modernism. Public participation may be advanced as part of a *"people first"* paradigm shift. In this respect public participation may challenge the concept that *"big is better"* and the logic of centralised hierarchies, advancing alternative concepts of *"more heads are better than one"* and arguing that public participation can sustain productive and durable change.

## Role of Community Participation

### *Public policy*

In some countries public participation has become a central principle of public policy making. In the UK it has been observed that all levels of government have started to build citizen and stakeholder engagement into their policy-making processes. This may involve large-scale consultations, focus group research, online discussion forums, or deliberative citizens' juries. There are many different public participation mechanisms, although these often share common features. Public participation is viewed as a tool, intended to inform planning, organising or funding of activities. Public participation may also be used to measure attainable objectives, evaluate impact, and identify lessons for future practice.

### *Participatory budgeting*

Participatory budgeting is a process of democratic deliberation and decision-making, in which ordinary city residents decide how to allocate part of a municipal or public budget. Participatory budgeting is usually characterised by several basic design features:

1. Identification of spending priorities by community members.
2. Election of budget delegates to represent different communities.
3. Facilitation and technical assistance by public employees.
4. Local and higher level assemblies to deliberate and vote on spending priorities.
5. The implementation of local direct-impact community projects.

Participatory budgeting may be used by towns and cities around the world, and has been widely publicized in Porto Alegre, Brazil, were the first full participatory budgeting process was developed starting in 1989.

### *Public Trust*

In recent years loss of public trust in authorities and politicians has become a widespread concern in many democratic societies. Public participation is a regarded as one potential solution to the crisis in public trust and governance, particularly in the UK, Europe, and other democracies. The idea is that public should be involved more fully in the policy process in that authorities seek public views and participation, instead of treating the public as simply passive recipients of policy decisions.

***Accountability and Transparency***

Public participation may also be viewed as accountability enhancing. The argument being that public participation can be a means for the participating communities to hold public authorities accountable for implementation.

***Participatory Development***

The desire to increase public participation in humanitarian aid and development has led to the establishment of a numerous context-specific, formal methodologies, matrices, pedagogies and ad hoc approaches. These include conscientisation and praxis; Participatory action research (PPA), rapid rural appraisal (RRA) and participatory rural appraisal (PRA); appreciation influence control analysis (AIC); *"open space"* approaches; objectives oriented project planning (ZOPP); vulnerability analysis and capacity analysis.

***Environment and Sustainable Development***

In recent years public participation has become to be seen as a vital part of addressing environmental problems and bringing about sustainable development. In this context the limits of solely relying on technocratic bureaucratic monopoly of decision making, and it is argued that public participation allows governments to adopt policies and enact laws that are relevant to communities and take into account their needs.

***Right to Public Participation***

In some jurisdictions the right to public participation is enshrined by law. The right to public participation may also be conceived of as human right, or as manifestation of the right to freedom of association and freedom of assembly. As such the Netherlands, Germany, Denmark and Sweden, have public participation and freedom of information provisions in their legal systems since before the Middle Ages. Democracy and public participation are closely connected democratic societies have incorporated public participation rights into their laws for centuries. Effective public participation depends on the public having accessing to accurate and comprehensive information. Hence laws regarding public participation often deal with the issue of the right to know, access of information and freedom of information. The right to participation may also be advanced in the context of equality and group rights, meant to ensure equal and full participation of a designated group in society.

***Rio Declaration on Environment and Development***

The Rio Declaration of 1992 enshrines public participation in its 27 principles. Principle 10 states that *"environmental issues are best handled with participation of all concerned citizens, at the relevant level"*. The Rio Declaration continues, drawing a close link between access to information and public participation: *"At the national level, each individual shall have appropriate access to information concerning the environment that is held by public authorities, including information on hazardous materials and activities in their communities, and the opportunity to participate in decision-making processes. States shall facilitate and encourage public awareness and participation by making information widely available. Effective access to judicial and administrative proceedings, including redress and remedy, shall be provided."*

### *Convention on the Rights of Persons with Disabilities*

The 2006 Convention on the Rights of Persons with Disabilities recognised that *"that disability results from the interaction between persons with impairments and attitudinal and environmental barriers that hinders their full and effective participation in society on an equal basis with others"* and that *"persons with disabilities continue to face barriers in their participation as equal members of society."* The Convention makes participation of disabled one of its principles, stating *"The principles of the present Convention shall be: ... Full and effective participation and inclusion in society"*, subsequently enshrining the right of disabled to participate fully and equally in the community, education, all aspect of life (in the context of habilitation and rehabilitation), political and public life, cultural life, leisure and sports.

## Role of Local Government

As central government responsibilities are developed to local authorities, new opportunities are created for citizens, NGOs and the private sector to participate in local government activities. As a result:

1. Efficiency can be improved in the allocation of resources by better matching services and investments to the needs of stakeholders and their willingness to pay.
2. Delivery of public services also can be improved. The skills required within the public sector at all levels are primarily those of political decision-making, planning and financing. While local governments can be assigned responsibility for provision of infrastructure and services, the private sector is often better able to carry out, manage and deliver these goods and services.
3. Other benefits include broadening accountability (as citizens are involved, mechanisms for accountability external to government are developed), by contracting the private sector, NGOs or community organisations to take on specific responsibilities, the need for multiple technical functions within local government is reduced.
4. Improving equity (in this, central governments can play an important role by providing local governments with guidelines, financial support and quality control related to redistribution objectives) and sustaining benefits.

In encouraging participation, local governments can act in one of three roles:

1. Intermediary
2. Creator of an enabling environment
3. Direct provider.

**Role 1: Intermediary**

Local governments can play an important role as intermediary between citizens and central government. Acting as intermediary, local governments can facilitate citizen access to information, resources and power controlled by the state, bilateral and multilateral donors, and others. This, in turn, should facilitate the flow of information on social, political or economic matters which can help local people make more informed decisions.

**Role 2: Creator of Enabling Environment**

For local citizens to participate in local government requires that there be an enabling environment-a social and political context that encourages, supports and facilitates such participation. An appropriate social and political environment creates expanded opportunities for initiative to be taken by previously marginalised or excluded groups, and provide them with the opportunity to express their opinions, take responsibility for decision making, implementation and operations, and make their voices heard. Local governments are increasingly called upon to enact and enforce legislation in the form of local ordinances and by laws.

Participation can influence this process in two ways:

1 By lobbying for changes in existing legislation.

2 By pressuring local governments to comply with such laws.

Equally important is the authority vested in local governments to decide who may or may not participate in specified development activities. While the creation of an enabling environment can potentially contribute to the achievement of many development objectives, it has most relevance in fostering greater equity and accountability of local government actions. It enables citizen demands for transparent decision making and operations to have an impact.

**Role 3: Direct Provider**

The greatest potential for participation by local citizens occurs when local governments provide services directly. This is increasingly the case when some specified responsibilities assigned to local governments can be contracted out to the private sector, NGOs, or community organisations. When such services are provided and produced locally, the geographical proximity of provider and consumer make participation that much easier, the demonstration effect of providing services on a timely and adequate basis community participation.

### Mechanisms for Encouraging Participation

The effective facilitation of participation by local governments requires a context of good governance. There are at least four broad interrelated mechanisms through which citizens can enhance the accountability of local governments.

#### *Public involvement in the legislative process*

Citizen participation in legislative functions provides the greatest potential for citizens to influence the development decisions of local governments. Just as policy-making is a legislative function, so too is deciding how, and how much, public revenue to collect and choosing how to spend it. Citizens can influence local governments' legislative processes indirectly through elections or the pressure of interest groups or directly, by being involved in decisions about specific applications of policies established by local governments. In order for citizens to make informed decisions and effectively influence local government decisions, local government decision-making must be transparent and formal channels need to exist for interest groups to influence policy in a transparent manner. An example of such transparency is the established requirement that communities have access to the financial accounts of irrigation projects in the Philippines and Indonesia. Public hearings at the local level, especially as part of planning and budget processes are another mechanism for facilitating transparent decision-making.

#### *Public Involvement in Executive Functions*

Providing labour and other resources in kind for the implementation of already-determined government sub projects at the community level. But direct citizen involvement in executive functions can involve more significant roles, such as the right to approve the work of contractors or executing agencies before final payments are made.

#### *Judicial Processes to Resolve Conflicts*

In some countries, the judicial systems can be used by citizens to hold local governments accountable. In such systems, citizens can bring a lawsuit or complaint that local governments have operated illegally to formal courts or arbitration and mediation commissions. For such systems to operate effectively, the legal framework within which local governments are supposed to operate must be clearly articulated and understood by citizens.

#### *Consumers as Financial Participants*

While financial transfers from central to local governments continue to play an important role in enabling the provision of goods and services at the local level, local governments increasingly need to generate more of their own revenues. Thus, local governments are increasingly requiring some payment by users for investment and services. When that happens, the role of citizens is transformed from passive beneficiaries to that of key decision-makers.

***Central-Local Government Linkages***

The comprehensive term *"decentralisation"* has been used to encompass a variety of alternative institutional structures. One type of decentralisation devolution holds the most promise for participation. In devolved systems, responsibilities for a range of operations encompassing more than one sector are assigned by the central authority to local governments.

**Scheme of State and Central Government in Education**

The Scheme is being conducted since 1986. The main objectives of the scheme are:

***Vocationalisation of Secondary Education***

Vocational Education will be a distinct stream intended to prepare students for identified occupations spanning several areas of activity. These courses will be provided in general education institutions after the secondary stage with flexible duration ranging from one to three years. The state Govt. has set up vocational education wing in Directorate of Education which is the implementing agency for this scheme in schools. The scheme also envisages involvement of voluntary or other Non-Government organisations in the programme that would be given financial assistance for specific innovative projects for conducting Vocational Education programme. The scheme has been implemented in 262 Higher Secondary Schools of M.P. At present nearly 14 thousand students are studying in these schools. The vocational courses are grouped under following major areas, viz. Agriculture, Business and commerce, Engineering and Technology; Health and Para-medical Services; Home Science; Services and others. The Vocational Education is imparted in the following trades in the schools of M.P.

***Operation Black Board Scheme***

This scheme is conducted since 1986. In this scheme the institutional equipment and instructional material are provided for the students studying in primary schools in M.P. Provision is made to provide salary of an additional Teacher to these Primary Schools enrolling 100 or more than 100 students for two years. The scheme was extended for middle schools in Ninth Five Year Plans. Govt. of India provided funds to equip such middle school with Institutional equipment, instructional material and pay the salary, allowances to Shiksha – Karmi Grade 2. At present scheme is conducted by Rajiv Gandhi Shiksha Mission.

***Jawahar Village Prosperity Scheme***

Under operation Black Board Scheme the Govt. of India has provided the 45 per cent fund of the total cost of construct school building. 15 per cent fund is provided by Department of Panchayat and social welfare. The rest 40 per cent has been contributed by School Education Department from its Plan limit. Under this scheme an aims is to construct school building for 1613 primary schools consisting two Class Rooms, one Varandah, one Teacher Room and separate toilets to boys and girls. In this scheme 1157 primary school building (Chhatisgarh) are to be constructed at the cost of Rs. two lakh each. For this purpose Govt. of India and social welfare department has released 45 per cent and 15 per cent funds respectively. The scheme is very useful for the department of school education.

***Improvement in Science Education Scheme***

The scheme is initiated since October 1987 to achieve improvement in quality of science education at the level of middle schools, High school and H.S. School. The main objectives of this scheme are to provide fund for science kits in middle schools, Books on Science in the libraries of high and Higher Secondary Schools, upgradation of laboratories of High Secondary schools, establishment of Laboratories in High Schools. The scheme also aims for the training of teacher. The Govt. of India has provided Rs. 12.2538 crores to achieve the objectives of this scheme. Out of this Rs 4.293 crores could not be utilised. To utilise the balance the permission of Govt. of India is awaited. For the re-provision in Budget the action is under consideration. For the non-utilisation of the balance of Rs 7.9608 crore the main reason is the registration of the cases in Bureau of Economics offence related to the suppliers. These cases are under consideration in different courts.

***Modernisation of Scheme of Madarsa Education***

This is a scheme of Govt. of India to initiate volunteering teaching of Science, Mathematics, Social Studies, Hindi and English in Madarsa and Maqtabs. In this scheme all such voluntary organisation/committees/trusts are competent to take part, which are registered according to the central/state govt. acts and are in existence for the last three years or more. Under this scheme the financial aid is provided for the purchase of Science kit, Mathematics kit, Books and salary of additional teacher in Madarsas/Maqlabs enrolling 40 or more than 40 students in each of them. Up till now the Govt. of India has Sanctioned Rs. 1,38,13800 in the form of Financial aid for 208 Madarsas. Including new 204 Madarsa the Govt. of India has sanctioned Rs. 220.968 crore for total 412 Madarsas for Financial year 2001-2002 and for its Budgetary provision a proposal has been submitted in Govt. of M.P. after budgetary provision and sanction the funds are to be disbursed to Madarsas. A proposal of Rs. 31,11,000 for additional 69 Madarsas and Rs. 16,43,000 for 36 Madarsas are under consideration of Govt. of India.

***Integrated Education for Disabled Children***

This scheme is sponsored completely by Govt. of India, with a provision of Financial Aid. The scheme has come in the control of school Education Department when it was transferred by Social Welfare Department in 1992. The aim of this scheme is to make efforts to bring all different disabled boys and girls that are studying in general/common schools of school Education Department in the mainstream and after linking them with mainstream of education for disabled children the goal of education for all be achieved by providing different economical facilities and educational guidance.

### *Computer Literacy and Study Scheme in Schools (Class Project)*

Class Project is a centrally sponsored scheme in full. This scheme was started in M.P. during 1996-97. During 1997-98 the scheme was named as revised class project. In initial year 1996-97 a provision was made to provide 125 computers in the Schools. For next year 1997-98 a provision was kept to provide computers in 175 H.S. School. The scheme is meant for H.S. School. At present the scheme is running in 398 H.S. school registering 40000 students. Under the scheme 417 teachers were trained which are providing training to students at present. In the scheme the computer Hardware and Software are also supplied. Initially the computer training was imparted by the computer trained teacher of the school.

### *Sanskrit Education Development Schemes*

The scheme is launched by Govt. of India to develop Sanskrit Education in the country during 1998-99. The scheme aims to award the well learned in Kalidas Samaroh in which training of Sanskrit teachers and various scholarships are included. In addition to the above aim the scheme aims to provide Grant in the form of salary of the teachers of Sanskrit primary schools as received by Govt. of India. In this scheme the Govt. of India sanctioned Rs. 73.03 lacs during 98-99 and this amount is fully utilised in 1999-2000 along with Rs. 46.50 lacs for Sanskrit studying boys and girls. Efforts are in progress to send the proposals for the budgetary provisions in first supplementary.

### *District Primary Education Programme*

This programme is being conducted in 33 districts of the state with the assistance of European community and World Bank, by Rajiv Gandhi Shiksha Mission. The total cost of the sanctioned project is Rs. 959.85 crores in which the share of the State Govt. is Rs. 143.98 crores.

### *Sarva Shiksha Abhiyan*

In this scheme Govt. of India has selected the 12 districts of state of Non-DPEP. Under this scheme all programmes of upgradation of primary schools are to be shaped or implemented. For this scheme 85 per cent amount will be available from Govt. of India and the State Govt. has provided 15 per cent remaining in the Budget of 2001- 2002.

### *Education Gwrantee Scheme*

Under the scheme to run EGS schools the State Govt. sanctions the funds from DPEP head. From this financial year the Govt. of India has taken a decision to initiate the implementation of EGS - AIE by extending this scheme. Facility of secondary education within three km and primary Education with in one km is to be provided in the initially run EGS school by Mission under this scheme. For this the total expenditure will theoretically be provided by Govt. of India with 75 per cent share and rest 25 per cent share by State Govt. This scheme is run by Rajiv Gandhi Shiksha Mission.

### *Information Technology Scheme*

The aim of this scheme is to provide information to every citizen on the cost which is least as possible as and to propagate the use of Information Technology up to 2003 in Govt. High schools/H.S. schools by setting a goal of computer Training in all such educational institutions.

### *Education Technology Scheme*

The Govt. of India provides the 75 percent of the total amount and the rest 25 per cent is provided by State Govt. from its own planning. Under the scheme the provision of Rs. Two crores was made in budget during 1999-2000 for the purchase of 1000 TVs and 5000 two-in-one but this amount could not be utilized due to the non-availability of the permission from finance development.

### *Free of Cost Distribution Scheme of Text Books*

The scheme is in force in which text books are distributed free of cost to the students of SC/ST communities studying in class 1 to 5 and to the all girls of backward and general categories, who are below poverty line and studying in class 1 to 3. Under this scheme free of cost text books are supplied by Text Book Corporation. For financial year a provision of Rs 6.29 crore is made in Budget.

### *Teacher Welfare Programme*

Under this programme the teachers are selected for state level and central level awards on the basis of their qualification and the excellent services rendered by them in the field of Education through Teacher Welfare Cell in the Directorate of Public Instructions. Every selected teacher is awarded Rs. 5000 cash, Shreephal and a shawl with a letter of appreciation by Honorable Governor of the state. For the selection of teachers for National award there is a state level committee in which a representative of Govt. of India is also included. For M.P. a proposal to award 12 primary teachers and six Middle school teachers every year is sent. The selected teachers are awarded Rs.10001 cash with a silver medal by Honorable President of India on every 5th September.

## Conclusion

Initiatives by central governments to decentralise significant responsibilities to local government are growing worldwide. As a result, local governments are playing an increasingly important role in the lives of their citizens in such areas as health, education and public works. They are also becoming more active in promoting local economic growth. Responsibilities that can be most successfully devolved from central to local governments are those requiring location-specific decision-making and quick response times, and which have low economies of scale. Other criteria include activities which do not significantly impact the priority objectives of the entire country; need close integration of cross-sector activities within the area of established local jurisdictions; do not require significant support from other government agencies ; and can be contracted to the private sector for technical design, implementation and operation.

## REFERENCES

1. Abraha, S., Beyene, A., Dubale, T., Fuller, B., Holloway, S., and King, E. (1991) 'What factors shape girls' school performance? Evidence from Ethiopia.' *International Journal of Educational Development,* 11(2): 107–118.
2. Academy for Educational Development (2002) *A Transnational View of Basic Education: Issues of Access, Quality, and Community Participation in West and Central Africa.* Washington, DC: Academy for Educational Development.
3. Bray, M. (1996) *Decentralisation of Education: Community Financing.* Directions in Development. Washington DC: World Bank.
4. Bray, M. (2003) 'Community initiatives in education: goals, dimensions and linkages 64 School Processes, Local Governance and Community Participation with governments,' *Compare,* 33(1): 31-45.
5. Jerry M. Silverman and David Gow with the assistance of John Frankenhoff, "*Participation and Local Government,*" 1995, The World Bank.

# 20

# Sarva Shiksha Abhiyan in India: Success and Constrains

*Dr. P.K. Ghoshal*

*"Education is the best friend. An educated person is respected everywhere. Education beats the beauty and the youth."*

**— Chanakya**

## Introduction

Education is a tool that can play a vital role in improving the socio-economic condition of the nation. It empowers citizens with analytical abilities, leads to better confidence levels and fortifies one with will power and goal setting competencies. Education involves not only textbook learning but also a growth of values, skills and capacities. This helps individuals to plan for their career as well as play a useful part in building a new society with progressive values. Hence, education results in changing both individual lives as well as that of the entire community for the better. The Right to Education has also been enshrined as a Fundamental Right by the Constitution of India. It states that, *"The State shall provide free and compulsory education to all children of the age of six to fourteen years in such a manner as the State may, by law, determine."* To promote literacy among its citizens, the Government of India has launched several schemes such as, Mid-day Meal Scheme and the National Programme for Education of Girls at Elementary Level (NPEGEL). One of the most fundamental and promising of these schemes is the Sarva Shiksha Abhiyan.

## Concept

Sarva Shiksha Abhiyan (SSA) is Government of India's flagship programme for achievement of Universalisation of Elementary Education (UEE) in a time bound manner, as mandated by 86th amendment to the Constitution of India making free and compulsory Education to the Children of 6-14 years age group, a Fundamental Right. SSA is being implemented in partnership with State Governments to cover the entire country and address the needs of 192 million children in 1.1 million habitations. The programme seeks to open new schools in those habitations which do not have schooling facilities and strengthen existing school infrastructure through provision of additional class rooms, toilets, drinking water, maintenance grant and school improvement grants.

**Importance of Sarva Shiksha Abhiyan Scheme**

Sarva Shiksha Abhiyan is a Indian Government programme aimed at the universalisation of elementary education *"in a time bound manner"*, as mandated by the 86th amendment to the India making free and compulsory education to children of ages 6–14 (estimated to be 205 million in number in 2001) a fundamental right. The programme was pioneered by Atal Bihari Vajpayee. The programme aims to provide useful and relevant free and compulsory elementary education for all children in the age group six to fourteen years under RTE Act. 2009. It is an initiative to universalise and improve quality of education. The programme has time-bound objectives on one hand SSA is a programme with its own targets, norms and process, on the other hand it is an umbrella programme covering other programmes like DPEP, Lok Jumbish and the operational black board, etc. The programme emphasises the need for a community-based planning process.

**Components of Sarva Shiksha Abhiyan Scheme**

The components of SSA include:

1. Preparatory activities for micro-planning, household surveys, studies, community mobilisation, school-based activities, office equipment, training and orientation at all levels.
2. Appointment of teachers.
3. Opening of new primary and alternative schooling facility like EGS/AIE centers.
4. Opening of upper primary schools.
5. Constructing additional classrooms, schools and other facilities.
6. Free textbooks to all children.
7. Maintenance and repair of school buildings.
8. Teaching Learning Equipment for primary schools on upgradation of EGS to regular schools or setting up of a new primary school and for new upper primary schools.

9. School grant.
10. Teacher grant.
11. Teachers' training.
12. Opening of SIEMAT.
13. Training of community leaders.
14. Provision for children with special needs.
15. Research, Evaluation, Monitoring and Supervision.
16. Management cost.
17. Learning enhancement programme.
18. Innovative activity for girl's education, early childhood care and education, interventions for children belonging to SC/ST, minority community, deprived children in urban areas and computer education specially for upper primary level.
19. Setting up of BRCs/CRCs.
20. Interventions for out of school children.

**Sarva Shiksha Abhiyan in India: Progress**

The Sarva Shiksha Abhiyan is to provide useful and relevant elementary education for all children in the 6 to 14 age. There is also another goal to bridge social, regional and gender gaps, with active participation of the community in the management of schools. Sarva Shiksha Abhiyan realizes the importance of Early Childhood Care and Education (ECCE) and looks at the 0-14 age as continuum. All efforts to support Pre-school learning in ICDS centres or special pre school centers in non-ICDS areas will be made to supplement the efforts being made by the department of Women and Child Development. Sarva Shiksha Abhiyan (SSA) has two aspects: (a) it provides a wide convergent framework for implementation of Elementary Education schemes. and (b) it is also a programme with budget provision for strengthening vital elementary, vital areas to achieve universalisation of Elementary Education. While all investments in the Elementary Education sector from the State and the Central Plans will reflect as part of the SSA framework, they will all merge into the SSA programme within the next few years. As a programme, it reflects the additional resource provision for UEE. Various objectives of Sarva Shiksha Abhiyan:

1. All children in school, education guarantee centre, Alternate School, '*Back to School*' camp by 2004.
2. All children must complete five years of primary schooling by 2007.

3. All children must complete eight years of Elementary Schooling by 2010.
4. Focus on Elementary Education of satisfactory quality with emphasises on education for life.
5. Bridge all gender and social category gaps at primary stage by 2007 and at Elementary Education level by 2010.
6. Universal retention by 2010.

SSA has been operational since 2000-2001 to provide for a variety of interventions for universal access and retention, bridging of gender and social category gaps in elementary education and improving the quality of learning. SSA interventions include inter alia, opening of new schools and alternate schooling facilities, construction of schools and additional classrooms, toilets and drinking water, provisioning for teachers, periodic teacher training and academic resource support, textbooks and support for learning achievement. The costs for SSA are shared by the centre and states in the ratio 85:15. In 2004-05, the central government imposed an education case of two per cent on all taxes to mobilise additional funds for SSA and the Mid Day Meal Scheme. In 2008-09, this surcharge was increased to three per cent. The National Mission for Sarva Shiksha Abhiyan under the chairmanship of the Prime Minister has overall responsibility of the programme. It comprises of a governing council, which is the apex policy planning body for elementary education and the executive committee, under the chairmanship of the Minister of Human Resource Development (MoHRD), which carries out all the functions of the Mission in accordance with the policies laid down by the governing council. The Mission coordinates with State Departments for Education and the Village Education Committees (VECs), created by the State Education Departments to manage the educational affairs of villages. Implementation at the district is overseen by the District Collector, Magistrate or the Chief Executive Officer of the zilla parishad. Social science institutes of national stature have been given the work of monitoring in states and union territories.

SSA was launched with the goal of universalising primary education by 2007 and elementary education by 2010. These deadlines have been extended to 2012. At the time of SSA's commencement in 2001 there were 3.40 crore out-of-school children between the ages of 6-14. Four years after the launch of SSA with more than 85 per cent of the funds utilised, 40 per cent of the children (1.36 crore) remained out of school. The proportion of children enrolled in school has climbed over the period 2002 to 2009, even as the child population increased. The ASER surveys (2005-2008) show that there has been a significant drop in out-of-school children over the four years 2005-2008, which does not necessarily translate into regular attendance. Additionally, the net enrolment ratio has improved only marginally more than gross enrolment ratio, indicating the need to focus on ensuring that children enroll in levels corresponding to the right age. Two of the poorest Indian states, Bihar and Rajasthan, showed the sharpest declines in the percentage of children out-of-school. Bihar, in particular, saw the largest drop of 8.9 per cent in out-of-school girls in the 11-14 age groups, which is usually the most difficult group to keep in school. It has consistently reduced out-of-school children in the same period. Though Rajasthan saw reduction of almost five per cent in out-of school children in the initial years, the percentage of truant children has crept back up. The top five recipients of central funds, Bihar, UP, West Bengal, Madhya Pradesh and Rajasthan received 50 per cent of the total central outlay. These states, however, accounted for 70 per cent of out-of-school children in 2005, implying the performance of the scheme in these states was not commensurate with the allocations.

Sarva Shiksha Abhiyan takes note of the fact that provision of elementary education is largely made by the government and government aided schools. There are also private unaided schools in many parts of the country that provide elementary education. Poorer households are not able to afford the fees charged in private schools in many parts of the country. There are also private schools that charge relatively modest fees and where poorer children are also attending. Some of these schools are marked by poor infrastructure and low paid teachers. While encouraging all efforts at equity and *'access to all'* in well-endowed private unaided schools, efforts to explore areas of public-private partnership will also be made. The Sarva Shiksha Abhiyan assigns greatest importance to the preparatory activities as these have been conceived as a necessary condition for quality implementation of the programme. Systematic mobilisation of the community and creation of an effective system of decentralised decision-making are part of the preparatory activities. Strengthening of the office of the District Elementary Education Officer has also to be undertaken in the preparatory phase in order to adequately equip it to handle the larger tasks during programme implementation. The success of Sarva Shiksha Abhiyan will depend on the quality of the community-based planning process. While SSA is formulated on the premise that the community can plan, it also accepts the tremendous requirement for developing capacities in communities to do so. The starting point for planning activities has to be the creation of a core group of governmental and non-governmental persons, entrusted with the task of implementing Sarva Shiksha Abhiyan. The State level Implementation Society has to exercise utmost caution and care in ensuring that the core team at the District and Block level is carefully selected and is committed to the task of Universal Elementary Education. Besides Education Department functionaries, these teams could comprise of faculty members of DIETs, BRCs, CRCs, NGO representatives, representatives of Teacher Unions, representatives of Women's Groups, representatives of Self Help Groups, retired and serving National and State Award winning Teachers, local literary figures, Panchayati Raj/Autonomous Council representatives, etc.

Each district will prepare a perspective Plan and an Annual Plan. The perspective Plan will be a Plan for universalisation within the timeframe of Sarva Shiksha Abhiyan. It will be based on the existing position with regard to attendance, retention, drop out and learning achievement. It will work out the total requirement for universalisation, spread over a number of years. Appraisal of District Plans is critical to the Sarva Shiksha Abhiyan. The National/State Mission will undertake Appraisal of plans with the assistance of resource teams constituted by the operational support unit of the National/State Mission. Appraisal teams will be jointly constituted by the National and the State level Mission. For non-governmental representatives in appraisal teams, besides the TA/DA as admissible for government servants, a modest honorarium will be available. Sarva Shiksha Abhiyan requires regular supervision of activities. Ideally, the CRCs, BRCs, DIETs have to be developed effectively to carry out supervision activities. Supervision teams will be periodically sent by the National/State Mission usually once in six months. The Sarva Shiksha Abhiyan allows States/UTs to have their own management structures, respecting the diversity that exists in these structures across the States. The States have to set up the State level Implementation Society.

The Sarva Shiksha Abhiyan will have a community-based monitoring system. The Educational Management Information System (EMIS) will incorporate provision for correlation of school level data with community-based information from micro planning and surveys. Besides this, every school will have a notice board showing all the grants received by the school and the details thereof. All reports sent to the Block and the District level with regard to enrolment, attendance, incentive, etc., shall be displayed on the school notice board. Reporting formats will be simplified so that the output is demystified and anyone can understand the data. The State Implementation Societies (SIS) will also undertake intensive monitoring. Representatives of the National Mission for UEE and National level institutions like NCTE, NIEPA, and NCERT will also undertake periodic monitoring and provide resource support to the SIS to strengthen appraisal and monitoring systems. Besides community-based monitoring, Sarva Shiksha Abhiyan will encourage independent research and supervision by autonomous research institutions. Institutions of proven excellence have been requested to take up State specific responsibilities. Since quality is a major concern under the Sarva Shiksha Abhiyan, its monitoring will be a priority. NCERT will undertake base line assessment of learning achievements at primary level in the non-DPEP States and at upper primary level in all states in order to provide a base line for the Sarva Shiksha Abhiyan.

Education of girls, especially those belonging to the scheduled castes and scheduled tribes, is the primary focus in Sarva Shiksha Abhiyan. Efforts will be made to mainstream gender concerns in all the activities under the Sarva Shiksha Abhiyan programme. The Sarva Shiksha Abhiyan recognises the need for special efforts to bring the out-of-school girls, especially from disadvantaged sections, to school. This would require a proper identification of girls who are out of school in the course of microplanning. The Education Guarantee Scheme and Alternative and Innovative Education scheme is a part of the Sarva Shiksha Abhiyan framework. States have their own norms for recruitment of teachers and a lot of diversity exists in payments being made to new recruits. In many cases the appointing authority is the local Panchayat. The States will be free to follow their own norms as long as these consistent with the norms established by NCTE. There will be no compromise on standards even though payments of less than the State pay scale as an interim measure may be adopted in states with large-scale vacancies. Rationalisation of existing teacher units will be a priority. The presence of the non-governmental sector has to be taken note of before working out vacancies.

**Financial Norms under Sarva Shiksha Abhiyan Scheme**

Sarva Shiksha Abhiyan is conceived as a long-term partnership between the Central and the State/UT governments. The procedure for release of funds incorporates this idea of a partnership. Under the programme of Sarva Shiksha Abhiyan, the districts will prepare their proposals through a community owned Pre-project phase, based on the Broad Framework for Implementation. The State level Implementation Society for Sarva Shiksha Abhiyan will forward these proposals to the National Mission of Sarva Shiksha Abhiyan for release after appraisal by a joint team. The Central government will release funds to the State government. The State government would be expected to transfer this to the State Implementation Society within thirty days. The State governments have to give written commitments regarding its contribution towards the Sarva Shiksha Abhiyan.

The assistance under the programme of Sarva Shiksha Abhiyan will be on 85:15 sharing arrangement during the IX Plan, 75:25 sharing arrangement during the X Plan, and 50:50 sharing thereafter between the Central government and State governments. The Government of India would release funds to the State Governments/Union Territories only and instalments (except first) would only be released after the previous instalments of Central government and State share has been transferred to the State Implementation Society. The support for teacher salary appointed under the SSA programme could be shared between the Central Government and the State government in a ratio of 85:15 during the IX Plan, 75:25 during the X Plan and 50:50 thereafter. All funds to be used for upgradation, maintenance, repair of schools and Teaching Learning Equipment and local management to be transferred to VECs/School Management Committees/Gram Panchayat/or any other village/ school level arrangement for decentralisation adopted by that particular State/UT. The village/school-based body may make a resolution regarding the best way of procurement. Other incentive schemes like distribution of scholarships and uniforms will continue to be funded under the State Plan. They will not be funded under the SSA programme.

**Sarva Shiksha Abhiyan Scheme: Constraints**

Educational outreach to disadvantaged groups and disabled children has been relatively limited, and the gender parity index remains poor in several states. SSA includes a grant of a maximum of Rs. 50 lakhs per district for designing and implementing innovative activities for girls' education, early childhood care and interventions for children belonging to SC/ST communities. The scheme also includes a provision for free textbooks upto Rs.150 per child for girls and SC/ST children. However, there were several states that did not provide free textbooks, some which provided cash in lieu of books, and many which provided them to ineligible students from the general and Other Backward Caste (OBC) groups. Approximately 7.5 lakh children did not receive free textbooks while 47. 5 lakh ineligible children received them. The SSA guidelines specify that the teacher-student ratio should be maintained at 1:40 in primary and upper primary schools and at least two teachers for every class in these schools. Many states violated this with ratios ranging from 1:60 to 1:130, while other schools were on record as having several teachers and not having a single student enrolled. Financial irregularities amounting to Rs. 472.51 crore in 14 states/UTs were observed, including nonadjustment of advances, loss of interest on funds kept in current account, excess payment of contingent grant, purchases made beyond delegated powers and non-refund of un-utilised balances.

**Conclusion**

Sarva Shiksha Abhiyan is Government of India's flagship programme for achievement of Universalization of Elementary Education in a time bound manner. 86th amendment to the Constitution of India has making free and compulsory Education to the Children of 6-14 years age group which is a Fundamental Right. Sarva Shiksha Abhiyan has been operational since 2000-2001 to provide the education for poor children in India. It is also an attempt to provide an opportunity for improving human capabilities to all children. Though the Sarva Shiksha Abhiyan is being administered through government and government aided schools, some private unaided schools are also actively involved in contributing towards universal elementary education. It is a valuable endeavour of the Government of India, in the universalisation of elementary education, which strives to help citizens to realise the importance of elementary-education. Right to education or SSA programme endows with life skills and quality elementary-education. This programmes focus on girls education at priority basis along with the children's requires special needs. It also offers a computer-education to eliminate the digital differences from outer world.

## REFERENCES

1. *Introduction of SSA,* Retrieved from http://kaithal.gov.in/images/ssa.pdf
2. *Sarva Shiksha Abhiyan (2013).* Retrieved from http://ssa.nic.in/
3. *Sarva Shiksha Abhiyan (2013).* Retrieved from http://mhrd.gov.in/schemes
4. *Sarva Shiksha Abhiyan Scheme Brief (2013).* Retrieved from http://cdf.ifmr.ac.in/wp-content/uploads/2011/03/Sarva-Shiksha-Brief.pdf
5. *Chapter I,* Retrieved from http://ssa.nic.in/financial-mgmt-docs/fm-manual-as-on-may18th/Pages-1%20to%20100-Revised%20Manual-FM-P.pdf
6. *Sarva Shiksha Abhiyan: A Programme for Universal Elementary Education Framework for Implementation,* Retrieved from http://sishusuchana.org/documents/programme/SSA.pdf

7. *Sarva Shiksha Abhiyan: Education for all,* Retrieved from http://www.archive.india.gov.in/spotlight/spotlight_archive.php?id=31
8. *Sarva Shiksha Abhiyan (2013*). Retrieved from http://www.pacsindia.org/sarva-shiksha-abhiyan

# 21

# Right to Education for Person with Disabilities

*Rakesh Joshi*

*"The goal of education is the advancement of knowledge and the dissemination of truth."*

**—John F. Kennedy**

## Introduction

Education for All means ensuring that all children have access to basic education of good quality. This implies creating an environment in schools and in basic education programmes in which children are both able and enabled to learn. Today, education is central to individual success, economic growth and innovation, and the flourishing of a democratic society. The Convention on the Rights of Persons with Disabilities is a wide ranging human rights treaty covering the full spectrum of civil, cultural, economic, political and social rights. The Convention does not establish new rights for persons with disabilities; instead, it elaborates on what existing human rights mean for persons with disabilities and clarifies the obligations of States parties to protect and promote these rights. The human rights imperative of a rights-based approach means that particular focus is given to discrimination, equality and the status of vulnerable groups. In order to ensure an environment conducive to the fulfillment of the rights of persons with disabilities, the Convention also includes articles on awareness-raising, accessibility, situations of risk and humanitarian emergencies, access to justice, personal mobility, habilitation and rehabilitation, as well as statistics and data collection. Articles 10 to 30 cover the rights guaranteed to persons with disabilities:

| *Articles* | |
|---|---|
| Article 10 | The right to life |
| Article 11 | Situations of risk and humanitarian emergencies |
| Article 12 | Equal recognition before the law |
| Article 13 | Access to justice |
| Article 14 | Liberty and security of the person |
| Article 15 | Freedom from torture or cruel, inhuman or degrading treatment or punishment |
| Article 16 | Freedom from exploitation, violence and abuse |
| Article 17 | Protecting the integrity of the person |
| Article 18 | Liberty of movement and nationality |
| Article 19 | Living independently and being included in the community |
| Article 20 | Personal mobility |
| Article 21 | Freedom of expression and opinion, and access to information |
| Article 22 | Respect for privacy |
| Article 23 | Respect for home and the family |
| Article 24 | Education |
| Article 25 | Health |
| Article 26 | Habilitation and rehabilitation |
| Article 27 | Work and employment |
| Article 28 | Adequate standard of living and social protection |
| Article 29 | Participation in political and public life |
| Article 30 | Participation in cultural life, recreation, leisure and sport |

**What is Disability?**

Disability is an evolving concept. The term disability is conventionally used to refer to attributes that are severe enough to interfere with, or prevent, normal day-to-day activities. According to the UN Convention on the Rights of Persons with Disabilities, "persons with disabilities include those who have long-term physical, mental, intellectual or sensory impairments which, in interaction with various barriers, may hinder their full and effective participation in society on an equal basis with others." Disabilities can be permanent, temporary, or episodic. The draft Cambodian Disability Law, states that, *"A person with disability is any citizen who lacks any physical organ or capacity or suffers any mental impairment, that causes restriction to his or her daily life or social activities and which significantly causes differences from non-disabled people, and who has a disability certification from the Ministry of Health."* Disability may involve physical, intellectual or sensory impairment, medical conditions or mental illness, and may be more or less visible to others.

The World Bank estimates that approximately 600 million people, or 10 per cent of the world's population, have a disability and that 80 per cent of these people live in developing nations. If families of persons with disabilities are included, at least 25 per cent of the world is directly affected by disability. Some women, men and children with disabilities are fully integrated in society, and are participating in and actively contributing to all areas of life. However, the great majority face discrimination, exclusion, isolation and even abuse. Disability is both a cause and a consequence of poverty. This relationship is particularly acute in developing countries. Studies show that 98 per cent of children with disabilities living in developing countries do not receive an education. The link between disability and poverty is not limited to developing countries. Despite great variations in wealth and quality of life across countries, persons with disabilities tend to experience greater social, political, and economic exclusion than persons without disabilities worldwide.

**Right to Education**

The right to education is ingrained at the international and regional level as a fundamental right. The right to education has also been included in the constitutions of at least 59 countries. Furthermore, the right has, even in countries such as India or the United States of America, where it has not been constitutionally entrenched, nevertheless been recognised as a legal right of fundamental importance. The importance of entrenching the right to education is based on certain premises.

1. It is a precondition for the excise and understanding of other rights. That is, the employment of a number of civil and political rights, such as freedom of information and the right to vote depend on a minimum level of education, including literacy. Economic, social and cultural rights, such as the right to choose work or to take part in cultural life, can also only be excised meaningfully once a minimum level of education has been achieved.

2. Through education individuals can be taught values such as broadmindedness and respect for human rights. Education, therefore, can strengthen a culture of human rights within and amongst nations.

The right to education is distinctive both a positive and a negative right, requiring helpful; state policies and financial investments in human and material infrastructure for its realisation and bringing forward liberal aspects of free choice with respect to people's received education. The right to education is recognised in Article 26 of the Universal Declaration of Human Rights (1948) (Universal Declaration) and Articles 13 and 14 of the International Covenant on Economic, Social and Cultural Rights (1966) (CESCR). The most relevant for the right to education are General Comments No. 3, No. 11 and No. 13. In the African region, the right to education is entrenched in Article 17 of the African Charter on Human and Peoples Rights (African Charter) (1981). Article 11 of the African Charter on the Rights and Welfare of the Child (1990) also provides for the right to education. International human rights law defines the right to education in a comparatively precise manner.

**International Human Rights Law**

The American Convention on Human Rights came into force in 1969. Article 26 of the American Convention, titled 'Progressive Development', sets forth the goal of protecting economic, social, and educational rights under the governance the Organisation of American States. The lobbying by the disability movement has certainly had some effect in influencing legislation. However, legislation which specifically pertains to adult education for disabled people is still rare. A 1996 UNESCO survey shows how only a quarter of countries surveyed had any policies for vocational education for young disabled adults beyond school leaving age. However, even in countries where laws for disabled people exist, they are not always applied. The Convention on the Rights of the Child adopted by the UN General Assembly in 1989 is a milestone of current children's policy and refers to all children and juveniles up to the age of 18. It serves the concrete implementation of the General Declaration on Human Rights of the United Nations with regard to children and commits politicians and legislation to acknowledge children as subjects of the law.

The United Nations Standard Rules on the Equalisation of Opportunities for Persons with Disabilities (1994) and the Salamanca Statement and Framework for Action on Special Needs Education (1994) reaffirm the rights of disabled people to equal opportunities, full participation in society, and equal partnership in the planning and implementation of those policies which affect their lives. The United Nations statement is an attempt to improve the status of disabled people by influencing the custom and practice of nation states. International bodies have sought to safeguard the rights of disabled people, one of them is the Declaration on the Rights of Disabled Persons: *Disabled persons have the right to medical, psychological and functional treatment, including prosthetic and orthetic appliances, to medical and social rehabilitation, education, vocational training and rehabilitation, aid, counselling, placement services and other services which will enable them to develop their capabilities and skills to the maximum and will hasten the processes of their social integration or reintegration.* In USA "The Persons with Disabilities (Equal Opportunities, Protection of Rights and Full Participation) Act, 1995, inter-alia and strives to promote empowerment of persons with disabilities.

In 1990, the Americans with Disabilities Act (ADC) was signed. As a result, the laws designed to prevent discrimination against persons with disabilities became more unified and comprehensive under a single status. The ADA served to strengthen the Rehabilitation Act of 1973 by extending the protections afforded to persons with disabilities by that status to cover the private sector, as well as state and local governments. Children with disabilities have a right to education. Since the UN Universal Declaration on Human Rights was released in 1948, there has been legislation on providing education for all children. The Convention on the Rights of Persons with Disabilities, which entered into force in 2008 and which was ratified by the UK in 2009, has 145 signatories (as at June 2010) including all PSA countries except Afghanistan and Zimbabwe.

## Legal Mechanism: Indian Perspectives

The Education Commission of 1966 (Kothari Commission) drew attention to the education of children with disabilities. In 1974, for the first time, the necessity of integrated education was explicitly emphasised under the scheme for Integrated Education for Disabled Children (IEDC). The Rehabilitation Council of India Act

1992 initiated a training programme for the development of professionals to respond to the needs of students with disabilities. The enactment of the People with Disability Act in 1996 provided legislative support. This act makes it mandatory to provide free education to children with disabilities in an appropriate environment until the age of 18 years. There are various National/apex-level institutes set up in India for disables, like as

1. National Institute for the Visually Handicapped (1982), an autonomous body in Dehradun
2. National Institute for the Orthopedically Handicapped (1982), Calcutta
3. Ali Yavar Jung National Institute for the Hearing Handicapped (1983), Mumbai
4. National Institute for the Mentally Handicapped (1984), Hyderabad
5. National Institute of Rehabilitation, Training and Research (1984), Orissa
6. Institute for the Physically Handicapped (1976), Delhi
7. Rehabilitation Council of India (1986), Delhi Converted into a statutory body under the Rehabilitation Council of India Act 1992. One objective is to prescribe minimum standards for education and training of various categories of professionals dealing with people with disabilities.

India is a signatory to the Proclamation on the Full Participation and Equality of People with Disabilities, signed at the launch to the Pacific Decade of Disabled Persons (1993 – 2002) in 1993. This, in addition to lobbying from non-government organisations, lead to the formulation of the Persons with Disabilities (Equal Opportunities, Protection of Rights and Full Participation) Act, 1995. This is the fundamental act in India protecting the rights of people with disabilities. This legislation is intended to be implemented and monitored through co-ordination committees, both at central and at state levels. The committees are required to have at least five representatives from the disability sector. India has launched a large programme initiative — Sarva Shiksha Abhiyan/SSA — which it calls its flagship EFA campaign.

**Right to Education Act, 2009**

The Right of children to Free and Compulsory Education Act has come into force from April 1, 2010. This is a historic day for the people of India as from this day the right to education will be accorded the same legal status as the right to life as provided by Article 21A of the Indian Constitution. Every child in the age group of 6-14 years will be provided eight years of elementary education in an age appropriate classroom in the vicinity of his/her neighbourhood. Any cost that prevents a child from accessing school will be borne by the State which shall have the responsibility of enrolling the child as well as ensuring attendance and completion of eight years of schooling. No child shall be denied admission for want of documents; no child shall be turned away if the admission cycle in the school is over and no child shall be asked to take an admission test. Children with disabilities will also be educated in the mainstream schools. RTE has been a part of the directive principles of the State Policy under Article 45 of the Constitution, which is part of Chapter 4 of the Constitution. And rights in Chapter 4 are not enforceable. For the first time in the history of India we have made this right enforceable by putting it in Chapter 3 of the Constitution as Article 21. This entitles children to have the right to education enforced as a fundamental right.

## Conclusion

Education is the backbone of any society. For providing education to disable persons both various international and national laws are implemented. The disabled ones too have a right to learn. Any effort on the part of the State to alienate them from their national counterparts, in the learning process, also results in the violation of their Right to education. The International human rights law prohibits this discrimination and advocates inclusive education. The right to education for persons with disabilities as well as Inclusive Education should be included in the Countries' National Plans for Education. In many countries, these plans tend to not include children with disabilities. Human rights monitoring can play a key role in supporting States to effectively implement the Convention at national level and in empowering persons with disabilities to become increasingly aware of their rights, therefore bringing about positive change in the lives of persons with disabilities across regions.

## REFERENCES

1. Annedore Prengel and Bernd Overwien, *Children and Right to Education*, Detailed available at http://www.swisshumanrightsbook.com/SHRB/shrb_02_files/347_10%20prengel%20overwien.pdf
2. K. Sujatha, *Education among Scheduled Tribes*, Detailed available at http://www.doccentre.net/docsweb/Education/Scanned_material/analysis_Tribals.pdf
3. Dr Niranjan Aradhya and Aruna Kashyap (2006), *The Fundamentals Rights to Education in India*, Detailed available at http://unesdoc.unesco.org/images/0015/001510/151010e.pdf
4. UNESCO (2007), Guidelines for Inclusion: Ensuring Access to Education for All, In *Right to Education: Emerging Scenario*, N. Sudarshan (Ed), First edition, The ICFAI University Press, Hyderabad, p. 3.
5. Rob Rich (2007), Equality and Adequacy in the State's Provision of Education: Mapping the Conceptual Landscape, In *Right to Education: Emerging Scenario*, N. Sudarshan (Ed), First edition, The ICFAI University Press, Hyderabad, p. 54.
6. Olof Sandkull (2007), Strengthening Inclusive Education by Applying a Rights-based Approach to Education Programming, In *Right to Education: Emerging Scenario*, N. Sudarshan (Ed), First edition, The ICFAI University Press, Hyderabad, p. 39.

7. *"Report of the United Nations High Commissioner for Human Rights on progress in the implementation of the recommendations contained in the study on the human rights of persons with disabilities"* (A/HRC/4/75, Para 19.
8. *Monitoring the Convention on the Rights of Persons with Disabilities: Guidelines for Human Rights Monitors*, Detailed available at http://www.ohchr.org/Documents/Publications/Disabilities_training_17EN.pdf
9. Giampiero Griffo and Francesca Ortali (2007), *Training Manual on the Human Rights of Persons with Disabilities*, Detailed available at http://www.aifo.it/english/resources/online/books/cbr/manual_human_rights-disability-eng07.pdf
10. *National Plan of Action for Persons with Disabilities, including Landmine/ERW Survivors 2008-11,* Detailed available at http://www.ohchr.org/Documents/Publications/Disabilities_training_17EN.pdf
11. *The Right to Education for Persons with Disabilities: Towards Inclusion,* Detailed available at http://www.the-monitor.org/index.php/publications/display?url=lm/2010/es/Casualties_and_Victim_Assistance.html
12. *Making education accessible and available to all persons with disabilities,* Detailed available at http://www.unesco.org/education/uie/confintea/pdf/8d.pdf
13. World Bank, *Disability and HIV/AIDS* (World Bank: 2004), online: World Bank/Home/Topics/Health/Public Health/ HIV/AIDS/Disability < www.worldbank.orgl>. [World Bank, Disability].
14. C. Lewis and S. Sygall, Loud, *Proud and Passionate: Including Women with Disabilities in International Development Programmes* (Oregon: MIUSA, 1997).
15. R. McCarthy, *"Sport and Children with Disabilities" in Sport in the United Nations Convention on the Rights of Persons with Disabilities* (International Disability in Sport Working Group, Centre for Study of Sport in Society, Northeastern University, 2007) at 13, online: International Platform on Sport and Development <http://www.sportanddev.org/data/document/336.pdf>.
16. *Sport and Persons with Disabilities: Fostering Inclusion and Well-being,* Detailed available at http://www.righttoplay.com/International/news-and-media/Documents/Policy%20Reports%20docs/Harnessing%20the %20Power%20-%20FULL/Chapter5_SportandDisability.pdf
17. *Disability and HIV Policy Brief,* Detailed available at http://www.who.int/disabilities/jc1632_policy_brief_disability_en.pdf
18. Shantanu Gupta (2009), *What are the different strategies and approaches to realise Right to Education (RTE) in India?*, Detailed available at http://www.right-to-education.org/sites/r2e.gn.apc.org/files/Shantanu_Gupta _RTE%20in%20India.pdf
19. Katarina Tomasevski (2007), Girls Education through a Human Rights Lens: What can be done Differently, What can be made Better, In *Right to Education: Emerging Scenario*, N. Sudarshan (Ed), First edition, The ICFAI University Press, Hyderabad, p. 73.

20. M Nowak 'The right to education' in A Elide et al., (eds) *Economic, social and cultural rights; A textbook* (2001) 245. See also K Tomasevski 'Removing obstacles in the way of the right to education' Right to Education Primes No. 1, 8-9; http:/ / www.right-to-education.org
21. Faranaaz Veriava and Fons Coomans (2007), The Right to Education, In *Right to Education: Emerging Scenario,* N. Sudarshan (Ed), First edition, The ICFAI University Press, Hyderabad, pp.119-120.
22. Aristotelis Stamoulas (2007), Forms of Infringement of the Right to Education in Contemporary Greek Educational Structures, In *Right to Education: Emerging Scenario*, N. Sudarshan (Ed), First edition, The ICFAI University Press, Hyderabad, p.156.
23. General Comment No. 3. The nature of states parties' obligations (art 2, Para 1 of the Covenant) (5th session, 1990) [UN Doc E/1991/23]. This General Comment explains terms such as 'to the maximum of available resources', achieving progressively the full realisation of the rights and all appropriate means.
24. General Comment No. 11 Plans of action for primary-education (21st session, 1999) [UN Doc E/C 12/1999/4]. This General Comment deals with the provisions in art 14.
25. General Comment No. 13. *The right to education (art 13 of the Covenant) (21st session, 1999)* [UN Doc E/C 12/1999/10]. This General Comment deals with the provisions in art 13.
26. Faranaaz Veriava and Fons Coomans (2007), The Right to Education, In *Right to Education: Emerging Scenario*, N. Sudarshan (Ed), First edition, The ICFAI University Press, Hyderabad, p. 120.
27. Tomasevski, Katarina, *Mamual on Right-Based Education*, UNESCO Bangkok, 2004, p. 3.
28. *Guidance Note: A DFID Practice Paper*, Detailed Available at http://www.dfid.gov.uk/Documents/publications1/eng-priv-sect-skills-dvmt.pdf
29. Lorna Jean Edmonds (2005), *Disabled People and Development*, Detailed available at http://www.adb.org/Documents/Reports/Disabled-People-Development/disabled-people.pdf
30. National Council on Disability 92007), Lessons for All of Us: Protecting the Right to Education for Persons with Disabilities, In *Right to Education: Emerging Scenario*, N. Sudarshan (Ed), First edition, The ICFAI University Press, Hyderabad, pp. 87-92.

# 22

# Women Education in India: Challenges and Progress

***Dr. S.K. Chaudhury***

"*An investment in knowledge pays the best interest.*"

**— Benjamin Franklin**

## Introduction

A woman is a female human. The term *woman* is usually reserved for an adult, with the term girl being the usual term for a female child or adolescent. Women are important in our society. Every woman has her own job or duty in this modern society in which men are still the *'stronger gender'*. The role of women in society has been greatly overseen in the last few decades but now it is coming to a more positive perspective. In the early days women were seen only as wives who were intended to cook, clean, and take care of the kids. They were not allowed to vote while men took care of having jobs and paying any bills that had to be paid. Women do not have the same position as men, though much progress has been made in the society to bring women to a stage where they have equal rights, equal pay, equal independence but still it is not achieved. Though it may seem that women have a great deal of freedom and independence, the overall condition of women in the world of today is not as it should be. Still the bird flies with only one wing as the other is hampered and not fully functional.

The men and the women are the two wheels of the society. If one of the two falls defective, the society cannot make progress. Hence we need education for the females as we need for the males. Women constitute almost half of the population in the world. But the hegemonic masculine ideology made them suffer a lot as they were denied equal opportunities in different parts of the world. The rise of feminist ideas has, however, led to the tremendous improvement of women's condition through out the world in recent times. Access to education has been one of the most pressing demands of these women's rights movements. Women education in India has also been a major preoccupation of both the government and civil society as educated women can play a very important role in the development of the country.

**Importance of Women Education**

Education is important for everyone, but it is especially significant for girls and women. This is true not only because education is an entry point to other opportunities, but also because the educational achievements of women can have ripple effects within the family and across generations. Investing in girls' education is one of the most effective ways to reduce poverty. Investments in secondary school education for girls yield especially high dividends. Girls who have been educated are likely to marry later and to have smaller and healthier families. Educated women can recognise the importance of health care and know how to seek it for themselves and their children. The education of parents is linked to their children's educational attainment, and the mother's education is usually more influential than the father's. An educated mother's greater influence in household negotiations may allow her to secure more resources for her children.

The effects of women's education on development constitute a significant area of research within international development. Increases in the amount of women's education in regions tend to correlate with high levels of development. Women's education increases the income of women and leads to growth in GDP. Other effects are related to social development. Educating girls leads to a number of social benefits, including many related to women's empowerment. Recent research in human development has established a strong link between women's education and international development. There are multiple ways researchers measure the effects of women's education on development. Both individuals and countries benefit from women's education. Individuals who invest in education receive a net monetary gain over the course of their lifetime. This individual monetary gain creates an increase in the overall economic productivity of a country. Women's education leads to significant social development. Some of the most notable social benefits include decreased fertility rates and lower infant mortality rates, and lower maternal mortality rates. Educated women are more likely to engage in civic participation and attend political meetings, and there are several instances in which educated women in the developing world were able to secure benefits for themselves through political movements. There are also benefits relating to the woman's role in the household. Educated women have been found to experience less domestic violence, regardless of other social status indicators like employment status. Women with an education are also more involved in the decision-making process of the family and report making more decisions over a given time period. There are also a number of other benefits for children associated with having an educated mother over an educated father, including higher survival rates and better nutrition.

**Disadvantages of Women Education**

The female education has some disadvantages too. It is found in Europe and America that the educated women do not want to bear children. They do not like their children. They leave them in the nursery, more out of their disgust than for any other reason. But the defect does not lie in education as a principle. The defect lies in the curriculums. If they learn what the males learn then naturally they will like to be like males. So, separate courses of study should be prepared for the females.

**Women Education: Progress**

The history of female education in India has its roots in the British Regime. Women's employment and education was acknowledged in 1854 by the East India Company's Programme: Wood's Dispatch. Slowly, after that, there was progress in female education, but it initially tended to be focused on the primary school level and was related to the richer sections of society. In 1878, the University of Calcutta became one of the first universities to admit female graduates to its degree programmes, before any of the British universities had later done the same. This point was raised during the Ilbert Bill controversy in 1883, when it was being considered whether Indian judges should be given the right to judge British offenders. Bengali women who supported the bill responded by claiming that they were more educated than the English women opposed to the bill and pointed out that more Indian women had degrees than British women did at the time.

Indian National Congress played a major role in emancipating women. Within a year of its formation in 1885, a Ladies Association was formed. By 1890s more and more highly educated women were visible in public sphere. Later prominent Indian women like Ramabai Ranade, Sarojini Naidu, Annie Besant, Rameshwari Nehru, Rajkumari Amrit Kaur, Aruna Asif Ali, Sucheta Kriplani, Usha Mehta, and Vilasini Devi Shenai played an important political and social role. After independence women's education, especially higher education, took off. Education started playing a great role in the emancipation of women from traditional dependencies. Women became more vocal, articulate and assertive. Our constitution granted equal rights to women and that included the Right to education. Jawahar Lal Nehru said, *"You can tell the condition of a nation by looking at the status of its women."* He understood that higher education for women was the need of the hour.

After India attained independence in 1947, the University Education Commission was created to recommend suggestions to improve the quality of education. However, their report spoke against female education, referring to it as: *Women's present education is entirely irrelevant to the life they have to lead.* It is not only a waste but often a definite disability. However, the fact that the female literacy rate was at 8.9 per cent post-Independence could not be ignored. Thus, in 1958, a national committee on women's education was appointed by the government, and most of its recommendations were accepted. The crux of its recommendations was to bring female education on the same footing as offered for boys. Soon afterward, committees were created that talked about equality between men and women in the field of education. Before and after Independence, India has been taking active steps towards women's status and education. The 86th Constitutional Amendment Act, 2002, has been a path breaking step towards the growth of education, especially for females. According to this act, elementary education is a fundamental right for children between the ages of 6 and 14. The government has undertaken to provide this education free of cost and make it compulsory for those in that age group. This undertaking is more widely known as Sarva Shiksha Abhiyan (SSA). Since then, the SSA has come up with many schemes for inclusive as well as exclusive growth of Indian education as a whole, including schemes to help foster the growth of female education.

According to last census held in 2001, the percentage of female literacy in the country is 54.16 per cent. The literacy rate in the country has increased from 18.33 per cent in 1951 to 65.38 per cent as per 2001 census. The female literacy rate has also increased from 8.86 per cent in 1951 to 54.16 per cent. It is noticed that the female literacy rate during the period 1991-2001 increased by 14.87 per cent whereas male literacy rate rose by 11.72 per cent. Hence the female literacy rate actually increased by 3.15 per cent more compared to male literacy rate. Historically, a variety of factors have been found to be responsible for poor female literate rate, viz

1. Gender based inequality.
2. Social discrimination and economic exploitation.
3. Occupation of girl child in domestic chores.
4. Low enrolment of girls in schools.
5. Low retention rate and high dropout rate.

If all women in India had completed secondary education, the under-five mortality rate would be 61 per cent lower, UNESCO has said. India and Nigeria account for more than a third of child deaths worldwide. If all women in both countries had completed secondary education, the under-five mortality rate would have been 61 per cent lower in India and 43 per cent lesser in Nigeria, saving 1.35 million children's lives. UNESCO's new analysis proves that in south and West Asia, and sub-Saharan Africa, nearly three million girls are married by the age 15 years — below the legal age of marriage. If all young women completed primary education, the number of child brides would be reduced by almost half a million. Completing secondary education would reduce that number by two million. In these regions, 3.4 million young women give birth by the age of 17 years. If all young women completed primary schooling, this would result in 340,000 fewer early births, and if they all completed secondary education, the total would fall by two million. Findings also show that a secondary, rather than a primary education, increases tolerance towards people of a different religion or those speaking a different language. In India, those with secondary education were 19 per cent less likely to express intolerance towards people speaking a different language compared with those with less than primary education. According to All India Survey on Higher Education (AISHE) 2010-11, at higher education level, 55 per cent of male are enrolled in under graduate and post graduate courses while only 45 per cent of female are enrolled in the same. Also, 62 per cent of male are enrolled in PhD while only 38 per cent of female are enrolled in the same. Historical and cultural factors act as prime reasons behind gloomy situation of women education in the country. The Indian government has expressed a strong commitment towards education for all; however, India still has one of the lowest female literacy rates in Asia. In 1991, less than 40 per cent of the 330 million women aged seven and over were literate, which means today there are over 200 million illiterate women in India. This low level of literacy not only has a negative impact on women's lives but also on their families' lives and on their country's economic development. Although literacy rates in India are low, there has been a concerted effort to encourage girls to attend school, which should lead to higher literacy rates in the future. In 1992-93, 75 per cent of boys and 61 per cent of girls aged six to ten years were attending school. A major educational problem facing both boys and girls in India is that although they may be enrolled at the beginning of the year they don't always remain in school.

### Efforts of Women Education

Women's education in India is one of the foremost concerns of the Government of India as well as of the society at large. It is due to the fact that at the present time, the educated women play a very significant role in overall development and progress of the country. The Department of Women and Child Development was set up in the year 1985 as a part of the Ministry of Human Resource Development, Government of India to give the much needed impetus to the holistic development of women and children. With effect from 30.01.2006, the Department has been upgraded to a Ministry by the Government of India. Besides, playing its nodal role, the Ministry implements certain innovative programmes for women and children. These programmes cover welfare and support services, training for employment and income generation, awareness generation and gender sensitisation. These programmes play a supplementary and complementary role to the other general developmental programmes in the sectors of health, education, rural development, etc. All these efforts are directed to ensure that women are empowered both economically and socially and thus become equal partners in national development along with men. The major schemes are the following:

1. *Mahila Samakhya Programme:* This programme was launched in 1988 as a result of the New Education Policy (1968). It was created for the empowerment of women from rural areas especially socially and economically marginalised groups. When the SSA was formed, it initially set up a committee to look into this programme, how it was working and recommends new changes that could be made.

2. *Kasturba Gandhi Balika Vidyalaya Scheme (KGBV):* This scheme was launched in July, 2004, to provide education to girls at primary level. It is primarily for the underprivileged and rural areas where literacy level for females is very low. The schools that were set up have 100 per ecnt reservation: 75 per cent for backward class and 25 per cent for BPL (Below Poverty Line) females.
3. *National Programme for Education of Girls at Elementary Level (NPEGEL):* This programme was launched in July, 2003. It was an incentive to reach out to the girls who the SSA was not able to reach through other schemes. The SSA called out to the "hardest to reach girls". This scheme has covered 24 states in India. Under the NPEGEL, "model schools" have been set up to provide better opportunities to girls.

The main strategies adopted by the Government for increasing female literacy in the country include:

1. National Literacy Mission for imparting functional literacy
2. Universalisation for Elementary Education
3. Non-Formal Education

The provision of educational opportunities for women has been an important part of the national endeavour in the field of education since India's Independence. Though these endeavours did yield significant results, gender disparity persists with uncompromising tenacity, more so in the rural areas and among the disadvantaged communities. This is not only a matter of national anxiety and concern but also a matter of national conscience. It is with this concern that the Government of India launched the National Literacy Mission in 1988 for eradication of adult illiteracy. Since women account for an overwhelming percentage of the total number of illiterates, the National Literacy Mission is for all practical purposes a Mission of imparting functional literacy to women. Literacy campaigns have heightened social awareness among women regarding the importance of education, both for themselves as well as for their children. Large numbers of women have been participating whole-heartedly in the literacy campaigns as learners and volunteers. The literacy campaigns have also motivated and encouraged women learners to educate their children, particularly girls by enrolling them in formal schools. The literacy classes conducted under literacy campaigns have given women as opportunity to break the isolation which is socially structured into their lives, giving them a chance to meet other women and learn collectively- rather than learn singly as individuals. Total literacy campaigns have provided illiterate adult women, who have been denied access to formal schooling, with a great opportunity for reading, writing, increasing awareness levels and skills training. Literacy campaigns have thus actively promoted gender equity and have sought to empower them as to decision making about themselves, their families and their communities.

In recent decades, the Government of India has instituted some educational programmes such as the National Literacy Mission, and the Sarva Shiksha Abhiyan in an effort to combat the scourge of illiteracy in the country. The rate of illiteracy is particularly high in rural areas, especially among socially marginalised minorities, women and people from lower castes. Recognising that persistent female illiteracy is a major impediment to women's empowerment, NIRANTAR – a national centre for gender and education has since 1993 been working towards helping rural poor women access literacy and educational opportunities, enabling their access to information and engendering educational processes. Sahajani Shiksha Kendra, the literacy and educational programme for women's empowerment was initiated in 2002, in an effort to empower women in Lalitpur district of the northern state of Uttar Pradesh.

The All India Women's Education Fund's Association's (AIWEFA) *'Computers For Schools'* project was launched by Smt. Sheila Dikshit, Hon'ble Chief Minister of Delhi, on Women's Day i.e., 8th March 2002. The project aims at creating computer awareness of and imparting basic computer training to Government MCD/NDMC Primary Schools. In May 2003, AIWEFA adopted a holistic and sustainable approach to area wise development in its *"Village Adoption Project"*. The programme lays thrust on literacy development, including providing extra support for children with less aptitude for education; health issues, hygiene and sanitation, vocational training to girls and women and imparting income generation skills. CARE's Girls' Education Programme (GEP) has been in operation for over 10 years and plays a vital role in achieving CARE's long term goal of reaching out to two million women, girls, and other marginalised people to enhance their abilities to exercise greater choice in personal and public spheres by 2014. CARE views education programmes for India's marginalised children as a critical component of the fight against poverty. GEP seeks to improve opportunities for girls and women through their increased participation in formal and alternative education systems. Udaan (Flight) school was piloted in Uttar Pradesh in the year 1999 in the district of Hardoi, through an accelerated learning model, for older out-of-school girls, ages 9-14, which allows students to complete primary school in 11 months in a residential setting. KGBVs are special residential schools started by the government under the Sarva Shaksha Abhiyaan (SSA) government umbrella programme, for older girls from socially disadvantaged communities who were never enrolled in or had to drop out of primary school. CARE builds the capacity of KGBV teachers in Uttar Pradesh and Gujarat to deliver quality education in an equitable manner. We provide training in mathematics, computers and language to addresses knowledge and skill gaps, and encourage schools to adopt more inclusive methods of instruction.

### Constraints of Women Education

There are several reasons for the low levels of literacy in India. Over one-third of the population is estimated to be living below the poverty line. Although school attendance is free, the costs of books, uniforms, and transportation to school can be too much for poor families. Poor families are also more likely to keep girls at home to care for younger siblings or to work in family enterprises. Negative parental attitudes toward educating daughters can also be a barrier to a girl's education. Many parents view educating sons as an investment because the sons will be responsible for caring for aging parents. On the other hand, parents may see the education of daughters a waste of money because daughters will eventually live with their husbands' families, and the parents will not benefit directly from their education. Also, daughters with higher levels of education will likely have higher dowry expenses as they will want. Another barrier to education in India is the lack of adequate school facilities. Many states simply do not have enough classrooms to accommodate all of the school-age children. Furthermore, the classrooms that are available often lack basic necessities such as sanitary facilities or water. In some states, the inadequate supply of classrooms is further compounded by the large increase in the number of school-age children due to high population growth rates. Lack of female teachers is another potential barrier to girls' education. Girls are more likely to attend school and have higher academic achievement if they have female teachers.

**Education and Human Rights**

Everybody has the right to education, which has been recognised since the Universal Declaration of Human Rights (UDHR) in 1948. The right to free and compulsory primary education, without discrimination and of good quality, has been reaffirmed in all major international human rights conventions. Many of these same instruments encourage, but do not guarantee, post-primary education. These rights have been further elaborated to address issues like quality and equity, moving forward the issue of what the right to education means, and exploring how it can be achieved. As a minimum: states must ensure that basic education is available, accessible, acceptable and adaptable for all. (4A scheme) The right of girls to education is one of the most critical of all rights – because education plays an important role in enabling girls and women to secure other rights. Education is one of the most critical areas of empowerment for women, as both the Cairo and Beijing conferences affirmed. It is also an area that offers some of the clearest examples of discrimination women suffer. Among children not attending school there are twice as many girls as boys, and among illiterate adults there are twice as many women as men.

**Conclusion**

Women education in India plays a very important role in the overall development of the country. It not only helps in the development of half of the human resources, but in improving the quality of life at home and outside. Educated women not only able to promote education of their girl children, but also can provide better guidance to all their children. Moreover educated women can also help in the reduction of infant mortality rate and growth of the population. Basic education provides girls and women with an understanding of basic health, nutrition and family planning, giving them choices and the power to decide over their own lives and bodies. Women's education leads directly to better reproductive health, improved family health, economic growth, for the family and for society, as well as lower rates of child mortality and malnutrition. It is also key in the fight against the spread of HIV and AIDS. Educating girls and women is an important step in overcoming poverty. Inequality and poverty are not inevitable.

## REFERENCES


1. Alma M. García (2004). *Narratives of Mexican American Women: Emergent Identities of the Second Generation,* Rowman Altamira.
2. A.M. Sultana (2011). *Women Education and Empowerment, Lambert,* Academic Publishing.
3. Alan R. Sadovnik, and Susan F. Seme (2002). *Founding Mothers and Others: Women Educational Leaders during the Progressive Era,* Palgrave Macmillan.
4. Barbara Miller Solomon (1985). *In the Company of Educated Women: A History of Women and Higher Education in America*, Yale University Press.
5. Barbara Anne Keely (1997). *Faith of Our Foremothers: Women Changing Religious Education*, Westminster John Knox Press.
6. Barbara Whitehead (1999). *Women's Education in Early Modern Europe: A History, 1500Tto 1800,* Taylor & Francis.
7. Carolyn M. Sampselle (1992). *Violence against Women: Nursing Research, Education, and Practice Issues*, Taylor & Francis.
8. Dorothy Moss (2006). *Gender, Space and Time: Women and Higher Education,* Lexington Books.
9. D.Bhaskara Rao, Digumarti Pushpa Latha (2003). *Women, Education and Empowerment*, Discovery Publishing House.
10. Dorothy Moss (2006). *Gender, Space and Time: Women and Higher Education,* Lexington Books.
11. Elizabeth M. King, M. Anne Hill (1997). *Women's Education in Developing Countries: Barriers, Benefits, and Policies,* World Bank Publications.
12. *Empowering Women through Education,* Retrieved from http://www.unfpa.org/gender/empowerment2.htm
13. *Female literacy in India,* Retrieved from http://www.nlm.nic.in/women.htm
14. *Female education (2013).* Retrieved from http://en.wikipedia.org/wiki/Female_education
15. *Girls' Education Programme, Retrieved from* http://careindia.org/educational
16. Gail Paradise Kelly and Carolyn M. Elliot (1982). *Women's Education in the Third World: Comparative Perspective,* SUNY Press.
17. Gail P. Kelly and Carolyn M. Elliott (1982). *Women's Education in the Third World: Comparative Perspectives,* SUNY Press.
18. *History of Women's Participation In Indian Education System,* Retrieved from http://education.sulekha.com/history-of-women-s-participation-in-indian-education-system_94364_blog

19. *Importance of girls'/women's education*, Retrieved from http://www.right-to-education.org/node/187
20. Jessica Enoch (2008). *Refiguring Rhetorical Education: Women Teaching African American, Native American, and Chicano/a Students, 1865-1911*, SIU Press.
21. June Purvis (1991). *A history of women's education in England*, Open University Press.
22. Linda Eisenmann (1998). *Historical dictionary of women's education in the United States*, Greenwood Press.
23. Linda Eisenmann (2006). *Higher Education for Women in Postwar America, 1945–1965*, JHU Press.
24. Linda Eisenmann (1998). *Historical Dictionary of Women's Education in the United States*, Greenwood Publishing Group.
25. Linda Eisenmann (1998). *Historical Dictionary of Women's Education in the United States*, Greenwood Publishing Group.
26. Marilyn Shear Goodman and Beth Creager Fallon (1995). *Pattern Changing for Abused Women: An Educational Program*, Volume 2, SAGE.
27. Mary Agnes Cannon (1916). *The Education of Women during the Renaissance*, National Capital Press.
28. Margaret Grogan and Charol Shakeshaft (2010). *Women and Educational Leadership*, John Wiley & Sons.
29. Mary Biggs (1996). *Women's Words: The Columbia Book of Quotations by Women*, Columbia University Press.
30. Mary Kelley (2006). *Learning to Stand and Speak: Women, Education, and Public Life in America's Republic*, UNC Press Books.
31. Penny A. Pasque and Shelley Errington Nicholson (2012). *Empowering Women in Higher Education and Student Affairs: Theory, Research, Narratives, and Practice from Feminist Perspectives*, Stylus Publishing.
32. *Radhakanta Swain, Essay on female education in India*, Retrieved from http://www.publishyourarticles.net/knowledge-hub/essay/how-to-write-an-essayarticle-on-female-education-in-india.html
33. R.K. Bhandari (2008). *Educational Development of Women in India*, Ministry of Education and Culture, Government of India.
34. Shireen J. Jejeebhoy (1995). *Women's Education, Autonomy, and Reproductive Behaviour: Experience from Developing Countries*, Clarendon Press.
35. S.P. Agrawal, and J.C. Aggarwal (1992). *Women's Education in India*, Volume 1, Concept Publishing Company.
36. Susan Hamilton and Janice Schroeder (2007). *Nineteenth-Century British Women's Education, 1840-1900*, Volumes 1-6, Taylor & Francis Group.
37. Susan Hamilton and Janice Schroede (2007). *Nineteenth-century British Women's Education, 1840-1900: Education of working women and of middle class girls*, Routledge.

38. S. P. Aggrawal (2001). *Women's Education in India, 1995-98: Present Status, Perspective Plan, Statistical Indicators with a Global View,* Concept Publishing Company.
39. S. Suguna (2011). Education and women empowerment in India, *ZENITH: International Journal of Multidisciplinary Research,* Retrieved from http://www.zenithresearch.org.in/images/stories/pdf/2011/Dec/zijmr/15_VOL%201_ISSUE8_ZEN.pdf
40. *Sahajani Shiksha Kendra: Literacy and Education for Women's Empowerment,* Retrieved from http://www.unesco.org/uil/litbase/?menu=8&programme =82
41. *The Hindu* (Sep 25, 2013). Female education linked to under-5 mortality rate, Retrieved from http://www.thehindu.com/news/national/female-education-linked-to-under5-mortality-rate/article5164829.ece
42. The role of women in education in India: a report of the National Seminar on the Role of Women in Education in India held from October 3 to 5, 1975, at the Lady Willingdon Training College, Madras-5, under the chairmanship of Dr. Mrs. Rajammal P. Devadass.
43. Yaduvansh Bahadur Mathur (1973). *Women's Education in India, 1813-1966,* Asia Publishing House.
44. Victoria A. Velkoff (1998). *Women's education in India,* Retrieved from http://www.census.gov/population/international/files/wid-9801.pdf
45. *Women's education and development (2013).* Retrieved from http://en.wikipedia.org/wiki/Women's_education_and_development
46. *Women in society,* Retrieved from http://www.gsl.k12.tr/socialexclusion/main.php?subj=woman.
47. *Women's Role in the Society*, Retrieved from http://www.anandaseva.org/yoga/womens-role-in-the-society.

# 23

# Tribal Education in India: An Overview

*P. K. Pandey*

"*The roots of education are bitter, but the fruit is sweet.*"

— ***Aristotle***

## Introduction

Education is the base of any society. It is one of the necessary conditions for advancing quality of life and freedom. In other words, universal access to quality knowledge and skills ensures that everybody has an equal opportunity to play a full part in work and society. It is essential for integrating the marginalised and vulnerable in society into the development process. Historical forces have largely influenced the policy-planning processes and growth trends in education, both in developed and low-income countries. These include colonial policies related to institutional structures, choice of providers, curriculum decisions, teacher recruitment, evaluation systems, certification and financing. Education in its broadest, general sense is the means through which the aims and habits of a group of people lives on from one generation to the next. Primary education consists of the first 5–7 years of formal, structured education. In general, primary education consists of six or eight years of schooling starting at the age of five or six, although this varies between, and sometimes within, countries. Under the Education for all programmes driven by UNESCO, most countries have committed to achieving universal enrolment in primary education by 2015, and in many countries, it is compulsory for children to receive primary education. Education and development are interconnected. It is helpful for converting unskilled persons into skilled person. It is also an important parameter in human development index.

**Who are Tribal's?**

Generally speaking by the term *"tribe"* means, a group of people that live at a particular place from time immemorial. Anthropologically the tribe is a system of social organisation which includes several local groups- villages, districts on lineage and normally includes a comman territory, a common language and a common culture, a common name, political system, simple economy, religion and belief, primitive law and own education system. Constitutionally a tribe is he who has been mentioned in the scheduled list of Indian constitution under Article 342 (i) and 342 (ii). Tribals are found in almost all the states of country. Currently there are between 258 and 540 scheduled tribe communities exists. The strength of these communities varies from 31 people of Jarwa tribe to over 7 million Gonds. Thus the Gonds are big tribal community. Whereas the small communities comprising less than 1000 people include the Andamanese, Onge, Oraon, Munda, Mina, Khond, Saora. According to recent study there are mainly six tribes in chhatfisgarh they are Gond, Baiga, Halba, Kamar, Bhunjia, Korwa.

**Tribal Community in India**

The India's tribal belts refer to contiguous areas of indigenous settlement of tribal people of India. The Tribal Belt of Northwest India includes the states of Rajasthan, Gujarat, Maharashtra, and Karnataka. The tribal people of this region have origins which precede the Vedic Indo-European people of the north and the Indian people of the south. The tribes of north-west India were once strong matrilineal societies. The changing fates and fortunes of these people have caused a gradual evolution to a more patriarchal code of living. The Central India Tribal Belt stretches from Gujarat in the west up to Assam in the east across the states of Andhra Pradesh, Chhattisgarh and Jharkhand. It is among the poorest regions of the country. The quality of life of tribal people during pre-independence period was more deplorable and their main occupation was hunting, gathering of wood and forest products and primitive shifiting cultivation. Due to destruction of forest and non-availability of proper facilities, tribal were forced to lead a miserable life. After independence with the adoptation of Indian constitution in 1950, special attention was given for the upliftment of the tribal people under the article 48. It was mandatory on the part of the state government to make all the efforts to improve economic, social, and educational standard of the tribal people. India is home to a large number of tribes with population of about 70 million. In terms of geographical distribution about 55 per cent of tribals lived in central India, 28 per cent in west, 12 per cent in North-East India, four per cent in South India and one per cent elsewhere. Each tribal communities are rich in there culture, folk tales, folk songs and folk stories.

**Tribal's in Tripura**

The indigenous people of Tripura comprise of 19 tribes, including the Tripra, Reang, Jamatia, Kaipeng, Naotia, Koloi, Halam, Hrangkhal, Mog and Bangcher. Kok Borok is the lingua franca of the tribal people and other dialects spoken in Tripura are of Tibeto-Burmese group. Tripura was a princely state that acceded to the Indian Union on October 15, 1949. It became a Union Territory on November 1, 1956 and a full-fledged State on January 21, 1972. The Tripuri people are the original inhabitants of the Kingdom of Tripura in North-East India and Bangladesh. The Tripuri people mainly speak various dialects called Kokborok, the standard dialect of the Debbarma tribe. The indigenous Tripuri people comprises various hill tribal communities viz., Tipra, Reang, Jamatia, Kaipeng, Noatia, Koloi, Halam, etc. who migrated to this land in successive waves in the ancient past. The Tripuris live on the slopes of hills in a group of five to fifty families. The Reang are the second most populous tribe of Tripura after the Tripuris. According to the legend, a Tripuri prince who was once exiled by the King made his way, along with his followers, to the Mayani Thalang area of Lushai hills and founded a state over there. He proclaimed himself King and his descendants too ruled over the break-away state for generations. The Reang tribe in Tripura, which practised shifting cultivation and still does to an extent, faces serious problems with the state government implementing measures to turn them into settled cultivators. *Jamatia* is another tribal group of Tripura, having a distinct feature of Mongoloid Origin. Their language is also similar with that of *Tripuris*. *Jamatia* were the major strength of Royal Army of Tripura Kingdom for which they were exempted from house taxes during princely-state. Earlier *Jamatias* had to live on Jhum cultivation. *Noatia* are one of the important tribal groups in Tripura._*Uchoi* is a separate tribe, live in Tripura since time immemorial. They have migrated in Tripura from Arakan Hill of Burma. *Mog* comprises 3.06 per cent population in total tribes of Tripura. By religion they are Buddhist. Their major concentrations are at Subroom and Belonia. Their language is grouped under Tibeto-Chinese family._*Chakma* are one of the major tribe of Tripura according to their population strength. They comprises 6.22 per cent population in total tribes of Tripura. *Chakma* are known to be the tribe of South-East Asia.

**Tribal Education**

The aboriginal tribes of India are the oldest inhabitants of the country. For millennia, tribal societies have been subjugated by more recently arrived groups; their land was taken away, they were pushed further into the hilly gorges and wilds, and they were forced to work for their oppressors often without payment. Today tribal groups, which number more than 40 million, require special attention from the government even though they live largely isolated from the national culture. Government planners see education as indispensable for helping tribal peoples cope with national integration. Education will also determine their prosperity, success and security in life. The tribes which remain either deprived of or negligent toward education will suffer the consequence.

Compared with the literacy rates of 29.34 per cent for the general population, literacy among tribal peoples in India is at most six per cent. The Union and the state governments have spent considerable sums of money for tribal youths' education, but the results are meager. The Commissioner for Scheduled Castes and Scheduled Tribes asserts that unless exploitation among the tribels is combatted and eliminated through education, no improvement in tribal welfare will occur. Within tribal areas, education can be the basis for integrated development.

The Janshala Programme is a collaborative effort of the Government of India (GOI) and five UN agencies – UNDP, UNICEF, UNESCO, ILO and UNFPA – to provide programme support to the ongoing efforts towards achieving Universal Elementary Education (UEE). Janshala, a community based primary education programme, aims to make primary education more accessible and effective, especially for girls and children in deprived communities, marginalised groups, Scheduled Caste/Scheduled Tribes/minorities, working children and children with specific needs. A unique feature of Janshala is that it is a block-based programme with emphasis on community participation and decentralisation. The blocks have been selected on the basis of different indicators such as low female literacy, incidence of child labour, and concentration of Scheduled Tribe (ST) and Scheduled Caste (SC) populations. The programme is being implemented in nine States of India - Andhra Pradesh, Jharkhand, Chhattisgarh, Karnataka, Madhya Pradesh, Maharashtra, Orissa, Rajasthan and Uttar Pradesh - with a total of 139 blocks including ten cities under the Programme. The Programme covers nearly three million children, and 58,000 teachers in 18,000 schools. Out of 139 blocks more than 75 blocks have substantial tribal population. The proportion of tribal children is 33 per cent of the total target group children in the project area.

An important development in the policy towards education of tribals is the National Policy on Education (NPE), 1986, which specified, among other things, the following: (i) Priority will be accorded to opening primary schools in tribal areas; (ii) There is need to develop curricula and devise instructional material in tribal languages at the initial stages with arrangements for switchover to regional languages; (iii) ST youths will be encouraged to take up teaching in tribal areas; (iv) Ashram schools/residential schools will be established on a large scale in tribal areas; and (v) Incentive schemes will be formulated for the STs, keeping in view their special needs and lifestyle. On the basis of census 2001, among all STs, 56.5 per cent of the population has been recorded as literate, which is higher than the national average for STs (47.1 per cent). The male literacy rate of 68 per cent and female of 44.6 per cent show high gender disparity in literacy. Among all STs, 62.7 per cent of the children in age group 5-14 years have been attending schools or any other educational institutions. Any *Kuki* Tribe has recorded the highest (77.6 per cent) and *Munda* the lowest (36.7 per cent) percentage attending schools or any other educational institutions. As regards level of education, merely

9.5 per cent of total literates among STs are having educational level of secondary and above. Among the major STs, *Tripuri* have 10.5 per cent of their total literates as matriculates, while among *Munda* (4 per cent), *Reang* (5.7 per cent), and *Mog* (6.5 per cent) this percentage is low.

**Status of Tribal Women**

Traditionally, most of the tribal population practiced shifting or Jhum cultivation and were termed Jhumias. Jhumia is a generic term used for tribal people dependent on shifting cultivation as the primary source of livelihood. The big concentration of Jhumia families was in Dhalai and South District. The popular image and perception of tribal women is that they enjoy much better social status than their non tribal counterparts as the tribal women have no fear of early marriage, no stigma of widow hood, have the freedom of divorce and remarriage, and earns in her own way to get economic independence. The importance of tribal women in their society is significant because of the fact that the tribal women work hard almost relentlessly and the family economy and management depend on them. The unrecognised role of a silent worker primarily because the tribal women are not empowered to take decision both inside and outside of her family which her ancestral property. Economic development is a problem of women in general and the tribal women in particular. The problem becomes more surmountable of backward hilly regions inhibited by tribal people who reflect the co-existence of many problems namely, economic, geographical and sociological.

**Factors affecting Tribal Education**

The reasons can be categorised as external, internal, and socio-economic and psychological. The external constraints are related to problems and difficulties at levels of policy, planning, implementation, and administration. Internal constraints refer to problems associated with the school system, content, curriculum, medium of instruction, pedagogy, academic supervision, monitoring, and teacher-related problems. The third set of problems relates to social, economic, and cultural background of tribals and psychological problems of first-generation learners.

One of the major constraints of tribal education at planning level is the adoption of a dual system of administration. The tribal welfare department deals with tribal life and culture and administers development work at the local level, including education. But the tribal welfare department lacks expertise in educational planning and administration in general and academic supervision and monitoring in particular. On the other hand, the education department is the sole authority for planning of educational development at state level. It formulates implementation guidelines and instructions regarding curriculum, textbooks, teacher recruitment, transfer policies, and so on. In this the department tends to formulate uniform policies for the entire state. The school calendar is a case in point, where vacations and holidays cater to the needs of the formal school set up in a non-tribal context, with little consideration for local context and tribals festivals. This lack of sensitivity to their problems and failure in understanding tribal social reality, coupled with faulty selection and appointment of teachers in tribal areas, have resulted in poor performance and teacher absenteeism in tribal schools. Some of the important factors are as below:

1. ***Social Factors:*** There is still a widespread feeling among the tribals that education makes their boys defiant and insolent and alienates them from the rest of their society, while the girls turn modern or go astray.
2. ***Nature of Habitat:*** Most of the tribal villages are scattered. This entails long travels to attend schools. Unless the school situated very close to their villages and its site approved by the local people the result shall not be encouraging.
3. ***Health Problem:*** Health is a prerequisite for human development and is an essential component for the well being of the mankind. Poor health is another major hindrance in the promotion and participation of tribal children in education.
4. ***Economic Factors:*** Some economic factors too are responsible for lack of interest shown by the tribal people in getting education. Since most of the tribal people are living in poverty, it is not easy for most of them to send their children to schools.
5. ***Environment of the Family:*** Surrounding or environments is one of the importance factors influence for the development of a person generally and particularly in educational development. Most of the tribal parents are agricultures and labours; they have little knowledge relating to modern world and modern environment.

In school tribal students are also facing various types of problems, like as

1. *Communication:* Communication one of the key factor affecting the development of tribal education. Students facing problem for discussing their doubt with teachers. So their doubt continuing and automatically tribal students became the last in the class.
2. *Number of Teachers:* Number of teacher also a problem in those areas. As tribal villages are generarally situate in isolate places or far ways and infrastructure is not good in those areas, so teachers do not want to join in those schools which present there.
3. *Language:* One of the major problems in tribal education is that of language. Medium of language in school and their own mother language is not same.
4. *Lack of interest in Formal education:* In many states tribal children are taught through the same books which from the curriculum of non-tribal children of the urban and rural areas of the rest of the state. Obviously, the content of such books rarely appeals to the tribal children who come from different cultural backgrounds.

5. *Suitable Teachers:* Lack of suitable teachers is one of the major reasons for the slow growth of education in tribal areas. Teacher in many times unable to understand the problems of tribal students if teacher not know their language.
6. *Attitude of Non-Tribal Teacher:* Non-tribal teachers have pessimistic ethnic stereotypes of their tribal pupils, which are known from their responses to a checklist of ethnic stereotypes administered to them. They too have low expectation of their tribal pupil's scholastic achievement.

**Constitutional Previsions and Government Initiatives**

The Scheduled Areas and Scheduled Tribes Commission, a Constitutional body to look into the tribal people's problems has come at a very vital juncture, when the rights and resources of the people of the country are under serious threat and at a time when the constitutional safeguards are being violated or attempted to be diluted. Article 21A of the constitution guarantees every child a fundamental right to free and compulsory education up to the age of 14 years. And according to Article 28 of Convention of Child Rights, States Parties recognise the right of the child to education........and on the basis of equal opportunise shall, in particular make primary education compulsory and available free to all; encourage the development of different forms of secondary education......, make them available and accessible to every child, and take appropriate measures such as the introduction of free education and offering financial assistance in case of need;....... take measures to encourage regular attendance at schools and the reduction of drop-out rates; ..........

The Right to Education Bill, 2008 aimed at shaping up the dream for free and compulsory education for children between 6 and 14. To provide the right to education is the most important duty of the government to guarantees the right of the citizen to live with dignity. Most of the States address the issues related to teachers' attitudes, medium of instruction, textbooks and materials, curriculum and pedagogy, and teaching-learning process in tribal areas. Assam was the first State to prepare teacher training modules and separate teaching learning materials for the Bodo tribal language in 1995. Bodo is also a medium of instructions in some districts of Assam. The work on tribal language materials was undertaken through DIET staff and BRC/CRC coordinators who belonged to the tribal community. In Madhya Pradesh teachers' handbooks called Bridge Language Inventory (BLIs) have been prepared in three tribal languages viz. Gondi (Shahdol and Betul district), Kuduk, (Raigarh) and Bhili (Dhar). Identified teachers were imparted training for use of BLISs in classroom transaction. In Karanataka a texbook for class I and II has been developed and introduced for Soliga language. A handbook has been developed for sensitisation of teachers towards social and cultural specificities of tribal societies. In Maharashtra tribal language dictionaries have been developed. Language resource groups have been set up for Bhili,

Pawara, Madia, Gondi etc. Bridge material has been developed in Dhule district. Kerala has developed bilingual language materials at district level in Kasarkode, Waynad, Malappuram and Palakkad. Cooperation is essentials for promoting education in the case of tribal students. Their funds are flowing a number of persons hand and at last that amount will get students hands. The delay of funds are creating problem, so the respective authorities need to be responsible for providing funds at right time at right hand.

**Conclusion**

Literacy rate among tribal's are very less. They lives in hilly areas and economically they are poor. They are facing various problems in school, like language, communication, lack of teacher, curriculum, communal attitude, etc. For increasing the literacy rate among tribals both Centre and State government's implemented quota in educational institution. In rural areas government-run various programmes for enrolling more students. Government of India and various state governments are already taken various steps for increasing education among the tribals.

## REFERENCES

1. *Adivasi (2011),* Detailed available at http://en.wikipedia.org/wiki/Adivasi
2. A.V. Yadappanavar (2003). *Tribal Education in India*, Discovery Publishing House.
3. Aref Abu-Rabia (2001). *A Bedouin Century: Education and Development among the Negev Tribes in the 20th Century*, Berghahn Books.
4. B.S. Bisht (2006). *Tribes of Uttaranchal: A Study of Education, Health, Hygiene, and Nutrition*, Kalpaz Publication.
5. Bibhuti Mishra (2004), *Reorienting Tribal education,* Detailed available at http://www.hindu.com/op/2004/08/03/stories/2004080300271300.htm
6. Chitrasen Pasayat (2006). *Development of tribal women: problems and potential*, Anmol Publications.
7. C.R. Bijoy (2003), *The Adivasis of India: A history of discrimination, conflict, and resistance,* Detailed available at http://www.pucl.org/Topics/Dalit-tribal/2003/adivasi.htm
8. Dr. Munjunda D.C. et at., (2008). *Ignored Claims: A Focus on Tribal-Education in India,* Gyan Publishing House.
9. Digumarti Bhaskara Rao (1998). *District Primary Education Programme,* Discovery Publishing House.
10. Dickson A. Mungazi (1991). *Colonial-education for Africans: George Stark's policy in Zimbabwe,* Praeger.
11. E.V. Rathnaiah (1977). *Structural Constraints in Tribal-Education: A Regional Study*, Sterling Publishers.
12. Edgar Thurston and K. Rangachari (1987). *Castes and Tribes of Southern India,* Volume 1, Asian Educational Services.

13. *Economic Review of Tripura,* Detailed available at http://destripura.nic.in/review2009_10.pdf
14. *Economic Review 2007-08,* Detailed available at http://india.gov.in/allimpfrms/alldocs/11887.pdf
15. *Education (2011*), Detailed available at http://en.wikipedia.org/wiki/Education
16. Govind Chandra Rath (2006). *Tribal Development in India: The Contemporary Debate,* SAGE.
17. Health status of primitive tribes of Orissa, *ICMR Bulletin,* Vol. 33, No.10, October 2003, pp.1-5.
18. *Education of Tribal Children in India,* Detailed available at http://www.culturalsurvival.org/publications/cultural-survival-quarterly/india/tribal-education-india
19. *India Tribal Belt (2013*). Retrieved from http://en.wikipedia.org/wiki/India_tribal_belt
20. Ibbetson and Maclagan (1996). *Glossary of the Tribes and Castes of the Punjab and North West Frontier Province,* Volume 1, Asian Educational Services.
21. Jebagnanam Cyril Kanmony (2010). *Dalits and Tribes of India,* Mittal Publications.
22. Justin B. Richland and Sarah Deer (2004). *Introduction to Tribal Legal Studies,* Rowman Altamira.
23. Kanchan Roy (1989). *Education and Health Problems in Tribal Development: A Study of National Integration,* Concept Publishing Company.
24. K. Sujatha, *Education among Scheduled Tribes,* Detailed available at http://www.doccentre.net/docsweb/Education/Scanned_material/analysis_Tribals.pdf
25. Khaken Debbarma (2011). *Status of tribal in Tripura State of North-East India-An overview,* Retrieved from http://khakendeb.blogspot.in/2011/05/status-of-tribal-in-tripura-state-of.html
26. Manmatha Kundu (2003), *Tribal Education: New Perspectives,* First edition, Gyan Publishing House, New Delhi, p.1.
27. Manmatha Kundu (1994). *Tribal education, new perspectives,* Gyan Publication House.
28. M. Soundarapandian (2001). *Tribal Development in India: A Case Study,* Anmol Publications.
29. Maenette K.P., A Benham and Wayne J. Stein (2002). *The Renaissance of American Indian Higher Education: Capturing the Dream,* Taylor & Francis.
30. Manmatha Kundu (2003), *Tribal Education: New Perspectives,* First edition, Gyan Publishing House, New Delhi, pp. 4-9.
31. Monali Ramesh Panchbhai (2010), *Health of Tribal Health education,* Detailed available at http://www.tribalzone.net/healthcare/healthcare17.htm
32. Nawal Kishore Ambasht (1970). *A critical study of tribal education: with special reference to Ranchi District,* S. Chand.

33. Nabakumar Duary (2010). *Education in Tribal India: A Study of West Bengal,* Mittal Publications.
34. Otto Friedrich Raum (1940). *Chaga Childhood: A Description of Indigenous Education in an East African Tribe,* LIT Verlag Münster.
35. Prakash Chandra Mehta (2006). *Development of Indian Tribes,* Discovery Publishing House.
36. P. Adinarayana Reddy (2004). *Education of Tribal Women,* Anmol Publications.
37. Philemon Andrew K. Mushi (2009). *History and Development of Education in Tanzania,* African Books Collective.
38. *Problems related to tribal peoples in Andhra Pradesh: A report to the scheduled areas and scheduled tribes commission*, Detailed available at http://www.samataindia.org/documents/triballandproblems.PDF
39. *Reservation in India (2011),* Detailed available at http://en.wikipedia.org/wiki/Reservation_in_India
40. Rabindra Nath Pati and Jagannatha Dash (2002). *Tribal and Indigenous People of India: Problems and Prospects,* APH Publishing.
41. Ranjit Prasad Singh (2010). *Personality of Tribal and Non-Tribal School Children*, Discovery Publishing House.
42. Sabyasachi Bhattacharya (2002). *Education and the Disprivileged: Nineteenth and Twentieth Century India*, Orient Blackswan.
43. *Satish Rastogi, Educational, socio-cultural and health care needs among scheduled tribes of Nandurbar District,* Maharashtra: A diagnosis by YCM Open Univ Nasik, India, Detailed available at http://pcf4.dec.uwi.edu/viewpaper.php?id=104&print=1
44. *Scheduled Tribes and Scheduled Casts (2011),* Detailed available at http://en.wikipedia.org/wiki/Scheduled_castes_and_scheduled_tribes
45. *Scheduled Tribes,* Detailed available at http://planningcommission.nic.in/plans/planrel/fiveyr/10th/volume2/v2_ch4_2.pdf
46. *Study the Dimensional Problem of Tribal Students in India with special reference to Kerala State*, 2011, Detailed available at http://www.belcampus.org/study-the-dimensional-problem-of-tribal-students-in-india-with-special-reference-to-kerala-state.html
47. *Study the Dimensional Problem of Tribal Students in India with special reference to Kerala State*, 2011, Detailed available at http://www.belcampus.org/study-the-dimensional-problem-of-tribal-students-in-india-with-special-reference-to-kerala-state.html
48. Sukanta Sarkar, Problem of education among tribal students in rural areas of Tripura, In *Development of Scheduled Tribes in India: Policies and Programmes*, Prof. D. Pulla Rao (Ed), Serials Publications, New Delhi, 2012, pp. 80-100.
49. Thakorlal Bharabhai Naik (1969). *Impact of Education on the Bhils: Cultural Change in the Tribal Life of Madhya Pradesh*, Sponsored by Research Programmes Committee, Planning Commission.

50. *Tripura (2011)*, Detailed available at http://en.wikipedia.org/wiki/Tripura
51. *Tripura to protect endangered tribes (2011)*, Detailed available at http://www.sify.com/news/tripura-to-protect-endangered-tribes-news-national-ldqtaohacjg.html
52. *Tribal of life and culture (2000),* Detailed available http://www.webindia123.com/bihar/people/tribes2.htm
53. *The agony of Tripura*, Detailed available at http://www.oocities.org/the_agony_of_tripura/
54. *Tribal education in India*, Retrieved from http://www.culturalsurvival.org/publications/cultural-survival-quarterly/india/tribal-education-india
55. *Tribal struggles for education*, Detailed available at http://www.mediaforrights.org/infopack/eng/tribalstruggle.pdf
56. *Tripura Tribal Areas Autonomous District Council (2011),* Detailed available at http://en.wikipedia.org/wiki/Tripura_Tribal_Areas_Autonomous_District_Council
57. *Vinoba Gautam, Education of tribal children in India and the issue of Medium of Instruction: A Janshala experience,* Detailed available at http://www.sil.org/asia/ldc/parallel_papers/vinoba_gautam.pdf
58. Vimal P. Shah and Tara Patel (1985). *Social contexts of tribal education,* Concept Publishing Corporation.
59. Vimal P. Shah (1982). *The educational problems of scheduled caste and scheduled tribe school and college students in India: a statistical profile*, Allied Publisher.
60. Vine Deloria Jr (2010). *Power and Place: Indian Education in America,* ReadHowYouWant.com

# 24

# Environmental Education: Needs and Progress

*Anil Chandra Basak*

*"The direction in which education starts a man will determine his future in life."*

**— Plato**

## Introduction

India is a country with the seventh largest landmass in the world. It is a land of ancient traditions. With over a billion people and at least 17 major languages, the diversity of India in terms of culture and biological wealth is enormous. In spite of rapidly changing lifestyles, the traditions of living in harmony with nature and of environmentally sound practices underpin the lives of most people. India continues to be rich in its biodiversity. Agricultural revolution has ensured that food-grain production has not just kept pace with the population increase, but has rather grown faster. With better nutrition and healthcare, the life expectancy has gone up by almost three times since the independence. The per-capita-income has grown almost 45 times during this period. The past forty years have seen growing international recognition that the challenges associated with environmental degradation and sustainable development have important implications for, and connections with, education and schooling. The concept of environmental education is now wide spreading national-educational-policies, curriculum documents, curriculum development initiatives and conservation strategies. Environment, as an interactive entity could be cited as the other side of life in the sense that the very basic support system for life is provided by environment only. Thus, considering the fast deteriorating environmental condition, it becomes necessary to make Environmental Education (EE) as a tool for life and learning right from one's childhood. Environmental concerns began to emerge in its present form due to the enormous technological growth and it application resulting in a drastic transformation of the environmental situation. Kirk (1985) described the nature study movements into some overlapping phases from 1860 onwards. Education has been identified as a critical driving force for change in the Asian and Pacific Region, and countries and regional organisations have adopted a range of strategies for implementing programmes in environmental education. Environmental education is now being seen as an instrument and a process that enables participation and learning by people of all ages, based on two-way communication rather than the old paradigm of a one-way flow of information, from teachers to pupils.

### Concept

Environmental education (EE) refers to organised efforts to teach about how natural environments function and, particularly, how human beings can manage their behaviour and ecosystems in order to live sustainably. It is a learning process that increases people's knowledge and awareness about the environment and associated challenges, develops the necessary skills and expertise to address the challenges, and fosters attitudes, motivations, and commitments to make informed decisions and take responsible action. It is a process that aims at the development of environmentally literate citizens who can compete in global economy, who have the skills and knowledge and inclinations to make well informed choices concerning the environment, and who exercise the rights and responsibilities of the members of a community. Environmental knowledge contributes to an understanding and appreciation of the society, technology and productivity and conservation of natural and cultural resources of their own environment. Environmental education focuses on:

1. Awareness and sensitivity about the environment and environmental challenges.
2. Knowledge and understanding about the environment and environmental challenges.
3. Attitude concern for the environment and help to maintain environmental quality.
4. Skills to mitigate the environmental problems and.
5. Participation for exercising existing knowledge and environmental related programmes.

### Importance of Environmental Education

Environmental education, together with sound legislation, sustainable management, and responsible actions by individuals and communities is an important component of an effective policy framework for protecting and managing the environment. Environmental Education is a new focus for education. It is a way of helping individuals and societies to resolve fundamental issues relating to the current and future use of the world's resources. However, simply raising awareness of these issues is insufficient to bring about change. Environmental Education must strongly promote the need for personal initiatives and social participation to achieve sustainability. Principles of Environmental Education are

1. It must involve everyone.
2. It must be life long.
3. It must be holistic and about connections.
4. It must be practical.
5. It must be in harmony with social and economic goals and accorded equal priority.

**Environmental Education in India: Progress**

The Indian Constitution laid down the responsibility of Government to protect and improve the environment and made it a *"fundamental duty of every citizen to protect and improve the natural environment including forests, lakes, rivers and wildlife"*. On this background Department of Environment was established by the Government of India in 1980 and a Ministry was formed in 1985. Comprehensive scheme of *'Environmental -Education, Awareness and Training'* was launched in 1983-84. Central Government recognises EE as a key to success of overall environmental strategy and decides to help in the setting up of a *"Centre of Excellence"*. These centres promote EE through developing resource material, organising training/awareness programmes, builds capacity in the field for sustainable development. These centres play the vital role in setting the pace and the agenda for EE. These centres are- Centre for Environment Education, C.P.R Environmental Education Centre, Centre for Ecological Sciences, Centre for Mining Environment, Salim Ali Centre for Ornithology and Natural History (SACON), Centre for Environmental Management of Degraded Ecosystems, Tropical Botanic Garden and Research Institute, Centre of Excellence in Environmental Economics, Foundation for Revitalisation of Local Health Traditions (FRLHT), Centre for Animals and Environment.

Environmental education has been an area of concern in all curriculum development programmes in India. The movement of Basic Education launched by Mahatma Gandhi in 1937 was perhaps the first serious attempt at relating education in schools to local environmental needs. The essential elements of Basic Education were: productive activity in education; correlation of curriculum with the productive activity and the social environment; and intimate contact between the school and the local community. The National Policy on Education, 1986 (NPE) states that *"Protection of the Environment"* is a value which along with certain other values must form an integral part of curriculum at all stages of education. Para 8.15 of the Policy states: *"There is a paramount need to create a consciousness of the Environment. It must permeate all ages and all sections of society, beginning with the child. Environmental consciousness should inform teaching in schools and colleges. This aspect will be integrated in the entire educational process"*. The national system of education, as defined in the National Policy on Education 1986, visualised a national curricular framework which contains a common core including several elements having direct bearing on the natural and social environment of the pupils, such as: Protection of the environment, content essential to nurture national identity, and inculcation of the scientific temper. These core areas are expected to occupy a place of prominence not only in the instructional materials, but also in the classroom and out-of-school activities. Following the National Policy on Education, NCERT brought out detailed curriculum guidelines and model syllabi for classes I to X reflecting these ideas. The approach strongly recommended adoption of innovative teaching and learning techniques.

In India, taking initiative from Stockholm summit 1972, it incorporated environmental concern in the Constitution through 42nd Amendment in 1976. Environment has become a priority in policy statements, Plans and Strategies especially after 1980 with the establishment of a full-fledged Ministry of Environment and forests. Increasing concern on Environmental Education (EE) in India gained its momentum while its importance was recognised by the Government and policy was planned subsequently to introduce EE in schools. It is by now every one's general perception, rightly that, increasing population, unplanned growth of urban areas, ill planned industrialisation and misconceived development paradigm have given rise to the contemporary environmental crisis world over. The Ministry of Environment and Forests (MoEF), Government of India started The National Environment Awareness Campaign (NEAC) in 1986 with the aim of creating environmental awareness at all levels of society. It is a multi-media campaign which utilises conventional and nonconventional methods of communication for disseminating environmental messages to a wide range of target groups. Under NEAC, the Ministry provides financial assistance to selected non-governmental organisations, education and training institutes, community organisations, etc. to create massive awareness among citizens of India. For the implementation of this Scheme in Maharashtra, Goa and Dadra Nagar Haveli, Bhartiya Agro Industrials Foundation (BAIF) has been working as a Regional Resource Agency (RRA) for since 1986. BAIF have been providing technical inputs in organising field demonstrations and mobilising NGOs for environmental awareness. Eco Clubs were constituted by MoEF with objectives to educate school children about their immediate environment and impart knowledge about the eco-systems, their interdependence and their need for survival, by involving them in various environmental activities through visits and demonstrations and to mobilise youngsters by instilling in them the spirit of scientific inquiry into environmental problems and involving them in the efforts of environmental preservation.

Centre for Environment Education (CEE) was created in recognition of the importance of environmental education in India's overall environment and development strategy. The result of a unique partnership between government and a non-governmental institution, CEE was established as a Centre of Excellence in 1984 by the Ministry of Environment and Forests (MoEF). CEE now works in the field of environment education and action for a wide range of sectors, target groups and geographical areas. The GLOBE is an International Science and Education Programme, which emphasises on hands-on participatory approach. India joined this programme in August, 2000. This programme unites students, teachers and scientists all over the world and targets school children. The students of Global Learning and Observations to Benefit the Environment (GLOBE) schools are required to collect data about various basic environmental parameters under the supervision of a GLOBE trained teacher. Through this they learn about scientific protocols and perform environmental learning activities, which have already been introduced as theory in the textbooks.

The National Policy on Education, 1986 (NPE) states that the *"protection of the environment is a value which must form an integral part of the curriculum at all stages of education"*. In order to provide interested persons an opportunity to learn in detail about specific environmental issues, there is provision of a course module through an Indira Gandhi National Open University (IGNOU) for *'Environmental Appreciation'*. Delivery of these courses is through distance-education mode. The Ministry of Environment and Forests, New Delhi accords high priority for the promotion of non-formal environment education and creation of awareness among all sections of the society through diverse activities. The project was launched to encourage and enhance public participation in activities that intended to conserve, protect, manage and sustain the environment. India has a vast network of NGO's that are actively participating in the creation of awareness on development and environmental issues. Working on their own and with Governments they are the backbone of the strategy to create greater environmental awareness, especially that leading to environmental action. Environmental-education in one or the other form was existed in school curriculum prior to the Honourable Supreme Court of India's directive on 18th December, 2003, to impart EE in educational institutes as a compulsory subject. But the way of imparting EE in school was not similar throughout the country and there was no definite standard too. So far no agreement had been arrived at as how to impart EE in regular school curriculum. Several discussions and suggestions had been forwarded, but no general consensus had derived at.

India believes that environmental education is a lifelong process to seek relevant solution to environmental and social issues. It strives to strengthen the individual and institutional capacity for nature conservation and environmental protection, by promoting education and awareness within the social structure. India seeks to mitigate environmental degradation by fostering teamwork and ecological sensitivity by initiating the process of discovering and appreciating the wonders of nature. There is growing awareness about environmental issues amongst stakeholders, individuals and communities. This increase in knowledge and awareness has been, by and large, the result of campaigns and education programmes run by major public interest groups concerned with the environment. These include non-governmental organisations (NGOs) at the international, regional and national levels, as well as groups concerned with the empowerment of marginalised sections of society, such as women, indigenous peoples, and youth groups, and other community-based organisations. Such organisations have worked to foster grassroots-based approaches to the protection and preservation of the region's environment. It must also be recognised by the Government of India and various State Governments that gone are the days when the role of NGOs was confined to capacity building, conscientisation, awareness raising and mobilising the community. Under this changing scenario, competent NGOs need to be involved in all the developmental fields including technical fields. Environmental education is being undertaken by some of the leading NGOs like Assam Science Society, Bombay Natural History Society, Centre for Environmental Education, Centre for Science and Education, Kerala Sastra Sahitya Parishad. They have a vast range of publications – books, posters, educational packages, bibliographies, magazines, etc.

Environmental education has an ability to solve the societal needs, the needs of a community problem and their solutions and workforce for tackling cooperative minds. EE is imparted as EVS, which forms a common component of syllabus, prescribed by the States and CBSE. In Karnataka textbooks and workbooks from classes I to IV, environmental studies are in use. The textbooks for environmental studies which are prepared by NCERT have taken cross Extra curricular approach to teaching environmental concepts through language, mathematics about the environment. In classes I and II there is no separate EVS book. For classes III and IV, EVS textbooks are available. EE has been further reinforced under the art of healthy and productive living (AHPL) for which a single teacher's handbook has been developed for classes I to V. The textbooks lay emphasis on raising awareness levels and sensitising children about environmental concerns. Emphasis has also been laid on the need to organise learning in local specific contexts, which will provide more meaningful experiences to children. Aspects of indigenous knowledge have also been introduced. There are references and suggestions for conducting activities in and outside the classroom. The NCERT textbooks for environmental studies generally take a comprehensive view of the natural, physical, social and cultural environment. The concepts of EE have been provided in the textbooks of science and social sciences in the states of Rajasthan and Madhya Pradesh.

### Challenges for Environmental Educators

There are many challenges for environmental educators in India. Apart from the obvious ones of helping strengthen environmental management and conservation, one of the important ones is to bring about awareness of the need that the country develops in less wasteful ways than is the current paradigm. EE is one of the tools that can help India achieve this goal. There are considerable initiatives in EE in India today. There are also several challenges. Some of these are:

1. The challenge, in a large and diverse country, to find the right blend between centralised and de-centralised efforts and approaches.
2. The challenge of reaching out to large numbers cost-effectively.
3. The challenge of making environmental considerations relevant and meaningful to various groups.

4. The challenge of putting EE on the agenda of educational decision makers.
5. The challenge of putting sustainable development concerns high on the agenda of policy makers, and
6. Finding and developing human and financial resources for EE.

**Conclusion**

Environmental education is increasingly a prominent part of primary, secondary and tertiary education in Asia and the Pacific. The formal education sector plays a vital role in environmental education and awareness by exposing the younger generation to the information, issues, analyses and interpretations on environment and development. Increase in environmental studies has been a response to the market realities, and also to the growing recognition of the environmental crisis and the management options available. In line with the growing interest and activity in environmental education, awareness and training, the demand for educational materials and study aids has also increased. Establishment of environmental study centres has helped a great deal in developing materials and study aids for both formal and non-formal environmental education. Such centres also provide students with information, insights and practical activities, and adult visitors gain information and advice. Government agencies as well as NGOs have developed a wide array of outdoor activities that expose youth and adults to different aspects of environmental awareness, action and understanding.

There are many constraints and barriers to the widespread adoption and practice of environmental education. In the formal education sector, class sizes are often large and teachers lack resources and experience in interactive pupil-centred teaching strategies. School curricula are also dominated by competitive academic curricula which prioritise end–of-course examinations and discourage the development of locally and personally relevant intellectual skills. Outside the formal education sector, environmental education is often poorly organised and resourced. Another common constraint is the lack of clear integration of environmental education objectives and programmes with national education and environmental policies

## REFERENCES

1. Anil Kumar De (2004). *Environmental Education,* New Age International.
2. Alan M. Voelker (1973). *Environmental education: planning priorities*: proceedings of the Environmental Education Workshop for Teachers and Teacher Trainers, at Madison, Wisconsin, May, 1971, University of Wisconsin Extension Duplicating.
3. C. P. Loubser (2005). *Environmental Education: Some South African Perspectives,* BPR Publishers.
4. C.J. Sonowal (2009). *Environmental Education in Schools: The Indian Scenario,* J Hum Ecol, 28(1), Retrieved from http://www.krepublishers.com/02-Journals/JHE/JHE-

28-0-000-09-Web/JHE-28-1-000-09-Abst-PDF/JHE-28-01-015-09-1863-Sonowal-C-J/JHE-28-01-015-09-1863-Sonowal-C-J-Tt.pdf

5. *Centre for Environment Education*, Retrieved from http://envfor.nic.in/about-ministry/center-environment-education.
6. David W. Orr (2004). *Earth in Mind: On Education, Environment, and the Human Prospect*, Island Press.
7. Edward A. Johnson and Michael J. Mappin (2005). *Environmental Education and Advocacy: Changing Perspectives of Ecology and Education,* Cambridge University Press.
8. Erach Bharucha (2005). *Textbook of Environmental Studies for Undergraduate Courses*, Universities Press.
9. *Environmental education,* Chapter fifteen, Retrieved from http://www.unescap.org/esd/environment/soe/2000/documents/CH15.PDF
10. *Environmental Education in India*, Retrieved from http://envis.maharashtra.gov.in/envis_data/newsletter/envlit/env_edu_in_India.html
11. *Environmental education*, Retrieved from http://www.wwfindia.org/about_wwf/enablers/environment_education/
12. *Environmental education what and why?,* Retrieved from http://www.colfinder.net/materials/Green_Teacher/m3/unit_1.pdf
13. *Environmental Education for a Sustainable Future: National Action Plan*, Retrieved from http://www.environment.gov.au/resource/environmental-education-sustainable-future-national-action-plan-5
14. G.V. Gopal and V.V. Anand, *Environmental-education in school curriculum an overall perspectives,* Retrieved from http://www.ces.iisc.ernet.in/biodiversity/sahyadri_enews/newsletter/issue22/art5.htm
15. H.N. Vishwanath (2006). *Models of Teaching in Environmental-Education,* Discovery Publishing House.
16. Harendra Chakhaiyar (2000). *Periwinkle Environmental Education Part IX*, Jeevandeep Prakashan Pvt Ltd.
17. Ian Robottom (1987). *Environmental-Education*, Deakin University.
18. Jack Rudman (2005). *Environmental-Education*, National Learning Corporation.
19. Kartikeya V. Sarabhai, Shivani Jain and Meena R. (2002). *Environmental Education: Some Experiences from India*, See http://www.greenteacher.org/images/EE%20Papers/Environmental%20Education%20-%20Some%20Experiences%20from%20India.pdf
20. Kirubakaran Samuel I. Sundar (2007). *Environmental-Education: Curriculam and Teaching Methods*, Sarup & Sons.
21. Joy Palmer (2002). *Environmental-Education in the 21st Century: Theory, Practice, Progress and Promise*, Taylor & Francis.
22. Joy Palmer, and Philip Neal (1994). *The Handbook of Environmental-Education,* Routledge.

23. Martin Storksdieck (2011). *Field Trips in Environmental-Education*, BWV Verlag.
24. Margaret G. Muthoka, Assumpta B. Rego and Zipporah K. Rimbui (1998). *Environmental education: essential knowledge for sustainable development,* Longhorn Publishers.
25. Martha T. Henderson (2011). *Environmental education,* Social Science Education Consortium.
26. P. P. Gokulanathan Pai (2000). *Environmental Education: A North-East India Development Perspective,* North-Eastern Hill University Publications.
27. Pankaj Srivastava, et al. (2002). *Environmental Education*, Anmol Publications Pvt. Limited.
28. Paul Hart (2003). *Teachers' Thinking in Environmental Education: Consciousness and Responsibility*, Peter Lang.
29. Patricia R. Simpson, Harold R. Hungerford and Trudi L. Volk (2011). *Environmental education: a process for pre-service teacher training curriculum development*, Unesco, Division of Science, Technical and Environmental Education.
30. R.A. Sharma (2009). *Environmental Education: Components, Problems, Management*, Surya Publication.
31. R.C. Sharma (1981). *Environmental Education*, Metropolitan.
32. Richard Robert Jurin, Donald Eugene Roush and Jeff Danter (2010). *Environmental Communication. Second Edition: Skills and Principles for Natural Resource Managers, Scientists, and Engineers*, Springer.
33. Robert B. Stevenson, Michael Brody, Justin Dillon and Arjen E.J. Wals (2013). *International Handbook of Research on Environmental Education*, Routledge.
34. *Role of NGOs in Imparting Environmental Education in India*, Retrieved from http://in.reset.org/blog/role-ngos-imparting-environmental-education-india.
35. Somenath Halder (2012). An appraisal of environmental education in higher school education system: A case study of North Bengal, India, *International Journal of Environmental Sciences*, Volume 2, No 4, 2, Retrieved from http://www.ipublishing.co.in/ijesarticles/twelve/articles/voltwo/EIJES3210.pdf
36. *The Importance of Environmental Education*, Retrieved from http://efs.tki.org.nz/Curriculum-resources-and-tools/Environmental-Education-Guidelines/The-Importance-of-Environmental-Education
37. V.C. Pandey (2007). *Environmental Education*, Gyan Publishing House.
38. V. Krishnamacharyulu and G. S. Reddy (2004). *Environmental Education: For B.Ed. Students of the Indian Universities,* Neelkamal Publications.

# 25

# Sex Education: Needs and Challenges

*Amitra Sudan Chakraborty*

*"Education's purpose is to replace an empty mind with an open one."*

**— Malcolm Forbes**

## Introduction

Education in its general sense is a form of learning in which the knowledge, skills, and habits of a group of people are transferred from one generation to the next through teaching, training, or research. A right to education has been recognised by some governments. At the global level, Article 13 of the United Nations' 1966 International Covenant on Economic, Social and Cultural Rights recognises the right of everyone to an education. Although education is compulsory in most places up to a certain age, attendance at school often isn't, and a minority of parents chooses home-schooling, e-learning or similar for their children. Human sexuality has biological, physical, emotional and spiritual aspects. The biological aspect of sexuality refers to the reproductive mechanism as well as the basic biological drive, libido that exists in all species, which is strongly influenced by hormonal levels. The emotional or physical aspect of sexuality refers to the bond that arises between individuals, and is manifested physically or through emotions such as love, trust and caring. There is also a spiritual aspect of sexuality of an individual or as a connection with others. Experience has shown that adolescents are curious about aspects of their sexuality as well as the nature of sexuality in general, and that many will seek to experience their sexuality in some way.

**What is Sex Education?**

Sex education is instruction on issues relating to human sexuality, including human sexual anatomy, sexual reproduction, sexual activity, reproductive health, emotional relations, reproductive rights and responsibilities, abstinence, and birth control. Common avenues for sex-education are parents or caregivers, formal school programmes, and public health campaigns. There are two aspects of sex education — one straightforward the other complex. On one hand, we have the biological nature of sexuality and gender, which for the most part, can be effectively explained within schools objectively and without too much controversy. The other issue, the one dealing with the physical impulses and feelings associated with sex pose much greater problems especially in a still sexually restrictive culture. This conflict leads to a state where students become adequately educated to what hormones are and how they work without getting guidance on how to deal with them in everyday life.

**Importance of Sex Education**

One approach to sex-education is to view it as necessary to reduce the risk of certain sexual behaviours and equip individuals to make informed decisions about their personal sexual activity. Sex-education can help with India's fight against AIDS. Government statistics indicate that 40 per cent of new sexually transmitted infections are in the 15-29 age groups. More than 31 per cent of all reported AIDS cases occur in this age group, which indicates that young Indians are a high-risk demographic. Children, especially girls, need to be provided sex-education to prevent them from falling prey to sexual abuse. Children need to know the difference between a good touch and a bad touch. This is important to prevent child prostitution and sexual abuse of girls. Sex- education must be made compulsory at the high school level. Surveys indicate that on an average, every urban student watches television for two hours daily. The foreign television channels, the vulgar scenes shown in Indian cinema and video albums create a negative impact on them. The movie and serials on the small screen stimulate the younger generation sexually. Thus in the absence of sound knowledge about sex they commit mistakes which result in unwanted pregnancies, HIV positive cases and other sexually transmitted diseases. In India, 15 per cent of the HIV/AIDS patients are actually children under 15 years of age. Sex education can help people to take decisions regarding health and sexuality. Teaching children about sex in classroom would encourage them to view it as a natural, normal and healthy part of life. Sex education should be introduced in schools and colleges. If children and youngsters learn about sex in scientific and objective way, they would be more careful before indulging in sex secretly. At least they would be careful to take precautions so as to avoid pregnancies and diseases.

Traditionally, adolescents were not given any information on sexual matters, with discussion of these issues being considered taboo. Such instruction as was given was traditionally left to a child's parents, and often this was put off until just before a child's marriage. Most of the information on sexual matters was obtained informally from friends and the media, and much of this information was of doubtful value. Much of such information was usually known to be deficient, especially during the period following puberty when curiosity of sexual matters was the most acute. This deficiency became increasingly evident by the increasing incidence of teenage pregnancies, especially in Western countries after the 1960s. As part of each country's efforts to reduce such pregnancies, programmes of sex-education were instituted, initially over strong opposition from parent and religious groups.

Unawareness and sex can be disturbing and at times, even a fatal brew for young minds. As such, this is what a survey of 35 sex education projects conducted in 1993, by the World Health Organisation (WHO), had to conclude about this issue. It clearly stated that sex education in schools did not encourage youth to have sex at an earlier age or more frequently. Contrarily, the survey revealed that early sex education discourages an early start of sexual activity, lessens sexual activity among youth and encourages those who are already sexually active to have safer sex. Adolescents, particularly in the age group of 16 to 19 years are spoiling their youth with early pregnancies, abortions, AIDS, mental tension and sexually transmitted diseases. Providing them with proper sex education can help tackle these problems to quite an extent. Adult-Education Programme also insists that pre-marital sex along with sex outside marriage is immoral, unethical and unhealthy. Consensual sex before the age of 16 *'amounts to rape'*. A nationwide study conducted by the Department of Women and Child Development stated that 53.2 per cent children have faced one or more forms of sexual abuse and more than half the perpetrators were known to them. Educating youth about sex is very essential, so that they can protect themselves against such abuse.

**Sex Education: Global Perspectives**

All over the world sex education is seen as an intrinsic part of public health. As the threat of AIDS looms large all over the world children are encouraged to know about use of condoms, disease. There is also an ugly reality that a number of children are victims of abuse and harassment. Substantial evidence of the effectiveness of comprehensive sex education has recently emerged. Comprehensive sex education addresses both abstinence and age-appropriate, medically accurate information about contraception. Comprehensive sex education is also developmentally appropriate, introducing information on relationships, decision-making, assertiveness, and skill building to resist social/peer pressure, depending on grade-level.

Sex education may be taught informally, such as when someone receives information from a conversation with a parent, friend, religious leader, or through the media. It may also be delivered through sex self-help authors, magazine advice columnists, sex columnists, or sex education web sites. Formal sex education occurs when schools or health care providers offer sex education. Sometimes formal sex education is taught as a full course as part of the curriculum in junior high school or high school. Other times it is only one unit within a more broad biology class, health class, home economics class, or physical-education class. Some schools offer no sex education, since it remains a controversial issue in several countries, particularly the United States. When sex-education is contentiously debated, the chief controversial points are whether covering child sexuality is valuable or detrimental; whether LGBT sex-education should be integrated into the curriculum; the use of birth control such as condoms and hormonal contraception; and the impact of such use on pregnancy outside marriage, teenage pregnancy, and the transmission of STIs.

Sex education in Africa has focused on stemming the growing AIDS epidemic. Most governments in the region have established AIDS education programmes in partnership with the World Health Organisation and international NGOs. Egypt teaches knowledge about male and female reproductive systems, sexual organs, contraception and STDs in public schools at the second and third years of the middle-preparatory phase (when students are aged 12–14). A coordinated programme between UNDP, UNICEF, and the ministries of health and education promotes sexual education at a larger scale in rural areas and spreads awareness of the dangers of female genital mutilation. The state of sex education programmes in Asia is at various stages of development. In Thailand has there been progress on sex education, with the boundaries being pushed forward with each revision of the curriculum. Thailand has already introduced sexuality education. The first national policy on sexuality education in schools was announced in 1938, but sex education was not taught in schools until 1978. Then it was called *"Life and Family Studies"*, and its content consisted of issues related to the reproductive system and personal hygiene. Indonesia, Mongolia and South Korea have a systematic policy framework for teaching about sex within schools. Malaysia and Thailand have assessed adolescent reproductive health needs with a view to developing adolescent-specific training, messages and materials.

Bangladesh, Myanmar, Nepal and Pakistan have no coordinated sex education programmes. In China and Sri Lanka, sex education traditionally consists of reading the reproduction section of biology textbooks. In France, sex education has been part of school curricula since 1973. Schools are expected to provide 30 to 40 hours of sex education, and pass out condoms, to students in grades eight and nine. In January 2000, the French government launched an information campaign on contraception with TV and radio spots and the distribution of five million leaflets on contraception to high school students. In Germany, sex education has been part of school curricula since 1970. Since 1992 sex education is a governmental duty by law. In Sweden, sex education has been a mandatory part of school education since 1956. The subject is usually started between ages 7 and 10, and continues up through the grades, incorporated into different subjects such as biology and history. In Switzerland, the content and amount of sex education is decided at the cantonal level. In Geneva, courses have been given at the secondary level first for girls since 1926 and compulsory programmes have been implemented at secondary level for all classes since the 1950s. In England and Wales, sex education is not compulsory in schools as parents can refuse to let their children take part in the lessons. The curriculum focuses on the reproductive system, foetal development, and the physical and emotional changes of adolescence. Almost all U.S. students receive some form of sex education at least once between grades 7 and 12; many schools begin addressing some topics in grades five or six. Virginia uses the sex education programme called *The National Campaign* to prevent teen and unplanned pregnancy. The National Campaign was created in 1996 and focuses on preventing teen and unplanned pregnancies of young adults. Sex education in Texas has recently become a policy of much focus in the state. With the rise of recent protests and proposed bills in the Texas House, the current policy has been the focus of much scrutiny. The Government of Victoria (Australia) developed a policy for the promotion of *Health and Human Relations Education* in schools in 1980 that was introduced into the State's primary and secondary schools during 1981. In New Zealand, sexuality-education is part of the Health and Physical-Education curriculum, which is compulsory for the first ten years of schooling (Years 1 to 10) but optional beyond that.

**Sex Education in India**

One issue that has received the most varied responses from different quarters of the society is the introduction of sex education in schools and other educational institutions in India. Even the apex court in the country has repeatedly been emphasising that it cannot bring sex education within the purview of fundamental rights, by making it a part of the right to education. The real problem is that there is no clear accord in India, over the issue of introducing sex education in educational institutions. The people opposing sex education point out that India is a traditional society and claim that promulgation of sex education will give youth undue fillip to take interest in the issue. On the contrary, a certain section of the intelligentsia and NGOs in India that have been working closely with different social groups opine that introducing sex education in school curriculum will play crucial role in checking the increase of rape cases and unwanted pregnancies in youth.

Sex-education has become a debatable issue. Many people feel that these kinds of delicate issues should be left to the parents. Parents feel embarrassed to talk openly with their children in this regard. Sex is still considered a taboo in the Indian society. It is considered that teaching our children about their sexuality can break down pre-existing notions of modesty and tear the moral fabric of our society. But with the alarming increase of AIDS, unwanted/unplanned/unwed pregnancies and other diseases related to sex, it is important that sex-education should be given importance in schools and colleges. Physical and mental changes in children start appearing with puberty. Sexual development begins much earlier than that. Many children find it strange or difficult to cope up with the changes. They grow up with curiosity stamped on their minds. So it is very important to provide them sex education. It makes growing children aware of the various changes taking place in their bodies and prepares them for responsible adulthood.

The lesson that Indian leaders seem to take from sex education: *Prevention is better than cure.* But this may not be the best formula for a country with a high incidence of child marriages and teenage pregnancies. Experts say that the case for sex education in India is quite different from in the West because it is *'legitimate'* here for young people to have sex. According to the National Family Health Survey conducted by the International Institute for Population Sciences (IIPS) and Macro International in 2005-06, 12 per cent women aged between 15-19 years are mothers. Youth in India needs sex education more than in any other country since child marriage ensures that you not only have sex at a young age, you also have teenage pregnancy. Contrast this with the received wisdom of our politicians. The Committee on Petitions headed by the BJP's Venkaiah Naidu is a cross-party group up of nine Rajya Sabha members. The Committee has said there should be no sex education in schools because it promotes promiscuity and India's *"social and cultural ethos are such that sex education has absolutely no place in it."* The Committee directed its outrage at the human resource development ministry's (HRD) Adult Education Programme (AEP). Launched in 2005 and backed by the National Aids Control Organization (NACO), the AEP's focus is safer sex, as well as the physical and mental development of 14-18 years old. But the Committee said that it was *"highly embarrassed"* by the HRD ministry's curriculum and insisted that pre-marital sex, together with sex outside marriage, is *"immoral, unethical and unhealthy"*. It also said that consensual sex before the age of 16 *"amounts to rape"*.

Sex Education in India is not widespread. A parliamentary committee, with a varied political membership, recently recommended that there should be no sex education in schools. Sex even if done at the proper time, with a proper person, in a proper place, is a topic that makes many Indians uncomfortable. The committee itself refused a power point presentation on the question *"after going through the hard copy because of its explicit contents. The Committee felt that it was not comfortable with it and could be embarrassing especially to the lady Members and other lady staff present."* The committee has recommended that chapters like *'Physical and Mental Development in Adolescents'* and *'HIV/AIDS and other Sexually Transmitted Diseases'* be removed from the general curriculum. In a recent report released by the Ministry of Women and Child Development on a Study on Child Abuse in India stated that 50 percent abuses are person known to the child or in a position of trust and responsibility and that more than 50 per cent of children have faced one or more forms of sexual abuse. More often than not, the child did not report the abuse at all. Meanwhile, efforts made by the Central Government to introduce sex education in schools countrywide have run into some trouble. Many Indian States like Gujarat, Madhya Pradesh, Maharashtra and recently Karnataka have banned the introduction of sex education in schools after protests from legislators who say it will corrupt young minds. Equipping children with the *"correct"* information or knowledge is a primary way to prevent abuse. World Vision India Experience in developing an Adolescent Girls Training module goes back to the 90's when the primary research was to prevent by education girls on transmission of HIV/AIDS. But it included other reasons like gender discrimination, poor access to health services, poor nutrition and in particular unsafe sex practices. Sexual abuse of girls and women including incest and rape, were additional factors which could not be ignored.

**Conclusion**

Sex-education is a debatable matter in various countries. In developed countries it is not a problem but developing countries facing more challenges for implementing it. Schools life remains an integral part of every child's development. Along with the academic subjects, sex-education should be given equal importance. Trained teachers, psychologists and medical consultants should deal with the subject. While imparting sex-education the boys and girls should be divided into two groups (one for boys and other for girls). They should be taught separately. This way the lady teachers should teach girls and male teachers should teach boys. Children will not feel embarrassed. They will freely clarify their doubts and queries. Due care should be taken about the contents of the subject. This should be decided by a team of doctors and psychologists of the respective field.

## REFERENCES

1. Alexandra M. Lord (2010). *Condom Nation: The U.S. Government's Sex Education Campaign from World War I to the Internet,* JHU Press.
2. Alesha E. Doan and Jean Calterone Williams (2008). *The Politics of Virginity: Abstinence in Sex Education,* Praeger Frederick A.
3. Clint Bruess and Jerrold Greenberg (2008). *Sexuality Education: Theory and Practice,* Jones & Bartlett Learning.
4. Clint E. Bruess, and Jerrold S. Greenberg (2004). *Sexuality Education: Theory and Practice,* Jones & Bartlett Learning.
5. David Campos (2002). *Sex, Youth, and Sex Education: A Reference Handbook,* ABC-CLIO.
6. Edward Hammond Clarke (2006). *Sex in Education: Or, A Fair Chance for the Girls,* J. R. Osgood.
7. Janice M. Irvine (2002). *Talk about Sex: The Battles over Sex Education in the United States,* University of California Press.
8. Jessica Fields (2008). *Risky Lessons: Sex Education and Social Inequality,* Rutgers University Press.
9. J. Mark Halstead, and Michael Jonathan Reiss (2003). *Values in Sex Education: From Principles to Practice,* Routledge Falmer.
10. Judy Hunter, and Sheila Phillips (2000). *Sex Education,* Folens Limited.
11. Karen Stabiner (2002). All Girls: Single-Sex Education and Why It Matters, Riverhead Books.

12. Kekla Magoon (2009). *Sex Education in Schools*, ABDO.
13. *Manish Rajkoomar, Is sex education necessary in School,* Retrieved from http://www.publishyourarticles.net/knowledge-hub/essay/is-sex-education-necessary-in-schools-essay.html.
14. Martha Cornog, and Timothy Perper (1996). *For Sex Education, See Librarian: A Guide to Issues and Resources*, Greenwood Publishing Group.
15. Morton Edward Crawford (1975). *Sex Education in Schools*, School Library Association of New South Wales.
16. Nancy Kendall (2012). *The Sex Education Debates*, University of Chicago Press.
17. Pankaj Arora (2009). Sex Education in Schools, Prabhat Prakashan.
18. Roger J. R. Levesque (2003). *Sexuality Education: What Adolescents' Rights Require*, Nova Publishers.
19. Rosemary C. Salomone (2005). *Same, Different, Equal: Rethinking Single-sex Schooling*, Yale University Press.
20. Sex Education in Schools, Church Information Office for the Church of England Board of Education, 1964.
21. *Sex education (2013).* Retrieved from http://en.wikipedia.org/wiki/Sex_education
22. *Sex education in India (2013).* Retrieved from http://hyd-n-spook.blogspot.in/2012/09/sex-education-in-india.html
23. *Sex Education in India - Need of the Hour (2013).* Retrieved from http://upscportal.com/civilservices/magazine/csm/january-2013/sex-education-in-india-need-of-the-hour
24. *Sex education in India*, Retrieved from http://lifestyle.iloveindia.com/lounge/sex-education-in-india-56.html
25. Sue Allerston, and Graham Davies (2001). *Sex Education*, Nelson Thorne.
26. Susan Prentice (1994). *Sex in Schools: Canadian Education and Sexual Regulation*, James Lorimer and Company.
27. Thomas Edwards Brown (1968). A guide for Christian sex education of youth, Association Press.
28. Theodore Frederic Tucker and Muriel Pout (1937). *Sex Education in Schools: An Experiment in Elementary* Instruction, G. Howe.
29. *Taboo sex education key to reducing child abuse*, Retrieved from http://www.worldvision.in/?1126
30. Times of India (Apr 26, 2009). *Sex education: Why India should go all the way,* Retrieved from http://articles.timesofindia.indiatimes.com/2009-04-26/view-from-venus/28022348_1_child-marriage-indian-women-education-classes
31. William Josephus Robinson (1916). *Sex Knowledge for Men: Including a Program for Sex Education of the Boy,* Critic and guide Company.

# 26

# Knowledge Society and Information Management: A Study of Contemporary Socio-economic Issues and Challenges

*Manzoor Hussain*

*"Education is simply the soul of a society as it passes from one generation to another."*
**— Gilbert K. Chesterton**

## Introduction

Knowledge society refers to that society where the process of generation and transformation of information has become fundamental source of productivity and power. The Internet is the biggest global network connecting 227 countries of the world. The population of Internet users worldwide was 1,733,993,741 covering 25.6 per cent of the world total population. The Internet users as on December 31, 2012 account for only 32.7 per cent of world's population of 6,930,055,154. Out of that 13.5 per cent of them are in Africa, 26.2 per cent in Asia, 61.3 per cent in Europe, 35.6 per cent in Middle East, with a population of 1,037,524,058; 3,879,740,877; 816,426,346; 216,258,843; 347,394,870; 347,394,870; 35,426,995 respectively.

This is the essence of global digital divide that needs to be transformed into global digital opportunity. There are different dimensions to digital divide such as economic level of individuals, economic prosperity of nations, ethnicity, age (young/old), rural/urban, gender, geographic location, quantitative and qualitative aspects, dial-up and broadband access. In Europe, the first wave of Information Society policy, that focused heavily on the liberalisation of telecommunications and the development of information and communication technologies (ICTs) was followed by a second phase, more concerned with the wider social aspects including issues of social cohesion and the digital divide. The Global digital divide designates countries as the units of analysis and examines the divide between developing and developed countries on an international scale. There are no doubt that a digital divide exists but its severity and depth is evaluated differently according to the indicators used to measure it. However, the implications of the new media need to be understood more deeply because of way in which innovations in digital technologies are contributing to the exercise and the distribution of power in society. A number of socio-economic issues are related with information management. The unequal access to information and communication technologies has led to the digital divide not only in developing countries but globally as well. ICTs are restructuring the global social and economic equation i.e., shifting from income divide to knowledge divide. Knowledge has become basic form of capital, and the economic growth is driven by the accumulation of knowledge. Although this knowledge society offers many potential benefits to developing and developed countries but its access, dissemination and control carries, at the same time the real danger of a growing digital divide/gap among and within nations. The computer is a target for unlawful acts viz., unauthorised access to computer/computer system/computer networks, theft of information contained in the electronic form, e-mail bombing, data diddling, salami attacks, logic bombs, Trojan attacks, internet time thefts, web jacking, theft of computer system, physically damaging the computer system. Computer crime refers to offences that are committed against individuals or groups of individuals with a criminal motive to intentionally harm the reputation of the victim or cause physical or mental harm to the victim directly or indirectly, using modern telecommunication networks such as Internet (Chat rooms, e-mails, notice boards and groups) and mobile phones- SMS/MMS. Such threats are detrimental to information management and pose real danger to socio-economic fabric of society.

**Nature and Scope**

Information management (IM) refers to the collection and management of information from one or more sources and the distribution of that information to one or more audiences. This sometimes involves those who have a stake in, or a right to that information. Management means the organisation of and control over the structure, processing and delivery of information. Information management is an interdisciplinary field that focuses on information as a resource, with greater emphasis on the acquisition and management of external information and to some extent the management of internal records and other documents It mainly deals with managing documented and explicit knowledge (that is, information), which can be easily transferred or shared within or outside the organisation. Information management is different than knowledge management which is generally thought of as the effort to make the knowledge of an organisation available to those within the organisation who need it, where they need it, when they need it, and in the form in which they need it in order to increase human and organisational performance. Information professionals play a key role ininformation management by imparting lifelong learning skills to the information audience. Direct access to information services has changed the role of information professional from traditional keepers to guides. Information literacy skills are needed to enable one to use information and information communication technology effectively and to access appropriate digital resources. In the current technological environment, libraries are passing through a challenging phase, which is posing serious threats to library and information centres and information professionals. This has created a shift in the role of information professionals which is now increasingly being dependent on ICT viz., internet, virtual reference services (via web-based chat, instant messaging, text messaging and e-mail), online or electronic services, online information literacy, artificial intelligence, and digital information systems. The technological innovations have created new issues and challenges to manage information. The World Wide Web (WWW), the one single development is having the greatest impact as a huge information resource and a channel of distribution. The present information environment is rapidly changing from conventional to digital information systems. Electronic information in terms of electronic books (e-books), electronic journals (e-journals), electronic theses and dissertations (e-thesis and dissertations), electronic learning (e-learning), electronic commerce (ecommerce), electronic banking (e-banking) and electronic repositories (e-repositories) are all systems that represent the present information environment. Technological tools connect institutions, nations, continents and integrate resources and services, and boundaries are blurred. This has increased competition among the global information players where only the best will survive by being effective in operation, marketing and creation of products and services through better information management.

Simultaneously, information management is facing tremendous challenges that pose serious threats to economic and social fabric of society. The biggest contemporary socio-economic issue of information management is the computer crime. It encompasses a broad range of activities. Generally, however, it may be divided into two categories: (1) crimes that target computers directly; (2) crimes facilitated by computer networks or devices, the primary target of which is independent of the computer network or device. Crimes that primarily target computer networks or devices include: computer viruses, denial-of-service attacks, and malware (malicious code). Crimes that use computer networks or devices to advance other ends include: cyber stalking, fraud and identity theft, information warfare, and phishing scams. For a variety of reasons the content provided by websites and other electronic communications could be distasteful, obscene, offensive or illegal. Internet pornographye specially child pornography; drug trafficking etc. are promoted through Internet to sell their illegal substances. Available literature suggest that some drug traffickers arrange deals at internet cafes, use courier Web sites to track illegal packages of pills, and swap recipes for amphetamines in restricted-access chat rooms. This mode of crime poses serious issues for information management.

**Theoretical Orientations**

Sociologists argue that communication media support shared aims which demonstrate a powerful collective representation. The Marxists see communication media as an exploitative tool by the elitist groups for socioeconomic and political control. The invention of mini-electronic and optical circuits capable of speeding the rate of information flow through networks has a big impact on society. Free flow of information has given fillip to criminal activities like cyber crime. As an illustration it is easier to steal a penny from millions of bank account owners using the internet than using physical robbery. Other sociologists like (Giddens: 1984) has provided structuration theory as a meta-theoretical social framework that argues that action and structure operate as a duality, simultaneously affecting each other. Similarly (Orlikowski: 1992) developed a structuration model of technology which made the claim that technology is both constituted by human agency and constitutes human practice. Wood proposed the Human Firewall theory and advocated that organisations must sensitise and educate users and evaluate their compliance with security policies and procedures. Social psychology is a tool to improve user security conduct (Kabay: 2002). In this context (Schlienger and Teufel: 2002) adopted a socio-cultural approach to information security and posited that the cultural theory can be used to enhance security at different cultural layers-namely, corporate policies, top management, and individuals.

**Knowledge Society, Information Management and Socio-Economic Issues**

The introduction of new information technology has a ripple effect, raising new social, economic, ethical and political issues that must be dealt with on the individual, social, and political levels. These issues have five moral dimensions: information rights and obligations, property rights and obligations, system quality, quality of life, and accountability and control. These five dimensions are shown in the below mentioned figure.

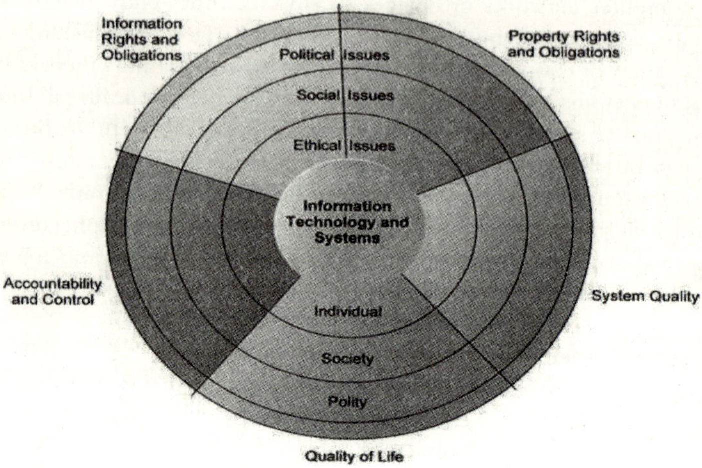


**Fig. 1. Showing Information Technology and Social, Economic, Ethical and Political Issues.**

*Source*: Cited in original from Chapter 4: Ethical and *Social Issues* in Information Systems, Retrieved from www.prenhall.com/.../pdf/laudon%20MIS10_CH-04%20FINAL.pdf

Free flow of information across boundaries have revolutionised the present era. ICTs are restructuring the global economic and social-equation and knowledge has become basic form of capital, and the economic-growth is driven by the accumulation of knowledge. Although this knowledge society offers many potential benefits but its access, dissemination and control carries, at the same time the real danger of a growing many socio-economic issues. Social dimensions of cybercrime are for reaching and are detrimental for overall social fabric of society. Cyber crime lead to social pathology and in fact distort social relationships of all – children, adults and the aged. Children and young people are targeted in the online environment that they inhabit, e.g., instant messaging, chat, and social networking sites; those that engage in offline abuse, create images and share them online with networks of like-minded individuals or are recipients and collectors of such material; or those that use the internet to link up and identify the best places in the world to travel to abuse children or young people or who use the internet to lure this vulnerable group into some form of exploitation. As with other forms of crime on the internet, this poses a challenge for law enforcement. The perpetrators harm or sexually-exploit children by transfer of illegal images of child sexual abuse when the public accidentally see such images. The nature of the technology which children often carry with them all the time, allows bullying to take place not only in school but continue outside. This can make the victim feel threatened and unable to escape the bullying, leading to a feeling of powerlessness.

The individuals or organised groups focus on particular issues through internet such as harm-based crime viz., racial or religious hatred, harassment, or political extremism. These perpetrators carry much type of frauds ranging from credit and debit card fraud, lottery scams, non-delivery fraud and frauds involving fake goods, such as watches or clothing, or more seriously of fake and unsafe pharmaceuticals. The cyber criminals use these offences on a mass scale, and conceal their real identities and locations. The motive data thefts are to secure private information and sell it either directly to those able to realise its monetary value through fraud, or to those who act as data brokers. They are targeted primarily for user names and passwords to enable criminals to access and control online accounts. Account holders reveal his private data through fake emails and websites or by infecting the account holder's computer with malicious software that automatically intercepts and forwards data to the criminal.

There is no structure for monitoring Internet businesses and the result is loss of revenue through missed taxes, piracy and intellectual property infringement. Similarly, loss of revenue can be caused through identity theft; unauthorised access to important information like trade secrets and through scams in which the victims willingly pay for undelivered services. Other financial losses are caused by denial of service attacks (DoS). In 2000, yahoo was hit by a DoS attack which caused their website not to be accessed for only two hours. Since yahoo received 50 million viewings per hour then, this attack is estimated to have cost them over $500,000 through missed revenue (Tushabe F and Baryamureeba V: Year N.A.). There is a lot of time and resource wastage through the management of cyber-crime. Since SPAM alone accounts for 90 per cent of the total email traffic, this means that 90 per cent of the time employees spend reading their mails is wasted. Additionally, over 33 terawatt hours of electricity are wasted every year. Facebook has 400 million active users with an average of 100 – 150 million unique users per month. Imagine how much time would be wasted if a spammer sent an email to all Facebook members. There are economic losses following fake visas, fake jobs and conferences, even fake marriages (on-line dating). Cybercrime is often correlated with negative effect on employees' productivity mainly due to security measures. Every second wasted performing these tasks are a second not spent working in a productive manner. Cyber-crime affects the poor and rich people slightly differently. Poorer people are more vulnerable to online exploitation that leads to evils like child labour, sexual exploitation and uncouth schemes related to immigration, fake visas, get-rich-quick-schemes etc. On the other hand, the rich people are more vulnerable to identity theft and damaged reputations. It is shocking to learn that in the United States alone, 10 million people have been victims of identity theft that resulted in a direct financial loss of $50 billion.

Cyber-terrorism is a big issue and it can be defined as an act of terrorism committed through the use of cyberspace or computer resources. The U.S.

Department of Defence notes that cyber space has emerged as a national-level concern through several recent events of geo-strategic significance. Among those are included the attack on Estonia's infrastructure in 2007, allegedly by Russian hackers. In August 2008, Russia again allegedly conducted cyber-attacks, this time in a coordinated and synchronised kinetic and non-kinetic campaign against the country of Georgia. Further one of the highest profiled banking computer-crime occurred during a course of three years beginning in 1970. The chief teller at the Park Avenue branch of New York's Union Dime Savings Bank embezzled over $1.5 million from hundreds of accounts. A hacking group called MOD (Masters of Deception), allegedly stole passwords and technical data from Pacific Bell, Nynex, and other telephone companies as well as several big credit agencies and two major universities. The damage caused was extensive, one company, South-western Bell suffered losses of $370,000 alone. In 1983, a nineteen year old UCLA student used his PC to break into a Defence Department international communications system. Between 1995 and 1998 the Newscorp satellite pay to view encrypted SKY-TV service was hacked several times during an on-going technological arms race between a pan-European hacking group and Newscorp. The original motivation of the hackers was to watch Star Trek re-runs in Germany; which was something which Newscorp did not have the copyright to allow. There are other issues of information management which have direct or indirect social implications. Information explosion refers too much inaccessible and irrelevant information. A lot of information is stored in computers, but it is very difficult or impossible to access it. But this information is not relevant to the needs or intentions of the people seeking information. Computer systems automatically capture or generate information such as access history, product purchase history, profiles of people segmented on the basis of various attributes (e.g., gender, income level, education level, ethnic origin, religion, etc.), and so on.

Digital divide is another issue which refers to the gap between the technology empowered and the technology excluded communities in the world. The developing world and transition economies-comprise the largest portion of the digital divide in knowledge society. While global-teledensity shows signs of improving the gap between those with and without access to the Internet continues to increase throughout the world. The *'digital divide'* has created a knowledge gap between information rich and information poor peoples, which has the potential to give rise to a new form of *'illiteracy'*. It restricts information and knowledge diffusion and limits the opportunities for economic-growth and wealth distribution. The 'digital divide' threatens to widen the already existing development gap between the rich and poor among and within countries. The majority of the world's people are not able to benefit from this revolution unless they are empowered to participate fully in the emerging knowledge-based information society. Internal divide is between digitally empowered rich and the disempowered poor; linguistic cultural divide between domination of Anglo-Saxon and the other world culture; divide in access of technology between the rich and the poor nation; and the divide between the values of ICT's driven affluent elite and conventional authority and hierarchies. In UK, for example, only four per cent of households in the poorest income quintile are connected to the Internet, compared to 43 per cent in the top quintile; in USA, the proportion of Afro - American families that are connected is half that for white families. Among developing countries, the digital divide sets apart the technologically more advanced countries from the less advanced ones. Whereas a few African countries with small populations still lack even one Internet host, in Singapore 98 per cent of households use Internet.

**Conclusion**

Information management has certain socio-economic issues and challenges that pose serious threats to economic and social fabric of society. Cyber-crime is posing great challenges to the socio-economic development of individuals, groups, communities and societies. Yet, less than half of it goes un-noticed or un-reported. There are intended and unintended consequences of ICT to include acts such as phishing, cyber-terrorism, electronic-spam mails, cyber-stalking and fake copy cat websites. The computer is a target for unlawful acts viz., unauthorised access to computer/computer system/computer networks, theft of information contained in the electronic form, e-mail bombing, data diddling, salami attacks, logic bombs, Trojan attacks, internet time thefts, web jacking, theft of computer system, physically damaging the computer system. The Internet is the biggest global network connecting individuals, groups, organisations and countries together. The unequal access to information and communication technologies has led to the digital divide not only in developing countries but globally as well.

## REFERENCES

1 Anttiroiko, A. (200). Toward the European Information Society, *Communications of the ACM*, Vol. 44, January, pp. 31–36.

2. Balakrishnan, N. (2001). Information and communication technologies and the digital divide in the third world countries: *Current Science.* 81(8): 966-972.

3. Balkin, J., Grimmelmann, J., Katz, E., Kozlovski, N., Wagman, S. and Zarsky, T. (2006) (eds) *Cybercrime: Digital Cops in a Networked Environment*, New York University Press, New York.

4. Bell, R. Garland, and Platt, R.B. (1997). *Bridging and signalling subsystems and methods for private and hybrid.* Retrieved from http://www.freepatentsonline.com/6606690.html

5. Chinn, Menzie D. and Robert W. Fairlie (2004). The Determinants of the Global Digital Divide: A Cross-Country Analysis of Computer and Internet Penetration. Economic Growth Center. Retrieved from http://www.econ.yale.edu/growth_pdf/cdp881.pdf

6. Csonka P. (2000). Internet Crime; the Draft council of Europe convention on cyber-crime: A response to the challenge of crime in the age of the internet? *Computer Law and Security* Report Vol.16 no. 5.
7. Dasgupta, S., S. V. Lall, et al. (2001) Policy Reform, Economic Growth, and the Digital Divide: An Econometric Analysis. *Washington, D.C: World Bank Working,* Paper No. 2567.
8. David Mann And Mike Sutton. (2011). "Netcrime". Bjc.oxfordjournals.org. http://bjc.oxfordjournals.org/cgi/content/short/38/2/201.Retrieved 2011-11-10.
9. Debal K, Singh Roy and Ms. Jitha, T.J. (2005) *Critique of knowledge society IGNOU, MSOE-003, Sociology of Development, Book-2.* New Delhi: IGNOU: 150-161.
10. DiMaggio, Paul et al. (2001). Social Implications of Internet, *Annual Review of Sociology*, Vol. 27, pp. 307-336.
11. Evers, Hans-Dieter and Gerke, Solvay (2004). Closing the Digital Divide: Southeast Asia's Path towards a Knowledge Society. Paper delivered at the Centre for East and South-East Asian Studies public lecture series *"Focus Asia"*, 25-27 May, 2004 Centre for East and South-East Asian Studies Lund University, Sweden www.ace.lu.se
12. Giddens, A. (1984). *The constitution of society*. Cambridge: Polity Press.
13. Government of India (2003). *India, 2003-04.* New Delhi: Publications Division.
14. Halder, D., and Jaishankar, K. (2011) *Cybercrime and the Victimisation of Women: Laws, Rights, and Regulations*. Hershey, PA, USA: IGI Global. ISBN 978-1-60960-830-9
15. Hazel, Hinderson (1999). Beyod Globalisation: Shaping a Sustainable Globals-Economy.
16. Kumarian West Hartford, CT. *Information Technology for Sustainable Development.* Canada: IDRC.
17. Henten, A. and Kristensen, T. (2000). Information Society visions of the Nordic countries, *Telematics and Informatics*, Vol. 17, pp. 77-103.
18. Henten, A., Skouby, K and Falch, M. (1996).European planning for an Information Society, *Telematics and Informatics*, Vol. 13 (2/3), pp. 177-90.
19. Houghton, J., and Sheehan, P. (2000). A primer on the knowledge economy.*Paper prepared for the National Innovation Summit*, Melbourne, Australia, February 2000.
20. Internet World Stats: 2010: *The Internet big picture world Internet users and population stats.* Retrieved January 9, 2010, from http://www.internetworldstats.com/stats.htm
21. Internet World Stats: 2011: *Usage and population statistics*. Retrieved December 31, 2011, from http://www.internetworldstats.com/stats.htm
22. Jaishankar, K. (Ed.) (2011). *Cyber Criminology: Exploring Internet Crimes and Criminal behavior.* Boca Raton, FL, USA: CRC Press, Taylor and Francis Group.

23. Jessop, Bob (2003). The state and the contractions of the knowledge driven economy. In Bryson, J.R. et al. (Eds.) *Knowledge, Space, Economy*. London: Routledge.
24. Kabay ME (2002).Using Social-Psychology to Implement Security Policies. In Bosworth S, and Kabay ME (eds) *Computer-Security Handbook*, 4th edition. John Wiley & Sons, Inc., USA,32.1-32.16.
25. Kinestin, S. (2003). CMTE: The Undergraduate Potential, *CMTE Postgraduate Conference*. Brisbane: Australia 19th May.
26. Loan, Fayaz: 2011: Gender Variability in Internet use of the college students. *Journal of society in Kashmir,* 1, 156-64.
27. Longe, O.B., Chiemeke, S.C., Damola, T (2008). Dealing with Malicious Insider Threats in Organizational information systems Using "Honeybaits". *Proceedings of the 2nd International Conference of the Int. Centre for IT and Dev.* Cameroon, December, 2008.
28. Lyon, D., (1998). *The information society: Issues and illusionism*, Cambridge: Polity Press.
29. Makori, E. O. (2009). Contemporary-issues in information management: A fresh look for information professionals. *International Journal of Library and Information Science* Vol. 1(6) pp. 082-091 Available online. Retrieved November 2009 from http://www.academicjournals.org/ijlis;www.academicjournals .org/ijlis/pdf/pdf2009/nov/makori.pdf
30. Mansell, R. (2002). From Digital Divides to Digital Entitlements in Knowledge Societies. LSE Research Online, May: 2008. Original citation: Mansell, Robin (2002) From digital divides to digital entitlements in knowledge societies. *Current sociology*, 50 (3). pp. 407-426. http://eprints.lse.ac.uk/3481/
31. Materska K (2004). Librarians in the knowledge age, *Emerald Insight.* Available online: http://www.emeraldinsight.com/researchregister.
32. Murphy, D. (2010). War is War. The utility of cyberspace operations in the contemporary operational environment Workshop Initial Impressions. United States Army War College: CSL. Retrieved from www.carlisle.army.mil/.../War%20is%20War%20Issue%20Paper%20...
33. OECD (2001). *Understanding the Digital-Divide.* Paris: OECD.
34. Official-Document. Gov. UK (2010). *Cybercrime strategy. Presented to Parliament by the Secretary of State for the Home-Department.* UK: TSO. Retrieved from www.tsoshop.co.uk © Crown Copyright 2010
35. Omekwuand et.al.(2006). "Roadmap to change: emerging roles for information professionals", *Library Rev.* 55(4): 267-277.
36. Orlikowski, W. (1992). The duality of technology: Rethinking the concept of technology in organisations, *Organisation Science*, 3(3), 398-427.
37. Parker, D (1983). *Fighting Computer-Crime* U.S.: Charles Scribner's Sons.

38. Schlienger and Teufel (2002). *Journal of Internet Banking and Commerce.* Retrieved from www.arraydev.com/.../Wada%20&%20Longe%20.
39. Silverstone, R. (1999). *Why Study the Media.* London: Sage Publications.
40. Tushabe F and Baryamureeba V. (Year N.A.) *Implications of Cyber Crime on Social-Economic Development.* Department of Computer Science: Makerere University Retrieved from cit.mak.ac.ug/staff/tushabe/implications Cybercrime.pdf
41. U.S. Department of Commerce, National Telecommunications and Information Administration (NTIA) (1995). Falling through the net: A survey of the "have nots" in rural and urban America. Retrieved from http://www.ntia.doc.gov/ntiahome/fallingthru.html.
42. Wada and Odulaja (2012). Assessing Cyber Crime and its Impact on E-Banking in Nigeria Using Social Theories, *African Journal of Computing and ICT Reference Format.* Vol 4. No. 3. Issue 2. pp. 69-82. Retrieved from www.ajocict.net/.../Wada_Odulaja-E-Banking_and_Cybercrime.
43. Warschauer, M. (2003). *Technology and Social Inclusion. Rethinking the Digital Divide.* Cambridge: Mass., MIT Press.
44. Weitzer, Ronald (2003). *Current Controversies in Criminology.* Upper Saddle River, New Jersey: Pearson Education Press. p. 150. Accepted 13 October, 2009.
45. Wikipedia (2012). *Information Management.* Retrieved 24 July, 2012 en.wikipedia.org/wiki/Informationmanagement.

27

# Value Education: Importance in Secondary Education

***Meenu***

*"Learning is a treasure that will follow its owner everywhere."*

**— Chinese Proverb**

## Introduction

Education can never be complete unless it equips the individual for meeting the real challenges of life, preparing him for his moral responsibilities as adult and helps him in achieving full growth. During the last few years, instead of helping the students to develop meaning and purpose of life, educational institutions have given more emphasis on achieving higher percentage of marks in schools and colleges keeping the development of human being aside. School is the common platform for all children coming from various backgrounds. In an interactive and learning environment of the school, where a child spends a maximum of eight hours of waking time, the human values can be easily evoked in him by making him *"experience"* and *"live"* the values. The youth of today have a lot of problems that they have to face and many of them do not have the skills to overcome the obstacles. It is evident that these youth need support in developing better values and morals. Value education is essentially *'Man Making'* and *'Character Building'* (Sridhar, 2001). Values are determinants of human behaviour. They play vital role in the lives of every individual. The phrase *'Value Education'* as used in the area of school education refers to the study of development of essential values in pupils and the practices suggested for the promotion of the same. Schools have the ability to stand up and take on these problems with their students. It is widely known that today's youth have to face more challenges and issues than any other past generations of youth (Kristo, n.d.).

## Importance of Secondary Education

Secondary education serves as a link between the elementary and higher education, and plays a very important role in this respect. This stage of education serves to move on higher secondary stage as well as to provide generic competencies that cut across various domains of knowledge as well as skills (NCERT, n. d.). Secondary education is a pre-requisite of any kind of development be it for the individual or for the nation as a whole. The self-confidence of an individual with secondary education is immense as compared to an individual with primary education or in some cases no education at all (Mallick, n.d.). It spreads over the ages of 15 and 16, and then to 17 and 18 in the senior secondary grades. These are the years of adolescence, and late adolescence. These are the years of transition; indeed, most crucial years of life. There are steady and fast changes in the body structure transforming to adult form and image of life. At this age, the bodily changes take final shape and stabilise. This is also the stage of emotional transformation and maturity that swings between joy and trauma. Secondary education essentially has to be the education of the adolescence (NCERT, n.d).

## Meaning of Value Education

Our values and morals are a reflection of our spirituality; our character. Values are generally loaded with affective thoughts about ideas, objects, behaviour etc. Sailaja (2001) values are those principles or standards, which help to better the quality of life. Values codify the dos and don'ts of behaviour. They form the basics of character formation and personality development. The values that spring from within or the core of the heart, like love, compassion, sympathy, empathy, tolerance, etc. lay the foundation for the external practiced values like honesty, discipline, punctuality and loyalty. The most important to remember is that "*values are priceless, while valuables are priced.*" In its full range of meaning, value education includes developing the appropriate sensibilities, i.e., moral, cultural, spiritual and the ability to make proper value judgment and internalise them in one's life. It is an education for becoming and involves the total personality of the individual. There are various categories of values such as traditional values, cultural values, political values, social values, moral values, professional values etc. (Trivedi and Pandey, 2004).

The definition of value education is educating the child to harmonise every aspect of his being viz. spiritual, physical, emotional, intellectual and psychological so as to develop his personality in a holistic manner. Value education means inculcating in the children sense of humanism, a deep concern for the well-being of others and the nation. This can be accomplished only when we instill in the children a deep feeling of commitment to values that would build this country and bring back to the people pride in work that brings order, security and assured progress. A person with proper values will not be afraid to face problems. He or she will expect and accept them as part of life. He or she will not give unnecessary importance to anything that happens in life. He or she will have complete faith in God. Such a person will be an example to the rest (Indrani, 2012). The purpose of the value education is for the development of body and mind to develop integrated and balanced personality. The purpose of value oriented education is to fight obscurantism, religious fanaticism and violence and promote and nurture critical thinking, reflection reasoning and built up a human reproach or life (Singh, 2013).

**Different Types of Values**

The Secondary-Education Commission (1952-53) laid special emphasis on the following values in the formation of character of the students:

1. Efficiency
2. Integrity
3. Discipline
4. Co-operation
5. Good Temper

Nevertheless creative thinkers and behavioural scientists suggest sets of important values in the information age like tolerance, objectivity, critical inquiry, equality of opportunity, self-esteem, sociability, honesty, caring, justice, trustworthiness, autonomy, benevolence, compassion, responsibility, courage, truthfulness, integrity, freedom of thought and action, human worth and dignity, responsible citizenship, patriotism, reasoned argument, respect for other's rights, courtesy, etc ( Sindhwani and Kumar, 2013).

**Importance of Value-Education in Schools**

Education from time immemorial has focused on values. Education is supposed to be a powerful instrument of change and has a progressive impact on human behaviour, but in actual practices, it is doing very little to cultivate moral, social, cultural and spiritual values in our youth. Education in general and value education in particular occupies a prestigious place in the modern context of the contemporary society. The factors like personal greed, meanness, selfishness, indifference to others interests and laziness are caused due to value crisis and erosion of values. The education for values related to habit formation of pupils necessitates a newer emphasis in bringing about a psychological change amongst learners. They should be trained in the process of practicing good habits and eliminating evil ones by an appropriate to real life situations. Education for values is a psychological affair. It is concerned with the world of emotions and expression, analysis and appreciation, interpretation and evaluation. It adheres to the wills and aspirations of the individual learner in relation to the group and vice versa. People will become aware of his inner self who awaits an appropriate pattern of efflorescence in terms of values and second he is blessed with making a comparative approach to learning the essence of values among teachers and friends (Chakrabarti, 1997).

Values form the core of educational goals and objectives. Building values is an integral factor in the process of internalisation of values because one can only give what one has within. Building values is somewhat similar to building a house, brick by brick. That is why Values Education is to be recognised as a fundamental need. Almost every education policy document has emphasised the role of education in fostering values. The National Curriculum Frame work for School-Education (2000) brought to focus the erosion of ethical, social and spiritual values and suggested the integration of values in the curriculum. The National Curriculum Framework (NCF), 2005 strongly advocates values like cooperation, respect for human rights, tolerance, justice, responsible citizenship, diversity, reverence towards democracy and peaceful conflict resolution (Central Board of Secondary Education, 2012).

### What Values Education Aims at Secondary Level

1. Holistic development of the child while addressing the head and the heart
2. Revisiting values and making everyone aware of eroding values
3. Creating balance between child and community
4. An education that connects the heart, head and hand
5. Inculcating the understanding of interdependence between family, society, nation and the world
6. Bringing in a pro-active social conscience
7. Improvement of the quality of education, and
8. Harmony and peace with self

### The Main Causes of Value Degeneration given by Indrani (2012) are

1. Lack of respect for the sanctity of human life
2. Breakdown of parental control of children in families
3. Lack of respect for authority seen through the brazen breaking of the law and total disregard for rules and regulations
4. Crime and corruption
5. Abuse of alcohol and drugs
6. Abuse of women and children and other vulnerable members of society, and
7. Lack of respect for other people and property

### Impact of Erosion of Values among Adolescents

Though every nation is worried about the continuous corrosion of values yet no serious action has been taken by any of the nations for the restoration of values. Even our current system of education is oriented towards giving knowledge and skills that would make students saleable products and nothing else. This education system has developed only cognitive aspect of a man and left effective and psychomotor aspects starving, which results in sordid rapes, heinous murders, treacheries, chicaneries, frauds and malpractices. Such a system of education is devoid of the primary human values of solidarity, justice, equality, brotherlihood, affection, generosity, empathy etc. Thus the problem of value crises seems to be inherent in the system of education itself. Human beings enjoy the maximum freedom and power for governing their habitat and environment. This power sometimes enables them to misuse the resources materialism has led us to degradation in our moral values. Due to the degradation in our values the juveniles becomes delinquents.

Thomas (2011) given the alarming number of juvenile arrests in recent years (Puzzanchera, 2009), as well as the appreciation that outcomes of deviant or delinquent activity are often of serious consequence to both the youth and to society, there is a growing interest in examining the factors that lead adolescents to engage in juvenile delinquency or deviant behaviour. Adolescence has been found to be a developmental stage during which youth are most responsive to reward (Galvan, Hare, and Parra et al., 2006). This increased reward response can lead individuals to engage in increasing amounts of risk-taking behaviour during adolescence. Cook (2006) found that nearly one in three girls and one in four boys reported being highly stressed. Suicide is the third-leading cause of death for people between the ages of fifteen to twenty-four and the sixth leading cause of death for five to fourteen years old. Among students nationwide, 5.4 per cent had not gone to school on one or more days in the last month because they felt unsafe. Between 15 and 25 per cent of students are bullied with moderate frequency. Lastly, he reported that more than half of sixth graders report peer pressure to drink beer, wine, or liquor and that one of every three sixth graders say they feel pressured to use marijuana (Cook, 2006).

**Role of Education for the Inculcation of Values**

Educational system should inculcate in the emerging individuals such type of human values so that they should follow the attributes like:

1. They will want peace and justice in a world that acknowledges the rule of law and in which no nation or individual need live in fear
2. Freedom and self-reliance to be available to all
3. The dignity and work of every person to be recognised and safeguarded
4. All people to be given an opportunity to achieve their best in life, and
5. They will seek equality before the law and the equality of opportunity for all.

**Primary Moral Traits given by Seetharam (2001) which the individual should have:**

1. To make right moral judgements

2. To postpone gratification of desires
3. To treat other human beings with dignity
4. To be flexible in making moral judgements
5. To be creative and dynamic in moral decisions

**Strategies to Promote Values for School Children**

Various strategies for motivating values among school children are:

1. Arrange debates, discussions, easy writing competitions etc. on the topics like national integration, literacy campaign.
2. Celebrating birthdays of national leaders, important persons and event.
3. Making the students responsible in various school management and college activities- student perception.
4. Organising morning prayers, celebrating certain social culture festivals, anniversaries, school day, teacher's day. Parent teacher association meetings etc. and encouraging values in the students by giving the talented and devoted person awards, gifts, titles and rolling shields etc.
5. Organising of science clubs, literary, associations, music centers, recreational centers and adult education programmes.
6. Generally, students are intrinsically motivated to pursue activities that are moderately novel, enjoyable, exciting, and optimally challenging. When schoolwork is too easy, students become bored. When tasks are too difficult, students become frustrated and anxious. Teachers should create classroom environments that provide students with opportunities to engage in interesting, personally relevant, challenging activities.
7. Immediate feedback enhances the psychological impact of the activity. When student perform some activity which are against the society norms then teacher should give the immediate feedback to the students.
8. Students are more likely to become engaged with material that is optimally challenging. Classroom activities should be appropriate to their current knowledge and skill levels. Material that is either too hard or too easy is anti-motivational. Ideally, teachers should deliver instruction that is just above the skill range of the students. The activity should be something that the students can master, but not without effort and appropriate strategy use (Morrone and Schutz, 2000). Ensure that your students are challenged (but not frustrated) by classroom activities.
9. Role of books: Books played a significant role in the ancient India in fostering values leading to harmonious and total personality development of people. Epics like Ramayana and Mahabharatha became sources of inspiration to millions of people who followed the path of righteousness. The story on Harichandra made great leaders like Mahatma Gandhiji to follow the path of truth. Therefore, good books have their own effect on the personality development of individuals.

Teachers and curriculum writers could also support character education through Reviewing instructional materials for themes relating to personal development and referencing such materials to specific learning objectives:

1. Reviewing national, state, and local documents for statements of goals relating to personal and social/cultural development.
2. Constructing a chart of ideas or concepts in various subjects that are focused on character themes.
3. Selecting methods and activities that involve students in the process of reflection about moral/ethical issues.
4. Teaching lessons that integrate character education with the content being taught.
5. Evaluating students learning for evidence of understanding of and personal growth in matters of character (Burrett and Rusnak, 1993).

Sridhar (2001) suggested the following methods and techniques for inculcation of values among adolescents:

1. *Classroom learning activities methods/approach:* This may include reading, listening, discussions, narration, direct presentation of ideas by the teacher and other strategies. These strategies should be used with any of the following sources of value education: (1) Biographies; (2) Stories; (3) Extracts form essays, articles, classics and news paper; (4) Parables, proverbs, quotations and poems; (5) Value/moral dilemmas; & (6) Classroom incidents/anecdotes/ conflicts. These sources can be used in many different ways to involve the learner in thinking and reasoning about values.
2. *Practical activities method:* Children should engage themselves in life related practical activities which will promote the application of principles and values in daily life.
3. *School campus/classroom maintenance activities*: (i) Social forestry/community development activities; (ii) Work experience related activities; (iii) Organizing campaigns on community sanitation, literacy, environmental awareness, AIDS prevention awareness; (iv) Yoga, meditation and prayer sessions; (v) Eradication of social evils campaign activities (gender inequality, dowry, alcoholism…); (vi) Co-curricular/self government activities; & (vii) Socialized techniques and activities

Brady (2008) Following are typical values clarifying strategies that exemplify the open ended and student centered nature of the approach:

1. *Y chart:* Students develop a list of actions that demonstrate a value (say care and compassion) by listing respectively in the three segments formed by the Y, what the value looks like (people helping, people giving), sounds like (gentle talking, 'come with us'), and feels like (warm, friendly).

2. *Values shield:* Students display what is meaningful to them by drawing symbols or pictures on a cardboard family crest. The crest is usually divided into six segments, and students complete each according to criteria provided (for example, what your family believes to be important; what you do to help others).
3. *Ranking:* Students are given numerous statements on an issue and asked to rank them in order of importance or commitment. Alternatively, they may be asked to generate a list before ranking (what qualities are most prized in a person; what is most feared; what comprises the greatest challenges to faith).
4. *PMI:* Students are required to list the positive (Plus), negative (Minus) and interesting (Interest) aspects of a nominated issue, thereby articulating their own values. For instance, the issues might be building high-rise structure in a local area, or logging a forest.

According to Central Board of Secondary Education the following ten basic themes may also form a part of Values Education in schools.

1. Think positive is a self-empowering concept that allows the student to have a positive self-image and values him/her and life in all forms.
2. Be compassionate and do no harm attempts to inculcate love, kindness and friendliness that are important to respond to intolerance and violence in society.
3. Discover inner peace enables an individual to understand the self at a deeper level of consciousness. It also addresses a person's spiritual needs.
4. Learning to live together seeks to promote the qualities of sharing, cooperation, mutual help, building trust and team work. Working harmoniously in groups with others reduces competition and emphasises the joy of working as a team.
5. Respect human dignity is based on the concepts of Human Rights and Justice. Its objective is to develop a consciousness that recognises rights of others along with ones own.
6. Be your true self builds behavioural skills such as time management, honesty and strength of character that are essential for resolving conflicts and for effective social interaction.
7. Developing critical thinking involves the ability to think with logic and reason. It also includes decision-making and is an important component of democratic institutions.

## Conclusion

Value development in children is like growing a plant. In this process, the society, parents, public servants, textbooks, media, and teachers play their respective roles. Nevertheless educational institutions can also play a significant role in die promotion of values. Value education is not a separate domain. No education is value-free and goals of education include the goals of value education itself. Therefore, value education is not to be taken as burden or as add on programme/activity. It does not have to be perceived as yet another task by schools already busy with the hard work of improving retention and academic achievement of students. The teacher should always play a proactive role in cultivating the minds of children and developing strong values in them. Every lesson, routine activity and environment becomes value-centric and the entire gamut of relationships and processes in the school is thereby strengthened and empowered. House is the first learning environment for the child and parents are the first teachers. They not only guide the child in its progressive path but also demonstrate the appropriate behaviour by their actions. Hence, both parents and teachers need to present themselves as role models, whom the children can look up to, for guidance.

## REFERENCES

1. Brady, L. (2008) Strategies in Values-Education: Horse or Cart? *Australian journal of teacher-education, 33*(5), 81-89. Retrieved January 30, 2014 from http://ro.ecu.edu.au/cgi/viewcontent.cgi?article=1504&context=ajte
2. Burrett, K., and Rusnak, T. (1993). Integrated character education. Indiana: Phi Delta Kappa Educational Foundation.
3. Central Board of Secondary Education (2012). *Values Education: A Handbook for Teachers.* Retrieved January 31, 2014 from http://cbseacademic.in/web_material/ValueEdu/Value%20Education%20Kits.pdf
4. Chakrabarti, M. (1997). *Value Education: Changing perspectives.* New Delhi: Kanishka publishers, Distributers.
5. Cook, J. (2006). *School counselors' role expands to address challenge of today's students.* Retrieved January 31, 2014 from http://www.azed.gov/character-education/files/2012/04/the-importance-of-values-in-schools-implementing-character-education.pdf
6. Galvan, A., Hare, T. A, Parra, C. E., Penn, J., Voss, H., Glover, G., et al. (2006). Earlier development of the accumbens relative to orbitofrontal cortex might underlie risk taking behavior in adolescents. *The Journal of neuroscience: The official journal of the Society for Neuroscience, 26* (25), 6885-6892.
7. Indrani, B. (2012 ). Importance of value education in modern time. *Education India Journal: A Quarterly Refereed Journal of Dialogues on Education, 1* (3). Retrieved January 31, 2014 from http://educationindiajournal.org/journal/63Beena%20Indrani.pdf
8. Kristo, J. (n.d.). *The Importance of Values in Schools: Implementing Character Education.* Retrieved January 29, 2014 from http://www.azed.gov/character-education/files/2012/04/the-importance-of-values-in-schools-implementing-character-education.pdf
9. Mallick, P. (n.d). *Essay on the importance of secondary education in India.* Retrieved January 31, 2014 from http://www.shareyouressays.com/98438/essay-on-the-importance-of-secondary-education-in-india

10. NCERT (n.d). Universalisation of secondary-education in India – vision. Retrieved January 31, 2014 from http://www.ncert.nic.in/departments/nie/dse/deptt/activities/pdfs/chapter_1.pdf
11. Puzzanchera, C. (2009). *Juvenile arrests 2008* (NCJ 228479). Retrieved from Office of Juvenile Justice and Delinquency Prevention, Office of Justice Programs, U.S. Department of Justice: http://www.ncjrs.gov/pdffiles1/ojjdp/228479.pdf
12. Role of Teachers and Parents in Imparting Values. Retrieved January 29, 2014 from http://www.ncte-india.org/pub/rimse/spk6.htm
13. Sailaja, B. (2001, November 18). Value Education. *Times of India.* Retrieved January 31, 2014 from http://timesofindia.indiatimes.com/city/hyderabad-times/Value-Education/articleshow/838583539.cms
14. Secondary Education Commission (1952-53). In Sindhwani, A., and Kumar, R. (2013). Values in Higher Education: Need and Importance. *Educationia Confab, 2* (2), 9-14. Retrieved January 30, 2014 from http://www.confabjournals.com/confabjournals/images/632013949362.pdf
15. Seetharam, A.R. (2001). Concept and objectives of value-education. Retrieved January 30, 2014 from http://www.ncte-india.org/pub/rimse/spk11.htm
16. Sindhwani, A., and Kumar, R. (2013). Values in Higher Education: Need and Importance. *Educationia Confab, 2* (2), 9-14. Retrieved January 30, 2014 from http://www.confabjournals.com/confabjournals/images/632013949362.pdf
17. Singh, S. (2013). Promoting values in higher education. In Sawhney and Bansal (Eds.). *Re-Imagining Teacher Education: Perspectives and Transformations.* Patiala: Twentyfirst Century Publications.
18. Sridhar, Y.N. (2001). *Methodology of value education.* Retrieved January 30, 2014 from http://www.ncte-india.org/pub/rimse/spk4.htm
19. Strategies to Increase the Intrinsic Value of Tasks in Your Class. http://www.gifted.uconn.edu/siegle/goalvaluation/goalva02.html
20. Thomas, A.M. (2011). *Parent and peer influences: their role in predicting adolescent moral values and delinquent behavior. Retrieved January 30, 2014 from* http://digitool.library.colostate.edu///exlibris/dtl/d3_1/apache_media/L2V4bGlicmlzL2R0bC9kM18xL2FwYWNoZV9tZWRpYS8xMjA1MTg=.pdf
21. Trivedi, A., and Pandey, P. (2004). Value education- as a part of course curriculum in home science extension and communication. In Pandya, R., and Mthur, A. (2004). *Imbibing Value Education: various perspectives.* Delhi: Kalpaz Publications.
22. Universalisation of secondary education in India – Vision. Retrieved January 30, 2014 from http://www.ncert.nic.in/departments/nie/dse/deptt/activities/pdfs/chapter_1.pdf

# 28

# Role of Management-Education for Sustainable Society and Sustainable Development: Limits and Possibilities

***Rajib Malik***

*"We need to secure the long-term future of our planet and its resources so future generations do not find themselves in a wasteland."*

**—World Bank Group Goals Document**

**Introduction**

Sustainable development recognises that growth must be both inclusive and environmentally sound to reduce poverty and build shared prosperity for today's population and to continue to meet the needs of future generations. It is efficient with resources and carefully planned to deliver both immediate and long-term benefits for people, planet and prosperity (Sustainable development, 2014). On the other hand, asustainable society is one that can progress without catastrophic setbacks in the foreseeable future. We can say that it is simply one that can avoid a devastating blow so that human society can continue its long journey to perfection *(Sustainable Society, 2013)*. Sustainable development means for considering the relationships of things to each other in order to propose viable solutions. As the Brundtland report puts it, *"sustainable development is not a fixed state of harmony but rather a process of change..."* It is a way of forcing ourselves to look at factors we might rather ignore in favour of short-term benefit, as in the case of a polluting industry that worries primarily about this year's profits, or a pension plan that doesn't account for the increase in the number of retirees relative to the number of subscribers *(Sustainable Development, 2012)*.

Management education involves teaching students the fundamentals, theories, and processes of business. It is typically prepares students for an occupation in business or a business-related field, or a teaching career in academia. Management education gives guidance on staffing, leading, planning, organizing or directing, and controlling an organisation or effort for the purpose of accomplishing an aim. Management Education in India is well developed as last few years and the demand of management education has bigger in India also due to the healthy economic growth for over a decade. In India, management education is seen as elitist *(Ravichandran, N, 2010)*. Often, young men and women are attracted to management education not because they need some education, exposure and experience to create something wonderful and hence useful to society but are usually motivated by the positive economic consequences associated with management education *(Ravichandran, N, 2010)*. The function of an effective management education is to instill in the managers, solidarity and dynamism. A durable society has to absorb new changes without losing its originality and ethos. In the state of constant flux the management and the industry has to respond to such a stimulus by a paradigm shift - to a new viewpoint or modification of its ideals. The important point is that these days, management education plays a vital role for attaining Sustainable Society and Sustainable Development.

**Methodology**

The study is based on secondary data. The study has dealt with Management Education for Sustainable Society and Sustainable Development. As the study is analytical, hence, in the course of analysing the issues, a number of text and references books, other published and unpublished documents from different sources and websites relating to the study have been considered. The analysis of the data has used in a conjunction with available literature. The collected and analyzed data has presented in tabular from in percentage as well as absolute figures as and where necessary.

**Analysis and Discussion**

Business is a key driver of economic development. Relationships between business and society are entering a new stage of development with an increasingly large number of interactions. It is argued that *"Partnerships with external organisations are keys to helping companies succeed at creating value through sustainable development strategies"* (Cook, E, 2010). Management education can play a vital role for development of business organisation and as well as society. The profitability and shareholder value alone do not represent the value of the company. To survive a company in long run is depend upon on its ethical and social responsibility. Again, globalisation is one of the key factors that prompted the calls for partnerships to achieve the potentials of sustainable development. Increasing demand for sustainable development during the last decades has initiated actions from governments as well as corporations and CSOs (Cerin, P. and Karlson, L. 2002). These can be strongly done through the application of management education.

A sustainable society is one that can progress without catastrophic setbacks in the foreseeable future. A sustainable society is simply one that can avoid a devastating blow so that human society can continue its long journey to perfection. A society running on a huge resource deficit is not sustainable. To build a sustainable society, a delicate balance between current needs and future needs has to be reached. Our capability is important to utilise the reserved resources and management education can be one way to do this. We could continue to use up all the reserved resources and let our children suffer the consequence of resource starvation. Or, we could aggressively move away from non-renewable resources and put ourselves on a sustainable footing once and for all (Sustainable society and sustainable development: limits and possibilities, 2005).

The function of an effective management education is to instill in the managers, solidarity and dynamism. Effective management education as a tool of social control has to perform two basic functions – firstly, to assimilate, preserve and transmit the useful elements of technology, and secondly, to develop convenient patterns of consumption and through this proper utilisation the civil society can be continuously developed (Sustainable Society through Effective Management Education, 2006-07). Education and training should contribute to all three axes of sustainable development, namely: The Social perspective – education and training strengthen social cohesion by investment in human capital; The Economic perspective – education and training contribute to building a knowledge society based on sustainable economic growth; and, The Environmental perspective – education and training are crucial for changes in citizens' behaviour on issues such as: consumption, transport, use of sustainable energies, etc.

Traditionally, sustainable development is conceptually considered in terms of three main pillars. These are Environmental sustainability, Economic sustainability and Social sustainability. The goal of environmental sustainability is to minimise environmental degradation and to stop and reverse the process that leads to environmental degradation. Economic sustainability is defined as the way to achieving economic growth whilst respecting environmental limits, finding ways to minimise damage to the natural world and making use of the earth's resources in a sustainable way. The social pillar of sustainable development is defined as a compilation of actions and efforts to promote development that does not deplete the stock of social and human resources but rather contributes to the enhancement of their potential (Inventory of innovative practices in education for sustainable development, 2008). There are various issues relating to different types of sustainable development. These issues are discussing below:

The concerning matters on today world concerning to Sustainable Society and Sustainable Development are: (i) Poverty and the Environment, (ii) Non-governmental Organisations on Development Issues, (iii) Foreign Aid for Development Assistance, (iv) Power, (v) Water and Development, (vi) Corporate Social Responsibility, (vii) Energy Security, (viii) Brain Drain of Workers from Poor to Rich Countries. Another important thing is that social sustainability effects are the intertemporal impacts of today's social security systems. There are several economic reasons for providing social security services by the state that base on some kind of market failure: (a) Social security is a public good. Social stability enhances economic productivity. But since this stability can be enjoyed by everyone without own contributions as long as someone else provides some kind of social security system, individuals find themselves in a prisoners' dilemma. (b). There are imperfect insurance markets. Asymmetric information implies moral hazard and adverse selection in insurance markets possibly entailing a sub-optimal amount of social security supplied to the market. But these market failures are just a necessary condition for public supply of social security systems. In addition it must be verified, that governmental intervention may improve this market failure and will not substitute state failure for market failure (Meyer, Eric C., 2010).

Sustainability effects on social capital accumulation involving more than one generation are unlikely, but not impossible. The impact of economic policy measures on social capital is indirect. For example, assume that the government constrains the application of some polluting production methods. This will induce depreciation of social capital as workers will be released or will have to be re-educated altering their social environment and their social ties. But this (transitional) depreciation of social capital and the readjustment of their social relations are politically intended and will be compensated by the improvement of environmental quality. Social capital will be regenerated by creating new social relations that are adapted to the new institutional environment. Nevertheless, structural frictions may persistently decrease an individual's

**Table 28.1: Various issues relating to sustainable development**

| | *Sustainable Development* | |
|---|---|---|
| *Environmental Pillar* | *Economic Pillar* | *Social Pillar* |
| Climate change | Sustainable consumption | Health and quality of life |
| Reduction of gas emissions | Sustainable production | Community cohesion |
| Biodiversity | CSR practices | Social equity |
| Energy efficiency | Urban and local development | Demography |
| Development of clean technology | Sustainable tourism | Management of migration and cultural diversity |
| Conservation of natural resources | Integration of environmental concerns in business decision-making (Green Business) | Equal opportunities |
| Waste management | Sustainable trade | Flexicurity |
| Pollution (water, air soil) | | Development of human capital and skills |
| Sustainable transport | | |

*Source*: http://ec.europa.eu/education/more-information/doc/sustdev_en.pdf

social capital, if it is unable to re-create new social ties, but it is unlikely that this will happen on an economy-wide scale (Meyer, Eric C., 2010).

There are various kinds of dimensions of sustainable development. These dimensions are directly interrelated to the social sustainability. Dimensions of Sustainable Development can be better implemented through utilization of effective of management education. The Dimensions of Sustainable Development have been discussed in below:

There are various principles for sustainable development. These are:( i) Balancing environmental, social and economic consequences, (ii) Considering impacts of change on different stakeholders, (iii) Corporate Social Responsibility, (iv) Life Cycle approach, (v) Benchmarking/Assessing sustainability and (vi) Cost/Benefit Analysis. Again, the management education can be developed by using the guidelines: Lifelong learning, Interdisciplinary approaches, Systems thinking, Partnerships, Multicultural perspectives, Empowerment, Innovation in the content, Innovation in the delivery method, Innovation in forging new partnerships and networks, Innovation at the institutional level, Innovation in addressing sustainable development.

There are various limitations of management education which gives resistance in sustainable development. Now-a-days, positioning in the management education sector rather involves effectively presenting institutional image and developing their position in the minds of the public than differentiation. In spite of the similarity of products in higher education, there are suggested key factors to be used by universities to occupy positions of distinctiveness: teaching led vs. research-led; science-based vs. arts based; basic teaching vs. higher level teaching. But even those factors cannot ensure totally differentiated positions of universities. Therefore, we can state that there are limitations in using the positioning concept in the real sense (differentiation) in the higher education sector. This is the basic limitation for the management education and as well as social sustainability. There are other limitations of management education for sustainable development: (i) Management education for sustainable development should be country and context based, (ii) Implementation of management education should be participatory (active) and inclusive. But in real case it is viable or takes time, (iii) Normally Management educa-

**Table 28.2: Dimensions of Sustainable Development**

| | |
|---|---|
| **Environmental** | Climate change, Energy efficiency, Conservation of natural resources, Waste management, Pollution, Sustainable transport, Global water crisis, Virtual water, Land use, Renewable raw materials, Use of biosphere reserves, Sustainable forest management, Genetic engineering etc. |
| **Economic** | Sustainable consumption, CSR practices, Urban and local development, and Sustainable tourism etc. |
| **Social** | Health, Community cohesion, Social equity, Equal opportunity, Development of human capital skills, Social justice, Human rights, Discrimination, Fair trade, Children's rights, Sustainable lifestyle etc. |

*Source*: Designed by author, available at http://ec.europa.eu/education/more-information/doc/sustdev_en.pdf

tion integrates formal, informal and non-formal learning which is uncomfortable for traditional learner, (iv) Management education should take into consideration existent local knowledge and skills, (v) Management education should integrate other social dimensions: migration, poverty, gender etc., (vi) Economic growth does not imply social equality that management education learn, (vii) For sustainable development, support on social mobility, indexes and data are mostly important. Management education where consume the concept at large and could not penetrate in depth (Poverty and Social Inequality and its Impact on Sustainable Development, 2008).

For today's economy, especially because of companies are looking for employees with more well-rounded skills than just narrowly focused in other engineering skills, management education become the pillar of success. Management education makes a person more flexible in diverse discipline, where employers might rely on that person to take on more responsibility. At present scenario, at most 25 per cent of management students are engineers due to their future prospect. Most of the management courses are aimed at all graduate disciplines. After obtaining a higher degree in technical course, management programme furnish their knowledge and skill in the area of business and social sustainability. According to Professor Victor Callan (University of Queensland's Graduate School of Management), Individuals are asked to assume more responsibility for enhancing their own career prospects, students chose to complete an MBA for many reasons. According to him, organisations want people with better skills in communication, leading change, entrepreneurship, and risk management (Management education offers skills advantages: academic, 2013). These skills and leading quality of the management people will help to form a sustainable society. On the other hand teachers and cooperation between universities and industry in the area of management education has greater role to make the sustainable society. Technology and IT application in management education can balance the different issues of social sustainability.

## Conclusion

The progress of management education in sustainable development remains erratically distributed and requires different approaches in different contexts. To build a sustainable society, the organization as well as management education need to take various initiatives like as: (a) Promote management education contribution to all of education and to achieving quality education, (b) Increase public awareness and understanding about sustainable development by mainstreaming and expanding the learning insights, (c) Mobilise adequate resources and funding in favour of education in sustainable development, (d) interweave of management education with national development policy and budgetary frameworks, (e) Develop and strengthen existing international, regional and national enabling mechanisms and cooperation for sustainable development that respect cultural diversity, (f) Support the incorporation of sustainable development issues using an integrated and systemic approach in formal education as well as in non-formal and informal education at all level, (g) Management education have to integrate into training, vocational education and workplace learning by involving civil society, public and private sectors, NGOs, and development partners, (h) Involve management education in key sustainable development conventions; for example, those focusing on biodiversity, climate change, desertification and intangible cultural heritage, (i) Intensify efforts in education and training systems to address critical and urgent sustainability challenges such as climate change, water and food security by developing specific action plans. Apart from this there is a need of support from all kinds of people and as well as government to go away for sustainable development.

## REFERENCES


1. Cerin, P. and Karlson, L. (2002), "Analysis – Business incentives for sustainability: a property rights approach", *Economical Economics*, Vol. 40, p. 14.
2. Cook, E. (2002) "Safe Climate, Sound Business", *Corporate and Environmental Strategy*, Vol. 20, p. 10.
3. Inventory of innovative practices in education for sustainable development (2008), available at http://ec.europa.eu/education/more-information/doc/sustdev_en.pdf
4. Management education offers skills advantages: academic (2013), available at http://www.uq.edu.au/news/?article=622
5. Meyer, Eric C. (2010), "Social Aspects of Sustainability", available at http://www-wiwi.uni-muenster.de/vwt/vwd/pdf/300.pdf
5. Poverty and Social Inequality and its Impact on Sustainable Development (2008), available at http://www. Un.ors/esa/dsd/ind
6. Ravichandran, N. (2009), "A perspective on management education in India", *The Financial Express*, 12th October, available at http://www.financialexpress.com/news/a-perspective-on-management-education-in-india/527793/
7. Sustainable Development (2012), *OECD Insights*, available at http://www.oecd-ilibrary.org/docserver/download/08121e.pdf?expires =1391148805&id =id&accname=guest&checksum=3A8AAA4ADB A801F09214030696ECF9EA
8. Sustainable development (2014), *World Bank*, available at http://www.worldbank.org/en/topic/sustainabledevelopment
9. Sustainable society and sustainable development: limits and possibilities (2005), available at http://www.hazelhenderson.com/recentpapers/sustainable_society.html
10. Sustainable Society through Effective Management Education (2006-07), available at http://poojas22.sulekha.com/blog/post/2007/06/sustainable-society-through-effective-management-education.htm
11. Sustainable Society (2013), available at http://www.sustainablesocietyusa.com/html/SustainableSociety/20070913/24.html
12. Sustainable Society (2013), available at http://www.sustainablesocietyusa.com/html/SustainableSociety/20070913/24.html

# Bibliography

Abbas, Khan M. (2007). *Teacher's Handbook of Curriculum Management*, First edition, New Delhi: Anmol Publisher

Abbas, Khan M. (2007). *Teacher's Handbook of Methods and Techniques,* First edition, New Delhi: Anmol Publisher.

Abbas, Khan M. (2007). *Teacher's Handbook of Measurement and Evaluation*, First edition, New Delhi: Anmol Publisher.

Abidi, Azra (2003). *Reformist and Conservative Teachers,* First edition, New Delhi: Anmol Publisher.

Adil, Khan M. (2007). *Teacher's Handbook of Health Education,* First edition, New Delhi: Anmol Publisher.

Adil, Khan M. (2007). *Teacher's Handbook of Elementary Science*, First edition, New Delhi: Anmol Publisher.

Agrawal, A.K. (2005). *Development of Educational System in India*, First edition, New Delhi: Anmol Publisher.

Ahmed, Shahzad (2004). *Islamic Education*, First edition, New Delhi: Anmol Publisher.

Ahmed, Shehzad (2007). *Teacher's Handbook of Educational Technology,* First edition, New Delhi: Anmol Publisher.

Ahmed, Shehzad (2008). *Teacher's Handbook of Information Technology,* First edition, New Delhi: Anmol Publisher.

Ahmed, Shehzad (2007). *Teacher's Handbook of Environmental Education*, First edition, New Delhi: Anmol Publisher.

Ali, Mahmood (2001). *Socio-Psychological Determinants of Educational Choice*, First edition, New Delhi: Anmol Publisher.

Ali, Mahmood (2001). *Psychological Aspects of Marking Behaviour in Educational System*, First edition, New Delhi: Anmol Publisher.

Anand, Sandeep (2007). *Educational Development and Technology*, First edition, New Delhi: Anmol Publisher.

Andrew Pollard, Jill Bourne (1994). *Teaching and Learning in the Primary School*, Routledge

Andrew J. Coulson (1999). *Market Education: The Unknown History*, First edition, Transaction Publishers.

Anil Kumar De (2004), *Environmental Education*, First edition, New Delhi: New Age International.

Andotra, Neetu & Pradyot Gupta (2008). *Elementary Education and Sarva Shiksha Abhiyan*, First edition, New Delhi: Anmol Publisher.

Anjanappa, M. (2006). *History of Education—A Study*, First edition, New Delhi: Anmol Publisher.

A.W. (Tony) Bates (2004). *Technology, e-learning and Distance Education*, Taylor & Francis

Bagulia, Abdul Mannan (2004). *Kothari Commission*, First edition, New Delhi: Anmol Publisher.

Bagulia, Abdul Mannan (2005). *Modern Education Audio-Visual Aids,* First edition, New Delhi: Anmol Publisher.

Barbara Bruns, Ramahatra Rakotomalala (2003). *Achieving Universal Primary Education by 2015: A Chance for Every Child*, Volume 1, World Bank Publications

Begum, Fahmeeda (2004). *Modern Teaching of Home Science,* First edition, New Delhi: Anmol Publisher.

Benakanal, V.A. (2006). *Models and Methods of Teaching*, First edition, New Delhi: Anmol Publisher.

Bhati, Anju (2012). *Curriculum Technology and Learning,* First edition, New Delhi: Anmol Publisher.

Bhatia, P.R. (2005). *Psychology of Teaching Learning Process*, First edition, New Delhi: Anmol Publisher.

Biloris Lyndem, Utpal Kumar De (2004). *Education in North East India: Experience and Challenge,* First edition, New Delhi: Concept Publishing Company

B. O. Igboabuchi, Eze Denco (1998). *Pre-primary education in Nigeria, Lincel,* Pennsylvania State University

Birendra Deka (2010). *Higher Education in India: Development and Problems*, First edition, New Delhi: Atlantic Publishers & Dist.

Carolyn M. Sampselle (1992). *Violence against Women: Nursing Research, Education, and Practice Issues*, Taylor & Francis.

Christine von Prummer (2000). *Women and Distance Education: Challenges and Opportunities,* Taylor & Francis

Chalam, K.S. (2003). *Introduction to Educational Planning and Management,* First edition, New Delhi: Anmol Publisher.

Chand, Tara (2008). *Educational Technology,* First edition, New Delhi: Anmol Publisher.

Chand, Tara (2003). *Principles of Teaching,* First edition, New Delhi: Anmol Publisher.

Chand, Tara (2006). *Educational Psychology,* First edition, New Delhi: Anmol Publisher.

Chand, Tara (2009). *Modern Child Psychology,* First edition, New Delhi: Anmol Publisher.

Chand, Tara (2009). *Development of Education System in India*, First edition, New Delhi: Anmol Publisher.

Chand, Tara et al. (2003). *Essentials of Instructional Technology*, First edition, New Delhi: Anmol Publisher.

Clint Bruess & Jerrold Greenberg (2008). *Sexuality Education: Theory and Practice*, Jones & Bartlett Learning

C. Naseema, V.K. Jibin (2013). *Eleventary Education and Children Rights,* First edition, New Delhi: Shipra Publication.

C. Naseema, V.K. Jibin (2013). *Comparative Education with Special Reference to Elementary Education,* First edition, New Delhi: Shipra Publication.

David Campos (2002). *Sex, Youth, and Sex Education: A Reference Handbook*, ABC-CLIO.

David W. Adams (1995). *Education for Extinction: American Indians and the Boarding-School Experience, 1875-1928,* University Press of Kansas

David Gillborn (2009). *Race, Ethnicity and Education: Teaching and Learning in Multi-Ethnic Schools*, First edition, Taylor & Francis

David L. Brunsma (2004). *The School Uniform Movement and what it Tells Us about American Education: A Symbolic Crusade*, R&L Education

David Sewart, Desmond Keegan, Börje Holmberg (1988). *Distance Education: International Perspectives,* Routledge

D.Bhaskara Rao, & Digumarti Pushpa Latha (2003). *Women, Education and Empowerment,* Discovery Publishing House

Denis Hayes (2005). *Primary Education: The Key Concepts,* Taylor & Francis

Desmond Keegan (1993). *Theoretical Principles of Distance Education*, Routledge

Desmond Keegan (1990). *Foundations of Distance Education,* Routledge

Desmond Keegan (1996). *Foundations of Distance Education,* Psychology Press

Dhanwant M. Desai (2007). *Universal, compulsory and free primary education in India*, Indian Institute of Education

Digumarti Bhaskara Rao (1998). *District Primary Education Programme,* First edition, New Delhi: Discovery Publishing House

Dorothy Moss (2006). *Gender, Space and Time: Women and Higher Education*, Lexington Books.

D. D. Aggarwal (2002). History and Development of Elementary Education in India, Sarup & Sons

Desai, Kashappa Goud H. (2009). *Pharmacy Education: Teaching and Research Guide*, First edition, New Delhi: Anmol Publisher

Dey, Suparna (2007). *Children and Adolescents,* First edition, New Delhi: Anmol Publisher.

Dutt, Suresh (2008). *Sociology and Education System*, First edition, New Delhi: Anmol Publisher.

Dutt, Suresh (1998). *Moral Values in Child Development,* First edition, New Delhi: Anmol Publisher.

Dutt, Suresh (1998). *Understanding Children,* First edition, New Delhi: Anmol Publisher

Dutt, Suresh (2003). *The Teacher and The Child Development,* First edition, New Delhi: Anmol Publisher.

Dutt, Suresh (1998). *Experiment in Teaching for Child Development,* First edition, New Delhi: Anmol Publisher.

Dutt, Suresh (1998). *Curriculum and Child Development,* First edition, New Delhi: Anmol Publisher.

Dr. B.A Benakanal (2008). *Models and Methods of Teaching,* First edition, New Delhi: Anmol Publisher

Dutt, Suresh (2003). *Teaching Methods and Child Development,* First edition, New Delhi: Anmol Publisher.

Edward Ebert, & Richard Culyer (2007). *School: An Introduction to Education,* First edition, Cengage Learning

Elaine Wilson (2009). *School-based Research: A Guide for Education Students,* First edition, New Delhi: SAGE.

Emily Davies (2007). *The higher education of women,* the University of Michigan

Elaine Wilson (2009). *School-based Research: A Guide for Education Students,* First edition, New Delhi: SAGE Publisher.

Eileen M. Byrne (1978). *Women and Education,* Tavistock Publications

Elizabeth M. King, & M. Anne Hill (1997). *Women's Education in Developing Countries: Barriers, Benefits, and Policies,* World Bank Publications

Fahimuddin (2003). *Nutritional Support to Primary Education,* First edition, New Delhi: Anmol Publisher.

Feeny, Stephanie, Galper, Alice, Seefeldt, Carrol (2010), *Counting issues in Early Childhood Education,* New Delhi: PHI Learning.

Frances R. Spielhagen (2008). *Debating single-sex education: separate and equal?,* Rowman & Littlefield Education, University of Michigan

Garry Hornby (2011). *Parental Involvement in Childhood Education: Building Effective School-Family Partnerships,* First edition, Springer.

Gail Paradise Kelly, & Carolyn M. Elliott (1982). *Women's Education in the Third World: Comparative Perspectives,* First edition, SUNY Press.

Gail P. Kelly, & Carolyn M. Elliott (1982). *Women's Education in the Third World: Comparative Perspectives,* SUNY Press.

Gerald Griggs (2012). *An Introduction to Primary Physical Education,* First edition, Routledge

Geetha, T.M. (2005). *Educating the Physically Handicapped,* First edition, New Delhi: Anmol Publisher.

Giridhar, D.P. et. al. (2005). *Teaching and Techniques in Technical Education,* First edition, New Delhi: Anmol Publisher.

Gupta, N.L. (2010). *Human Values for the 21st Century,* First edition, New Delhi: Anmol Publisher.

Gupta, Sunit et al (1997). *Higher Education towards 21st Century*, First edition, New Delhi: Anmol Publisher

Hall, G.S. (2005). *Encyclopaedia of Educational Problems*, First edition, New Delhi: Anmol Publisher.

Heblikar, Chaya A. (2008). *Child Development—Moral Judgement,* First edition, New Delhi: Anmol Publisher.

H.N. Vishwanath (2006). *Models of Teaching in Environmental Education*, First edition, New Delhi: Discovery Publishing House

Husain, M. (2009). *Encyclopaedia of Elementary Education,* New Delhi: Anmol Publisher.

Husain, M. (2008). *History of Elementary Education*, First edition, New Delhi: Anmol Publisher.

Husain, M. (2004). *Distance Education: Theory and Practice,* First edition, New Delhi: Anmol Publisher.

Husain, M. (2004). *Open and Non-Formal Education,* First edition, New Delhi: Anmol Publisher.

Husain, M.(2004). *Media and Distance Education*, First edition, New Delhi: Anmol Publisher.

Husain, M. (2004). *Distance Education through Television*, First edition, New Delhi: Anmol Publisher.

Ian Robottom (2010). *Environmental Education,* Deakin University

James, William (2004). *Special Education and Social Development,* First edition, New Delhi: Anmol Publisher.

James, William (2004). *Evolution and Development of School Education,* First edition, New Delhi: Anmol Publisher.

Jagannath Mohanty (1987). *Education in India: impact of democracy,* First edition, New Delhi: Deep & Deep,

James, William (2004). *History of University Education,* First edition, New Delhi: Anmol Publisher.

James, William (2005). *History of Ancient Education*, First edition, New Delhi: Anmol Publisher.

James Arthur, Teresa Cremin (2006). *Learning to Teach in the Primary School,* Taylor & Francis

Janet Moyles (2007). *Beginning Teaching, Beginning Learning: In Primary Education,* 3rd edition, McGraw-Hill Companies

Janet R. Moyles (2002). *Beginning teaching, beginning learning in primary education,* 2nd edition, Open University Press,

Janice M. Irvine (2004). *Talk about Sex: The Battles over Sex Education in the United States*, University of California Press

James Arthur, Teresa Grainger, David Wray (2006). *Learning to Teach in the Primary School,* Psychology Press

Janet Moyles (2007). *Beginning Teaching, Beginning Learning: In Primary Education,* McGraw-Hill International

J.C. Aggarwal & S Gupta (2008). *Secondary Education and Management,* First edition, New Delhi: Sipra Publication

Jeanne H. Ballantine (2008). *Schools and Society: A Sociological Approach to Education,* Pine Forge Press.

Jeanne H. Ballantine, Joan Z. Spade (2011). *Schools and Society: A Sociological Approach to Education,* First edition, Pine Forge Press.

Joy Palmer, Philip Neal (1994). *The Handbook of Environmental Education,* Routledge

Joy Palmer (2002). *Environmental Education in the 21st Century: Theory, Practice, Progress and Promise,* Taylor & Francis

Joanna Glover, Stephen Ward (1998). *Teaching Music in the Primary School,* 2/e, Continuum

Johri, P.K. (2005). *Foundations of Education,* First edition, New Delhi: Anmol Publisher.

Johri, Pradeep Kumar (2005). *Educational Thought,* First edition, New Delhi: Anmol Publisher.

Johri, Pradeep Kumar (2005). *Modern Distance Education,* First edition, New Delhi: Anmol Publisher.

Joshi, Sneha M. & K. Pushpanadham (2010). *Value Based Leadership in Education: Perspective and Approaches,* First edition, New Delhi: Anmol Publisher.

June Purvis (1991). *A history of women's education in England,* Open University Press

Kalavathi, B.K. (2007). *Reading Readiness of Children,* First edition, New Delhi: Anmol Publisher

Kapahi, C. K. (2013). *New UGC 12th Plan Grants, Guidelines and Model Curriculum,* First edition, New Delhi: Anmol Publisher.

Kaur, Prithpal (2010). *Empowerment of Physically Handicapped and Disabled Persons,* First edition, New Delhi: Anmol Publisher.

Kaushik, Vijaya K. (2004). *The Essentials of Teaching & Learning,* First edition, New Delhi: Anmol Publisher.

Kaushik, Vijaya K. (1997). *Principles of Education,* First edition, New Delhi: Anmol Publisher.

Kaushik, Vijaya K.(1998). *School Administration Organisation,* First edition, New Delhi: Anmol Publisher.

Kaushik, Vijaya K. (1997). *Modern Methods of Teaching,* First edition, New Delhi: Anmol Publisher.

Kaushik, Vijaya K. (1997). *Education: Theory and Practice,* First edition, New Delhi: Anmol Publisher.

Kaushik, Vijaya K. (1997). *Modern Media and Education,* First edition, New Delhi: Anmol Publisher.

Kaushik, Vijaya K. (1997). *The Social Context and Education,* First edition, New Delhi: Anmol Publisher.

Kaushik, Vijaya K. (1997). *Fundamentals of Secondary Education,* First edition, New Delhi: Anmol Publisher.

Kaushik, Vijaya K. (1997). *Education and Social Thought,* First edition, New Delhi: Anmol Publisher.

Kaushik, Vijaya K. (1997). *Education and Social Change,* First edition, New Delhi: Anmol Publisher.

Kaushik, Vijaya K. (2007). *Child Development through Education,* First edition, New Delhi: Anmol Publisher.

Kaushik, Vijaya K. (1998). *Principles of Secondary Education,* First edition, New Delhi: Anmol Publisher.

Keith Harry, Magnus John, Desmond Keegan (1993). *Distance Education: New Perspectives,* Secend edition, Routledge

Khan, Md. Abbas (2005). *Modern Adult Education*, First edition, New Delhi: Anmol Publisher.

Kumar, S. et al. (2005). *Ancient Educational Philosophy,* First edition, New Delhi: Anmol Publisher.

Kumar, S. et al. (2005). *Aims of Education*, First edition, New Delhi: Anmol Publisher

Kumar A P , Sharma S C , Gundur N S (2013). *Universitites and Higher Education System in India*, First edition, New Delhi: Anmol Publisher.

Lal, J.P. (2008). *Educational Measurement and Evaluation*, First edition, New Delhi: Anmol Publisher.

Lal, Madan (2007). *Essentials of Educational Technology*, First edition, New Delhi: Anmol Publisher.

Laxmi Devi, et al. (1998). *Policies and Programmes Related to Child Development*, First edition, New Delhi: Anmol Publisher.

Leena Datta Bharali (2010). *History of Higher Secondary Education in India,* First edition, New Delhi: Anmol Publisher.

Lee Ayers Schlosser, Michael R. Simonson (2006). *Distance Education: Definition and Glossary of Terms,* IAP

Linda Eisenmann (1998). *Historical Dictionary of Women's Education in the United States*, Greenwood Publishing Group

Loknath Mishra (2013). *Internationalization of Higher Education,* First edition, New Delhi: Shipra Publication.

Martha T. Henderson (2011). *Environmental education, Social Science Education Consortium,* University of Michigan

Martha Cornog & Timothy Perper (1996). *For Sex Education, See Librarian: A Guide to Issues and Resources,* Greenwood Publishing Group

M. Dash (2000). *Education in India: Problems and Perspectives,* First edition, New Delhi: Atlantic Publishers & Distribution

M.F. Cleveland-Innes, D.R. Garrison (2010). *An Introduction to Distance Education: Understanding Teaching and Learning in a New Era,* Taylor & Francis

Michael G. Moore, William George Anderson (2003). *Handbook of Distance Education*, L. Erlbaum Associates

Michael G. Moore (2007). *Handbook of Distance Education*, First edition, L. Erlbaum Associates

Michael Grahame Moore (2013). *Handbook of Distance Education,* Third edition, Routledge

Michael G. Moore, Greg Kearsley (2011). *Distance Education: A Systems View of Online Learning,* Third edition, Cengage Learning

Michael G. Moore, Greg Kearsley (1996). *Distance education: a systems view,* Secend edition, Wadsworth Pub. Co

Michael Grahame Moore, William G. Anderson (2003). *Handbook of Distance Education,* Second Edition, Routledge

Michael G. Moore (1996). *Distance Education: A Systems View,* Second edition, WADSWORTH Incorporated FULFILLMENT

Morton Edward Crawford (1975). *Sex Education in Schools,* School Library Association of New South Wales

Michael Anthony Rose (2009). *Why School?: Reclaiming Education for All of Us,* First edition, The New Press.

Naik, S.P. (2003). *Perspectives on Comparative Education,* First edition, New Delhi: Anmol Publisher.

Naik, S.P. (2003). *Role of Evaluation in Education,* First edition, New Delhi: Anmol Publisher.

Naik, S.P. (1998). *Reforms in Modern Education,* First edition, New Delhi: Anmol Publisher.

Naik, S.P. (2003). *Education for 21st Century,* First edition, New Delhi: Anmol Publisher.

Nanda, V. K. (1997). *Science Education Today,* First edition, New Delhi: Anmol Publisher.

Nanda, V. K. (1997). *Teaching in Urban Schools,* First edition, New Delhi: Anmol Publisher.

Nanda, V. K. (1997). *Theory of Distance Education,* First edition, New Delhi: Anmol Publisher.

Nanda V. K. (1997). *Environmental Education,* First edition, New Delhi: Anmol Publisher.

Nanda, V. K. (1997). *Perspectives of Rural Education,* First edition, New Delhi: Anmol Publisher.

Nanda, V. K. (1997). *Health Education,* First edition, New Delhi: Anmol Publisher.

Nanda, V. K. (2008). *Adult Education and Human Resource Development,* First edition, New Delhi: Anmol Publisher.

Nanda, V. K. (1998). *Teaching of General Science in Elementary Schools,* First edition, New Delhi: Anmol Publisher.

Nanda, V. K. (1998). *Typology of Distance Teaching Systems,* First edition, New Delhi: Anmol Publisher.

Nanda, V. K. (2002). *Educational Technology for Adults,* First edition, New Delhi: Anmol Publisher.

Nanda, V.K. (1998). *Principles of Child Development*, First edition, New Delhi: Anmol Publisher.

Nanda, V.K. (2004). *Child Development Counselling*. First edition, New Delhi: Anmol Publisher.

Nanda, V.K. (2008). *Nutrition and Health for Child Development,* First edition, New Delhi: Anmol Publisher.

Nanda, V.K. (2003). *Teaching Methodology and Child Development,* First edition, New Delhi: Anmol Publisher.

Nanda, V.K. (2003). *Development of Interactive Abilities in Children*, First edition, New Delhi: Anmol Publisher.

Nanda, V.K. (2005). *Education in Emerging Indian Society,* First edition, New Delhi: Anmol Publisher.

O.P.Gupta (1993). *Higher Education in India since Independence: U.G.C and its Approach*, First edition, New Delhi: Concept Publishing Limited.

Patel, Mushtaq Ahmed I. (2008). *Audio-Visual Programmes in Teaching at Schools,* First edition, New Delhi: Anmol Publisher.

Pawan Agarwal (2009). *Indian Higher Education: Envisioning the Future,* First Edition, New Delhi: SAGE Publications Pvt. Ltd.

Pedro Noguera (2003). *City Schools and the American Dream: Reclaiming the Promise of Public Education*, First edition, Teachers College Press.

Pankaj Arora (2009). *Sex Education in Schools,* Prabhat Prakashan

Philip G Altbach (2010). *A Half-Century of Indian Higher Education,* First edition, New Delhi: SAGE Publisher.

Prabhakaran, Wilson (2012). *Methods in Behavioural Research,* First edition, New Delhi: Anmol Publisher.

Qureshi, M.U. (2006). *New Media and Educational Planning,* First edition, New Delhi: Anmol Publisher.

Qureshi, Hasnain (2004). *Modern School Education,* First edition, New Delhi: Anmol Publisher.

Qureshi, M.U. (2005). *Problems of Indian Education,* First edition, New Delhi: Anmol Publisher.

Qureshi, Muniruddin (2004). *Education for All in the New Millennium,* First edition, New Delhi: Anmol Publisher.

Qureshi, Muniruddin (2005). *Social Aspects of Education,* First edition, New Delhi: Anmol Publisher

Rai, Sudhir (2011). *Problem of Child Abuse in India,* First edition, New Delhi: Anmol Publisher

Ram Nath Sharma, Rajendra Kumar Sharma (2005). *History of Education in India*, First edition, New Delhi: Atlantic Publishers & Dist.

Ram Nath Sharma & Rajendra K.Sharma (2004). *Problems of Education in India,* First edition, New Delhi: Atlantic Publishers & Dist

R. C. Sharma, C. L. Sapra (2008). *Wastage and stagnation in primary and middle schools in India,* National Council of Educational Research and Training

Reddy, P. Adinarayana (2004). *Total Literacy Campaign: Problems and Prospects,* First edition, New Delhi: Anmol Publisher.

Reddy, P. Adinarayana (2004). *Education of Tribal Women,* First edition, New Delhi: Anmol Publisher

R.N. Misra (2010). *Women Education and Development,* First edition, New Delhi: Discovery Publishing House

Robert B. Stevenson, Michael Brody, Justin Dillon, Arjen E.J. Wals (2013). *International Handbook of Research on Environmental Education,* Routledge

Rosemary C. & Salomone (2005). *Same, Different, Equal: Rethinking Single-sex Schooling,* Yale University Press

R.S.Bhatia (2009). *Psychology of Teaching Learning Process,* First edition, New Delhi: Anmol Publisher.

Sagar, J. Vidya (2003). *Scientific Attitude and Higher Education,* First edition, New Delhi: Anmol Publisher.

Sahu, Sachindra Mohan (2005). *Education of Children with Special Needs,* First edition, New Delhi: Anmol Publisher.

Sarah Mondale, Sarah B. Patton (2002). *School: The Story of American Public Education,* First edition, Beacon Press.

Salim, A. Abdul (2001). *Educational Development in India,* First edition, New Delhi: Anmol Publisher.

Sareen, N. (2005). *Information and Communication Technology,* First edition, New Delhi: Anmol Publisher.

Saxena, Ravi (2006). *Health and Physical Education,* First edition, New Delhi: Anmol Publisher.

Selvam, S.K. Panneer (2013). *Lesson Plan Writing by Software Package,* First edition, New Delhi: Anmol Publisher.

S. P. Agrawal (2001). *Women's Education in India, 1995-98: Present Status, Perspective Plan, Statistical Indicators with a Global View,* Concept Publishing Company

S. P. Agrawal, & J. C. Aggarwal (1992). *Women's Education in India,* Volume 1, New Delhi: Concept Publishing Company

S. L. Sharma (2009). *Educational Management: A Unified Approach of Education,* First edition, New Delhi: Global India Publications

Selvam, S.K. Panneer (2013). *Teaching Learning with Multimedia,* First edition, New Delhi: Anmol Publisher.

Senapati, Tilottama (2006). *Curriculum Development in Population Education,* First edition, New Delhi: Anmol Publisher.

*Sex Education: Gender Politics and Schooling,* Routledge, University of Michigan

Sengar, Shailendra (2008). *Introduction to Information Technology,* First edition, New Delhi: Anmol Publisher.

Sengar, Shailendra (2008). *Library and Information Science,* First edition, New D[illegible] Anmol Publisher.

S[illegible]si, N. (2005). *Social Foundations of Education,* First edition, New Delhi: Anmol Publisher.

Sharma, Dinesh C. (2006). *Management of Distance Education*, First edition, New Delhi: Anmol Publisher

Sharma, S.R. (1994). *Research in History of Education*, First edition, New Delhi: Anmol Publisher.

Sharma, S.R. (2003). *Teacher Training and Educational Research*, First edition, New Delhi: Anmol Publisher.

Shireen J. Jejeebhoy (1995). *Women's Education, Autonomy, and Reproductive Behaviour: Experience from Developing Countries*, Clarendon Pres

Sharma, Seema (2004). *Modern Teaching of History*, First edition, New Delhi: Anmol Publisher.

Sharma, Sita Ram et al. (1998). *Historical Perspectives of Education*, First edition, New Delhi: Anmol Publisher.

Sharma, Sita Ram et al. (1998). *Textbooks and Schools*, First edition, New Delhi: Anmol Publisher.

Shridhar Nath Mukerji (2006). *Secondary Education in India*, University of Michigan

Sharma, Sita Ram et al. (1998). *Textbooks and Education in India*, First edition, New Delhi: Anmol Publisher.

Sharma, V.S. (2010). *Environmental Education*, First edition, New Delhi: Anmol Publisher.

Shrivastava, S.K. (2006). *Comparative Education*, First edition, New Delhi: Anmol Publisher.

Singh, Bharat (2004). *Modern Education Theory and Practice*, First edition, New Delhi: Anmol Publisher.

Singh, Bharat (2004). *Modern Educational Measurement & Evaluation System*, First edition, New Delhi: Anmol Publisher.

Singh, Bharat (2004). *Dalit Education*, First edition, New Delhi: Anmol Publisher.

Sonkar, Satish (2000). *Physical Education and Sports in Elementary Schools*, First edition, New Delhi: Anmol Publisher.

Sonkar, Satish (2000). *Physical Education and Sports in Secondary Schools*, First edition, New Delhi: Anmol Publisher.

Srivastava, Gouri (2001). *Education in India: In Historical Perspectives*, First edition, New Delhi: Anmol Publisher.

Sue Davies, Cathy Lubelska, & Jocey Quinn (1994). *Changing the Subject: Women in Higher Education*, Taylor & Francis

Susan Anne Capel (2004). *Learning to Teach Physical Education in the Secondary School: A Companion to School Experience*, First edition, RoutledgeFalmer

Sudhanshu Bhushan (2009). *Restructuring Higher Education in India*, First edition, Jaipur: Rawat Publication.

Theodore Frederic Tucker & Muriel Pout (1937). *Sex Education in Schools: An Experiment in*

*Elementary Instruction*, Second edition, G. Howe

Thomas Edwards Brown (2010). A guide for Christian sex education of youth, Indiana University, Association Press

Thakur, Sadhana (2013). *Modernization and Dalit Education*, First edition, New Delhi: Anmol Publisher.

Thomas, J.A. (1998). *Education and Economic Development,* First edition, New Delhi: Anmol Publisher.

Tony Bates (2005). *Technology, E-Learning and Distance Education*, Secend edition, Routledge

Trilochan Singn Bakshi & Zeev Naveh (1980). *Environmental education: principles, methods, and applications,* Volume 1978, Plenum Press

Usmani, B.D. (2004). *Women Education in Twenty First Century,* First edition, New Delhi: Anmol Publisher.

V.C. Pandey (2007). *Environmental Education*, First edition, New Delhi: Gyan Publishing House

Veer, Udai (2004). *Modern Basic Education,* First edition, New Delhi: Anmol Publisher.

Venkataiah, S. (2000). *Computer Education*, First edition, New Delhi: Anmol Publisher.

Venkataiah, S. (2000). *Teacher Education,* First edition, New Delhi: Anmol Publisher

Venkataiah, S. (2000). *Vocational Education,* First edition, New Delhi: Anmol Publisher

Venkataiah, S. (2000). *Adult and Modern Education*, First edition, New Delhi: Anmol Publisher

Venkataiah, S. (2000). *Women and Child Education,* First edition, New Delhi: Anmol Publisher.

Venkataiah, S. (2000). *Management and Quality Education,* First edition, New Delhi: Anmol Publisher.

Venkataiah, S. (2000). *Primary and Secondary Education*, First edition, New Delhi: Anmol Publisher.

Venkataiah, S. (2000). *High and Distance Education,* First edition, New Delhi: Anmol Publisher.

Verghese, B.V. (2003). *Evaluation in Primary Education,* First edition, New Delhi: Anmol Publisher.

Verma, Romesh (2005). *Distance Education in Technological Age*, First edition, New Delhi: Anmol Publisher.

Vivian Parker Makosky (1991). *Fact book on women in higher education, American Council on Education,* University of Michigan

Vimala Ramachandran (2004). *Gender and Social Equity in Primary Education: Hierarchies of Access,* Firstr edition, New Delhi: SAGE.

V. P. Matheswarn (2005). *Distance Education: Student Support Services*, First edition, New Delhi: Anmol Publications Pvt. Limited

V. R. Taneja, S. Taneja (2000). *Educational Thinkers*, First edition, New Delhi: Atlantic Publishers & Dist

Walter Leal Filho, Farrukh Tahir, Maik Adomssent (1998). *Distance education and environmental education*, Peter Lang, University of Michigan

World Bank (2010). *Primary education in India*, World Bank, University of Michigan

Yaduvansh Bahadur Mathur (2008). *Women's Education in India, 1813-1966*, First edition, Asia Publishing House

Zakia A. Siddiqi, Anwar Jahan Zuberi (1993). *Muslim Women: Problems and Prospects, Aligarh Muslim University*, India. University Grants Commission, M.D. Publications Pvt. Ltd.

# Index